AUGUSTUS AND THE PRINCIPATE

ARCA
Classical and Medieval Texts, Papers and Monographs

35

General Editors: Francis Cairns, Robin Seager, Frederick Williams
Assistant Editors: Neil Adkin, Sandra Cairns

ISSN 0309-5541

AUGUSTUS
AND THE PRINCIPATE
The Evolution of the System

W. K. LACEY

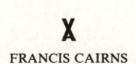

FRANCIS CAIRNS

Published by Francis Cairns (Publications) Ltd
c/o The University, LEEDS, LS2 9JT, Great Britain

First published 1996

British Library Cataloguing in Publication Data

A catalogue record for this title is available
from the British Library

ISBN 0-905205-91-X

Printed in Great Britain by
Redwood Books, Trowbridge, Wiltshire

CONTENTS

FILIIS NOSTRIS
ALASTAIR JONATHAN ET SEBASTIAN
MORTE PROPERA PEREMPTIS

PREFACE

I was in Form VI when (Sir) Ronald Syme's *Roman Revolution* appeared. Thirty years later when I came to Auckland University, in which Syme had been simultaneously both M.A. student and teacher, I found myself faced for the first time with the task of presenting to students a rational account of Augustus and the governmental structure he created which we call the Roman Empire.

The studies in this book are attempts to suggest answers to questions, some asked by students, some by myself, to which the accounts commonly offered by the text books have seemed to be unsatisfactory for a variety of reasons — abuse or neglect of the evidence and scenarios which defy common sense or the normal patterns of human behaviour.

Since 1939 we have all had to face, at least via the news media, the implications of civil war, even when we have not had to face it in person. This was what the much-admired 'nobles' of the Roman 'Republic' gave their people, and was an essential factor in the Romans' acceptance of Augustus, which ancient writers recognised, modern often ignore.

Sir Ronald Syme vindicated Tacitus as an historian who went back to the primary sources; the implications of this perception have also not been fully explored in relation to Tacitus' account of Augustus.

A welcome development has been that students of Ancient History are nowadays presented with the evidence, not just with modern syntheses. The fresh minds of students often supply insights from other disciplines on the implications of what they find. I have learned much from mine. This has unfortunately been accompanied by campaigns conducted by education authorities against the ancient languages, so that source materials have to be presented in English. I have therefore translated Latin and transliterated Greek as well, and offered comment on interpretations when this seemed useful. There is probably too much for some and too little for others.

Criticism of the sources, which has often amounted to a rewriting, and assumptions about the prevalence of a Westminster-type style of debate, seem to me to have gone beyond reason. I do not believe that anyone, and certainly not Augustus, put on record what everyone would recognise as simply untrue. Nor do I think it reasonable to dismiss Cassius Dio as unreliable because he followed the tradition of history set by Thucydides in using speeches to present what modern historians present as syntheses of the factors in a situation. The reactions of people in general to an event, or set of events, seem to me to be the most incontrovertible facts.

A number of these studies are based on contributions to journals made over a period of some twenty years; I have in most cases added new insights which have been published since the original papers were written, but I am conscious that I have not been able to read all that has been written on this field.

I have had the benefit of discussion with members of A.S.C.S. at A.U.L.L.A. conferences, Auckland University staff and members of Auckland Classical Association, to whom almost all these studies have been read; in particular Richard Allison, Janet Smale and Tom Stevenson, who have between them read and commented on the whole text. I also wish to thank Michael Crawford and Terence Volk for help in the area of numismatics, Graeme Clarke, Barbara Levick, Nicholas Purcell and the late Elizabeth Rawson for encouragement and criticism, and Robin Seager, who has saved me from a number of errors. Those that remain are my own.

I also record my thanks to Auckland University for periods of leave, the British School at Rome, St Catharine's College Cambridge and St John's College Oxford for hospitality, and the Universities of Alberta and Oxford for invitations to visit and offer seminars.

Some chapters in this book are based (more or less closely) on my earlier papers in: *JRS* 64 (1974) (chap. 3), *Antichthon* 19 (1985) (chap. 4), *Classicum* 23 [IX.2] (1983) (chap. 6), *JRS* 69 (1979) (chap. 7), and *Antichthon* 14 (1980) (chap. 9). I am grateful to the various editors for permission to re-use this material.

My deepest debt of gratitude is to my wife for a lifetime of support.

Auckland, 1995

ABBREVIATIONS

Works of Reference

ANRW: H. Temporini, W. Haase (edd.) *Aufstieg und Niedergang der römischen Welt.* Berlin and New York: Walter de Gruyter 1972–

CAH X: *Cambridge Ancient History* Vol. X. Cambridge 1934

CAH X²: *Cambridge Ancient History* Vol. X. *The Augustan Empire, 43 B.C.– A.D. 69.* 2nd edn Cambridge 1996

FGH: F. Jacoby *Die Fragmente der griechischen Historiker.* Berlin and Leiden 1923–

FIRA: S. Riccobono *et al.* (edd.) *Fontes Iuris Romani Anteiustiniani.* 2nd edn, Florence. Vol. I (1941), II (1940) III (1943)

LSJ: H.G. Liddell and R. Scott, rev. H.S. Jones *Greek-English Lexicon.* 9th edn, Oxford 1940

OCD: *Oxford Classical Dictionary.* (2nd edn, N.G.L. Hammond and H.H. Scullard. Oxford 1970)

OLD: *Oxford Latin Dictionary.* Oxford 1968–82

RE: Pauly–Wissowa *Realencyclopädie der classischen Altertumswissenschaft.* Stuttgart 1894–

Coins and Inscriptions

BMCRE: H. Mattingly *et al. Coins of the Roman Empire in the British Museum* Vol. 1. London: Trustees of the B.M. (repr.) 1965

BMCRR: H.A. Grueber *Coins of the Roman Republic in the British Museum.* Vol. 2. London: Trustees of the B.M. (repr.) 1970

CIL: *Corpus Inscriptionum Latinarum*

E–J: V. Ehrenberg and A.H.M. Jones *Documents illustrating the Reigns of Augustus and Tiberius.* Oxford 1949, 2nd edn 1976

ILS: H. Dessau *Inscriptiones Latinae Selectae.* 3 vols (1892–1916). 2nd edn, Berlin: Weidmann 1954

R.g.: *Res Gestae Divi Augusti.* Text of Brunt and Moore. Oxford 1967

RIC: H. Mattingly and E.A. Sydenham *The Roman Imperial Coinage.* London: Spink 1923

RIC I²: *The Roman Imperial Coinage.* Vol. I. Revised edition by C.H.V. Sutherland, London: Spink 1984

SEG: *Supplementum Epigraphicum Graecum*

Books and article collections

The following books are referred to throughout in abbreviated form.

Brunt and Moore: P.A. Brunt and J.M. Moore (edd.) *Res Gestae Divi Augusti. The Achievements of the Divine Augustus* Oxford 1967 (notes)

Gagé *Res Gestae*: J. Gagé (ed.) *Res Gestae Divi Augusti*. 3rd edn Paris: Société d'édition «Les Belles Lettres» 1977

Holmes *Architect* I and *Architect* II: T. Rice Holmes *The Architect of the Roman Empire*. 2 vols Oxford 1928, 1931

Jones *SRGL*: A.H.M. Jones *Studies in Roman Government and Law*. Oxford: Basil Blackwell 1960

Millar and Segal: F. Millar and E. Segal (edd.) *Caesar Augustus. Seven Aspects*. Oxford: Clarendon Press 1984

Raaflaub and Toher *BRE*: K.A. Raaflaub and M. Toher *Between Republic and Empire. Interpretations of Augustus and his Principate*. Berkeley: U. of California Press 1990

Scullard *Festivals*: H.H. Scullard *Festivals and Ceremonies of the Roman Republic*. London: Thames and Hudson 1981

Syme *Aug. Ar.*: R. Syme *The Augustan Aristocracy*. Oxford 1986

Syme *History*: R. Syme *History in Ovid*. Oxford 1978

Syme *Rom. Rev.*: R. Syme *The Roman Revolution*. Oxford 1939

Syme *Tacitus*: R. Syme *Tacitus*. 2 vols, Oxford 1958

Weinstock *Divus Julius*: S. Weinstock *Divus Julius*. Oxford 1971

Zanker *Images*: P. Zanker *The Power of Images in the Age of Augustus*. E.T. Alan Shapiro. Ann Arbor: U. of Michigan 1988

Sundry

E.T.: English Translation

LCL: Loeb Classical Library

Latin authors as in *OLD*; Greek authors as in LSJ

Journals as in *L'Année Philologique*

All dates B.C. unless otherwise indicated.

INTRODUCTION

Students of Augustus should begin with Tacitus. The opening of *Annals* in particular, it is argued in these studies, is not just a few preliminary remarks but a penetrating insight into the system established by Augustus which we call the Principate. Augustus called it *res publica* (the same expression which Cicero and his contemporaries had used for their system of government), and retained in it as many features of the previous form as he could without putting into the hands of potential rivals the tools by which they might overthrow his regime.

It is necessary therefore to look first at the opening of Tacitus *Annals* Book 1 and to discuss the realities lying behind the expression *res publica* so that Augustus' changes can be studied in their contexts. The remainder of this Introduction outlines the particular aspects of the Principate which are discussed in these studies.

Tacitus *Annals* 1. The opening chapter is about power; the sequence of kings, consuls, brief interludes of rule by dictators, decemvirs or military tribunes followed by brief arbitrary rule (*dominatio*) by Cinna and Sulla then the extra-legal power (*potentia*) of Pompeius, gave way to that of Caesar; the forces of Lepidus and Antonius succumbed to those of Augustus. He took under his control (*imperium*) everything in a state of exhaustion from civil wars. Only the consulate — that is the period of rule by consuls — was characterised by *libertas*.

In this political context *libertas* probably does not mean "freedom" as we understand that word, but "independence". This is the meaning (e.g.) in Servius Sulpicius' letter to Cicero in 45 (Cic. *Fam.* 4.5 esp. 3):[1] What Caesar had robbed Servius and Cicero of was the prospect of exercising *libertas* in public affairs and the concerns of

---

[1] *In re publica, in amicorum negotiis libertate sua usuri.* Servius Sulpicius is speaking of the grandchildren which Tullia's death had deprived Cicero of.

their political allies (*amici*), along with the right to hold public offices in due order. This did not deny personal freedom; after all staying away from the Senate House was always an available option, as was retiring to their country estates (although that amounted to a self-imposed *exilium* (exile) as in the famous example of Scipio Africanus);[2] in the case of those who did not have a senatorial family tradition, *libertas* enabled them to decide not to proceed with a senatorial career, like Ovid, or, in an earlier age, Cicero's friend Atticus, though the latter had remained very much in touch with the political scene.[3]

Such people (*equites*) could make money in business, banking and contracting, but men of senatorial family felt a moral imperative to lead the political life of their ancestors; for them public office was the sole road to wealth — or any kind of financial standing. This was the *libertas* which Sulla and the dynasts who followed him had sought to deny those not in their *factio* (clique) and the independence in public life which Augustus did not restore. This is Tacitus' point.

A rising tide of *adulatio* (fawning flattery), Tacitus continues (*Ann.* 1.1.2), which rose during Augustus' Principate, gradually destroyed the line of distinguished writers of history; thereafter there was no recovery under Augustus' dynasty "through fear of living and hatred of recently deceased emperors". That is why Tacitus, after the Flavian dynasty, says he can research the records without ill-feeling or partiality.

The power theme returns in chapter 3 with an account of Augustus' chief lieutenants and destined successors in public life; at the end "how few there were" he exclaims, "who had seen *res publica*", which might be taken to mean "public business in public hands".

Between these chapters lies chapter 2, a masterpiece, whose literary skill has tended to divert attention from what is a penetrating insight into Augustus' Principate. It requires detailed translation:

---

[2] At his villa at Liternum. H.H. Scullard *Scipio Africanus: Soldier and Politician* (London 1970) 223 and 290 n.179.

[3] And C. Maecenas in Augustus' own circle (or clique). Maecenas virtually ruled Rome without official office, unless that of *praefectus* or prefect, during the civil war period. See Syme *Rom. Rev.* 233 (during the war in Sicily), 292 (during the Actium and Egyptian campaigns), "Maecenas controlled Rome and Italy, invested with supreme power but no title". Syme exaggerates; Dio 51.3.4f. for example shows that Maecenas required the support of Agrippa to control the troops. Cf. Vell. 2.88.

The deaths of Brutus and Cassius left the nation without an army;[4] when (Sextus) Pompeius was suppressed around Sicily, Lepidus discarded and Antonius killed, even Julius Caesar's partisans had no surviving leader except the (young) Caesar; he abandoned the designation 'triumvir', always declaring[5] "I am consul", and "a tribune's rights are all I need for looking after the common people";[6] he won the hearts of the troops by his gifts, ordinary people by a reliable supply of food, the entire nation by the pleasure of relief from civil wars; he then gradually encroached, drawing into his own hands the responsibilities of the Senate, magistrates and laws without opposition since all the most defiant had perished in battle or proscription, while the rest of the nobility had prospered financially and in political success in proportion to their readiness to serve the regime;[7] prospering in the revolution they preferred the safety of the present to the perils of the old order.

The provinces too had no objection to the state of affairs; rule by the Senate and People had earned their hostility on account of the generals' rivalries, the rapacity of their governors and the failure of the laws to provide any retribution, since these were thrown into chaos by violence, party interest and, to cap it all, bribery.

These two magisterial sentences have seldom received the close attention they deserve, even from editors of Tacitus.[8] In this series of studies it will be suggested that the manner in which Augustus exercised his leadership as Princeps was an unfolding, evolving process of encroachment,[9] and not, as usually interpreted a matter of

---

[4] There is some prejudice here. The armies of Brutus and Cassius in 43 were initially as illegal as those of Octavian until like his they were made legal some months later, later in fact than those of Octavian; they had been raised by their commanders on their own initiatives in provinces not formally allocated by the Senate. They were made legitimate after Antonius' defeat round Mutina.

[5] Tacitus uses a present participle, possibly for merely literary reasons, but the repetitive sense should not be discounted.

[6] As argued in chap. 4 below.

[7] "Serve the regime"; Tacitus uses the prejudicial word "servitude", but few contemporaries would have seen their competing for the traditional magistracies as servitude, even if they were conscious that their electoral success was due to their being acceptable to Augustus and his governing circle (*amici*). The term *amici* describes a man's political allies to those allies; they look more like a *factio* or clique to others, especially historians with the advantage of hindsight.

[8] "In a manner peculiarly Tacitean it represents the gradual and calculated encroachment of Augustus on the power of the Senate and People" (F.R.D. Goodyear *The Annals of Tacitus Books 1–6* I (Cambridge 1972) 101). Most modern interpretations go back ultimately to F. Haverfield 'Four notes on Tacitus' *JRS* 2 (1912) 195–7: "Tacitus is talking about titles." Rather he is using Augustus' own words to explain how Augustus managed to win from his contemporaries their acceptance of his encroachments on their traditional privileges.

[9] It is often if not always difficult to be certain of the impetus behind a new encroachment: did it come from Augustus himself or his immediate circle of *amici* or

two 'Settlements', in 27 and 23.

Tacitus in fact suggests at least three stages; the first was to abandon the name or designation (*nomen*) of triumvir. This should probably be dated to the *coniuratio* (solemn league) of 32, when "all Italy" took an oath to support and defend the young Caesar, whom we call Octavian, against his enemies.[10] He never formally released them from the obligations of this oath, though he kept it well in the background; it gave him no constitutional or traditional power. He preferred to advertise his status as consul (till mid-23), then the rights of a tribune — all he needed to protect the common people, or so he said.[11] But neither of these or any other office annulled or changed the oath all had taken to support him, nor is there a vestige of evidence that he ever released the communities from their oath. Quite the reverse in fact occurred: he quietly converted the oath of support into the soldiers' oath, for all soldiers now made him and not their commanding officer for the time being the subject of their oath of obedience. Nor was it forgotten by the civil population; everyone renewed the oath of support in AD 14 to accept Tiberius' succession.[12]

Augustus' claim to rule as no more than consul, it will be argued,[13]

---

from below — from the *plebs* preferring his government to that of potential noble competitors, or Senators trying to win his attention or approval to further their own careers, or even from magistrates voluntarily ceding powers or rights? For example the *iiiviri monetales* (or *a a a f f*), the board of three in charge of the mint, ceded to Augustus the right to put their own names and family insignia on coins. Whose was the initiative? We cannot be sure; see A. Wallace-Hadrill 'Image and authority in the coinage of Augustus' *JRS* 76 (1986) 66–87. It seems to me probable that at different moments the impetus will have come from different directions, from Augustus himself perhaps early in the Principate; but later the continuing pressure of the position and power of the Princeps made Senators first acquiesce for the sake of peace and stability then wish to collaborate, promote and perpetuate his powers in the interest of their own careers. It is in fact an aspect of *adulatio*, but encroachment was, like the tide, probably inevitable and irresistible. Tacitus' verb *insurgere* is a metaphor from such natural phenomena as rivers and winds (*OLD s.v.*) which the Romans thought of rather than the Mediterranean tide when seeking a metaphor for an irresistible force.

[10] The terminal date for the triumvirate I take to be 31st December, 33, but as it was an office that had to be laid down it went on past that date in effect; see chap. 1. The importance of the *coniuratio* (the solemn league) of 32 is usually downplayed, but see A. Momigliano in *OCD* 149 *s.v.* Augustus. For the interpretation of the *coniuratio* here adopted see Brunt and Moore 67f. While not quite the same as the military oath it has much the same effect: "I will spare neither spirit nor life nor children ... I will endure every danger ... I will be the personal enemy ... I will pursue and resist by land and sea with arms and 'iron'" does not fall far short of swearing to obey the orders of the commander-in-chief.

[11] That this is the right interpretation is argued in chap. 4 below.

[12] Tac. *Ann.* 1.7.2.

[13] In chap. 3 below.

was confirmed by his action of placing the provinces — by which is meant the decision as to who was to govern them — into the hands of the Senate at the so-called 'First Settlement' in January, 27. His claim to be the champion of the common people derived from activating his powers of a tribune in 23 in the so-called 'Second Settlement'.[14] This is the point from which Tacitus traces his "gradual encroachment"; it was in fact a start in the evolution of the Principate, not the end of the process.

Encroachment will be detected in many spheres. A detailed account will be given for the *tribunicia potestas*, and for the promotion of the cults in public and private religion with which Augustus had been associated during his fight for supremacy: Apollo his special deity, then Roma the goddess of the site of the city, and the deities and cults of the *compita*, which were intended to present the idea of the city-dwellers as one big family with one family cult, of which Augustus became acknowledged as the priest and father-figure, or *Pater Patriae*.[15]

Augustus' own account of his rise to supremacy is very different — naturally. In *Res gestae*, in the first sentence he claims to have brought the *res publica* from subservience to the arbitrary rule of a clique (*dominatione factionis*) into independence (*libertas*). This is propaganda, of course, but the use of the words *res publica* here and in chapter 34, where he claims to have handed it back to the control of the Senate and People, shows the enduring importance of this idea in political discourse. Tacitus on the other hand nowhere uses this key word till the end of his account of Augustus' chief collaborators in his rule as Princeps, and only then to deny that there had been a (true) *res publica* after the start of the civil wars (*Ann.* 1.3 *fin.*). Significantly however he puts it into the mouths of those who speculated about the succession (4 *fin.*) and into both the favourable and unfavourable assessments of Augustus' career (9.3, 5 and 10.1, 2, 5, 7). The idea of *res publica*, he saw, was clearly far from dead in AD 14.

Res publica, literally 'public business', was how the Romans had always described their constitution in so far as they had one. It was the opposite of *res privata* 'private business'. *Res publica* was a bit like 'democracy' nowadays; everyone is for it, but what people mean by it differs widely. Before the civil wars, in the period we usually call the

---

'Republic' or 'Republican period', Rome's *res publica* was run by a tight oligarchy of self-styled *nobiles* (nobles), ennobled by being the descendant of a consul. Noble families felt honour bound to hold the consulship in each generation, so, as there were only two consuls elected each year, competition was fierce, and *novi homines* (newcomers) at best unwelcome. *Nobiles* competed in making a show of their wealth and power, the latter being evidenced in the number of *clientes* (adherents) they could call on as escorts, voters and, in the last turbulent years, bully-boys and soldiers.

Policy was made, in theory, by the People's Assembly after approval by the Senate, but in practice conclaves of nobles meeting in private, often on social occasions, made decisions which would then be proposed in the Senate, supported by the first speakers, the ex-consuls (*consulares*) whose mana (*auctoritas*) was instrumental in seeing them through the Senate. The People's Assembly (theoretically sovereign) could overrule the Senate, but it was often by-passed, most significantly in the important area of choosing the provincial governors who were also the army commanders.

The nobles never achieved a philosophy of empire; governing a province and commanding an army was the prime way of enrichment, since even without intimidation and extortion a governor's allowance (known as *ornatio*) was certainly sometimes excessive and probably if not provably always so; and the opportunity to obtain and reward supporters by offering jobs was always present. Similarly, decisions to extend the empire were often made for no better reason than that a clique (*factio*) among the nobles wanted an opportunity for enrichment by the spoils of war. This was how all the great noble houses had become great. So, the empire was territorially disconnected, badly and unpredictably governed, and randomly extended. The northern party of Italy, the rich Po valley for example, was left open to raids from the Alpine tribes while the Senators as governors were milking the wealth of the more settled districts of Asia Minor, and extending the empire there.

Nor had the oligarchy of the nobles any philosophy of government for Italy. Italian manpower had been exploited unscrupulously for two centuries and more till the 'allies' revolted in the Social War (91–89), and despite bitter resistance from the nobles obtained an equality in the franchise. Even then, however, their votes, whether for elections, legislation or the great issues of peace and war, could only be exercised in Rome itself, so that only the rich or landed gentry could in fact exercise their rights. Besides, the nobles imposed on the peoples of Italy who had fought hardest, backing the nobles' opponents in their fight for their rights, a 'peace' which involved widespread confiscations of lands and property and disfranchisement. That was under Sulla the dictator (82–79).

The *res publica* of the era before the civil wars had therefore meant different things to different people: to the nobles and their adherents independence in competing for wealth, power and status against equals, and combining to keep the rest of the world in its place — down. To the leaders of the Italian towns who began to enter the lower ranks of the governing class in Rome (*domi nobiles*) it meant winning the favour of a noble patron who would promote their interests while pursuing his own, but no freedom to aspire too high or independently without meeting strenuous opposition, which required extreme ability to overcome. To the commercial class outside the Senate (Knights or *equites*) — merchants, bankers, contractors — it meant the chance to join the Senators in exploiting Rome's subjects, and to acquire country estates, while keeping the Senators sweet with loans and bribes, and a weather eye open for shifts of power to ensure they were favoured and not victimised in the nobles' quarrels. They had little ability to influence policy, though this power grew with the increase of their number after the Social War, and their enrolment in the thirty-one 'rural' tribes for voting purposes.[16]

To the common people it meant grinding poverty, and a vote of little value because it was easily circumvented both in the voting on legislation, since those who lived in Rome were mostly lumped together in four of the thirty-five tribes (voting units), and in the voting at elections, since they were enrolled in the lower '*classes*' which almost never voted when the Senate and Knights voted together, as they usually did. Some men obtained a pittance for dancing attendance on a noble, making up his retinue, and occasionally risking a split head by brawling with other nobles' retinues or gangs. Some must have had small workshops, and small-scale businesses or trades, but there is next to no information about their activities. The nobles had little or no interest in them, since they purchased slaves or trained their own to do the work done nowadays by professionals like doctors, teachers, accountants and secretaries, skilled people such as hairdressers and clothes-makers, and semiskilled or unskilled workers — for menial tasks like house maintenance, cooking,

---

[16] A result of the Social War which the nobles of Sulla's clique had tried but failed to overturn.

cleaning, waiting at table, estate work, gardening, carrying litters and letters, and keeping the door. The state provided very little employment: the city's infrastructure of services was small, and by the start of Caesar's civil wars very run down, and there was little new construction or maintenance.[17]

The food supply of the common people of the city had been regarded as a political football by rival noble factions, who had used it in their own interests. Expressing discontent by demonstrations was virtually the only means by which the common people could exert any sort of pressure, since the nobles had hijacked their representatives the tribunes into serving their own interests. The theatre, races and other shows which were part of the religious calendar gave them their only opportunity to cheer or jeer at the political élite.

Julius Caesar belonged by family to the losing party in the civil wars of 88–82. In the face of bitter opposition he rose to the consulship, and started a series of wars: first with the peoples of Gaul by which he became enormously rich and powerful, then the first of the civil wars of 49–45 when his enemies tried to crush him by political manoeuvring. In this war the towns of Italy showed what they thought of the nobles: they joined Caesar virtually without exception. However, after his victory, it became evident that Caesar had no ideas for a long-term political settlement, except the 'clemency' of an all-powerful, eventually lifelong dictator, with an all-embracing reform programme to be carried out by others while he went on new campaigns. He was murdered by those who had been his friends and protégés on the Ides of March, 44.

This was the heritage which fell to Caesar's heir, the dictator's great-nephew, C. Octavius, whom we call Octavian until 27 (he called himself Caesar), then Augustus. At the age of eighteen he was in a situation in which political loyalties, polarised in the civil wars of Caesar, were further polarised by his murder; some applauded the assassination of a 'tyrant' and anticipated the return of *res publica*, that is the nobles' power; others were determined to bring the 'murderers' to justice; others held every point of view between. Many, especially farmers and landowners, were appalled at the thought of another civil war, and more confiscations; others, no

---

[17] Constructing and reconstructing the city's services, and ensuring an adequate supply of food and water offered an opportunity to win popular support which Augustus and his *amici* did not neglect.

doubt, were on the look-out for opportunities for loot;[18] to others any change would have to be for the better.

Exhibition/Showmanship. This was endemic in the nobles' *res publica*. Senators climbing the political ladder (*cursus honorum*, the prescribed sequence of offices) had to give shows. A mean outlay brought little thanks; lavish shows, well staged, enhanced the credit of those already well thought of, though they often did little for those already in bad odour. Another opportunity for exhibition and winning popular favour occurred when a Senator returned to Rome from governing a province. There were well-established parameters for claiming honours and for the Senate and People to accept the claims or reject them. Such occasions gave some indication of popular feeling, however much stage management took place. They therefore provided a sort of touchstone for estimating the amount of support a leader actually had at any given moment.

The forms remained substantially the same throughout the period from before Caesar crossed the Rubicon till the death of Augustus, but the uses to which the forms were put did change. Augustus used them first in his claim to a share in the leadership of Caesar's partisans, then to the sole leadership of the party and sole command of the state's armed forces. He pursued his claims both before and after his victory with such regularity and lavish expenditure that the common people hardly missed the shows which used to be given by rival nobles competing in claims to glory and the enhancement of their pedigrees.

Initiatives in presenting these spectacles changed too: in the 'Republic', when nobles claimed the right to put them on for their own glory and their families' advancement, their claims were open to challenge, and were challenged. Octavian/Augustus first used such honours in his outmanoeuvring of his rivals for Caesar's heritage, then after his victories found the Senate and People offering him new and unprecedented honours which he was able to modify and thus seem less autocratic.[19] Eventually he was able to use his own and his destined successors' returns to the city and departures to establish claims to leadership through successes in the military sphere.

The first study in this book traces the uses made of returning to the city as a means of managing public opinion, and the way returns

---

[18] Cf. what Tacitus says (*Ann.* 1.4) about people's expectations as Augustus' life drew to a close.

[19] The point is well made by Zanker *Images* 2f.

illustrate the changing nature of the style of leadership from what we
call 'republican' conventions to those of what we call the Principate.

Octavian/Augustus in 44 had no assets except the fact of his adoption
— "a name" as contemporary detractors expressed it. The story of
the next fifty years is of how he established a new form of *res publica*,
not as free as the old one for the nobles because he drew up limits
outside which independent action was not permitted. But he
maintained a peace which even a stern critic like Tacitus said was of
benefit to the subject peoples (*Ann.* 1.2). It was a monarchy in a sense,
as contemporaries (and Tacitus) recognised,[20] but it was in another
sense still a *res publica*, now governed by a new oligarchy which had
gone through the traditional series of magistracies (*cursus honorum*)
and won honours in the traditional pursuits of the army and the law,
not in complete independence but with the approval of Augustus —
Princeps as he called himself.[21]

In the simplest analysis Octavian/Augustus fought his way to the
position of Princeps without scruple or pity; civil war, as Tacitus
remarked (*Ann.* 1.9.3), does not admit of civilised behaviour.
Whether he could have worked in a system in which he was not sole
ruler is a matter of psychology, guesswork or the political philosophy
of the observer and other imponderable factors; whether a less
ruthless or less crafty man could have done it remains in the same
field of guesswork. What we can observe are his methods, and they
are the subject of the second study. They were tailored to the
traditions (*mores maiorum*) of the *res publica* and the sentiments of
the people which demanded caution. That is why they succeeded.

The foundations of this new *res publica* were not easily laid. All victors
in civil wars have to face a range of difficulties: partisans must be
rewarded, neutrals must be persuaded that the new order will offer
stability, security and an opportunity to pursue their chosen careers,
opponents — or such as have survived — must be reconciled,
muzzled or dealt with in a way that does not arouse resentment
among the uncommitted. So, while Sextus Pompeius' followers
could be treated as pirates or runaway slaves,[22] those of Antonius
had to be said to be the dupes of the Egyptian Queen who had

[20] And Dio 53.11–19, esp. 17 and 19.
[21] *R.g.* 13; 30.1; 32.3 for example.
[22] *Id.* 25.1; cf. Syme *Rom. Rev.* 233.

bewitched him;[23] the common people, once violently hostile,[24] had to be wooed by great public works which required labour and stimulated trade and restored and later improved the city's infrastructure and services. They could be impressed too by the magnificence of the works of the dynasty, the completion of the works begun by Julius Caesar for example and the huge *Mausoleum* built in the Campus Martius beside the *via Flaminia*,[25] the Great North Road. There were besides the splendour and variety of the victory memorials in the Forum[26] and numerous statues, some of stone,[27] others of silver, standing, riding, or chariot-driving.[28] A magnificent new temple to Apollo was rising on the Palatine Hill in gratitude for the victories of Naulochus and Actium over Pompeius and Antonius.[29] Octavian's triple triumph in 29 was unparalleled in the amount of booty distributed among the army and people.

This all appeared to presage a monarchical state. The young Caesar (as he still then was) had other plans; Zanker has described the major change in policy which then took place, as represented in the monuments.[30] He abandoned the nobles' traditional self-glorification and replaced it with religious devotion, accepting from the Senate a commission for a wholesale restoration of the temples of the Roman gods in 28 (*R.g.* 20). The poets blamed the civil wars on the anger of the gods for their neglect.[31] Octavian himself said he was consul and to prove it shared the *fasces* with his colleague in 28 in the traditional manner, and dismantled the surviving traces of the emergency measures of the civil war period. The process culminated in January, 27, when he put the question of the provinces for the consuls to the Senate — i.e. who would command the armies. This is the subject of the third study.

The results, the so-called 'First Settlement', lasted four years, for most of which Augustus as he now was stayed out of the forefront of

---

[23] Though some were put to death (*Rom. Rev.* 299f.) including the last survivors among Caesar's assassins.

[24] E.g. in 40, Dio 48.31; App. *B.C.* 5.67f.

[25] Zanker *Images* 72-7, esp. 73: "The monument was first of all a demonstration of the patron's great power."

[26] *Id.* 80f.

[27] More than life size, *id.* 76.

[28] He melted down more than 80 of them, *R.g.* 24.2.

[29] He had claimed the patronage of Apollo since the battles round Philippi against Caesar's assassins. See Zanker *Images* 49f.

[30] *Id.* 85-9.

[31] See (e.g.) Syme *Rom. Rev.* 447.

politics, being either in Gaul or in Spain or ill. Exactly what prompted the 'Second Settlement' in 23 is unknown, and strenuously discussed. In the fourth study it is argued that Tacitus tells us what happened — that Augustus said all he needed to protect the *plebs* were the rights of a tribune (*se ferens ... tribunicio iure contentum*); in 23 there was no law, no *senatus consultum*; that is why scholars cannot find one.

Whether he was trying to extract himself from open leadership as consul, with its accompanying burdens, or to create a position outside the constitution which would enable him to pursue a policy of encroachment (which was what happened) remains an open question. He nowhere states what he intended. But Tacitus saw it as the point from which his encroachments began. And Octavian still had to win acceptance as Princeps.

Agrippa's position after 27. Agrippa was Augustus' chief associate, the architect of his victories and agent for reconciling the *plebs* through work on the infrastructure of the city and the public services, and his fellow-consul for the two restoration years 28–7. In our sources he remains a shadowy figure, but after 27 did he remain outside the structures of the new *res publica* or come within them? and if so in what role? This question is the subject of the fifth study. It cannot be answered by the traditional methods of enquiry for lack of evidence. The scientific method of inductive reasoning from a hypothesis is attempted to see if a reasonable account emerges; this hypothesis is that Agrippa remained within the traditional forms by taking — or being given — a prefecture of the fleet and coasts, with powers derived from the precedents of Cn. Pompeius with his protracted commands and extensive powers.

The Principate. Whether he intended it or not, Augustus' withdrawal from the consulship produced a period of unrest which lasted till 19. The electoral assemblies (*comitia*) made it clear that they wanted Augustus to have consular *imperium*, not merely to have the rights of a tribune to defend the people's interests. In 19 the Senators formally accepted this, recalled him to the city and confirmed that his *imperium* though perhaps titularly proconsular was the equal of that of the consuls in the city. In a real sense this was the true start of the Principate, as Augustus now did step outside and above the constitution. This is the theme of the sixth study.

Augustus' creeping progress or encroachments, the uses to which he put his tribunician power and the use he made of the religion of the families, are the subjects of the next two studies. Tribunician power was originally not highly regarded, but it steadily advanced in importance till it became the mark of the destined successor to Augustus' position. Romans had traditionally looked to their family gods to watch over their food supply and protect them. The priest in this cult was the father (*paterfamilias*) of each family. Augustus cultivated the idea of the citizens of Rome as one big family with their local deities at the crossroads and himself as the food provider, until eventually he found them willing — or rather, eager — to accept him as the father figure for the whole city — *Pater Patriae*, in 2 BC.[32]

The climax, and anticlimax, of 2 BC. This year was (briefly) the apogee of Augustus' success. After being hailed as *Pater Patriae* he introduced his second grandson (adopted as a son) to public life, and with an unprecedented series of shows dedicated a great new temple to Mars Ultor, Mars the Avenger (of Caesar). This was to be the focus of a new era in Rome's military glory, glorifying the ancestors' achievements and especially his own family (the Caesars) and looking forward to the future. Now, if it was not already clear, he made it plain that he planned that his grandsons (adopted sons) should succeed him as Princeps, or joint Principes,[33] though they were still very young and immature, and lacking experience. But something happened, or was made to happen,[34] which caused him to explode with rage, banish his daughter Julia his only child and mother of his grandsons, and cause M. Antonius' surviving son to kill himself.

Various theories have been put forward to explain Augustus' unrelenting anger at Julia; in the ninth study it is argued that some act of folly on her part caused or brought out into the open popular

---

[32] For Augustus as *Pater* because he was an ideal benefactor, T.R. Stevenson 'The ideal benefactor and the father analogy in Greek and Roman thought' *CQ* 42 (1992) 421–36. A part is also played by his oak-wreath or *corona civica* "for saving citizens' lives", which was originally seen as a deed analogous to the giving of life by procreation.

[33] They were now *principes iuventutis* (Principes of the Officer-cadets), a distinction seen by Ovid as foreshadowing their future as Principes of their seniors (*senum*); see chap. 9.

[34] Scholars who believe in the view that Augustus' household was the scene of bitter rivalries between the *amici* of Julia and those of Livia naturally think it was made to happen, but there is no evidence.

speculation (or gossip) that her two sons, who were Augustus' pride and joy, were not legitimate and thus could not in law succeed him as of right.[35]

Julia was banished and damage control contrived, but Augustus did not dare expose Gaius Caesar his elder 'son' to the glare of the consulate to which he had been prematurely elected, and sent him off with senior advisers to win military honours. Lucius Caesar the younger 'son' received the same treatment, but both boys died; and to secure the succession of the Caesars Augustus had to turn to his surviving stepson Tiberius, adopt him as Tiberius Caesar and restore his public image by conferring on him military and civil honours.

Other encroachments. In the tenth study Augustus' creeping progress from 23 is briefly traced in various fields as he gradually took the public activities of the new *res publica* more and more into his own hands. His growing predominance was responsible for that 'fawning flattery' (*adulatio*) which Tacitus recognised as the curse of Rome in his own day.[36] *Adulatio* had destroyed free discussion of the business of the state (*res publica*) and undermined the morale of the governing class. That is why Tacitus hated it so much.

Augustus' last years were spent in weathering storms caused by a major revolt in the Balkans, and a severe defeat East of the Rhine. Despite his increasing age — he was over 75 when he died — his leadership remained unchallenged at home and he died in his bed.

★

Since these studies were completed I have been privileged to see 'Tacitus' view of Augustus' place in history', the contribution of G.R. Stanton to the still unpublished Edwin Judge Festschrift *Ancient History in a Modern University* shortly to be published in Sydney. Stanton argues that Tacitus saw in Augustus the second of the Caesars; he was therefore encumbered with much of the baggage of the first (Julius); he pleads for the abandonment of the term "the Republic" to describe the Romans' political organisation.

I agree, and think that greater clarity of thought is obtained by

---

[35] This would destroy all he had worked for, especially the stability and certainty for the future offered by the dynasty of the Caesars.

[36] But care is needed. The story of Apudius (or Pacuvius) in Dio 53.20.2f. (dated in 27), if true, shows that *adulatio* was not brought about by Augustus' long Principate; cf. the story of Zarmarus' self-sacrifice (dated in 20), *id.* 54.9.10.

always speaking of *res publica*, the public business, to describe how the Romans thought of their governmental system. The public business was managed by small cliques of competing nobles till Julius Caesar started the civil wars in 49. War lords took over the public business till 28 when Octavian, the surviving war lord, step by step handed the public business back to the traditional managers (except for the armed forces, whose management he kept in his own hands). This had important implications — possibly inevitable ones — for the civil parts of the government because of the Roman traditions of patronage and clientship, and the imbalance created between the Princeps and the other leading personages. In any case it merely confuses the issue to talk about the Republic being restored or not restored, being a myth, mirage or façade. The Republic is a modern idea with modern baggage, much of it imported from the French and American revolutions against monarchies. The Romans talked of their public business, the business of the body politic. We should, as Stanton says, do the same.

Many topics are not studied in this book; finance, details of campaigns, legislation and the attempted reform of the upper class, the composition of the party which supported Octavian/Augustus resolutely, achievements in building, literature and art which made this a Golden Age, etc. All these matters have been studied elsewhere. The notes are intended simply to indicate the point at issue, and to name the source, without extensive bibliography. For the ancient sources, I have always tried to understand the implications of what they say rather than discard the evidence without carefully weighing it when it is a statement of fact. Dio's speeches I regard as like those of Thucydides.[37] They express sentiments thought by the historian to be appropriate to the situation at the time, and illustrate possible courses of action which a contemporary speaker might have put forward. Inscriptions and coins I regard as intended to plant ideas in the minds of those who saw or handled them; they must show at least the face of probable truth. In regard to modern work, I have done no more than record what I know I have taken from others. In the immense volume of work on this period I have no doubt that I have not acknowledged all that I ought, and from time to time have supposed that the view I have taken is original when it is not. To those to whom I have not given the credit that is their due I apologise.

---

[37] Even the long speeches in book 52 setting out the alternatives open to Octavian as seen through third-century eyes. But see *CAH* X^2 71.

Postscript

While my MS was still with the press, the second edition of *Cambridge Ancient History* X became available. I can thus take at least some preliminary notice of the chapters by J.A. Crook on 'Political history, 30 B.C. to A.D. 14' (70–112) and 'Augustus: power, authority, achievement' (113–146). The account in these two chapters of the evolution of Augustus' *res publica* (Principate) seems to me entirely correct, along with Crook's preference for simple explanations of the evidence and his refusal to be beguiled by ingenious theories. Of some details I remain unconvinced: I still believe that the 'restoration of the *res publica*' is an interpretation of the whole course of 28–7 (as Augustus said in *R.g.* 34) and not a *relatio* (motion) before the Senate on January 13th, 27 (*CAH* X² 78, chap. 3 below), and I see no cause to abandon either the view (based on Tacitus) that there was no formal conferment of *trib. pot.* in 23 (*CAH* X² 86, chap. 4 below), or the view on Julia's adulterous behaviour given in chap. 9. Nor is there new evidence to destroy the hypothesis (which is the simplest explanation) about Agrippa's position after 27 offered in chap. 5.

CHAPTER 1

COMING HOME *

**Continuity and change in the traditions of the *res publica*
from before the Civil Wars to the death of Augustus**

The metamorphosis which Roman Senators habitually underwent
from proconsul or propraetor *cum imperio* (with the right to demand
compliance) to *privatus* (private citizen) took place on returning to
the city after handing over their province (*provincia*). Specifically
they crossed from *militiae* to *domi* (active service to home service) at
the *pomerium* (the sacred boundary of the city)[1] and then became
eligible to resume their life in the *res publica* as Senators. The Senate
could extend a tenure of *imperium* temporarily within the city, to
allow a general who had received the salutation of *imperator* to
progress in triumph to the Capitol and offer his laurels at the shrine
of *Iuppiter Optimus Maximus* where his *imperium* had originally
received its divine sanction.[2] Otherwise they simply dismissed their
lictors, donned civilian dress (the toga), as a symbol of laying down
their *imperium* and went to sacrifice on the Capitol, though it is not
certain that all did so. We should note that this laying down of
imperium was a positive act; it was not simply coming home when
their tour of duty was over. It is indeed one of the peculiarities of the
Roman system that, although offices were allocated for a specific
period of time, they — or at least those carrying *imperium* — did not
just expire, they were laid down. See below.

---

* Parts of this study were offered at a series of seminars given in Oxford to mark the
retirement of Professor Robin Nisbet, and in Sydney to mark that of Professor Edwin
Judge. These will appear in the *Festschrift* volumes. I have to thank speakers, most of
whom I did not identify at the time, for their valuable comments.
  [1] Gell. 15.27: *quia exercitum ... intra urbem imperari ius non sit.* The extension of
the tribune's *ius auxilii* beyond the *pomerium* to a mile beyond the walls seems not to
have affected this rule.
  [2] J.S. Richardson '*Imperium romanum*: empire and the language of power' *JRS* 81
(1991) 1–9 for stress on the right to take *auspicia*, conferred by a *lex curiata*, as
validating *imperium* by divine sanction.

The *imperium* of the annual magistrates was different, since their *imperium* was *domi* as well as *militiae*, and did not lapse or have to be revived at the *pomerium* whether they were leaving the city or entering it. This applied regularly to consuls and praetors, and to the emergency magistrates appointed to deal with perceived crises, dictators, their masters of the horse, and in the triumviral period the triumvirs *rei publicae constituendae (iiiviri r.p.c.)*, the "triple dictatorship" as M.P. Charlesworth described it.[3] But *domi* was *domi*,[4] not *militiae*, consequently even consuls did not bring troops into the city, except briefly when a state of emergency had been declared (by the so-called *senatus consultum ultimum (s.c.u.)*, which asked the consuls and others to see to it that the *res publica* came to no harm). The creation of a dictator, or the election of *iiiviri r. p. c.* seems to have been seen as the equivalent of declaring a state of emergency, or perhaps martial law. But this was by *mos* (custom)[5] not by any *lex* (law) we know of. And it seems to have been tacitly agreed — perhaps because disputing with a man with an army is often not profitable — that in these circumstances arms within the city were acceptable.

It follows that, since returning to the city was equivalent to making a political statement or a claim to rank (*dignitas*) and/or fame (*gloria*), the manner in which such claims were made, and were responded to, illustrates the state of the *res publica* at the time. The late 'Republic', with its intense competition for *dignitas* and *gloria*, set the scene for the triumviral and Augustan ages: the place at which a returning citizen was met — the further from the city the more honourable[6] — and the numbers and quality of the people turning out to greet him,[7] became the criteria by which a return was judged,

---

[3] *CAH* X 19.

[4] C. Marius caused great offence by coming to the Senate straight from his triumph in his triumphal robe: he left, changed to a senator's toga and returned. Plut. *Mar.* 12.5. Cf. the shock of Caesar's use of Cn. Pompeius' 'veterans' in politics in 59; they were too obviously soldiers.

[5] "The Romans ... were a conservative people ... devoted to the worship of law and order"; *mos maiorum* was "a vague ... concept ... a subject of partisan interpretation, of debate and fraud" (Syme *Rom. Rev.* 153). True, but it could arouse support, and public sentiment and opinion counted.

[6] Some evidence in T.E.V. Pearce 'Notes on Cicero, *In Pisonem*' *CQ* 20 (1970) 313f.; from earliest times Dion. Hal. 2.34.2; Plut. *Numa* 7, to later empire; and for the Republican period G.D. Holland *Returning to the City in the Late Republic*, Unpublished Research Essay for M.A. Degree, University of Auckland 1986, p.32. Add Cicero's jibe, *Phil.* 2.78 "As Caesar returned from Spain you went further than anyone else to meet him" (*obviam longissime processisti*). Caesar honoured Antonius for doing so, Plut. *Ant.* 11.1.

[7] Sulla (e.g.) escorted Cn. Pompeius into the city in 79 (Plut. *Pomp.* 13.4).

and his *dignitas* and *gloria* accordingly enhanced — or not.[8] The periods for which we have reasonable amounts of information are those in which there were political struggles and vigorous competition for *dignitas* and *gloria*, and, in consequence, returns to the city often provoked controversy as claims, especially for triumphs, were made and challenged. After Julius Caesar's assassination, the manner and style of the competing factional leaders' returns to the city illustrate not just their understanding of the political situation, but their regard for tradition (*mores maiorum*) and for the susceptibilities of their contemporaries; analysis of these suggests that the usual interpretations are open to criticism both before the passing of the *senatus consultum ultimum* in March 43 and the formation of the triumvirate later that year, and at its end in 32.

The manner in which Octavian/Augustus returned to the city after his victory at Actium casts considerable light on each occasion in turn, and perhaps on the interpretation of his position he then wished to convey. Towards the end of his Principate the *profectio* (departure) of Gaius Caesar became a precedent for the formal *profectio* and *adventus* (arrival) adopted by later emperors setting out for visits or tours to the provinces. Under the 'Republic', several provincial governors returned to the city every year; statistical accuracy is not attainable, but when there were about twelve provinces, between three and six tenures would expire each year if tenures averaged between two and four years, so between three and six governors came home, less a few who did not return because they had died on service overseas.[9] In *pro Murena*, Cicero gives an account of the return of a propraetor who did not ask for a triumph, but aspired to the consulship in elections which were coming up: L. Licinius Murena had been in Transalpine Gaul, where he had commanded the troops he had levied in northern Italy (*Mur.* 42); he had served in Gaul from the end of his praetorship (which was in 65) till 63, when he was returning to stand for the consulship of 62 (*ibid.* 68). His reception was orchestrated by him and his political *amici* (allies):[10] I quote:

---

[8] If he was ignored, like Piso (below), or met only by people of no *dignitas* (rank), Cic. *Mur.* 69, contrasted here with Murena's honourable reception.

[9] Appius Claudius Pulcher (e.g.) who died in Macedonia (*Rom. Rev.* 21), and others like M. Licinius Crassus who fell at Carrhae.

[10] For returns prepared by correspondence to maintain contacts, Cicero *Fam. passim* esp. 15 and 2 (to Caelius); Caesar ran a postal service to Gaul, in 58–50; Pompeius Magnus wrote to Cicero about Appius Claudius, Cic. *Fam.* 3.10.10. It does not seem rash to suppose that most proconsuls wrote such letters.

Many people went out to meet him when he returned; that always
happens to men who want to stand for the consulship; is any one not
met on his return? Who comprised the crowd? I can't give an exact
count, but there were many there, as you'd expect when a consular
candidate was arriving. What of it? If I add the point — a perfectly
normal one — that many were invited to come; that's no offence, nor
is it extraordinary; in our community we're often asked to come and
escort the sons of nobodies at night from the most outlying suburbs;
people naturally did not resent turning out in the middle of the
morning to the Campus Martius to meet a man of his reputation.
(68–9)

Cicero was no doubt exaggerating, as he often did. But the truth
about the socio-political custom is indisputable. Cicero continues:

Members of all the *societates* (syndicates) of *equites* (businessmen)
came — many of them are sitting here on the jury — so did many
Senators of the highest reputation. Of course, every candidate for
office was there, the people who never allow anyone to enter the city
without a reception. Even Postumus our accuser came to meet him,
with a large escort — why be surprised at Murena's large turnout? I
don't mention [which of course means that he is about to do so] his
clients, neighbours, fellow-tribesmen, all the old soldiers who served
with Lucullus, who had come at that time for his triumph. [All whose
officium (duty) called on them to be there as we might say.] (*ibid.* 69)

The implications of Cicero's account are clear — even allowing for
exaggerations. Everyone *cum imperio* who wanted to make an
impression arranged — or had his friends and supporters (*amici*)
arrange — a formal return to the city. The first element was the
reception outside the *pomerium*. Duty (*officium*)[11] brought many
people out; on Cicero's list are kinsmen (of course), *amici*, and those
of lower status (*tenuiores amici*) who would benefit directly or
indirectly from honours bestowed on the returning proconsul/pro-
praetor, whether the honour was immediate (a triumph) or prospective, such as a consulate gained at least partly on the strength of
achievements in the province from which he was returning. This
would lead to jobs and salaries for his *amici*, especially when a
governorship was in prospect.

Cicero does not include — perhaps because it was too obvious to
contemporaries if not to us — that the numbers of people at the
reception and at the public meeting (*contio*) (if any) which followed
were swelled by those who simply wanted to show approval of the

---

[11] For *urbana officia*, Nepos *Att.* 4.3, N.M. Horsfall *Cornelius Nepos: A Selection*
(Oxford 1989) n. *ad loc*, with bibliography, esp. C. Nicolet *The World of the Citizen in
Republican Rome* (E.T. London 1980) 357.

person being received and support for the honours he was seeking; his popularity if you like — or esteem, or mana. Analysis must leave room for some people to act spontaneously — choice after all was the essence of *res publica*.

The reception included a speech, or could do so if one of the magistrates or a tribune with the right of doing business with the People (*ius agendi cum populo/plebe*) invited the proconsul to speak, or the proconsul could progress directly to the temple of Jupiter on the Capitol where he had received the divine ratification of his *imperium*, sacrifice there and then return to his own house, still with an escort. We do not know how many proconsuls actually went to sacrifice on the Capitol, but it is prudent not to assume that no religious act took place when none is recorded. There is, for example, the most meagre amount of information about consuls' *eiuratio* (taking the end-of-term oath) but it must normally have taken place; Cicero's words not the fact of his *eiuratio* in 63 were what aroused commentators' interest (*Fam.* 5.2.7; *Pis.* 6) He could address the Senate later when asked his advice (*sententia*) and the People or *plebs* when someone with the *ius agendi* gave him a *contio* (meeting at which to speak). This made up the full programme — reception, procession to the Capitol, sacrifice, escorted return home, a speech either at the reception or later when invited to address the Senate or a *contio* or, of course, both. A triumph was often crowned by the erection of a building, often a temple, to honour the family of the *triumphator*.[12]

The programme was not necessarily continuous; those seeking a triumph postponed crossing the *pomerium* till the day of the triumph. A friendly consul could — and would — call a meeting of the Senate outside the *pomerium* to hear an account of the returning *imperator*'s (general's) achievements. The Senate could then appoint a day for the triumph and approve the retention of the *triumphator*'s *imperium* within the *pomerium* in order to complete the triumph on the Capitol.[13]

If the consul was not friendly the *amici* of the would-be *triumphator* had to obtain the Senate's approval in his absence. This took longer, sometimes much longer, even several years when an *imperator*, for whatever reason, had enemies in sufficient numbers in high enough

[12] Zanker *Images* 66 *et alibi*. Julius Caesar made it fashionable. Cf. also *id*. Chap. 1.

[13] Triumphs in the 3rd and 2nd centuries are known to have been challenged, like that of Marcellus, because the capture of Syracuse did not end the war in Sicily. He triumphed at the Alban Mount, was later given an *ovatio* on returning to Rome, Plut. *Marc.* 22.

places. The years around 63 — some of the few about which we have
a quantity of information — offer a number of examples: L. Lucullus
was kept waiting from 66–63 by the friends of Pompeius, and allowed
to triumph only to assist his old lieutenant Murena to defeat Catilina
in the consular elections; Metellus Creticus waited from 66 to 62; Q
Marcius Rex, it is generally agreed, was still waiting when he died in
61. Some, like C. Antonius in 63, did not pursue their claim beyond
the salutation by their troops; others, like L. Manlius Torquatus, did
not proceed beyond the vote of a thanksgiving (*supplicatio*) by the
Senate (also in 63). These struggles may reflect the nature of this
period, and its political disharmonies. Similarly C. Pomptinus,
whose triumph, even when granted, was controversial,[14] waited from
61 to 52 and P. Cornelius Lentulus Spinther who returned from
Cilicia in 53 waited till 51.[15] Cicero himself was frustrated, at least
partially, by the Civil War.[16] He waited from 50 till 47 before he gave
up hope, dismissing his lictors[17] and entering the city in a toga after
his interview with Caesar on the latter's return from his victories at
Alexandria and Zela in Asia Minor.

Romans serving in the provinces without *imperium* could also
return with honour, like C. Cassius, who as proquaestor had taken
over Syria after M. Crassus' defeat at Carrhae,[18] or without honour,
as Cicero mocked P. Clodius' explanation of why he had not received
a welcome on returning from his quaestorship in Sicily.[19] On his own
return from Sicily where he had been quaestor, he stopped in
Campania, and made no attempt to make a show when he found that
no one was interested in what he had achieved there (*Planc.* 64f.).

Metellus Numidicus and Cicero offer two examples of prominent
men without *imperium* receiving a civic welcome on their return to
the city. Both had been exiled, Metellus through the enmity of C.
Marius, Cicero through that of P. Clodius. Their reception was
similar to that accorded to successful proconsuls and propraetors. In
Metellus' case, from the scrappy sources of the first decade of the last
century BC, we hear only that the crowd which came to meet him was
so great that daylight ran out before he had ceased greeting those

---

[14] Cic. *Att.* 4.18.4; *Q. fr.* 3.4.6. For the results, Dio 39.65.

[15] Cic. *Att.* 5.21.4.

[16] His return anticipated with interest in 50, *Att.* 7.7.5; he was warmly received,
Fam. 16.11.2.

[17] Whether at once, with Caesar's leave (E. Rawson *Cicero: a portrait* (London
1975) 208), or on crossing the *pomerium* is uncertain.

[18] He beat off a Parthian invasion of Syria, Cic. *Fam* 15.14.3.

[19] Cic. *Att.* 2.1.5. Clodius said he had been in a hurry and arrived after dark.

who came (App. *B.C.* 1.33), and that he was escorted to the Capitol to sacrifice to Jupiter after making an address to the People, and from there was escorted home (Gell. 13.29.1). The accounts are incompatible since his address to the People could not have been held after dark, nor the sacrifice to Jupiter. Either there is exaggeration or invention from what ought to have happened, or the welcome extended to a second day. The former is more likely.

There are much fuller accounts of Cicero's return in 57, all directly or indirectly from his own pen. The best is probably that written to Atticus in the heat of his elation (*Att.* 4.1) since there was no point in trying to deceive Atticus. He had proceeded from Brundisium up the *via Appia*, receiving deputations[20] from the citizen colonies (*coloniae*) and self-governing boroughs (*municipia*) on the way; he can therefore not have travelled fast, since greetings would be exchanged, and Cicero was not conspicuous for his brevity when exchanging compliments. Outside the city gates the Senate (*Pis.* 52)[21] and everyone known to his *nomenclator* (servant to remind him of people's names) except those unable to disguise their enmity came to greet him in person. When he entered the city through the *Porta Capena* the vantage points along the road, the steps and podiums of the temples were crowded by people applauding and cheering. This reception continued as he progressed through the Forum to the Capitol, where he presumably sacrificed to Jupiter. This imitation of a triumphal procession can hardly have been coincidental, though his civilian dress and lack of *imperium* (and lictors) made the occasion quite different. And, like a triumph or the return of a successful proconsul, it must have been orchestrated and organised by Cicero's *amici* and supporters or Clodius' enemies, and supported by them.[22]

[20] So many that they seemed like a continuous procession (*perpetuum agmen*) Cic. *Pis.* 51; R.G.M. Nisbet *Cicero, in Pisonem* (Oxford 1961) p.113.

[21] "Senate came to meet him" suggests (though it does not prove) that it decided to do so. Normally this was only done at triumphs, Jos. *B.J.* 7.125, but this return was modelled on a triumph; the building to be erected was his house — and at public expense. This was unique, Cic. *Pis.* 52 *fin.* See also Pearce 'Notes on Cicero' (cited n.6.).

[22] Note how receptions could be enhanced by the assent of the uncommitted. Their support guaranteed the recipient's charisma. For many, coming to cheer was a voluntary act, not just fulfilling *officium*. Cicero's returns now, in 49, on August 31st 44, December 9th, 44 and the demonstration in 43 (below) should warn modern scholars against underestimating his enduring charisma and decrying his achievement in 63. Contemporaries did not think that he exaggerated, or even invented, the Catilinarian conspiracy, even if he praised his achievement excessively.

Less welcoming receptions were also prepared. Verres had tried to outmanoeuvre his enemies, we are told, by getting the *civitates* (communities) of Sicily to send embassies to Rome to praise him.[23] So did Appius Claudius[24] Cicero's predecessor in Cilicia. In neither case were the precautions successful; prosecutors were awaiting both on their arrival. Gabinius on his return from Syria had to face a similar reception.[25]

Others, fearing prosecution, returned home quietly so as not to arouse enmity. Q. Cicero is an example: M. Cicero had warned him not to make tactless remarks, especially in letters, which might land him in trouble (*Q.fr.* 1.2.1–11), and not to get the backs up of influential men in case their enemies attacked them both (*id.* 13).[26] In his exile M. Cicero was terrified this might happen (*Att.* 3.9.1, 3.17.1). In fact Q. Cicero was warmly received. Even the harmless Q. Minucius Thermus, governor of Asia in 51, was advised not to make enemies but to take thought for a quiet life (*Fam.* 2.18).[27]

By contrast, in *in Pisonem* Cicero gives a splendid satirical account of a man returning without glory; it would be unwise to accept it all as literally true,[28] but it gives an account of what the audience knew was the reverse of honourable. Piso, Cicero alleges, had stolen out of Macedonia to escape his soldiers' anger (*Pis.* 92). It appears that he had won some successes at the start of his tenure, and had been saluted *imperator*, but after subsequent reverses he lost face and left surreptitiously, *crepidatus imperator* (a general in slippers), not in military array — *caligatus* (in military boots); he avoided the limelight on his journey to Rome, bypassing Brundisium and all populous places (*id.* 53), using a circuitous route which kept him clear of the *municipia* (self-governing boroughs) and even the houses of his friends to stay the night. He travelled mostly by night, lurking in pubs by day — more like the corpse of a criminal than an *imperator*

---

[23] Cic. *Ver.* 2.2.145 statues; *id.* 154 triumphal arch; *id.* 154, statues in Rome; *id.* 150 another by farmers; *id.* 168 by the leading business men (*negotiatores*).

[24] Cic. *Fam.* 3.8.2f.; 3.10.6 deputations from *civitates* of Cilicia. The abuse was widespread, stopped by Augustus, Dio 56.25.6.

[25] Cic. *Q.fr.* 3.1.24; Gabinius returned at night; *Pis.* 51: impossible for Piso to return (though he did).

[26] Cf. Cicero's warning to C. Cassius that his distinguished return (*clarum reditum*) might be tarnished while his kinsman Q. Cassius was being prosecuted, a "most unfortunate moment" (*tempus alienissimum*) Cic. *Fam.* 15.14.4.

[27] Cicero cannot have been the only Roman (or governor) to have written streams of letters to *amici*, men with *auctoritas* and *potentia*, e.g. *Fam.* 15, esp. 3 to M. Cato, 7 to C. Marcellus, 8 to C. Marcellus his father, 12 to Aemilius Paullus.

[28] "An amusing invention", Nisbet *In Pisonem* (n.20) p.114.

from Macedonia (*id.* 53). On his arrival at the city nobody met him. The report of his arrival with lictors bearing the insignia of a triumph aroused no interest even among those who had served with him in Macedonia, not even among those standing for office, though they had been forewarned and invited to come. His escort changed into civilian garments at the Esquiline Gate, not the *Porta Triumphalis*, by which governors of Macedonia usually returned (*id.* 54f.). Again the truth is not the point; the point is what Cicero's audience would understand as portraying the disgraceful.[29]

Returns of these sorts reflect the flavour of the late 'Republic', an age of intense political competition and rivalry, of self-glorification to enhance personal *dignitas* and the *gloria* of the family. More sinister were the hostile returns, marches on the city to rectify political injuries and political defeats by force of arms. Sulla started it, in 88, and his example was quickly followed by his enemies and by his own repeat performance in 82. By Plutarch's account, the civil population put up a resistance to Sulla's force on the first occasion (*Sulla* 9.6), but on the others, though pillage and rapine took place, and there were casualties in the clashes of the legions, the civil population is not said to have taken any part. The nervousness with which the return of Pompeius from his Mithridatic wars (in 62) was anticipated stems from these violent returns to the city and the civil wars they precipitated,[30] in which Pompeius himself had won the nickname of "teenage butcher",[31] the known enmity of L. Lucullus and his supporters, the recent abortive coup of L. Catilina and the measures taken to thwart it. But his return was peaceful, ostentatiously so, and brought out the usual welcome: large crowds, escorts from the towns of Italy, audience by the Senate, allocation of days for his triumph, and the triumphal progress to the shrine of *Iuppiter Optimus Maximus*.[32]

The opposite occurred in 49, with Julius Caesar's return from his Gallic wars, when the enmities were so bitter, and the pursuit of *dignitas* and *gloria* so unrelenting, that civil war resulted.[33] In the

[29] Piso's mana is what is at issue; if *candidati* ignored him, he had none, cf. Cic. *Mur.* 68–9, quoted above; similarly for those who did not perform *officium* (if true). If not true, the allegation still shows how people could register disapproval — by boycott. The Esquiline Gate route lay through a squalid part of the city, was reached through a cemetery (a point I owe to an unknown speaker at the Oxford seminar).

[30] Plut. *Pomp.* 9–14 etc.

[31] *Adulescentulus carnifex*, Helvius Mancia *ap.* Val. Max. 6.2.8.

[32] Plut. *Pomp.* 43–5.

[33] M. Gelzer *Caesar, Politician and Statesman* (E.T. Oxford 1968) 169–94 for a detailed account.

wars the movements of prominent citizens to and away from the city were seen as important, since to leave and stay away demonstrated criticism of Caesar, to come to Rome, and especially to attend the Senate, signified support for him. Cicero's agonies on this point are familiar enough.[34] No less important were the movements of Caesar's leading lieutenants during the fighting, and immediately after it. Cicero attacked M. Antonius in another satirical sketch for the way he returned to the city from a visit to Caesar after the Munda campaign in 45, though he, Antonius, had taken no part in the campaign and was *privatus* (a citizen without office). However, he had previously been Caesar's master of horse, and was then a candidate for the consulship of 44 (*Phil.* 2.76); he had made a quick tour (*cucurristi*)[35] through the *municipia* and colonies of Gaul, not even dressed like a Roman in a toga and senator's shoes, but wearing slippers and a Gallic cloak, though these were boroughs which senators regularly visited to canvass for votes. On his return to Rome, he stopped at *Saxa Rubra*, nine miles up the *via Flaminia* (Cicero actually says he kept out of sight boozing in a squalid pub (*cauponula*) for two hours till it was dark). He then hired a fast carriage, arrived in the city in a whirl in disguise and went straight home to surprise his wife (*id.* 76f.).

Cicero claims this was irresponsible and induced an atmosphere of panic in the city and alarm throughout Italy (*id.* 77). However that may be, Antonius was summoned by a tribune (unnamed) before a *contio*, and in answer to a question said he had come back on private business (*rei tuae causa*) (*id.* 78), a response which set tongues wagging, or so Cicero says. The whole story is doubtless much misrepresented, but it does show how important the comings and goings of major political figures were thought to be, even when at the time they had no official position or *imperium*.[36]

Part of the crisis precipitated by Julius Caesar's murder arose from the fact that political action would have to take place in Rome, whereas the armies, whose consent was required for any political settlement to hold, were mostly elsewhere; many were in Macedonia preparing for Caesar's Parthian expedition; many were in Italy, and

---

[34] *Att.* books 8 to 10 *passim*.

[35] Lit. "you ran" — or perhaps "jogged".

[36] Nic. Dam. *frr.* 32–3 Jac., Jane Bellemore *Nicolaus of Damascus, Life of Augustus* (Bristol 1984) 14–17 (text and translation), 89 (commentary), for C. Octavius' unwanted welcome before Caesar's death from the charlatan 'son of Marius', who had a "large following" and pestered Octavius till he reached home.

in colonies of veterans. The arbiters of the issues not present in Rome would have to move there or forfeit their opportunity to influence the course of events, and also satisfy the aspirations of the troops.

First among these was Caesar's heir, the young C. Octavius. I don't think we need the advantage of hindsight to recognise this. His return to the city was characteristic of the man, young, middle-aged and old, cautious to discover the lie of the land and decisive in action when he had analysed the situation. On the Ides of March he was with the army in Macedonia, training for the Parthian campaign. On the news of Caesar's death and his own adoption he crossed to Italy, avoiding Brundisium at first, but when he had news which encouraged him to believe that Brundisium was friendly and that Caesar's veteran soldiers would welcome him he went there and was welcomed by them. He sacrificed, announced his claim to Caesar's name (App. *B.C.* 3.11),[37] collected funds and set out for Rome in a sort of *profectio* (ceremonial departure). As he travelled towards Rome he gathered a following, and discovered that Caesar's old soldiers were looking for a leader to avenge him (*id.* 12). He reached the Naples area on April 8th 3 weeks later (Cic. *Att.* 14.10.3). He remained in this area for some days making soundings through Balbus and other old friends of Caesar (*ibid.*). He sought support from Cicero and Philippus his stepfather, and quite certainly from others, and it would be unreasonable not to suppose that he also made arrangements for financial support should he need funds to pay Caesar's legacies. Some of his entourage made remarks about his intentions which upset Cicero, but Octavius had arranged the three essentials before he approached Rome — political support, financial resources, the backing of troops.

He arrived in Rome with an escort of *amici*, as was only to be expected, but apparently without organising a big reception.[38] Cicero had anticipated that L. Antonius, who was tribune, would present him to a *contio*, and was anxious to know what he would say (*Att.* 14.20.5 and 14.21.4, written on May 11th). This proves that his arrival was going to be a matter of public importance.[39] Octavius had told his *amici* that he would accept his inheritance — they were already calling him "Caesar" (Cic. *Att.* 14.12.2) and laying claim to it

[37] Nic. Dam. *fr.* 51 Jac.: Bellemore *Nicolaus* (n.36) 22–4, 96; Dio 45.3.2.

[38] "Only a few *amici*", Dio 45.5.2.

[39] Apparently M. Antonius did not think so. He tried to ignore him (App. *B.C.* 3.13).

was his first public act the day after he arrived.[40] He made the prescribed declaration in the Forum before the acting *praetor urbanus* (president of the civil law courts), C. Antonius, and perhaps on this occasion requested that a *lex curiata* be passed to ratify his adoption, which required such a law because it would involve a *detestatio sacrorum*[41] (renunciation of his own family's cults).

The next day the young Caesar was presented to a *contio* by L. Antonius. At it he made remarks which upset Cicero (*Att.* 15.2.3, May 18th). This declaration of his intentions in personal and public life completed his return and laid the foundations for his political future.[42]

M. Antonius' return to Rome for the debate on June 1st produced the first use of force against the city.[43] There had been no declaration of a state of emergency or the creation of any special magistracy (Antonius himself had recently abolished the dictatorship). His force (or escort) was one of veteran soldiers. We do not know the numbers, but they are described as *tantam frequentiam militum veteranorum* (so huge a crowd of veteran soldiers) by Brutus and Cassius in a letter to Cicero (Cic. *Fam.* 11.2); nor do we know where they were encamped, but they frightened off Cicero, who had planned to attend the meeting (*Att.* 14.14.6, 17.2), as well as the 'liberators' and the consuls designate, A. Hirtius and C. Pansa (Cic. *Phil.* 1.6, *Att.* 15.5.2). There were indeed so many absentees that Antonius did not have the full meeting (*frequens senatus*) which he required for the business he had in mind, which was to alter the provincial allocations for himself and others.

Although Cicero drew a marvellous picture of the scene in the *Second Philippic* (108f.; he was not actually there, so he is using his imagination or the words of others), the fact is that Antonius had to put his measure through the popular Assembly, which he did despite being unable to comply with the requirement of three *nundinae* (market days)[44] notice of his measure. An irregular measure of the

---

[40] He organised his own *amici* to come to the Forum with their followers (App. *B.C.* 3.14) — *clientes* perhaps? He also took care to arrive before two *dies fasti* when public business could be conducted.

[41] Gaius, *Inst.* 1.99; Gell. 5.19; cf. J.A. Crook *Law and Life of Rome* (London 1967) 112; *RE* iii 1331 (Hübner) etc.

[42] For the subsequent rebuff by M. Antonius, Holmes *Architect* I 14 with refs; Syme *Rom. Rev.* 115.

[43] It was certainly an act of intimidation, if not of war, and comparable to Julius Caesar's use of Cn. Pompeius' veterans in 59, Cic. *Vat.* 5.

[44] Roughly three weeks in modern calculation. It is sometimes forgotten that this

Assembly was presumably easier to get away with than an irregular *senatus consultum*. He did not get away with it, of course, since Decimus Brutus refused to make way for him in Gaul at the end of the year, but it is likely that the legal nicety was not the principal reason for this. It gave him room for justifying himself, however, and putting Antonius in a bad light.

Festivals of various sorts occupied much of June and July, with Antonius' attempts to thwart Octavian's exhibition of his father's golden chair and the diadem offered at the *Lupercalia* at the games for Caesar's Victory and *Venus Genetrix* at the end of July. These formed the background to L. Piso's speech on August 1st which Cicero declared was an important factor in his decision to return to the city.

Cicero's return on August 31st was not without ceremony. He made a point of appearing formally in a toga and senator's shoes, in broad daylight, as he emphasises in *Phil*. 2.76; he received a considerable reception at the gates, perhaps the *Porta Capena*,[45] the same gate by which he had entered on his return from exile — was he making a point in so doing? We do not know (Plut. *Cic*. 43.4). As he had previously let it be known that his roving embassy (*libera legatio*) would last till the end of M. Antonius' consulate (on December 31st),[46] his return at this time indicated that he would take part in the Senate's routine debate on the *res publica*, on September 1st. When Antonius changed the agenda, however, Cicero stayed away to show his displeasure. This enraged Antonius,[47] who left the city and was not in the Senate on September 2nd, when Cicero delivered what he subsequently wrote up as the *First Philippic*.

The autumn of 44 saw a series of comings and goings by Antonius the consul, and by Octavian. In all cases they appear to have been escorted by armed men. When Antonius appeared on September 19th, to reply to *Philippic I*, he had a strong bodyguard openly under arms (*Phil*. 2.112). Octavian also had a bodyguard when he returned to the city on November 11th while Antonius was in Brundisium meeting the legions from Macedonia. On this occasion he did not enter the city until invited in by Cannutius the tribune (App. *B.C.*

---

lex lacked the validity of one properly carried with due notice. The issue of legality is not as clear as *Rom. Rev.* 163 (e.g.) indicates.

[45] *Phil*. 1.10 for Piso's speech. For Cicero's reception Plut. *Cic*. 43.4; though *Porta Capena* is not actually named, Cicero will have come up the *via Appia*.

[46] Cic. *Att*. 15.25; Plut. *Cic*. 43.2.

[47] Cic. *Phil*. 1.12f., believed at least by Plutarch, *Cic*. 43.5.

3.41), and when he did enter, his bodyguard were armed but their weapons were concealed — how well we cannot say — and they were not in full military uniform. When he addressed the *contio* in the Forum neither he nor the tribune used the official speaker's *rostra*; they stood on the podium of the temple of Castor and Pollux. Nor was any formal motion or vote (*plebiscitum*) moved. Were these concessions to soothe public opinion?[48] There was certainly some toning down of the breaches of the *mores maiorum*.

After Octavian withdrew North, Antonius returned, again with at least a praetorian cohort under arms (App. *B.C.* 3.45) for a debate on November 24th, which was aborted, and again on November 28th for a meeting of the Senate at night after his failure to win the mutineers at Alba Fucens (*ibid.*); these were the two occasions he tried, but failed, to stop legions going over to Octavian, as he did to get the Senate to declare him a rebel.[49] Antonius made no attempt to pretend that there was not a war situation in existence, despite the lack of any declaration of a state of emergency (by a *senatus consultum ultimum*), and the Senate's refusal to sustain his accusation of rebellion against Octavian.

These further three marches on the city in order to force resolutions through the Senate show both Antonius' view that there was a war situation, and his lack of respect for the *mores maiorum* (traditions) in regard to returning to the city.[50]

Cicero's planned return to Rome was timed for December 9th, the day before the new tribunes entered office; the choice of date can hardly have been accidental, but we have no information on his reception. He said he wanted to meet C. Pansa, the consul designate; we do not know if they met, and if they did what views they exchanged. Ten days later the tribunes announced a meeting of the Senate to discuss the protection of Pansa and Hirtius his colleague when they entered their office on January 1st. Talks had obviously taken place, and there must have been at least some element of propaganda in the agenda, since it implied much more than it said.[51]

---

[48] But the speech was not conciliatory Cic. *Att.* 16.15.3. Cf. *Rom. Rev.* 125. And gestures towards Caesar's statue could be made more effectively from there, as the statue stood close by — much closer than it did to the *rostra*. I owe this point to a speaker at the Oxford Seminar.

[49] Often confused in text books, but Holmes *Architect* I 32–4 gives a clear account.

[50] The reverse of the picture in *Rom. Rev.* 125f. For *mos maiorum* n.5 above.

[51] It implied that the new consuls were under threat, and by implication that a state of emergency should be declared (by *senatus consultum ultimum*) to bring troops into the city.

Cicero was seen going to the Senate House, and this prompted a large attendance.[52] Can we seriously believe either that Cicero was unprepared, or that he had not let it be known that he would attend for this piece of business? I for one think not.

He treated the Senate to the *Third Philippic Oration* (*Fam.* 11.6a; *id.* 8) and the People's Assembly to the *Fourth Oration* in the afternoon. Both will have been written up, but both show clear signs of premeditation,[53] leading as they did to his proposal for a state of emergency to be declared which would legitimise bringing troops into the city to protect the consuls. However, it was not till after the envoys had returned from their unsuccessful mission to Antonius (Dio 46.31.2) on February 1st or 2nd, 43, that the *senatus consultum ultimum*, as proposed by Cicero on January 1st (*Phil.* 5.30) was passed, and the state of emergency (or state of war) declared which regularised the action taken in response to the *Third Philippic* of bringing troops into the city to protect the consuls and Senate *domi*, with arms inside the *pomerium*.

Once the fighting began, the customary honours associated with returning to the city became exaggerated and inflated competitively in the same way as the other honours the *res publica* had recognised: Cicero frankly admitted that the honours proposed for the deceased Servius Sulpicius were unprecedented (*Phil.* 9.3); the 50-day thanksgiving (*supplicatio*) for the relief of the Mutina garrison in April was also unprecedented (App. *B.C.* 3.74);[54] the demonstration of support which Cicero received as a *privatus* (citizen without office) — huge numbers escorting him from his house to the temple of Jupiter on the Capitol to give thanks for the victory, thence to the *rostra* (Cic. *ad Brut.* 1.3.2, and cf. *Phil.* 14.16f.) — was also highly unusual for a *privatus* (even allowing for some exaggeration).

After the siege of Mutina, when the generals returned, the brutal realities of civil war became apparent. Octavian came first, in August, 43 (App. *B.C.* 3.88f.), to demand the consulate. He did however make some concessions to propriety: he halted his men outside the *pomerium*, beyond the Quirinal Hill in the first place, and later moved them to the Campus Martius, and even withdrew them from there while the election was held in the usual place. When the

---

[52] Cic. *Fam.* 11.6a (Shackleton Bailey 356) 2f.

[53] The elaborate details of the *s.c.*s proposed cannot possibly have been drafted *ex tempore*.

[54] Fifty days was longer than for any of Caesar's victories. Did Cicero remember his words in *Prov.* 27?

people came out from the city to meet him in the customary manner they were reassured by messages conveyed by an advance guard comprising cavalry. Appian (*B.C.* 3.92) says he entered the city with a "sufficient" guard and saw to the safety of his female relatives[55] (did they need it, or was this propaganda?), obtained money for his troops and withdrew for the consular elections.[56] After these, Octavian entered the city with his consular *imperium* and took the *auspicia* in the customary way, and with the propitious omens duly reported by Suetonius (*Aug.* 95) and others (Dio 46.46.2, Obsequens 69).

The entry of the three prospective triumvirs later in the year, after their compact at Bononia, was more blatantly uncompromising. They entered the city on successive days each with his praetorian cohort and one legion and occupied strategic sites. Octavian came first, presumably as consul, but no ancient account of their entry survives; as it was known that there would be proscriptions it is not likely that they were welcome. At a meeting of the People's Assembly the law making them triumvirs was proposed and passed without the customary three *nundinae* between proposal and ratification (App. *B.C.* 4.7). Tradition was again broken on January 1st, 41, when L. Antonius triumphed on the first day of his consulate, and demanded gifts of crowns from each of the tribes (Dio 48.4.6, who adds that the triumph was entirely undeserved).[57]

In 41, when Octavian returned from the victory at Philippi, Dio records only that he "did what was customary for a victory" (48.5.1) — presumably a sacrifice at the temple of Jupiter — but his reception in the city is not noticed. In the diplomatic skirmishing before the Perusine War both L. Antonius and Octavian, the one consul, the other triumvir, entered the city under arms; L. Antonius even addressed a *contio* in military uniform, another unprecedented violation of tradition. But the city was under military occupation, and the troops at least partially out of control.[58]

Octavian was welcomed when he returned from the Perusine War (in 40). This must have been organised, likewise the decree which

---

[55] His mother and sister were in the *aedes* of the Vestal Virgins, which could have been seen as a place of asylum.

[56] The legal question 'after a *s.c. ultimum* which named a propraetor as one of those asked to see that the *res publica* come to no harm, could that propraetor cross the *pomerium* without losing his *imperium*?' appears not to have been asked, then or since. Academic at the time, probably, since arguing legal niceties with generals backed by armed troops is not likely to be very profitable.

[57] Given as *ex Alpibus*, *CIL* I² pp.50, 179.

[58] Dio 48.12 (sacrilege and temple-robbery).

granted him the right to wear a laurel crown on all occasions when *triumphatores* customarily wore theirs (Dio 48.16). The citizens also ostentatiously resumed wearing their togas to symbolise the return of peace. No source suggests what might have lain behind this propaganda, but the demonstration must have been organised, since, though the fighting in Italy had died down, Sextus Pompeius was still astride the routes by which the city's food supply would arrive, and there was hunger in the city (Dio 48.18.1). Perhaps it was the first peace demonstration.

The longing for peace was illustrated the next year (39) on two occasions, the first when the population flocked out of the city to meet the triumvirs after the compact at Brundisium, and escorted them at their triumphal *ovatio*.[59] The second was when the news of the compact reached at Misenum between Sextus Pompeius and the triumvirs was made known. Antonius and Octavian proceeded towards the city to the accompaniment of sacrifices in their honour as saviours, but they did not receive a formal welcome in Rome because they avoided one by entering secretly at night (App. *B.C.* 5.74). The expectation of a restored food supply was clearly uppermost in the citizens' minds, as well as the restoration of exiles and the once proscribed.

These receptions differed from those of the 'Republic' before the civil wars in that the initiatives seem to have lain not with the recipients but with the Roman populace, though this may be deceptive, and the supporters of the Caesarian party may have been behind them. We cannot be confident either way, as the sources are only Dio and Appian, and not the contemporary Cicero's letters. They are however part of the trend pointed out by Zanker,[60] of the Senate and People apparently taking initiatives in bestowing honours rather than the leading citizens asserting claims to honours, gaining the Senate's assent and erecting lasting memorials to their own families.

Novel, or exaggerated, honours greeted Octavian on his return from the victory over Sextus Pompeius in 36. The citizens' progress "a very long way" out from the city to welcome him[61] wearing festal garlands, the escort to the temples, then to his house, are traditional.

---

[59] *CIL* I[2] pp.50, 180: "*quod pacem cum ... fecit*" in each case.

[60] Zanker *Images* 92, esp. after 27. Cf. A. Wallace-Hadrill 'Roman arches and Greek honours' *PCPhS* 36 (1990) 158, which compromised "the republican aristocratic tradition of self-assertion".

[61] *hoti porrōtatō*, Appian *B.C.* 5.130. Cf. Zanker *Images* Chap. 2.

So is his speech outside the *pomerium* (Dio 49.15.3), but many honours were novel, some suggesting triumphs — e.g. the right to ride into the city on horseback (as those receiving an *ovatio* did), to wear the laurel crown (of the *triumphator*) on all occasions, to celebrate the victory of Naulochus annually on September 3rd in the temple of Jupiter with his family (Dio *loc.cit.*). Appian in his account dates his speeches to the Senate and People the following day, but he also says that Octavian had had them written down and circulated, and included a justification of all his actions since he first entered the public arena. Along with another *ovatio* he was given new and augmented honours, as was M. Agrippa (Dio 49.14.3f.), who was voted the *corona rostrata*, a gold crown with ships' prows.

Octavian's reception on the three occasions when he returned to the city from his Illyrian campaigns in 35, 34 and 33[62] is nowhere described. The Senate offered him a triumph, in 35 (Dio 49.38.1), or 33 (App. *Ill.* 28); this reversed the traditional order of events, in which the would-be *triumphator* asked the Senate to approve a claim and name a day or days. No doubt Octavian's friends prompted the Senate, but his postponement of its celebration casts doubt on how far he organised it; could one ask for a triumph not now but some time in the future?[63] Another novelty was the vote of honours to the women of his family; as Rice Holmes remarks (*Architect* I 133), this smacks of the idea of a royal family. On this visit Octavian also inaugurated his second consulship (of 33), if only for one day, possibly with enough time to enable him to associate himself with M. Agrippa at the start of his aedileship, and with the campaign of building amenities for the populace of the city on which the ex-consul (*consularis*) turned aedile embarked. Returning from his campaign of 33 Octavian dedicated his spoils from Illyricum to the colonnade and libraries of the *Porticus Octaviae*, another public amenity, but following in the tradition of using spoils to enhance the *gloria* of his own family.

Returning to the city to lay down *imperium* became a crucial point at issue in 33/32. According to Dio, Octavian, who had transacted business in the city on the last day of 33 (49.43.7), was not in the city

---

[62] Dio describes a *profectio* for Britain early in 34 "in emulation of his father" (49.38.2), but says he was diverted from Gaul to Illyricum. Cf. App. *Ill.* 24–7.

[63] No examples; the difficulty was usually to obtain 'a day' so that the would-be *triumphator* could celebrate and then resume his place in the *res publica*. But a *iiivir* was not inhibited in crossing the *pomerium*.

on the first day C. Sosius took the chair (50.2.3)[64] and was keeping a watch on things from outside it, but, obviously, from not far off. In the debate which followed, Sosius, a partisan of Antonius, attacked Octavian, but was prevented from taking action against him — presumably by moving the sort of motion that Cicero moved in the *Third Philippic Oration* — by the veto of a tribune. Later,[65] after considering the situation, Octavian entered the city with troops, and summoned the Senate. He appeared at the meeting with an armed escort; Dio's expression[66] need mean no more than lictors with axes, but it might have been a full general's bodyguard (*cohors praetoria*). His *amici* carried concealed daggers. How well concealed? We do not know; perhaps not too well, and if not too well, did he need a full *cohors praetoria*? In any case, lictors with axes or a *cohors* both proclaimed that the 'emergency' magistracy, the triumvirate, was still in existence. This is the essential point.

Most modern writers call this a *coup d'état*,[67] and there has been an interminable debate on the date at which the triumvirate ended with a view to establishing whether Octavian's whole position was based on an illegality or not.[68] But the debate, I suggest, is a complete waste of time, because, though magistracies always had a terminal date attached to them, they did not terminate until the magistrate had been succeeded or brought his *imperium* formally to an end. Consuls in the city went to the temple of Jupiter and took an oath that they had kept the laws; proconsuls went to sacrifice at the temple, surrendering their *imperium* as they crossed the *pomerium*, unless the Senate had extended it to allow them to triumph, as we have seen.

This I think is how we should view the end of the triumvirate; whether or not the 31st of December 33 was the terminal date, as I think virtually certain, everybody knew that it had not expired since neither surviving triumvir had surrendered his *imperium*, nor would their *imperium* expire till they did, and had successors appointed to

---

[64] Sosius is named second on the *fasti*; Dio mentions the unwillingness of Domitius Ahenobarbus, his colleague, to become involved in the quarrel, so the date may be February 1st; cf. Holmes *Architect* I 141, J.M. Carter *The Battle of Actium* (London 1970) 186. M. Reinhold *From Republic to Principate* (Atlanta Ga. 1988) 88f. for refs to other discussions of the date. Syme reverses the order of events (*Rom. Rev.* 276–8), though Dio is explicit in stating that Sosius made the first move.

[65] Dio (*loc. cit.*) says *husteron*, so probably not next day.

[66] *Phrouran tōn stratiōtōn* (50.2.5).

[67] Except those who accept Mommsen's view (*Staatsrecht* II 2, 720f.) on the end of the triumvirate, which lies at the base of this argument. Reinhold *Republic to Principate* (n.64) 236 n.52 for a list of discussions.

[68] Holmes *Architect* I 231–45, and above.

their province(s) (*provinciae*).[69] Sosius and his fellows understood
this perfectly well. In the first place they attended the meeting called
by Octavian; they would not have done so had his summons been
clearly *ultra vires* — staying away was a traditional form of protest.[70]
In the second place, those who arranged the furniture in the Senate
House had placed a third curule chair between those of the consuls,[71]
apparently without protest from Sosius or anyone else. This can only
mean that the Senators were prepared to receive Octavian as
triumvir.

On the other hand they may have come expecting Octavian to
resign, or, if he was not going to resign immediately, to indicate the
steps he would take towards that end. But Octavian said he was not
going to resign, and gave as his reason — however tendentious —
"since Antonius is not prepared to come to the city or lay down his
imperium though the time of the triumvirate has expired".[72] Livy's
words are said to have derived from Augustus' own autobiography,
but in any case they mean he would not resign unless Antonius did so
too, in the only known way, which was to come to Rome for the
purpose.

Octavian seems to be on surprisingly good ground here, though
precedents were few. No one but Sulla had given up an emergency
dictatorship; he had done so (Plut. *Sulla* 34.3) by dismissing his
lictors and walking in the Forum in a toga with his *amici*. Lepidus
had also come to Rome when stripped of his share in the triumvirate
and sent there by Octavian wearing civilian dress,[73] hence we must
assume without his lictors, thus indicating his surrender of *imperium*.
So, Octavian was taking a stand on precedent in arguing that the
requisite act was to appear in Rome in a toga without lictors and
accept successors in his *provincia(e)*, or have it/them renewed by the
Senate, or at least make a start on the process.

Antonius had in fact perhaps already done this in the dispatches he

---

[69] Or had them renewed. A point often overlooked. Resignation as *iiivir* was
meaningless unless arrangements for governing the provinces (hence commanding the
armies) were made.

[70] Many examples; for Caesar's lack of support in 59, Plut. *Caes.* 14.8. More
recently, M. Antonius' failure to get a quorum in 44 (above).

[71] Dio 50.2.5.

[72] Livy's words (Epit. 132): *cum M. Antonius ... neque in urbem venire vellet neque
finito triumviratus tempore imperium deponere.* I have translated the ablative absolute
"though": it could equally well be "since" (causal) or "when" (temporal), which offer
different nuances, but without affecting this argument. Holmes *Architect* I 243 for the
view that Augustus' autobiography is the source.

[73] App. *B.C.* 5.126, the only source to offer this important point.

had sent, asking for the ratification of his reorganisation of the provinces East of the Hellespont, dispatches Sosius had suppressed (Dio 49.41.4).[74] If the Senate ratified the reorganisation, Antonius could simply remain in Egypt, and ask the Senate to appoint a new proconsul to Macedonia — in effect go into *exilium* (exile) without formally terminating his *imperium*. Or he could ask to be recognised as proconsul of the whole area. But Sosius, it may be supposed, knew that neither the Senate nor the *populus Romanus* would accept giving away the provinces East of the Hellespont, especially Asia with its lucrative revenues. He therefore adopted the best method of defence, which was to attack Octavian for not surrendering his *imperium* as after the defeat of Sextus Pompeius he said he would "when Antonius returned from the Parthian business" (App. *B.C.* 5.132), a task which Antonius claimed to have accomplished at his triumph in Alexandria. Sosius was anxious to publish this dispatch, Octavian to suppress it (Dio 49.41.5). An attack of this sort would explain Octavian's line of defence, or counter-attack, demanding Antonius' appearance in Rome as *privatus*, to resign *more maiorum*. In his defence of himself, he could also have pointed out that he had a triumph to organise, and could not be expected to lay down his *imperium* before that.

Dio's account of Octavian's proceedings (50.2.3–7) makes it clear that it was not his summons of the Senate, nor the defence of his own position (*id.* 5), which was "temperate", nor his criticisms of Sosius and Antonius which provoked a walk-out. He was heard in silence (*id.* 6). What caused the walk-out was his calling a second meeting at which he promised documentary proof of Antonius' wrong-doing.[75] Dio may not be telling the whole truth, but his account is detailed, and logical, and if the *mores maiorum* on laying down *imperium* are weighed carefully, it seems to me to correspond to what could be expected.

But this threat was what caused Sosius, Domitius and some 300 senators to leave before the meeting Octavian called, not openly, by walking out of the Senate House, but in secret (Dio *id.* 6) — skulking if you want an emotive word — and Octavian said "good riddance", at least later. They claimed that Octavian was using force against the *res publica* — a very successful piece of propaganda that almost all

---

[74] By Dio's account they did not arrive till 32, when Sosius was consul.

[75] Or perhaps "crime", mentioned in Tac. *Ann.* 2.3.1; Vell. 2.82.3; Reinhold *Republic to Principate* (n.64) App. 7. But giving away provinces was certainly an act which was illegal unless and until sanctioned.

modern scholars have swallowed. Opinion in the Senate however was pretty evenly divided; the 300 senators who left with the consuls represented about half of the normal total, but it is generally supposed that the Senate was greatly swollen at this time to as many as 1000,[76] which would make Sosius' supporters about one third. At all events, after this exodus no more is heard of demands that Octavian should resign his position as triumvir without also demanding that Antonius should do so too.

Apart from the streams of mostly undeserved triumphs,[77] the next significant return to the city was Octavian's after Actium and the seizure of Egypt; it led ultimately to the settlement of 27, at which Octavian did precisely what he demanded that Antonius should do in 32; he put his *provincia* in the hands of the Senate by inviting it to discuss the consular provinces. and thus by this act, as I argued as long ago as 1974, 'restored the *res publica*' because it invited the Senate to nominate the commanders of the legions.[78]

But this happened later. In 32, nothing is heard of Octavian's movements after the departure of Sosius, Domitius and the other senators who supported them; if there was a celebration of the *coniuratio Italiae* (Italy's united oath of support) in Rome it is not mentioned in our sources.[79] The simplest explanation is that there was none, and that Augustus' words in *Res gestae* (25.2) are a simple statement of fact, "all Italy swore to support me",[80] and the process probably began in Rome with the consuls L. Cornelius and M.

---

[76] Suet. *Aug.* 35.1. More than 700 fought with Octavian at Actium (*R.g.* 25), whence the traditional figure of 300 who left with Sosius and Domitius. Cf. *Rom. Rev.* 278 n.3.

[77] Syme (*Rom. Rev.* 327) calculated ten before the Battle of Actium, but most had already taken place. The *Acta* record L. Antonius' plus nine others since January 1st, 41, plus three ovations. Ventidius Bassus' in 38 was very well deserved: "first of all the Romans to triumph over the Parthians" Gell. 15.4.4.

[78] 'Octavian in the senate, January 27 B.C.' *JRS* 64 (1974) 176–84.

[79] "Of the manner in which the measure was carried out there stands no record at all" *Rom. Rev.* 284. Nor is the date certain, and opinions have differed; Rice Holmes *Architect* I 143f. and 247–51, Carter *Battle of Actium* (n.64) 195, etc. But in Rome opinion moved so much in Octavian's favour that, when he was ready to take the field, he made a formal *profectio* from the temple of Bellona, using the ancient ritual of the *fetiales*, Dio 50.4.4f.

[80] *Iuravit in mea verba tota Italia*, with reservations about the word 'all' — *tota*. Virgil (*Aen.* 4.275) certainly thought that *Italia* included the Roman People. *R.g. loc. cit.* for Augustus' stress on the number of men of quality (senators and priests) who followed him. For the oath Brunt and Moore 67f. See also Richard Gordon *et al.* 'Roman inscriptions 1986-90' *JRS* 83 (1993) 136 for the oath taken in ?6/5 at Conobaria in Baetica as a recapitulation of the oath of 32, *q.v.* for further bibliography.

Valerius Messalla (or perhaps only L. Cornelius, who became consul on July 1st, Messalla not until November 1st[81]); they succeeded Sosius and Domitius, who were deemed to have resigned by leaving Italy without being allocated a province, and without holding the Latin festival.

The strongest supporting evidence that this is the essential truth lies in the words of Tacitus (*Ann.* 1.7),[82] who echoes Augustus' expression in describing how first the Senate under the consuls then the People and the army accepted Tiberius as his successor. If the consuls of AD 14 were not following a precedent, how, we may ask, did they strike exactly the same formula?[83] They had not yet seen *Res gestae*!

The manner in which the peoples of Italy were induced to give their adherence to Octavian's forces might be deduced by analogy from how the British crown obtained the adherence of the Maori peoples to the Treaty of Waitangi in New Zealand in 1840. Then, commissioners were sent round the country visiting every substantial settlement, summoning meetings and trying to persuade each group of chiefs to add their signatures. Where this was refused at first, the commissioners did their best to obtain a favourable response and then left. So perhaps Octavian and/or his agents may have toured Italy, perhaps with latent, even blatant, threats (Dio 50.6.3).

In the opinion of some scholars[84] the *coniuratio*, with its oath of support, effectively ended the triumvirate; Octavian no longer needed triumviral powers, since the oath was *sine die* and the obligations could be terminated only by the commander in whose *verba* the oath had been taken.[85] Under it he obtained control of everything.[86]

Octavian returned to the city from his victories at Actium and in

---

[81] So *Fasti Venusini, CIL* I² pp.66 and 160.

[82] *Consules primi in Tiberii Caesaris verba iuravere* (The consuls took the lead in swearing to support and defend Tiberius).

[83] As there was neither *praefectus annonae* nor *praefecti praetorio* in 32, the consuls must also have spoken for the *populus* in its role as the military classes. I find no difficulty in this even if we cannot be sure of the exact words of the oath. A.H.M. Jones *Augustus* (London 1970) 37f., has argued that E–J 315 (*ILS* 8781) is an echo, so also Syme *Rom. Rev.* 288 and n.3; Brunt and Moore *loc. cit.* (n.80 above).

[84] E.g. Gagé *ad loc.* I agree, and this seems not incompatible with the formal annulment (in 28) of all the acts of the *iiiviri* not already ratified as legal. F. Millar 'Triumvirate and Principate' *JRS* 63 (1973) 50–67, esp. 59–61.

[85] Did Augustus ever terminate it? The actions of the consuls in AD 14 (above) may suggest he did not, though he kept it latent after the Actium campaign.

[86] *Rerum omnium potitus*, Augustus' own expression, *R.g.* 34.1.

Egypt some 3 years after the *coniuratio Italiae*. The thanksgivings
and honours voted after each of the three successes reported were so
overwhelming that Dio at one point abandoned the attempt to give a
complete account (51.19.3). Many were without precedent too: to
give two examples, sacrifices involving the whole *populus* were led by
his consular colleague (Dio 51.20.3 and 21.2); at Octavian's triumphal
procession he and the magistrates followed his chariot instead of
leading him home as normal (51.21.9). It therefore comes as quite a
surprise to read that the one honour explicitly stated by Dio to have
been rejected was a civic reception outside the *pomerium* (51.19.2): by
senatorial decree the Vestal Virgins, magistrates and population of
the city with their wives and families had been ordered to go out to
meet him. This seems innocuous enough in comparison with other,
more adulatory, honours of a Hellenistic type, but it was selected to
be declined. We should ask why.

Any number of answers are possible, but the reception of returning
imperatores had been a political rather than a religious act despite the
traditional sacrifice. Those who went to meet a returning general
with their *clientes* had claimed to be *amici*, or to wish to become
amici, or were seeking to profit from the popularity and mana of the
imperator. The choice of not taking part had always been available;
overt *inimici* stayed away,[87] and were expected to, so that, by
commanding everyone to take part, the Senate had sought to deprive
people of their freedom of political association which was the essence
of *res publica*.[88] By declining this honour Octavian avoided the
appearance of compelling everyone to proclaim their political
support, and avoided the open assertion of a one-party state, which
ancient political philosophy called despotic rule (*regnum*). With
characteristic perspicacity Octavian saw this as important.

There was perhaps a religious element too; when Cicero described
the procession to meet him in 57 as "Rome virtually uprooted herself
from her dwelling place",[89] he was using strong language. On that
occasion the Vestal Virgins had stayed at their post. To command
them to leave it was to tamper with the worship of the gods of the city
herself (the *di patrii*).[90]

Octavian's return was preceded by ceremonies declaring the return

---

[87] Cic. *Att.* 4.1 (e.g.).

[88] Cic. *Fam.* 4.5.3 (written by Ser. Sulpicius Rufus) makes the point particularly
explicit.

[89] *ipsa Roma prope sedibus suis convulsa: Pis.* 52, Nisbet *In Pisonem* (n.20) p.114 for
parallel examples.

[90] For his sensitivity to them and enhancement of their importance, see below.

of universal peace: the temple of Janus was closed *ex senatus consulto* (Dio 51.20.4). Peace was always "secured by victories" and this decree, despite the continuing warfare on the Rhine frontier (*ibid.*), is said to have pleased Octavian more than any of the other honours.[91] The Senate is unlikely to have made it without prompting, but Octavian was not the proposer, and was not present himself. In 28, the *augurium salutis*, also taken only in peace-time, was taken. Octavian was probably present himself.[92]

Octavian's triumph, August 13-15th, 29, was preceded by honours to his *legati* — the unprecedented honour of a dark blue pennant for Agrippa[93] for example (Dio 51.21.3), distributions of money to the troops and to the city *populus* and the remission of *aurum coronarium* (gold for crowns) to the cities of Italy (*ibid.* 3f.). This sharing out the rewards of victory made him very popular, more especially as it produced a cut in interest rates (*ibid.* 5). This was Octavian's most spectacular return to the city and he never tried to triumph again.[94] Octavian seems to have stayed in or near Rome for the rest of 29 and for most of 28,[95] claiming the government of the new *res publica*, as he would have called it, was consular.[96] The most obvious evidence of this was his sharing the *fasces* with Agrippa his consular colleague (Dio 53.1.1), declaring all unratified acts of the triumviral period null and void[97] from the end of 28, and taking the traditional consular oath (*eiuratio*) at the end of the year.

When, in January 27, he ended the tenure of his extraordinary command by putting the question of the consular provinces to the

---

[91] Dio 51.20.4. *Parta victoriis pax*, *R.g.* 13, meant peace after fifteen years of civil wars, proscriptions, conscription, confiscations of land for veterans, compulsory levies of money, famine etc. It did not inhibit aggression — precisely the opposite, C.M. Wells *The German Policy of Augustus* (Oxford 1972) 8 *et alibi*.

[92] Last taken in 63, Dio 37.24.1; for 28 Suet. *Aug.* 31.4 and J.M. Carter *Suetonius, Divus Augustus* (Bristol 1982) 135; not taken again till Claudius' day, Tac. *Ann.* 12.23. Nor is it listed in *R.g.* as an achievement.

[93] To add to the golden *corona navalis* awarded for the victory at Naulochus; to be worn on the occasion of triumphs, Dio 49.14.3; Vell. 2.81.3; Virg. *Aen.* 8.684.

[94] Celebrations went on till August 28th: the Temple of *Divus Iulius* was dedicated on August 18th, the statue of *Victoria* in the *curia Iulia* on August 28th, E-J pp.50f.

[95] It is probable that he absented himself from the three triumphs of 28, dated May 26th, July 14th, August 16th, *Acta Triumph.* in *CIL* I² p.180, E-J p.35.

[96] It is suggested that when Tacitus wrote (*Ann.* 1.2.1) *consulem se ferens* (saying "I am consul") he is quoting, as he is argued to have been in the next phrase *(se) tribunicio iure contentum* ("I am content with the rights of a tribune"), see chap. 3 and chap. 4 below. For the importance of sharing the *fasces*, Syme *Tacitus* 365, *Aug. Ar.* 1f.

[97] Above and n.84. All his own acts had been ratified by January 1st, 29 (Holmes *Architect* I 172). This decree was therefore more of an amnesty for his agents, their beneficiaries, and his old opponents.

Senate, he could claim to have taken the step which he blamed Antonius for not having taken in 32. Henceforth, he could claim, he held his *provincia* because he had been appointed to it by the Senate in the way traditional for the *res publica*.

New arrangements were made (though it is unlikely that the system was immediately brought into effect) for the departure of governors to the provinces, and for their return to the city, but they upheld the *mores maiorum* in respect of the *pomerium*: proconsuls, who had the *auspicia* (divine sanction), were not to wear military uniform, but had lictors, and bore their insignia continuously from crossing the *pomerium* till they returned to it: propraetors — strictly Augustus' lieutenants of propraetor's rank (*legati Augusti pro praetore*) — had no lictors, but wore military uniform and a sword, and had the right to command troops and impose capital punishment (*ius gladii*) from the time they entered their province until they left it, and no longer (Dio 53.13.3–8). When, therefore, they returned to the city they could not be generals with *imperium* (*imperatores cum imperio*).[98] These provisions were pretty certainly not drawn up all at once but evolved; proconsuls of Africa with their armies were exceptions for the time being,[99] but these rules illustrate how important returning to the city was for the management of the new *res publica*, as it was for the old. They made the military threats to the *res publica* of the last century virtually impossible except from the Princeps himself. Octavian, now Augustus, left Rome in the summer of 27, probably before June, and moved to his newly granted *provincia* of Gaul,[100] thence to Spain. For his *profectio*, he symbolically set in hand repairs to the *via Flaminia*, the main road North. This act, and the addition of his own statue at the Mulvian Bridge, where the road crosses the Tiber outside the city, and an arch at Ariminum,[101] advertised his commitment to the northern frontiers of Italy as in the triumviral period.

Victories in Spain, and its pacification after two hundred years,[102]

---

[98] Logically, not being *suis auspiciis*, they could not triumph as they could not return the *auspicia* to Jupiter. Augustus took 20 years to establish a formula to enable *legati* to win an equivalent honour, the *ornamenta triumphalia*, of which the first recipients were from his own family. See below and n.128.

[99] Two triumphed, one in 21, one in 19, *CIL* I² p.181, E–J p.36.

[100] Dio (53.25.2) adds Britain, and as part of Caesar's legacy; this may well have been mentioned; cf. Hor. *Carm.* 3.5.3f. about adding Britain to the empire. Augustus did no more than receive fugitive kings, named in *R.g.* 32.1. He will most probably have left before July 4th, the date of M. Crassus' triumph.

[101] *R.g.* 20.5, Suet. *Aug.* 30, E–J 286 (= *ILS* 84) for the arch.

[102] Vell. 2.90. There had been six triumphs *ex Hispania* in the last decade. Hor. *Carm.* 3.14 comparing Augustus with Hercules, benefactor of mankind.

preceded Augustus' next return. He was saluted *Imperator VIII*, though Dio says explicitly that this was for M. Vinicius' successes in a 'German' war (53.26.4);[103] the temple of Janus was again closed, and a triumph voted before Augustus' planned return some time in the early European spring of 24.[104] Dio's account (53.26.5) implies that Augustus himself closed the temple in 25, but the vote must have been in his absence, since he was coming home for the marriage of Julia his daughter to Marcellus, his nephew, very early in 24, but was not able to reach the city in time through ill health (Dio 53.27.5). Though Dio lists many honours both before and after this return to the city, he offers no description of how he was received apart from noting that no triumph was held (53.26.5).[105] The populace however received a cash distribution (*congiarium*) which was as large as that distributed at his triumph in 29. It was from his own pocket he emphasised:[106] did he say so at the time? It is hard to believe that he did not.

But why no triumph? A number of reasons may be suggested: he was in poor health, a triumph was a physical strain; uncertainty about when he might arrive made organising a triumph difficult; the new outbreak of fighting might have been known, or rumoured, and the amount of spoils available might have provoked odious comparisons with 29; the discharged veterans did not need or want to come to Rome, they had been given settlements at *Augusta Emerita* in Spain (Dio 53.26.1). To judge from what followed, though, Augustus may be thought to have wished to start making triumphs unfashionable. He had reasons; apart from the earlier plethora (20 plus 3 ovations since 44) which had cheapened the honour, the unfortunate episode of M. Crassus' claim to the *spolia opima*[107] which had

---

[103] It was in the Alps; the theme of Italy's northern border again. A mistake by Dio; the main focus was actually on Augustus, so T.D. Barnes 'The victories of Augustus' *JRS* 64 (1974) 21.

[104] He arrived before June 13th, the date of the Latin festival; he was absent, 'ill', not 'in Spain' as in 26 and 25, *CIL* I² p.58. Dio 53.28.1 suggests early in the year.

[105] Horace celebrated his return (*Carm.* 3.14); Livia and Octavia are to lead the mothers of soldiers who have come through in a public celebration, with the girls and boys. Horace's private celebration recalls the civil wars in the vintage of the wine — the Social War, Spartacus' revolt, the campaign of Philippi. The message is clear; Augustus gave Italy rest from wars. Cf. E. Fraenkel *Horace* (Oxford 1957) 288–91.

[106] *R.g.* 15.1, Brunt and Moore 57–9 (excursus on his finances); add the fact that his income also included an *ornatio* of his provinces. That was why the treasury (*aerarium*) was normally in low water.

[107] *Spolia opima*, the reward of the general who killed the opposing general in battle with his own hand. Augustus had managed to cheat Crassus only by fraudulent manipulation of the evidence. Syme *Rom. Rev.* 308 and n. *ad loc.*

embarrassed him in 28 could not recur if triumphs became obsolete or nearly so. In 24 nobody knew that seventeen years would elapse before the next one from Augustus' province.

Nothing is known of Augustus' movements between his return from Spain in 24 and his resignation from the consulate in 23, nor is his return from the Alban Mount after resignation described, though his motive for resigning at the Alban Mount is of enough interest to provoke a note from Dio.[108] After his resignation we do not know his movements either. It is hard to believe that he was not present at the games given by Marcellus as aedile, the *Ludi Romani*, which took place from September 5th to 19th, and that they did not take place in the Forum under the awning which provided shade for the People throughout the summer (Dio 53.31.3). Why were these games so memorable? The reason given by Dio seems very inadequate.[109] It has been suggested that they might have been the first occasion on which *pantomimi* appeared at the *Ludi Romani*.[110] To judge by their later popularity, this would have been a truly memorable occasion. But they may also have been memorable because of Marcellus' death, since it appears probable that it occurred before Augustus' birthday on September 23rd.[111] He thus crossed the *pomerium* as proconsul for these games, and must have done so also for Marcellus' funeral, since he gave the eulogy for him "as was customary" (Dio 53.30.5) which must mean in the Forum. On crossing the *pomerium* he appears not to have dismissed his lictors or acted as if his *imperium* was in danger of lapsing. In his view, then, it did not lapse (or else he was conscious that technically it had, but decided that the needs of the *res publica* were overriding — compare what he said at Primus' trial, below). In the view of others, perhaps, it did lapse, but as they had not the power to press the point, they made do with verbal protests. Certainly we have to explain why he seems to have been unpopular with the Senators now, at the precise time when his resignation from the

[108] "Lest he be prevented"; how? A veto? Popular demonstrations? Riots? We know that the *populus* disliked the move. And we have no information on how his *suffectus* (replacement) was received.

[109] The appearance of an *eques* on the stage as a dancer, also of a woman of note (both unnamed).

[110] E.J. Jory 'The literary evidence for the beginnings of Imperial pantomine' *BICS* 28 (1981) 147f. He has noted (unpublished lecture, 1990) that performances by *pantomimi* may go back to the second century. But Pylades and Bathyllus by innovative ideas may have developed and popularised an existing genre.

[111] The evidence is that in 13 the dedication of the Theatre of Marcellus preceded the birthday of Augustus on September 23rd. The natural date for the dedication was the tenth anniversary of his death. Hence between September 19th and 22nd.

consulate should have made him popular. Resistance to him in 23 would also explain the steps he took to clarify the issue of the nature of his *imperium* in 19 (see chapter 6). In any analysis, however, his returns in 23 reveal a willingness to encroach — set in motion, that is, the 'creeping progress' or encroachment in his position and power as Princeps.

Augustus certainly left Rome that wet and fever-ridden autumn, since we know that he had to return from Campania to face the demand that he become dictator to deal with the crisis in the grain supply. His reception on this occasion was without precedent; the delegation met him with twenty-four lictors, the symbols of a dictator's (or triumvir's) office (Dio 54.1.3), and the *populus* was present en masse. Whether they met inside or outside the *pomerium* is unknown. Almost certainly outside. But he must have entered the city. Augustus must have stayed in Rome for much of 22, as is argued in chapter 6. Certainly he was still in Rome on September 1st, as he dedicated the temple of Jupiter Tonans that day (E–J p.51). But not for long, as he was in Sicily when the consular elections reached an impasse, presumably shortly after that (Dio 54.6.1–3).[112] It is suggested that he met Agrippa in Sicily (he had been in Lesbos),[113] and there arranged Agrippa's marriage to Julia. Augustus then moved to the Aegean area to "settle accounts with the Parthians", while Agrippa moved to Rome. Presumably he was welcome, at least to those fed up with the riots, and those whose election as consuls for 20 he effected. But we have no information.

Augustus returned to the city in 19. Before this he had taken a ninth salutation as *Imperator* (presumably for the Parthian 'victory')[114] and received in Athens the embassy sent by the Senate after riots broke out in the city when Augustus' refusal of the consulship for 19 was reported, and there had been murders (Dio 54.10.1–2).[115] He appointed Q. Lucretius Vespillo, one of the envoys, to be the colleague of C. Sentius Saturninus, the one consul, who must by then have been in office since the Senate had voted him a bodyguard, which he refused. Augustus then moved to Campania.

---

[112] Not Samos, as stated in *CAH* X² 89.

[113] The nature of his *imperium* has been much discussed. See chap. 5 below.

[114] On May 12th, 20. Barnes 'Victories' (n.103) 21f., citing the evidence. We do not know what celebrations, if any, took place in Rome on this occasion.

[115] It is unclear from Dio whether the riots preceded or followed the rejection of Egnatius Rufus' candidature, which he omits here. If the latter, these events took place in 19, if Velleius' account (2.92) is correct, and Sentius was already consul when he rejected Egnatius. The rejection might also have been the spark for the riots.

In *R.g.* Augustus devotes a whole chapter and a bit (11 and 12.1) to his reception in Rome. He stresses its uniqueness, the dignity of the members of the delegation[116] and the distance they travelled to meet him,[117] as well as the altar of *Fortuna Redux*, sited just outside the prestigious *Porta Capena*, and the annual sacrifice to be made there by the *pontifices* and Vestal Virgins.[118] It was all designed on the most honorific scale. After agreement with the delegation Augustus returned to Rome, entering the city by night in order to frustrate demonstrations (Dio 54.10.4). The first, small, temple of *Mars Ultor* on the Capitol was dedicated on May 12th (E–J p.48), either in his absence or in 18.

It was perhaps these two receptions — by the *populus* in 23, by the Senate in 19 — which gave Augustus the confidence to continue his policies of not triumphing[119] (despite the return of the standards and the humbling of the Parthians so often portrayed on the coins), and of implementing his plans for social reforms as a prelude to the Secular Games in 17, and the advertisement of a new era.

Agrippa also returned to Rome in 19 from the final conquest of Spain, but he again refused the honour of a triumphal entry to the city despite the offer made by the Senate on Augustus' own motion (Dio 54.11.6).[120]

After the Secular Games, the new *saeculum* opened with new campaigns. Freed from the wars in Spain, and the commitment of troops to them, Augustus turned again to the northern frontiers of Italy, and was himself in the area for most of 16–13. Not quite all the time, however. Dio records (54.19.7) prayers for his return, prompted by bad omens; perhaps these were the same as the votive games (*ludi votivi*) given in 16 for his return (E–J 34); they were perhaps also connected with his salutation as *Imperator* (the tenth) by the end of

[116] One consul, Q. Lucretius, representatives of the colleges of praetors and tribunes and *principes viri* = ?*consulares*?

[117] A journey of three days at least. Horace and his friends took four days to reach a point in Campania short of Nola where Augustus' house was (*Sat.* 1.5.1–46). But they were not hurrying.

[118] The Vestal Virgins were normally not expected to appear at other than the most important celebrations.

[119] Dio mentions an ovation (54.8.3). It seems generally agreed that this is an error, but he may be reporting a vote of the Senate that was not accepted by Augustus. See also chap. 6 below.

[120] Agrippa's persistent refusal to hold a triumph has never been satisfactorily explained. Perhaps it cannot be. A possible line of thought is that, as he had been awarded almost unique honours during the civil wars (the *corona rostrata* and blue pennant) he did not care to accept what had been devalued in his youth. So Dio 54.12; cf. J.-M. Roddaz *Marcus Agrippa* (Rome 1984) 409. See also chap. 5 below.

the year.[121] He certainly returned in 13. The consuls gave votive games (E–J 36), and Dio records that the Senate decreed an altar to be put up in the Senate House for his return (54.25.3); and when Augustus declined the honour the Senate decreed the erection of the *Ara Pacis Augustae*, to be put up in the Campus Martius (*R.g.* 12.2); this took place on July 4th (E–J p.49). He actually arrived a bit earlier, however; the news of his impending arrival was a matter of pride to Cornelius Balbus, who was giving games at the time (Dio 54.25.2), since he thought that his games would see Augustus returning. Augustus, however, again avoided a reception by arriving at night. This can be interpreted as avoiding interrupting the games or as snubbing Balbus, but it is of little importance. Dio now adds that henceforth Augustus made a point of returning to the city by night whenever he left, even to go to the suburbs and anywhere else, in order not to give offence.[122] That is, he avoided overexposure,[123] taking people away from their everyday activities and occupations so often that they would get fed up with him and his honours.[124] On this occasion, though, he did not neglect the routine; after a levee (*salutatio*) on the morning after his return he performed the rite of offering the laurel wreath from his *fasces* at the temple of Jupiter, and the following day convened the Senate. (Dio 54.25.4f.) This was correct *more maiorum*; religious business always took priority.

In 13, his provinces were renewed for another five years, and he settled time-expired veterans in Italy and the provinces on lands purchased for the purpose. Dio says (54.25.6) that this move, and the new terms of service for the legions, pleased landowners because they now knew that their lands would not be compulsorily acquired for

[121] These are the first recorded; 16 is also the last recorded celebration of the festival commemorating the victory at Actium, celebrated every four years from 28 by the priestly colleges in turn (Dio 53.1.4–5). The *pontifices*, we may guess, celebrated in 24, the *augurs* in 20, the *xvviri* required Agrippa's financial support this year: we do not know if the *viiviri* acted in 12. The salutation IMP X was for victories in Rhaetia, Barnes 'Victories' (n.103) 22, but not attested till 13/12 (*ILS* 5816).

[122] For holidays etc., as all Romans of any means did, especially in the hottest months. For villas of Augustan date on the Bay of Naples, J.H. D'Arms *Romans on the Bay of Naples* (Cambridge Mass. 1970) *passim*; Suet. *Aug.* 72.2 mentions more strictly suburban villas at Lanuvium, Praeneste and Tibur. *Id.* (53.2) says Augustus also entered or left every city or town in the afternoon or at night, and (82) preferred to travel by night and at a leisurely pace, taking two days to reach Praeneste or Tibur.

[123] Z. Yavetz 'The personality of Augustus' in Raaflaub and Toher *BRE* 21–41 has stressed Augustus' *humanitas*: this was an aspect of it.

[124] Cf. Suet. *Aug.* 40.2, reduction in the number of grain distributions to reduce the diversion of the *plebs* from their jobs — clear evidence (if true) that the *plebs* included many workers; all were not unemployed — or unemployable.

veteran settlements in the future. Lepidus the *Pontifex Maximus* died
this year; Augustus was not elected to succeed him till March 6th the
following year (E–J p.47). There was much building work to do.[125] In
September, the Theatre of Marcellus was dedicated, probably on the
tenth anniversary of his death, and Augustus' fiftieth birthday was
celebrated by games given by the praetor, Iullus Antonius (Dio
54.26.2); the beast-hunts given on this occasion may have been in
connexion with the dedication, as they are inappropriate for a
birthday. For the dates, see above and note 111.

Shortly after, early in 12, Agrippa died. By Dio's account he had
left for Pannonia on hearing of a revolt in the winter, but had not
reached the province when the rebellion subsided so that he returned
to Italy, but died in Campania on the way back to Rome. Hearing of
his illness, Augustus dashed to his bedside, but arrived too late. He
had been giving a gladiatorial show at '*Panathenaia*' (Dio 54.28.3).
Dio may have made an error here, translating *Quinquatrus*, a festival
of Athena/Minerva, as *Panathenaia*;[126] the Quinquatrus games were
held from March 19th for five days. This time-frame fits well.
Augustus returned to Rome, escorting the bier; naturally he received
no formal welcome. He gave the funeral laudation himself (*ibid.*)[127]
and Agrippa's ashes were buried in Augustus' own family Mausoleum (*ibid.* 5). In 12, Tiberius and Drusus, Augustus' stepsons,
took over as field marshals and went campaigning while Augustus
himself remained in Rome, very active (Dio 54.35); he may have
stayed all year completing unfinished business as Agrippa's executor
and as the new *Pontifex Maximus*, with the building activity which
that involved. There was a cash distribution (*congiarium*) this year
too (*R.g.* 15) which was given as a testamentary gift from Agrippa
according to Dio (54.29.4). If Dio is right, it was not a concomitant of
the celebrations which must have taken place when Tiberius and
Drusus returned to the first gift of *ornamenta triumphalia*[128] and
another salutation as *Imperator* for Augustus.[129] He was using his

[125] The new entrance to his house containing the Vesta shared by his family and the
city. See chap. 8.

[126] I owe this suggestion to Mr N. Purcell.

[127] E–J 366 for fragments.

[128] The first recipients, Suet. *Tib*. 9.2. Dio says triumphal honours for Tiberius in
12 (54.31.4); 54.33.5 in 11 for Drusus, but he should mean *ornamenta*. Augustus'
congiarium was of 'victory' size, the same as in 29 and 26.

[129] Dio 54.33.5; cf. the three salutations attested between January 1st, 12 (*IMP XI*)
and January 1st, 8 (*IMP XIV*). One must belong to Drusus' *ovatio* (Suet. *Claud.* 1), one
to that of Tiberius (Vell. 2.96.3). The first grants of *ornamenta triumphalia* are
obviously appropriate for the other. This analysis involves believing that Dio has

stepsons' returning to the city to advertise his (and the *res publica*'s) new field marshals.

Augustus went to the northern frontier again in 10, but, despite the triumphal ovations of Drusus from Germany (Suet. *Claud.* 1) and Tiberius from Pannonia and Dalmatia, on January 16th, 9 (Vell. 2.96.3), Dio makes little of their joint return to the city, commenting only that they "carried out the decrees made in honour of their victories" (54.36.4).[130]

Augustus went North again in 9 (Dio 55.2.2). He moved to Gaul while Drusus launched a new offensive in Germany and Tiberius went first to Illyricum, but hastened back at the end of the year to take over Drusus' forces after the latter's death (September 14th). Augustus' own return to Rome was for Drusus' funeral, undertaking what must have been a severe physical ordeal for a man of fifty-four as he escorted the bier from Ticinum in the Po valley to Rome in the company of Tiberius;[131] he did not himself enter the city, but delivered a eulogy in the Campus Martius. The eulogy in the city was delivered by Tiberius. Augustus made much of not crossing the *pomerium* because he was in mourning and would have been unable to go to Jupiter's temple on the Capitol to give thanks for their victories (Dio 55.2.2). As Tiberius did not have the *auspicia* he was not similarly handicapped.[132]

Later, in 8, after ending his period of mourning, Augustus entered the city, celebrated the victories of 9 and dedicated his laurels at the shrine of Jupiter Feretrius. Dio (55.5.1) mentions this without trying to explain why this shrine and not the usual *Iuppiter Optimus Maximus* was chosen, but he says that Drusus' death had caused Augustus to tone down the celebrations (*ibid.* 2).[133]

---

telescoped the honours of 11–9, subsuming the grants of *ornamenta* into the ovations of 10 and 9 respectively. Since Augustus was boosting the honours of his stepsons at this moment, two sets of honours seem quite plausible.

[130] Because of the telescoping (last note). Tiberius' ovation is mentioned incidentally by Dio (55.2.4). Neither ovation is in the *ACTA* in *CIL* but they are conjectural at this point.

[131] Tac. *Ann.* 3.5.1 with Suet. *Tib.* 7.3. Tacitus' words *urbem intravisse* echo Cicero *quoad urbem introisset* when he meant crossing the *pomerium* at the end of a governorship (*Fam.* 1.9.25), but it seems that Tacitus did not mean "crossed the *pomerium*", or he made a mistake.

[132] Note how funerals, part of family *religio*, take precedence over everything else, even public *religio*, when entering the city.

[133] Augustus was neither surrendering *auspicia* nor renewing them: perhaps this was why it was not essential to go to *Iuppiter Optimus Maximus*. He had built the new shrine to Jupiter Feretrius to hold Romulus' *spolia opima*, and possibly those of Marcellus and Cossus.

Augustus stayed in Rome long enough to hold the census he mentions in *R.g.* 8.3, not noticed by Dio, who turns to electoral malpractice and legislation about the evidence of slaves. A new topic begins (Dio 55.6) with the renewal of Augustus' command for ten years (despite the fact that he was by now fifty-five years old). This introduces a campaign against the Sugambri, clearly intended to commemorate Drusus. There was a *profectio* of Augustus himself, Tiberius and Gaius Caesar against 'the Gauls'; Tiberius crossed the Rhine, while Augustus and Gaius remained in Gaul training the troops, who were given gifts for Gaius' first military experience (he turned twelve this year!) (*id.* 4). The campaign brought salutations as *Imperator* to Augustus (XIV) and Tiberius (II), a memorial funeral mound (*honorarius tumulus*) for Drusus was constructed, Tiberius was elected to a second consulship and awarded a triumph. Augustus himself was honoured by votive games for his return (E–J 38) and it was decreed that his birthday was to be celebrated annually with races (Dio *loc.cit.* 6). Dio then records that Sextilis was renamed August this year (*ibid.*). The election and all the honorific votes took place after Augustus' *profectio* if Dio is maintaining a chronological order. Nor did Augustus return to the city for Maecenas' funeral. The contrast with Agrippa's and Drusus' funerals is marked.

Augustus remained in Gaul while Tiberius returned to triumph on January 1st, 7. This triumph tends to be played down by modern scholars,[134] perhaps because they know what was to come next. But at the time the Senate and Roman People had cause to witness an impressive celebration:

1. The first curule triumph from Augustus' vast *provincia* since 26 — now nineteen years ago, and the first from anywhere since 19 — twelve years ago.
2. It was the first ever from Germany,[135] and the first over Germans, named as such, since that of M. Claudius Marcellus in 222, who had claimed *spolia opima*.
3. It had traditional (what modern scholars call 'Republican') elements, and Tiberius did not cross the *pomerium* till the day of the triumph, when he became *suis auspiciis*.[136]

---

[134] E.g. H.H. Scullard *From the Gracchi to Nero* (4th edn London 1976) 263f. Totally ignored by Syme *Rom. Rev.* 391.

[135] *Acta Triumphorum* are not extant; *de Germaneis* is a conjecture, but deducible from Vell. 2.97 and Dio 55.8.2.

[136] As consul; this must be crucial. Whether or not he had actually taken the *auspicia* before triumphing is open to debate. He convened the first meeting of the

4. To triumph on January 1st may have reminded people of C. Marius, the great conqueror of a German menace, though in his case his German triumph was yet to come.[137]

Besides, the triumph was commemorated by a building project in traditional style — restoration of the Temple of Concord in his own name and that of Drusus.[138] Less traditional elements were the banquet to the Senate on the Capitol, and by his mother Livia to the women (unspecified by Dio) at a venue unknown to him.[139] Apparently, however, there was no *congiarium* to the *plebs*. He was not their *patronus* — yet.

Augustus was not present.[140] It has been argued that this was because of the quarrel which came to the surface in 6, in which case it was already simmering. It might, on the other hand, be argued that Augustus decided to stay away so as not to distract the *plebs* from Tiberius' hour of glory; or for rather less creditable motives such as being himself unwilling to walk before or behind Tiberius' chariot with the Senators, or simply not knowing what part would be appropriate for him as proconsul of the provinces in and from which Tiberius was triumphing. What, moreover, should he wear? Should he too be wearing the garb of *triumphator* which had been voted to him whenever anyone wore triumphal robes? Assertions of jealousy or ill-feeling seem rather too simplistic.

The exact reverse could be argued; the reign of peace inaugurated when Augustus returned later in 7 with a major celebration could be seen as complementing, or following on from, Tiberius' triumph,

---

Senate outside the *pomerium* (Dio 55.8.1). In any case, his *imperium*, now being consular, did not lapse on crossing the *pomerium*. The status of the Capitoline Hill in regard to the *pomerium* was in any case ambiguous (information Mr Nicholas Purcell). It was not included in the ancient *Roma quadrata*, L. Richardson *A New Topographical Dictionary of Ancient Rome* (Baltimore 1992) 70.

[137] Marius' German triumph was *e Cimbris et Teutonis, CIL* I² p.195 (his *elogium*). Less welcome precedents for a January 1st triumph were L. Antonius (*ex Alpibus*, 42), L. Marcius Censorinus (*ex Macedonia*, 39).

[138] A temple with long associations with the *res publica* and conservative politics, Zanker *Images* 21; Carter *Suetonius, Augustus* (n.92) 131. The colonnaded square of the *Porticus Liviae* was also dedicated this year, by Tiberius and Livia. She presented it to Augustus. It occupied the site of the mansion of Vedius Pollio, demolished in 15 by Augustus on the death of Vedius, who had left it to him, as an example of his hatred of luxury (*luxus*). Dio 54.23 for Vedius, 55.8.2 for the portico, Ov. *Fast.* 6.637–48 for the dedication and moral.

[139] It was held on her initiative, and private, Dio 55.8.2. Presumably this was why the venue was not recorded. She was stressing the achievements of her sons.

[140] Proved by the votive games of *ILS* 95 (= E–J 39).

especially if Janus' temple was now closed.[141] Moreover, the
celebration of a sort of requiem for Agrippa five years after his death
might be seen as complimentary to the man who was moving into
Agrippa's position as son-in-law, and was destined perhaps already
to receive *tribunicia potestas* as much as reminding people of the
natural father of Augustus' adopted sons. Looking back from 7, as
contemporaries did, the complimentary intention seems much more
likely than rivalry, but there is no certainty, and gossip is probable.

The status of Tiberius' triumph as a major contribution to the *Pax
Romana* is confirmed by one of the Boscoreale cups. It forms the
subject of the scene following that in which Drusus sponsors a
legation of Gallic chiefs bringing children to Augustus. One of the
Boscoreale children has the same face as the child on the north face of
the *Ara Pacis Augustae* who balances the oriental child who follows
Agrippa on the south face. The association is obvious.[142]

Gaius Caesar probably returned with Tiberius, as it is unlikely that
he returned on his own; if so, he took part in the triumph. Very
shortly after, Tiberius, now *IMP II*, held *ludi votivi* for Augustus'
return *ex senatus consulto* (E–J 39), and returned to the North. When
Augustus returned, a big festival was held by Cn. Piso the consul and
Gaius Caesar deputising for Tiberius (Dio 55.8.3). This is remarkable
for a twelve-year-old child, but it may seem a little less bizarre if we
reflect that Tiberius had become his brother-in-law by his marriage.
Augustus' return was publicity-conscious. He made public property
the *Campus Agrippae*[143] and the *Diribitorium*,[144] which Agrippa had
built (Dio 55.8.3f.). The demobilisation programme detailed with
loving care in *R.g.* 16.3 was started, to confirm the theme of peace.[145]
Later he gave a gladiatorial show, perhaps in the new year (6) on the
anniversary of Agrippa's death, at which everyone except Augustus
himself and his two sons wore black — a remarkable performance
(Dio 55.8.5). These ceremonies seem to be proclaiming Tiberius as

[141] 8 or 7, Syme *Aug. Ar.* 68. But surely not before Tiberius' triumph and Augustus'
return in 7.

[142] A. Kuttner 'Lost episodes in Augustan history: the evidence of the Boscoreale
cups and the *Ara Pacis*' *AJA* 91 (1987) 297f.

[143] Though the Portico of Polla, Agrippa's sister, was unfinished, Dio 55.8.4.

[144] Used for marshalling the electoral assembly for voting purposes. It was almost
a wonder of the world (Pliny *Nat.* 36.102), as it had an exceptional span, needing
enormously long beams. Never replaced when burnt in Titus' principate.

[145] Especially as it confirmed the hopes aroused in 13, when the new pay
arrangements for troops were made (Dio 54.25.6); emphasis on sending the troops
home (*in sua municipia*), with rewards paid by Augustus out of his own pocket. So
Brunt and Moore 59.

the new Agrippa, and guardian of the heritage of the Caesars. Was Augustus also making a farewell to campaigning, and was this intended to be a last return *ex provincia*? He was fifty-six years old, an era of peace was being inaugurated, which was not to be broken till Gaius Caesar's formal *profectio* in 2.[146] By then Tiberius had gone into self-imposed exile, from which he was to make an ignominious return.

Augustus did not go campaigning again. As he become *senex* on September 23rd, 3, he was deemed too old.[147] He did however make a formal *profectio* to Ariminum to support the campaign against the Pannonian rebels in AD 8, and was welcomed, with sacrifices, on his return (Dio 55.34.3). He probably never left Italy except for visits to Capri and other offshore islands on vacation (Suet. *Aug.* 98f.) and possibly for the voyage to Planasia to see Agrippa Postumus; but as this was a secret voyage, if it actually occurred, there were naturally neither celebrations for his *profectio* nor for his return.[148] Visits to Naples for the quinquennial games in his honour are recorded by implication on their foundation in 2 (Dio 55.10.9) and on their fourth celebration in AD 14 (Suet. *Aug.* 98.5). But nothing is known of how, if at all, he was welcomed on his return on the former occasion, and after the third celebration, if he went to it in AD 10. He might have been too preoccupied that year.

Receptions for others recorded in the later years of Augustus' principate seem to be restricted to those for members of the imperial family arriving in triumph[149] or deceased;[150] for others, it must be

[146] The year 1, the traditional date, comes from Xiphilinus' abridgement of Dio (55.18), where he resumes after the suicide of Phoebe, which was in 2 (Boissevain's edn of Dio, II 492–3), but it is by no means certain that Dio had started a new year. Evidence for 2 comes from J. Pollini *The Portraiture of Gaius and Lucius Caesar* (Fordham, N.Y. 1987) 32–5, 53–5. The altar from *Vicus Sandaliarius* is dated 2 (*AUGUSTUS XIII M. PLAUTIUS SILVANUS*). If the scene is of a *profectio* (and Pollini's arguments seem convincing), Gaius left in 2. But not necessarily at the start of the year (as Pollini). The names of the *coss. ordinarii* were often used throughout the year. A *profectio* for Gaius at the end of the year — the first ever from the new shrine of Mars Ultor — would make a splendid finale to the year, repairing perhaps some of the damage done by Julia. Cf. Syme *Aug. Ar.* 89 and nn.55, 56. For *profectio* and *adventus*, J. Rüpke *Domi Militiae* (Stuttgart 1990) 125 and 215–7. Cf. Jasper Griffin *Latin Poets and Roman Life* (London 1985) 61, quoting as an example for *profectio* Livy 42.49; for *adventus* Weinstock *Divus Julius* 289f.

[147] Seneca (*de brev. vit.* 4.3f.) says he was already wanting release from public duties. Next year Dio (55.10.18) says he was "too old" to campaign in Armenia.

[148] Mentioned by both Tacitus (*Ann.* 1.5) and Dio (56.30.1).

[149] Tiberius' triumph in AD 11 was preceded by his reception in AD 9 as described by Dio (56.1.1f.). The celebrations were muted by the news of Varus' disaster announced five days after Tiberius completed his work in Pannonia/Dalmatia (Vell.

assumed that those who received *ornamenta triumphalia* had receptions staged[151] or at least planned by their *amici*. The emphasis on celebrating military success goes well with the Romans' general militaristic ethos, but it is simply not known whether returning proconsuls from the civil provinces were normally received, and whether they made the traditional sacrifices at *Iuppiter Optimus Maximus* on their arrival. Roman conservatism, especially in religion, makes it likely that they did, and their normal social behaviour and the customary attendance of *clientes* makes it likely that all returning Senators had escorts and at least a modest reception organised by their *amici*. As long as there was real electoral competition too,[152] promoting a patron's electoral chances cannot be wholly discounted as a real motive. Augustus, perhaps, had to be impressed at least as much as coevals and equals.

Augustus' return from the quinquennial games at Naples was his last — as a corpse. Roman funerals had always impressed outsiders with their majesty[153] (Polybius 6.53–4). Augustus' funeral[154] was made especially honourable by the pall-bearers,[155] *decuriones* (councillors) of the *municipia* (boroughs) lying between Nola and Bovillae, *equites* from Bovillae, Senators from the vestibule of his house on the Palatine Hill through the Forum, where two eulogies were spoken, to the Campus Martius where he was cremated. His ashes were then taken to the great Mausoleum which he had completed perhaps in 28 and already contained the ashes of Agrippa, Drusus and the sons whom Augustus had adopted. The *populus Romanus* was prevented

---

2.117.1). Much of what Dio reports may only have been voted. Augustus' welcome (going out of the city, escorting him "from the suburbs" to the *Saepta Julia* in the Campus Martius and giving him a *contio*) seems likely to have taken place. Tiberius dedicated the Temple of Concord (vowed in his second consulate, E–J p.45) on January 16th before leaving for Germany in AD 10. For his triumph Suet. *Tib.* 17.

[150] The deaths of L. and C. Caesar were formally recorded (E–J p.50 August 20th, p.47 February 22nd) and their remains received (Dio 55.12.1). Xiphilinus' abridgement of Dio gives no details of the dedications in the Senate House of their golden shields and spears, given when they were enrolled in the *iuventus*.

[151] Deduced from Tacitus *Agricola* 40. They averaged more than one per year for a time; Velleius lists six between AD 4 and 9 (2.104.2 etc.); Dio adds more, and that Augustus and Tiberius both took the title of *Imperator* for that of Sentius Saturninus (55.28.4–6).

[152] Proved by laws against bribery and the accusation of the consuls in 8, Dio 55.5.3.

[153] Polyb. does not consider those whose bodies have to be brought back.

[154] Suet. *Aug.* 100.

[155] Cf. Drusus' pallbearers: officers as far as winterquarters, then leading men of each *civitas* (Dio 55.2.1).

from making a demonstration, or getting out of hand, as they had at Caesar's funeral fifty-seven years before, by a strong presence of troops — a point on which Tacitus exercises his ferocious irony (*Ann.* 1.8 *fin.*). The proposals rejected reflect perhaps the growth of that fawning flattery (*adulatio*) which is the target of Tacitus' most withering scorn, since all breached the *mores maiorum* in the state's political or religious life, or both. But they are not really more outlandish than the proposals made in the aftermath of the victories at Actium, Alexandria and Egypt which exhausted the patience of Dio (51.19.3).

Tiberius' arrival on this occasion — his first appearance in the city as the surviving partner in Augustus' honours — was simply as leader of the party escorting Augustus' corpse. In an edict — presumably issued from Nola — he had refused to undertake any business other than escorting the corpse.[156] Arriving in this way he avoided a personal reception, thus offering perhaps a first glimpse of his dislike of crowds and of the pomp associated with receptions. His arrival in the role of chief mourner was possibly an appropriate note for the gloomy principate about to begin.

Augustus' management of the *mores maiorum* for *principes viri* returning to the city reveals his many political skills. His initial modesty and subsequent avoidance of seeming more insensitive[157] than his rivals and choosing less offensive ways of breaching these *mores* in the triumviral period was skilful; his use of them to put Antonius in the wrong in 32 was masterly. Throughout his life he seems to have managed to gauge popular opinion correctly as he returned to the city in the guise successively of Caesar's avenger, defender of Italy, bringer of peace.[158]

At his triumph he used his return to the city to assert the nobility of his family in the tradition of the *nobiles*, outdoing all rivals in *gloria*, but taking care in so doing to see that the citizens at large shared the benefits of his success. While accepting, and responding to, unprecedented demonstrations which he had not planned, as in 23 and 19, when he himself held the initiative he avoided giving the citizens a surfeit of displays; he put these on when he had a point to make or relatives to promote.

---

[156] Tac. *Ann.* 1.7.6 (Furneaux) and note *ad loc.*, H. Furneaux *The Annals of Tacitus* (2nd edn, Oxford 1896).

[157] It was not difficult to be less insensitive than M. Antonius, compared by Plutarch with Demetrius Poliorcetes (*Dem.* 1.7f.).

[158] At home. Cf. *R.g.* 13, *Rom. Rev.* 303f.

Whether the predominance of military occasions reflects the ever-present chauvinistic imperialism of the Romans or the prejudices of our sources[159] is not possible to determine, but it is certain that to be seen as a successful commander-in-chief was an essential part of the role of the Princeps, and of any successor.[160] Returning to the city and being received, remained, as it had always been, an important element in this, and especially for the religious life of the *res publica*.

The institution of *ornamenta triumphalia* renewed the possibility of honourable receptions for *nobiles*, which must have pleased them. The inauguration of the Temple of Mars Ultor provided a venue for the gods' share in celebrating military exploits, and a more valid one than the great shrine of *Iuppiter Optimus Maximus*, since *legati* were not able to return the *auspicia* they had not received.[161] But they could and presumably did return to the temple from which they had set out, to render thanks to the god who had blessed their departure.

---

[159] Or both. For Roman imperialistic chauvinism Wells *German Policy* (n.91) chap. 1.

[160] Hence the intensive campaigning after Agrippa's death.

[161] Augustus' generals fought under his *auspicia*; Fraenkel *Horace* (n.105) 431, Weinstock *Divus Julius* 112, both quoting Mommsen *Staatsrecht* I³ 94. Cf. *R.g.* 4.2, Suet. *Aug.* 21.1.

CHAPTER 2

MANAGING THE *RES PUBLICA*

In 'The historians and Augustus'[1] Emilio Gabba has outlined the various assessments of Augustus which have prevailed during and since his day. *Prudentes*, men of sense, had expressed opposite views before Tacitus wrote *Annals* 1.9 and 10. Many of his actions were open to two interpretations; some championed liberty, others peace. Many crimes have been committed in the name of both. In Britain, the view of Syme, that Augustus' "ability and greatness will all the more sharply be revealed by unfriendly presentation" (*Rom. Rev.* 7) has often been misunderstood.[2] His book is seen as identifying Augustus with the dictators of 1939, who totally lacked Augustus' statecraft, resembling him only in his ruthlessness to opponents and the aggressive imperialism which was characteristic of almost all Romans we know of.

Times change; in our age, when everyone claims to be democratic, and all political systems claim to represent the people, constitutions and laws are said to be for academics; the right to govern comes out of the barrel of a gun — or so we thought till 1989/90, when it became clear that a government must also have the hearts of those whose hands are on the trigger.[3] If not, the power of the people from whom the soldiers have been recruited can overcome a government which has forfeited its mandate to rule, and states, even the superstate of the USSR, can disintegrate, peacefully or not, depending on whether the

[1] In Millar and Segal 61–88.
[2] Z. Yavetz 'The *Res Gestae* and Augustus' public image' in Millar and Segal 1–36, 25f. quotes H.E. Steier *Augustusfriede und römische Klassik* in *ANRW* II.2 (1975) as an example.
[3] Cf. P.A. Brunt 'The Roman Mob' in *Studies in Ancient Society* ed. M.I. Finley (London 1974) 101 (= *Past and Present* 35 (1966)): "The main cause of the fall [of the Roman 'Republic'] must ... be found in agrarian discontents; it was the soldiers, who were of peasant origin whose disloyalty to the Republic was fatal". True, but they needed disloyal leaders to lead them. Cf. Syme *Rom. Rev.* 352, "the veterans were the strongest pillar of [Augustus'] military monarchy".

people did, or did not, have common sympathies. The heart of the common man and woman matters. Augustus seems to have understood this. His opponents did not.

Augustus' regime was a success for the vast majority of the population in that for a hundred years it ended the civil wars, which had brought appalling consequences similar to those our century is having to watch. The purpose of this chapter is to suggest that Augustus' success owed much, if not most, to his methods, together with his ability to survive illnesses till the age of seventy-five.

His methods were based on a cold realism in identifying the essential in each situation ("From the beginning his sense for realities was unerring", Syme *Rom. Rev.* 113), his caution and his gift for public relations. In part this is shown in his choice of effective catchwords or slogans; as Syme put it "It might be hard to resist the deceitful assertions of a party who claimed to be the champions of liberty and the laws, of peace and legitimate government" (*Rom. Rev.* 152). In part he understood the Romans' innate conservatism, so that he made constant appeals to the *mores maiorum* (tradition), and took care as far as possible to disguise his own breaches of these by specious (and often effective) excuses like loyalty to his parents.

In part he played on their religious conservatism, reviving half-forgotten rituals and neglected priesthoods and building or rebuilding temples old and new; there was an element of a religious zealot about his religious revival after the Actium victory.[4] One objective of this might have been to enable ordinary citizens to accept that the civil wars were the result of the gods' anger at their fathers' neglect (venial perhaps and understandable) and not of their own greed and ambition (less venial and more shameful).

In part he played on the pride of the noble families, inviting the children who had survived the civil wars to pursue under his leadership a career which superficially resembled that pursued by their ancestors, thus establishing a group of political allies (*amici*) connected by marriage, which many were invited to join. In principle it was an association like the *amici* of a 'Republican' *nobilis*, though this screen grew thinner as the years passed, and was effectively dropped by the promotion of Gaius and Lucius Caesar to the status of *principes iuventutis*. But by then it was too late to think of an alternative while Augustus lived, or even after his death, however much gossip there may have been (Tac. *Ann.* 1.13.2).

---

[4] Zanker *Images* chap. 4, esp. 102–110.

In part it was the personal relationships he cultivated, a modest demeanour, way of life and manners (Suet. *Aug.* 72–5).[5] True, he was prone to losing his temper when provoked in the Senate House (*id.* 54) and lost control completely when he felt himself severely injured by Julia (Dio 55.10.14) and those who interceded for her (Suet. *Aug.* 65.3), but he valued the restraint of Maecenas (Dio 55.7.1–2) and the advice of Athenodorus on restraining himself from intemperate responses;[6] most of his outbursts were brief, and "nobody was endangered by their independence or defiance" (Suet. *Aug.* 54 *fin.*).

His caution and restraint in dealing with literary and verbal assaults has been pointed out:[7] the total of those known to have been punished by him on this score is Cassius Severus and three *equites*, of whom two were punished very lightly. As the third was Ovid we get the impression of a harsh and unfeeling master, but Ovid was not gagged in his writing, nor was he prevented from addressing leading citizens to procure his recall, and though he found Tomis unattractive, it was not a barren island, but on a coast which is now regarded as a very pleasant place for a summer holiday.

All the time, though, a hallmark of his methods was caution in making preparations and waiting for the right moment for effective action. Loyalty to his supporters maintained a solid party base.[8] While he used money lavishly, he did not do so wastefully, as M. Antonius did, but in a calculating manner, to win and maintain support. Tacitus describes him as "winning the hearts of the troops with gifts, the people (sc. of Rome) with food" (*Ann.* 1.2). All parties used deceit and cruelty in civil wars which "do not admit the arts of civilisation" (*ibid.* 9.3); moreover, everyone found the sweet taste of

---

[5] Good discussions by Z. Yavetz 'The personality of Augustus' in Raaflaub and Toher *BRE* 21–41, emphasising *"humanitas"*, and A. Wallace-Hadrill 'Civilis princeps: between citizen and king' *JRS* 72 (1982) 32–48, stressing *recusatio* as a distinctive part of the style of the Princeps, which was such a marked contrast with the *nobiles'* relentless pursuit of *gloria*.

[6] Plut. *Mor.* 207C (= *Apophthegmata Augusti*) esp. 7, the counsel of Athenodorus: "When you are angry, recite the alphabet before you speak." Augustus valued this advice. Cf. his own sayings quoted by Suet. *Aug.* 25.4.

[7] K.A. Raaflaub and L.J. Samons II 'Opposition to Augustus' in Raaflaub and Toher *BRE* 417–454.

[8] Suet. *Aug.* 66, even when he objected to supporters' way of life, as that of Vedius Pollio, on whom see Zanker *Images* 137, or to aspects of their character, as Maecenas' inability to hold his tongue (Suet. *Aug.* 66). The case of Castricius (*id.* 56.4) — the only guilty man whom Augustus intervened to save — is particularly illuminating. Cf. Macrobius *Sat.* 2.4.27. Earlier, for his gathering support, *Rom. Rev.* 234–9. Salvidienus was an exception; for his treachery, Vell. 2.76.4, *Rom. Rev.* 220 and n.6 for refs.

peace seductive (*ibid.* 1.2). Many of those outside their ranks hated the nobles;[9] the peoples of Italy had suffered from Sulla,[10] and when they heard the threats of Pompeius and his circle in 50/49, they could see the nobles had not changed. Many must have felt they could not lose by backing first Caesar, then his heir.

Pietas erga parentem — the duty he owed to his father (Tac. *Ann.* 1.9.3 and 10.1) — is given as his first policy statement by both friendly and unfriendly critics. *Pietas* was a highly rated virtue, needing no apology, and loyalty to Caesar was a programme with a mass appeal; it is important not to forget that 'Caesar' was what Octavian as we call him always called himself from the time of his adoption until he became Augustus — throughout his battle for supremacy.

Taking up Caesar's inheritance has been seen as rash; not to have done so would have been pusillanimous. It is argued (chap. 1) that in fact he felt his way cautiously before going to Rome for the first time after the Ides of March. Having claimed his inheritance, he vowed to avenge his 'father'; he said so in a speech in the Forum, and by giving Caesar's Victory Games (*Ludi Victoriae Caesaris*) and those of Ancestress Venus (*Venus Genetrix*) in July he reaffirmed his sonship (cf. *Rom. Rev.* 117). Towards vengeance he moved relentlessly, accepting support where he could get it, matching deceit with deceit, and ruthlessness and lack of scruples with equal measures, if not greater.

But caution was never absent from Octavian's manoeuvring: he never tried to face M. Antonius as consul with inadequate arms in the autumn of 44 during his rebellion, for example, or challenged the consular *imperium* head-on in the city; when courting Cicero and others whom Antonius' carelessness about the feelings of other people had alienated (so that, for example, Antonius could not get a *frequens senatus* (i.e. a Senate with a sufficient quorum) or one which would back his attacks on Octavian) he avoided becoming involved with M. Brutus and C. Cassius and their illegal usurpations East of the Adriatic; A. Hirtius and C. Pansa, with whom he associated and campaigned, were as good Caesarians as Antonius himself. After the relief of Mutina in early 43, he avoided collaborating with Decimus

---

[9] For whom Syme "has a curious affection", A.H.M. Jones *Augustus* (London 1970) 187. So have many of his followers.

[10] It is surely no accident that Augustus' principal assistants came from Etruria which had felt the harshest treatment in Sulla's revenge on those who had opposed him.

Brutus, Caesar's assassin; before joining forces with M. Antonius and M. Lepidus as triumvirs he took care to obtain a position (as consul), and to make clear his programme of punishing the murderers.

Caesar was avenged at the battles at Philippi. Afterwards, Octavian had no choice but to allow M. Antonius the task of completing the mission to avenge the defeat of Crassus at Carrhae which Caesar was about to undertake at the time of his murder. The execution of the compact at Bononia, and the rewarding of Caesar's (and their own) veteran soldiers — apparently a much more intractable task — was left to Octavian. Yet it offered unusual opportunities: for the unpleasant parts of the task he could plead his commitment to his partners; for the rewards he gave, he could claim the credit for himself. Even those who allocated the confiscated lands did not commend their work (Tac. *Ann.* 1.10.2), but the recipients must have done so. The opposition of Antonius' brother Lucius and wife Fulvia simplified Octavian's task of presenting himself as the veterans' true friend. The dead and disfranchised had no vote, so it was the veterans who had received farms who could be called on ten years later to endorse the unanimity of Italy in the face of invasion by forces said to represent the East.

As for those who accused him, justifiably, of brutality, Octavian could conjure up Cicero's pictures, of Antony the butcher of Pharsalus (*Phil.* 2.71) and of the centurions and men of the legions at Brundisium (*Phil.* 5.22, repeated in 12.12 and 13.18), though it is not clear that he actually did so even in the battle of words, insults and allegations which preceded the Actium campaign.

The welcome Octavian received after the Perusine War might have been inspired as much by fear as by favour. However, when Sextus Pompeius, who was immensely popular, perhaps because he alone of the leaders at the time had had no share in the proscriptions, used attacks on the city's food supplies to press his claim for a higher political status, he laid himself open to Octavian's counter-attack: that he was a pirate supported by slaves and criminals, and an enemy of Italy and its peoples. After Pompeius' death, for which Octavian was able to disclaim responsibility, he was able to build up a new people's champion, Agrippa his friend and the chief commander of his forces by land and sea.

Agrippa was ideally suited to this role: he was a *novus homo*, entirely without ancestral baggage, disliking the *nobiles* and disliked by them, hence with a ready appeal to the *plebs*. His naval victories

off Sicily revealed that Lepidus, as Syme put it (*Rom. Rev.* 346)
"lacked capacity", had nothing to offer but his family's past
distinction, and could be easily discarded. Agrippa's victory off
Naulochus in 36 was a — perhaps the — most important turning-
point in Octavian's rise to supremacy. After it, the welcome he
received showed that for the present he had the support of the *plebs*,
since he had removed the spectre of famine and starvation for the
moment.

From now on the city's food supply became a constant, and well-
advertised plank in Octavian's appeal, and Agrippa became the
instrument for providing the *plebs* with a share in the amenities of a
great city — paved streets, water-supply, fountains, drainage,
granaries, facilities for recreation and baths. All of these had been
neglected by the Senatorial government before the civil wars.[11]

As 'Protector of Italy' Octavian was able to play on popular
nationalism to launch campaigns to make Italy more secure from the
North in what were actually limited and cautious initiatives against
the peoples living East of the Alps in what is now Slovenia and
Croatia. To counter earlier accusations of cowardice, his own valour
was well publicised, and his two wounds, and the greatness of the
victories. But the campaigns were limited in their objectives,
probably quite unnecessary, and certainly of no lasting effect. The
Senate voted him a triumph, however. That was the main point. As
the defender of Italy and Roman tradition he could face Antonius,
now able to be represented as the instrument of Cleopatra, monarchy
and the East.

Every aspect of public life could be pressed into service in the battle
of words which ensued. Octavian's triumph could be contrasted with
that of Antonius, held in Alexandria, from which Italy and Rome
had gained no benefit. Octavian's and his friend Agrippa's resources
were being spent on amenities for Rome, Antonius' resources on
revelling with Cleopatra.[12] When Antonius' friends Domitius and
Sosius tried as consuls in 32 to destroy Octavian's power-base and
reallocate his provinces, they had no answer to his demand that
Antonius should do the same. They failed to hold the Latin festival, a
traditional obligation, and ran away, abandoning the gods of Rome,
even Jupiter from whom they had received the sacred *auspicia* and
whom they had a duty to defend — for what? To serve the gods and

---

[11] Zanker *Images* 20f.
[12] *Id.* 71 *et al.*

queen of Egypt, who had been seen in Rome as Caesar's mistress, and who rumour said had as her strongest oath "as surely as I shall one day give judgement in the Capitol" (Dio 50.5.4).

Nobody laid a hand on the consuls as they fled; their supporters were let go too; how different from the Pompeian threats! When those antagonised by Antonius' indifference to the sympathies of others betrayed the whereabouts of his will, Octavian was able to prove the truth of the charge that he had abandoned Rome for Alexandria as the capital of the world they knew. It was little wonder then that when an invading armada threatened Italy, the communities of Italy rallied to Octavian's banner, though many were reluctant, and perhaps few really spontaneous, as Octavian later claimed (*R.g.* 25). How much of his propaganda did they believe? How whole-hearted was their support? We cannot say. Certainly Octavian was not short of troops, but very many perhaps were like the man with the talking raven (or crow) which cried "Hail, Caesar, victorious commander". When Octavian rewarded him generously, a disappointed partner revealed that he had another bird which cried "Hail, victorious commander, Antonius".[13] In other words, they did not care deeply; they would support the winner, and hope to live in peace. All governments are oligarchies, as Syme remarked;[14] one tends to be much the same as another; it produces good executives and bad ones. The old oligarchy had ruled badly, almost exclusively in its own interests; a new one might do better; at least the promise of peace could be made to sound more convincing.

In the war of Actium, Antonius was in fact defeated as much by his own carelessness about what others thought, and the resulting desertions, as by Agrippa's seamanship and leadership. Italy was said to have triumphed, and by blaming all on Cleopatra's seduction of Antonius, Octavian was able to show the mercy which had been Julius Caesar's undoing. To prevent the latter, a new slogan had to be found.

It was, of course '*res publica*', the restoration of the authority of the Senate over the armed forces. "I am consul" he said; unfortunately Tacitus does not tell us when (*Ann.* 1.2.1).[15] Octavian's refusal to

---

[13] Macrobius *Sat.* 2.4.29.

[14] *Rom. Rev.* 7, "In all ages, whatever the form and name of the government ... an oligarchy lurks behind the façade."

[15] *consulem se ferens* (calling himself consul) Tac. *Ann.* 1.2; Tacitus does not date his description but in three documents of 32/31 Octavian calls himself no more than 'consul' or '*consul designatus*', F. Millar 'Triumvirate and Principate' *JRS* 63 (1973) 50-67, 58. But he was not then in Rome. The claim to be consul (sc. and no more than

hurry back from Egypt reflects his caution. Besides, it gave time for animosities to cool in Rome, or new enemies to show their hand. He also had time to undo Antonius' reorganisation of the Roman provinces east of the Hellespont, re-establish provincial governments in Syria, Cyprus, Cyrene and Asia,[16] and kings where appropriate, and reward other supporters. He could begin to demobilise huge numbers of troops and establish new colonies to be new centres of his own supporters: twenty-eight in Italy, others in eleven provinces (*R.g.* 28.1). He had time to think out how '*res publica*' might be re-interpreted. Not Caesar's way however; the 'clemency' of an all-powerful dictator would not do. He would claim to be consul and to have saved the citizens' lives;[17] an oak wreath could be voted him by the Senate, and coins issued OB CIVES SERVATOS[18] to convey the message. He would also appeal to the *mores maiorum*, and declare that he took no office contrary to the ancestors' traditions. But for two years he avoided the pressures of Rome, not returning to triumph till August, 29.

Display was traditional, and designed to influence the *populus Romanus*.[19] Octavian's triumph was itself a masterpiece, unrivalled in magnificence, taking Octavian beyond the achievements of other *nobiles*.[20] But it was also unprecedented in the rewards it brought to others,[21] and this enabled him to present himself as one who shared the fruits of victory in a way the nobles never had in the past. And he used his welcome to assert a Roman's right to freedom of action

---

consul) is obviously more relevant and appropriate when people could accuse him of being something more — triumvir perhaps.

[16] Note the large issue of coins *ASIA RECEPTA* between 29 and 27. *RIC* I² 276; *id.* p.31.

[17] We do not know when he adopted this theme. The oak wreath was a traditional honour; it imposed moral obligations on the giver. It is incredible that a decision to adopt it was thought up in the hurly-burly of debate in the Senate in January, 27. True, Octavian did have time to think in 29–8, but he had much more time, and to plan his course for 29–8, which is logical and coherent, before he came back to live in the city.

[18] Sextus Pompeius had already used this legend on his coins, M.H. Crawford *Roman Republican Coinage* (Cambridge 1974) 511 no.1 etc., reflecting or perhaps promoting his appeal. Augustus' coins with this legend did not appear for some years, probably not till 19 or later. See chap. 7 below.

[19] Werner Eck 'Senatorial self-representation: developments in the Augustan period' in Millar and Segal 129f.

[20] *R.g.* 4.3: nine kings or sons of kings were led before his chariot; they included two of Cleopatra's children by Antonius.

[21] Suet. *Aug.* 41 — even the veterans already settled in colonies received a bounty in 29, *R.g.* 15.3.

(chap. 1), and his spoils to publicise his piety[22] and not a taste for high living.[23]

A year and a half — August, 29 to January, 27 — were now taken up in dismantling the inheritance of the triumvirate (some would say the triumvirate itself); those who had not read the signs of the times correctly — C. Cornelius Gallus and M. Crassus, who thought that the age for competition and self-glorification was not yet over — had to be made to suffer for their misjudgement. Peace was gained by victories, but now the victories belonged to the Caesar.[24] Politically, the grand gesture of inviting the Senate to resume control of the provinces and their armies was carefully prepared and carried out (chap. 3), as later was the assumption of the guise of 'popular' leadership adopted in 23 (chap. 4). This followed a new proclamation of peace with victories and the closure of Janus' temple, ephemeral though it proved to be, and another sharing in the rewards of victory (in 24) — out of his own pocket, as he took care to advertise (*R.g.* 15). The people learned the benefit (to them) of a salutation as *Imperator*. They received as much as at his triumph. But Augustus himself was mostly abroad.[25] The proconsul of the last days of the 'Republic' who remained in Rome had been an improper innovation of the Pompeian party; Caesar's work had still to be consolidated by his heir. The reconstruction of the *via Flaminia* was visible proof to the citizens of his plan to guarantee the safety of Italy from the North; compelling other *triumphatores* to spend their booty on other roads (Suet. *Aug.* 30) showed the populace his interest as much as theirs.

[22] Eighty-two temples restored in 28 (*R.g.* 20.4); so were the gifts presented to *Iuppiter Optimus Maximus*, *Divus Julius* (whose temple he completed, and the basilica Julius had begun between the temples of Castor and Pollux and Saturn in the Roman Forum, *id.* 20.3), and the shrines of Vesta, Mars Ultor and Apollo. These are deities special to the city of Rome, and those to whom he felt a special affinity. Cf. Brunt and Moore 62f. (n. on *R.g.* 21.2). The choice of Apollo as the deity to whom a temple should be built on the Palatine Hill to mark the site of a lightning-strike is most unusual (Suet. *Aug.* 29.3); Jupiter was the god of lightning, and Jupiter Tonans was vowed in gratitude for Augustus' preservation in Spain (Suet. *Aug.* 29.3, *R.g.* 19.2). But Palatine Apollo was very special; it was virtually part of Augustus' own house, especially when he had added to the front the *atrium* or portico with his own Vesta, *Lares* and *Penates* and those of the city. Cf. Ov. *Fast.* 4.949–54: "Vesta, Apollo and Augustus share the one house". It was almost compulsory to pass through this portico to reach Apollo's temple by the main entrance. The Senate often met there in Augustus' last years. My thanks to Mr N. Purcell for help with this note.

[23] For the contrast between Augustus' simple mode of life and the nobles' luxury cf. (e.g.) Plut. *Luc.* 39–41 with Suet. *Aug.* 72f.

[24] Eck 'Senatorial self-representation' (n.19) 131 and others.

[25] "Of the 18 years after Actium, he was in Rome for about 7", F. Millar 'State and subject: the impact of monarchy' in Millar and Segal 37–60, 43.

"An absent consul was an impropriety" (*Rom. Rev.* 337), especially when there was no emergency. A permanent consul was also a denial of *res publica*. Augustus' announcement that he would look after the *plebs* by his powers as a tribune, after he resigned the consulate, followed naturally from a populist (*popularis*) programme (chap. 4). It was not necessarily either forced on him by plots or a sudden decision or a reaction to his illness.[26] The great demonstration which met him when summoned back to handle the food crisis in 23 (chap. 6) showed that some Senators' unwillingness to accept his new status was not shared by the populace at large. Careful preparation perhaps hindered, perhaps assisted, by ill-health had worked. He could leave Rome again to complete M. Antonius' undone task of squaring accounts with the Parthians, restore Rome's honour by recovering the standards lost by Crassus and Antonius and releasing prisoners, and escape the pressures of Rome.

For this task patience, caution and threats were his weapons; he actually busied himself with paying off old scores and rewarding old services in the the Aegean area (chap. 6), so demonstrating without ostentation that his proconsular *imperium*, whether greater because it was so conferred by law or greater by virtue of his superior prestige or mana (*auctoritas*), was effective in provinces governed by other proconsuls.[27] He also concerned himself, in all probability, with the new temple to *Roma et Augustus* in Pergamum (chap. 6, with n.60 for the coins). Three and a half years later he could return to Rome, his mission accomplished; Roman honour was restored, Parthia was claimed to have been humiliated, and this was publicised, and illustrated by the coins. Another salutation as *Imperator*, a holiday with games and other benefits for the populace was in prospect.

While he was away, for three years from 26 the *res publica* had run without Augustus; the great prize, the one consulate available, went consistently to members of Augustus' party, until 23, when two old opponents who had fought with Brutus at Philippi became consul: first, Cn. Piso replaced the Terentius Varro Murena, thought to be kinsman to Maecenas, who was first elected, then L. Sestius replaced Augustus himself when he resigned on recovering from the disease he

---

[26] Cf. E. Badian '"Crisis theories" and the beginning of the principate' in G. Wirth (ed.) *Romanitas–Christianitas: Untersuchungen zur Geschichte und Literatur der römischen Kaiserzeit, Johannes Straub zum 70. Geburtstag gewidmet* (Berlin and New York 1982) 18–41 esp. 28f.

[27] He started issuing orders to proconsuls from 27, Dio 53.15.4. Examples in Millar 'State and subject' (n.25) 48 etc.

had thought fatal. At this point Augustus cautiously introduced a new element into his position, dressed up as a power he already had, the power without the office of a tribune, the tribunician power; it was enough to protect the People when he was no longer consul, or so he said (chap. 4). There was also a plot — whether in 23 or 22 is immaterial for this discussion — and a challenge in a law court, after which the great proconsul went East to do what Antonius had failed to do, as we have seen.

While he was away his caution paid off again; the Senators found they could not win the support of the electoral assembly, and Rome was again torn by rioting as the leaders of the rival senatorial factions competed for the consulships. Year after year the people elected one of Augustus' men consul,[28] and kept the other place for Augustus. From a safe distance in the eastern Mediterranean he refused every time, once (for 21) compelling them to make their own choice, once (for 20) sending Agrippa to make sure two were chosen, once (for 19) nominating one of the delegates who came to Athens to see him (Dio 54.10). While awaiting Augustus in 19 the consul in Rome, C. Sentius Saturninus, dealt with Egnatius Rufus, leader of a new popular front. Suetonius says (*Aug.* 19.1), and Tacitus indirectly implies (*Ann.* 1.10.4), that the hand behind the blow that struck him down was Augustus'; it would be surprising if it were not. But Sentius got the blame.

In dealing with the Senate Augustus was no less cautious. It had been usual under the 'Republic' for the consuls to hold a levee or *salutatio* at their houses, at which friends and supporters (*amici*) were expected, and others tolerated or welcomed. Public business was discussed at these levees before the Senate met or a public meeting (*contio*) was held; agreement on a programme or a step to be taken could be planned, or even achieved. Augustus experimented with various committees for preliminary discussions of this sort[29] in which Senators played a leading part. Augustus continued to hold these till he was over seventy (Dio 56.26.2). He did not cease till AD 12, when he also apologised to the Senators for ceasing to attend public banquets.

He tried to treat the Senate as tactfully as he could, being cautious in making changes to its membership, duties, privileges etc. They

---

[28] They were military men: M. Lollius (21), P. Silius Nerva (20), C. Sentius Saturninus (19) — *Rom. Rev.* 372. This means that only Augustus' party had any political appeal at all.

[29] John Crook *Consilium Principis* (Cambridge 1955) chap. 2.

were and remained an élite, but they were expected to behave responsibly. At meetings he greeted members individually before the start, genuinely seeking views by altering the order in which he asked for opinions (*sententiae*) (Suet. *Aug.* 35.4); he tolerated a modicum of dissent and interruption (*id.* 54, Dio 54.16.3–6), and when the introduction of a new tax on legacies to fund army pensions met with resistance, he invited the Senators to think of some better way (Dio 55.25.4 and 56.28.4). This does not mean that he had an open mind on the subject, only a less than dictatorial method of government. Yavetz has recently given a good assessment of the 'ordinariness' of Augustus, and what the Romans called '*humanitas*', courtesy.[30] This does not mean that he was soft on real opposition and plotting, real or suspected. He struck swiftly and hard when he detected this.

He showed caution and patience in carrying through legislation: he may have planned a programme of social legislation[31] before it was implemented in 18 on the heels of the Senate's welcome in 19 and the votes that year and the next (18) that he should be supervisor of morals (*R.g.* 6.1). He had planned for Secular Games in 22;[32] they were postponed till 17, at which time the completion of Caesar's work (in 19) had been capped (in 18) by the sort of moral reforms which Caesar had attempted (Suet. *Jul.* 43). Virgil's *Aeneid* had also appeared,[33] paving the way for a new age of peace, merciful rule of the nations, and re-establishment of concord with the gods.

This was attractive propaganda, and fell on receptive ears. The *plebs* had long hated the nobles, and with good reason. Livy's *History* was retelling the story of the harsh debt laws of the early 'Republic'; the memory of the Gracchi was still alive. In populist tradition they were represented as having been killed by the nobles for championing the land rights of the common people and the conscript soldiers who had been expelled from their ancestral lands by the rich foreclosing on debts incurred while on service, or by force (App. *B.C.* 1.7–11). Marius Gratidianus, who had abolished the fraudulent currency and was worshipped for doing so,[34] was still remembered. Sallust's

---

[30] Yavetz 'Personality' (n.5).

[31] *Rom. Rev.* 443 quoting Prop. 2.7; Livy *Praef.* 9. But this has been doubted.

[32] They were due in 39, and possibly mooted (*Rom. Rev.* 218 and n.2), but that year's promise of peace was unfulfilled. For 22, *Rom. Rev.* 339 quoting H. Mattingly 'Virgil's Golden Age, sixth *Aeneid* and fourth *Eclogue*' *CR* 48 (1934) 161–5.

[33] Themes like the Golden Age, *Aen.* 6.791–853; *Rom. Rev.* 462, but Syme's whole chapter is relevant.

[34] Z. Yavetz *Julius Caesar and his Public Image* (E.T. London 1983) 55f. For Marius, Weinstock *Divus Julius* 295.

denunciations, especially Marius' speech (*Jugurtha* 84) and the *Second Letter to Caesar*,[35] were not long published. The clearest evidence of their attitude comes from Caesar's life and death, from the common people's initial reaction to his generosity (Suet. *Jul.* 10–11) to their rage after his funeral (*id.* 85) — and these people were not his soldiers.[36]

Like Caesar, Augustus was a consistent benefactor of the *plebs*: the public works he and his principal ally, M. Agrippa, constructed included many public amenities: better water supply, better drains, baths, protection from fire for all, as well as porticoes and libraries for the better-off rather than temples to extol a noble family's glory. Later, after the death of his son-in-law Marcellus, he built the Theatre of Marcellus, and provided the sort of entertainments the people enjoyed, and enjoyed them with them. He also distributed cash to celebrate his own victories, and later his family's achievements. He took charge of the city's food supply, from the twelve distributions of the year he resigned the consulship to the supplementation of the supply whenever there was a shortage, from 18 (*R.g.* 18). Granaries too, like the *horrea Agrippiana*, provided work in the construction and in the porterage for the grain.[37]

Augustus seems to have remembered that many of the common people had work to do, and not just the semi-servile duties of a client. Buildings needed workers, who were paid, so did other trades serving a great city's life. It is commonly suggested that Juvenal's jibe that all the city dwellers wanted was bread and circuses (*Sat.* 10.81) is true. Two measures of Augustus suggest this is not entirely so; one was his attempt to change the system of distributing the corn so as not to make people leave their work so often,[38] the other Augustus' own avoidance of making people attend on him in great receptions too

---

[35] I accept the arguments of M. Gelzer *Caesar, Politician and Statesman* (E.T. Oxford 1968) 183, n.1 on its genuineness; the nobles were 'greedy, proud and useless'. Syme, who denies the genuineness of the attribution, accepts the description "arrogant and exclusive, corrupt and incompetent" *Aug. Ar.* 12.

[36] The feeling did not die. Eighty-two years after the battles at Philippi, despite twenty-three years of rule by the grim and gloomy Tiberius, and four by the mad Caligula, the people still wanted a Caesar to rule, not the nobles of the Senate (Joseph. *A.J.* 19.227–8). For a recent discussion, T.P. Wiseman *Death of an Emperor* Exeter Studies in History 30 (Exeter 1991) 91 comm. *ad loc.* Even Tacitus admits that the nobles had ruled badly (*Ann.* 1.2.2).

[37] G.E. Rickman *Roman Granaries and Store Buildings* (Cambridge 1971) 8–11, 79, 86 *al.*

[38] Suet. *Aug.* 40.2, though he had to give the idea up.

frequently (chap. 1).[39] For some people the corn ration may have been simply a way of compensating city dwellers for the higher cost of food in the city, comparable not to an unemployment dole but to a food subsidy to help low wages or keep them low.

Nor is the idea of the city composed of *insulae* (apartment blocks) which are rabbit-warrens of single-room dwellings with a constantly shifting population perhaps generally true. While there will certainly have been some tenements like that, some bad *insulae*, probably some bad districts, the citizens could not have been registered *vicatim* (street by street) as they were, and drawn their food ration by *vici* (by streets) had the majority of the population not been stable, or reasonably so. Augustus' organisation of the city by *vici* must have helped to promote this stability, to the satisfaction of many, if not most of the population.[40]

The ordinary citizen's religious life also became more relevant. Those who lived in the *vici* had no lands producing food; their *Lares* and *Penates* had no permanent home save in the city; any tomb they had was communal, a niche in a building for storing urns (*columbarium*) or in a crowded cemetery; they joined a *collegium* (association) if they could, to procure a decent burial. The sacrifices of the aristocrats had ignored the common people: *favete linguis* — do us the favour of not speaking — had been their part in the state's religion. Augustus filled the void by promoting the shrines of the *Lares Compitales*, where there were gods of their own street with a place to worship them, *Augustales*, a priesthood to which they could aspire, festivals like Compitalia and Augustalia (see chap. 8) and officers drawn from their own community and social class, the *Vicomagistri*. By adding his own statue in the guise of *Liber Pater*, god of abundance, to those in the shrines of the *Lares Compitales* he easily became associated with the grain supply which the *plebs* ate. From there, his transition to the status of *paterfamilias* presented no difficulty. But the process had been cautious and slow; the first libations to Augustus' spirit (*Genius*), when libations were to be poured after dinner, were decreed in 30, after the capture of Alexandria (Dio 51.19); his nomination as *Pater Patriae* was in 2; his caution helped to explain why, by then, it was the act of the whole

---

[39] Cf. Suet. *Aug.* 89, he warned the praetor giving games not to allow his name to become too hackneyed in the speeches at the opening of games. But his homecomings were always celebrated, Suet. *Aug.* 57.

[40] The rebuilding of his house after fire should be significant for his popularity; everyone contributed, Suet. *Aug.* 57.

nation (*populus universus*).[41]

"The Doom of the *Nobiles*" is the title of the penultimate chapter of *The Roman Revolution*. It sounds impressive, and some families did die out, some ("all the most defiant", Tac. *Ann*. 1.2.1)[42] the victims of the civil wars who fell in battle or proscription. But families had always died out. The consular *fasti* of early Rome contain names unknown in the second century BC; some of the families then famous had disappeared by the time Caesar crossed the Rubicon; the *nobiles* themselves had destroyed others in the factional victory of Sulla — that of C. Marius for example, though he was not an old noble. In *Roman Revolution* 377 Syme mentions people who began to discover or invent illustrious ancestors, and in *Augustan Aristocracy* points to families which simply petered out, the last recorded member dying at an unknown date "probably from disease". Augustus had nothing to do with these.

Many of the nobles who survived in fact prospered "in proportion to their willingness to serve the regime" (Tac. *Ann*. 1.2). Apart from those who had always backed him, noble names start appearing in the consular *fasti* from 23, with L. Sestius and Cn. Piso; from 18 to 13 only two *novi homines* appear, both men of military distinction; there are eleven *nobiles* (*Rom. Rev*. 372f.). "Conspicuous among [them] are men whose fathers through death or defeat in the civil wars had missed the consulate" (*ibid*.), and the honour of the office was enhanced by 12-month tenures; there are only four *suffecti* (replacements) between 19 and 6, of whom two were required to replace men who had died. From 5, the number of *suffecti* again rose; Syme attributes this to Augustus' need for more allies in a "bid for the support of the *nobiles*" (*ibid*.) for his 'sons'. A new nobility arose from the remains of the old; those who refrained from overambition and palace-politics enjoyed several generations of assured honours

---

[41] Cf. Yavetz 'Augustus' public image' (n.2) 14, for the *equites*.

[42] The Latin *ferocissimi* is usually translated as if it were an unambiguously laudatory word — "high-spirited," "true republican" Penguin, Everyman translators, "boldest spirits" J. Jackson in LCL, "men of spirit" Michael Grant; but *ferox* is an ambiguous word, taking its tone from the standpoint of the observer. Derived from *ferus* 'a wild beast', it means (*OLD*) "having a violent or savage nature", "bellicose", "defiant", "self-assertive", the opposite in fact of *civilis*, *humanus* — civilised, humane, the qualities appropriate to a political leader of a civilised state. H.W. Traub 'Tacitus' use of *ferocia*' *TAPA* 84 (1953) 250–261 argued that Tacitus' use of *ferocia* is derogatory, but F.R.D. Goodyear *The Annals of Tacitus* I (Cambridge 1972) 105 note *ad loc.* offers the laudatory "boldest", mistakenly.

with a lower age for eligibility for office, but not necessarily military distinction.[43]

Military distinction was the field in which Augustus was most unwilling to move, even cautiously; he was of course right in this, since the unbridled quest for military distinction had created an unwieldy empire, with many areas only partially under control, and it was the rivalries of the military *principes* which destroyed the government by the Senate and People. Till the death of Agrippa in 12, he, or Augustus himself, had the command of the largest armies in the state, following a policy of consolidation in Spain, the Alpine region and the borders and frontiers of Syria. This was followed by a planned drive to push the frontier of Italy further North and East, to the sources of the Rhine and Danube, across the Rhine and down the Danube valley.[44] No excuse was needed for these incursions; the Germans were always potential invaders of Italy; both at the time of the Pannonian revolt in AD 6, and after the disaster of Varus in AD 9, the old bogey of a German invasion of Italy was raised (Dio 55.30.1 and 56.23.1). Augustus decided not to triumph again after 29, but to be content with salutations as *Imperator*, with holidays and games for the people. This decision should have roused some interest in view of the long-established Roman traditions of military glory and the frequent celebrations of victory by the Augustan regime (*R.g.* 4.1f.). There is no certainty as there is no evidence, but one consideration might be suggested, which, if relevant, throws light on the public relations aspect of the Principate as interpreted by Augustus.

In the rules (*mores maiorum*) applying to a triumph, the *triumphator* made his way to the Capitol where the triumph finished at the Temple of *Iuppiter Optimus Maximus*. There the *triumphator* dedicated his laurels and returned the *auspicia* he had been granted. If the *triumphator* was not consul he thereupon became *privatus*. Augustus it is suggested had no intention of becoming *privatus* — not because

---

[43] Quite the reverse. *Rom. Rev.* 326–330. Augustus deliberately denied such people large military commands. Some of the old aristocracy survived several generations, and Nero murdered many. Junia Calvina survived till AD 79; she was Augustus' last descendant. Cn. Calpurnius Piso (cos. 23) had at least three generations of descendants, Vipstanus Messalla was four generations from Messalla Corvinus (cos. 31); he died of disease. A cousin was consul in AD 73. A descendant of M. Aurelius Cotta was consul in AD 94. Syme, *Aug. Ar.* index.

[44] C.M. Wells *The German Policy of Augustus* (Oxford 1972) chap. 1: expansion on this front took place when there were troops available following careful planning, *op. cit.* 12f.

he feared he might be prosecuted (like Caesar in 49), but because the process of reinstituting his *imperium* might cause embarrassment, discussion perhaps of its proper limits in time and space, conceivably even of the need for it in the light of the peace proclaimed and the success claimed in the triumph.

Moreover, challenged or not, the act of revival would draw attention to the existence of the *imperium proconsulare maius* which Augustus was so keen not to advertise that he left it out of *Res gestae*. Renewals of the tenure of his *provincia* (which is what A.H.M. Jones has argued was what was renewed at intervals)[45] were much less embarrassing, and much less liable to raise questions. By not triumphing, questions about his *imperium* need never arise.[46] *Mutatis mutandis* the same might be true for Agrippa after his consulate. If reviving *imperium* were an embarrassment for Augustus, how much more so for Agrippa? It were surely much better not to allow his *imperium* to lapse, and if this is so the case for a *provincia* for Agrippa after 27 becomes stronger.[47]

In 12 Agrippa's death compelled Augustus to find a new field marshal or field marshals. Cautious as ever, he looked within his own family and picked on the two Claudii, Livia's sons, Tiberius and Drusus. They were immediately put in charge of the armies. Whether because of the removal of the objections of Agrippa (of which there is no direct evidence), or because Augustus decided for other reasons to restore incentives for the ruling classes to win military distinction, he introduced the new distinction of the honours (but not the reality) of a triumph (*ornamenta triumphalia*), and made the two Claudii the first recipients. Whether this was another cautious step in creating a royal house, or an olive branch to the nobles to enable them to recover access to military glory, we cannot say. But it represented a new era in the awarding of honours.

---

[45] 'The *Imperium* of Augustus' in *SRGL* 3–17.

[46] This does not explain his decision not to triumph in 24, when he was consul, and as a result his *imperium* would not have lapsed. But in 24 there were other factors to consider: he was ill, and a triumph involved considerable physical effort; moreover the troops who would have taken part had been given farms in Spain, and might not be very interested in coming over to Rome for the ceremonial of a triumph at an unpredictable time (because of Augustus' illness); there was also the consideration that the show could not have stood comparison with that of 29, going on for three days and showing the spoils of Egypt and kings as prisoners etc. The *plebs* might have regretted the show, but they were handsomely compensated in the *congiarum*, which was the same size as that given at the triumph in 29.

[47] See chap. 5. Jones '*Imperium*' (n.45) 8f. has argued that *imperium* without a *provincia* in which to exercise it was nonsensical.

The honour came to be given to *legati* (lieutenant generals) on quite a generous scale in the wars which followed, while the curule triumph was reserved for those who were *suis auspiciis* (supreme commanders) — that is for the imperial family. This too could be claimed to be *more maiorum* (traditional).[48]

It would be a mistake to regard *ornamenta triumphalia* as an insignificant honour. Tacitus never refers to them disparagingly.[49] After 2, they were awarded by the Senate sitting in the Temple of Mars Ultor on a motion from the emperor. But the honour of a curule triumph granted to Tiberius while he was enjoying the *auspicia* of a consul in 7, and a second one while he shared the *imperium* of Augustus in AD 11, marked him out for succession as certainly as did the grant of *tribunicia potestas*.

Planning for the succession was the sphere in which Augustus' care and concern had most trouble. *Atrox fortuna*, as he called his ill-luck (Suet. *Tib*. 23), destroyed his plans. He was a Roman, and having assumed responsibility for Julius Caesar's heritage he owed it to his ancestors (whom he was later to commemorate in his Forum) to leave behind a new *paterfamilias* to carry on the worship of his *Lares* and *Penates* and remember the ancestors at *Parentalia* and *Lemuria*.

And he owed it to Rome. His victories at Actium and Alexandria would be of little profit if his death led to a new round of civil wars.[50] His own attempts to get a child from Livia were vain. This must have been surprising as well as disappointing since they had both had children with different partners. The impetuous passion with which he had snatched her from Tiberius Claudius Nero (Suet. *Aug*. 62) lasted all his life. Many Romans would simply have divorced. Augustus chose to adopt his kin, first his grandsons, with their father Agrippa as their guardian, and after his death, Tiberius, until he in turn was adopted after Julia's disgrace made his adoption possible because of the resulting divorce, and the grandchildren's deaths.

Augustus was also concerned that the new *res publica* should have

[48] Cf. the 'research' on the basis of which Augustus disallowed the grant of *spolia opima* to M. Crassus. Syme *Rom. Rev*. 308 and n.2.

[49] Eck 'Senatorial self-representation' (n.19) 142f., *q.v.* for the bronze statues in the Forum Augustum (*statua aenea*) which were later awarded for services other than military. Cf. A. Gerber and A. Greef *Lexicon Taciteum* (Leipzig 1877–1883) *s.v. triumphalia*. Only in *Agricola* (40.1 and 44.3) does he use the expression *ornamenta triumphalia* in full; elsewhere, *triumphalia* without noun eight times, with *insignia* twice, *decus* four times, *honos* once, always either admiring or respectful. *Agr*. 44.3 — *consulari et ornamentis triumphalibus praedito quid aliud fortuna adstruere potest?* — is obviously unstinted praise.

[50] Suet. *Aug*. 28: his wish for the future includes posterity.

new blood; he tried to stimulate the birthrate among the governing classes by the Julian Laws of 18 and the Papian/Poppaean of AD 9, and when he brought in the inheritance tax (*vicesima hereditatum*) in AD 6, with its ratification in AD 13, he directed it so as to support families with children by making it not payable on legacies within the family, only to others.[51] He built the temple of *Iuventas* (*R.g.* 19.2), and reorganised the *iuventus* (cadets), making it identical with the *turmae equitum* (state cavalry),[52] and granted the members privileges like special seats in the theatre (Tac. *Ann.* 2.83), permitting them to attend the Senate (Suet. *Aug.* 38.2) to learn the protocol. Chosen members sang Horace's *Carmen Saeculare* at the Secular Games in a choir with girls of comparable age and standing.[53] In his censorships he regulated their activities, reinstituting their annual parade[54] and watching it himself. He organised performances of the 'Troy Game' (*lusus Troiae*), traced by Virgil to the days of Aeneas;[55] it evidently contained an element of risk (though the emperor's grandson Gaius Caesar took part at the age of seven, Dio 54.26). Some time before AD 4 a certain Nonius Asprenas fell and was crippled (Suet. *Aug.* 43.2), and Asinius Pollio the historian made such a fuss when his grandson broke a leg that Augustus abandoned the game,[56] thus showing his responsiveness to pressure.

Augustus also used the *iuventus* to bring forward his grandsons; they were unanimously chosen *principes iuventutis* (chief cadets) by the *equites Romani* (Roman Knights) (*R.g.* 14), and received gifts of silver shields and spears which were laid up in the Senate House after their deaths. The appellation was part of Augustus' plan for their advancement to lead the state (Ovid *Ars* 1.96), and is widely publicised on coins[57] and inscriptions.[58] The statues in the porticoes

---

[51] C. Nicolet 'Augustus, government, and the propertied classes' in Millar and Segal 89–128, 109f.

[52] Yavetz 'Augustus' public image' (n.2) 16 and n.113; H. Furneaux *The Annals of Tacitus* (2nd edn, Oxford 1896) n. on *Ann.* 2.83.

[53] E–J 32.

[54] *Transvectio equitum* on July 15th. Dion. Hal. 6.13.4; cf. Hor. *Carm.* 1.8; 3.2; 3.24; *Sat.* 2.2.9–13 for riding and the manly sports appropriate to the youth.

[55] *Aen.* 5.545–603 and R.D. Williams *The Aeneid of Virgil Books 1–6* (Basingstoke and London 1972) 433–438 (nn. *ad loc.*).

[56] Suet. *Aug.* 43, J.M. Carter *Suetonius, Divus Augustus* (Bristol 1982) 158. It is not known how long the ban lasted. Perhaps Gaius Caligula revived it, Dio 59.7.4.

[57] *RIC* I[2] 198f. C CAESAR; 205–212 C L CAESARES, E–J 66 for the legend; gold *aurei* and silver *denarii*; the *denarii* 199, 207, 208 are classed as 'common'. Cf. chap. 9 n.80 for the view that the inventiveness goes out of the Augustan coinage after the C L CAESARES issues.

[58] E–J 63a and 65, a very beautiful piece of work.

of the Forum of Augustus were put there to remind future
generations of what their ancestors had achieved (Suet. *Aug.* 31.5),
and in *Res gestae* Augustus writes (8.5) of transmitting exemplary
practices for imitation.[59] But Augustus' planning failed in this case,
and he had to fall back on his middle-aged stepson and his middle-
aged *amici.*

We are told that Augustus did not approve of his successor (Suet.
Tib. 21 etc.; Tac. *Ann.* 1.10.7); stories were told of Augustus'
consistent preference for Tiberius' brother Drusus, but before his
withdrawal to Rhodes in 6 Tiberius had been chosen to succeed to the
leadership of the party. His sudden, to Augustus inexplicable,
withdrawal to Rhodes was an injury which Augustus found hard to
forgive, though in the end he had to. For succession had to be
through the family; the family "was the kernel of a Roman political
faction" (*Rom. Rev.* 157), and in fact Suetonius' *Lives* contain
extracts from quite a number of letters which show no signs of ill
will.[60] Rumour said that Augustus had gossiped about alternative
successors;[61] one at least was both a better man than Tiberius, and
willing to try, but Augustus had planned otherwise, and despite
reservations saw that Tiberius took over. His caution did not allow
an alternative experiment.

---

[59] Yavetz 'Augustus' public image' (n.2) has argued that *Res gestae* is addressed to
the youth.

[60] *Aug.* 76; *Tib.* 21 etc.

[61] Tac. *Ann.* 1.13. If Augustus did, surely others must also have done so.

CHAPTER 3

OCTAVIAN IN THE SENATE, JANUARY 27 *

Reviewing Peter Sattler's *Augustus und der Senat* (1960), J.P.V.D. Balsdon remarked[1] that the background to the events which marked the establishment of the Principate is a field which has been ploughed, even deep ploughed, times without number. This must be agreed, but much of the ploughing has been concerned with the question, 'By what legal right did Octavian/Augustus govern before, during, and after the events in which he claimed to have "transferred the *res publica* into the discretionary power of the Senate and Roman people"?'[2] The interest of this particular question has somewhat

---

* An earlier version of this study appeared in *JRS* 64 (1974) with the same title. I am grateful for permission to use the material, which has required some modifications in detail; the basic thesis as to what happened on the Ides of January 27 remains unaltered.

[1] Review of P. Sattler *Augustus und der Senat: Untersuchungen zur römischen Innenpolitik zwischen 30 und 17 v. Chr.* (Göttingen 1960) in *Gnomon* (1961) 393–6. For a more favourable view of Sattler, P.A. Brunt, *JRS* 51 (1961) 234f. Sattler's views on the opposition to Augustus have been taken up and amplified by W. Schmitthenner 'Augustus' spanischer Feldzug und der Kampf um den Prinzipat' *Historia* 11 (1962) 29–85. Their basis is a belief in Dio's basic veracity, at least in the narrative. Less confident is F. Millar *A Study of Cassius Dio* (Oxford 1964). But all historians should heed what Tacitus tells us about his predecessors in imperial history (*Annals* 1.1); they were Dio's predecessors too, and Dio was less perceptive, and less Roman, than Tacitus.

[2] *Res gestae* 34. Cf. the valuable summaries by G.E.F. Chilver 'Augustus and the Roman Constitution 1939–1950' *Historia* 1 (1950) 408–435; more recent but more discursive, E.T. Salmon 'The Evolution of Augustus' Principate' *Historia* 5 (1956) 456–478. Both reveal how much tilling has been in the same furrow — *imperium, potestas, auctoritas*. A new line of thought was suggested by Sir Frank Adcock 'The interpretation of *Res Gestae Divi Augusti* 34.1' *CQ* 1 (1951) 130–5, but it did not convince Salmon ('Evolution' 457 n.7), and another by A.H.M. Jones (*Augustus* (London 1970) 46, and *A History of Rome through the Fifth Century* (2 vols London 1968–70) II 25; 41) which does not convince me. Both involve a formal vote to give Octavian overriding powers. P. Grenade *Essai sur les origines du Principat* (Paris 1961) adopted a similar but more sweeping view on the totality of Octavian/Augustus' legally bestowed powers. For a favourable review J. Béranger, *Gnomon* (1961) 387–93,

declined recently, perhaps rightly so, in an age in which there is a score of Octavians in the world, governing by right of victory in a civil war, and the governed populations tolerate these rulers without constantly examining their constitutional credentials, because they have one all-important virtue — they have put a stop to the massacres which seem to be the invariable accompaniment of civil wars.3

This "forking over of one portion of the field" (to borrow again from Balsdon) seeks in the first place to look closely at the events surrounding the 'transfer', and to enquire whether the hypothesis that Octavian used the normal senatorial procedures of the *res publica* of Cicero's day to effect that 'transfer' clarifies our understanding of what occurred, or not.

A second consequential hypothesis is that the arrangements made for governing the provinces follow naturally from the experience of the fifteen years of bloody civil wars which were formally brought to an end in 28, so that they were accepted because they offered a formula which might prevent civil wars starting again.

In the *res publica* of Cicero's day, as common sense would lead us to expect — and enquiry where that is possible confirms the expectations of our common sense — the Senate discussed what was put before it, and the resolution (*senatus consultum*) (or sense of the meeting (*auctoritas*) as the case may be) which resulted from a debate reflected the feeling of the House on the subject under debate. The formal summons to Senators seems always to have been to discuss the *res publica*, or *summa res publica* — either the *res publica* without limitations or restricted to particular business (*aut infinite de re publica, aut de singulis rebus finite*) as Gellius puts it (14.7.9) — and this appears to have been the case even when the actual subject of the proposed discussion had been announced formally or informally in

---

for a hostile one, P.A. Brunt *JRS* 51 (1961) 236–8. A. Momigliano *OCD* 149 (s.v. *Augustus*) for an entirely different view, that the *coniuratio* of 32 made those who took the oath Octavian's clients, and the oath was a substitute for his triumviral powers (which by implication simply lapsed).

    3 See Millar *Study of Cassius Dio* (n.1) 118 for Dio. For this reason, I share Syme's view of Augustus' interpretation of his *imperium*: review of H. Siber *Das Führeramt des Augustus* in *JRS* 36 (1946) 155–7, despite the theoretically valid but arm-chair objections of Salmon 'Evolution' (n.2) 465; cf. *Rom. Rev.* 307, "had the question [of the name of Octavian's powers] been of concern to men at the time". It wasn't. Their concern was peace. Cf. *id.* 324.

advance.[4] A debate might be opened by a speech from the presiding consul[5] (or other magistrate); this might be general in character, or lead up to a proposal he wished to have debated or approved by *senatus consultum*;[6] or the consul might invite one of the *consulares* to address the House,[7] or to say what he thought about the *res publica* — i.e. propose a topic for debate; he could also allow motions and counter-motions or rival motions to be proposed as the debate progressed.[8] When strong feelings were aroused and the interests of differing factions clashed debates might go on for days or even months, especially when there was a variety of conflicting proposals.[9] The consul could also allow (or perhaps could not prevent) disputes

[4] Examples of formal announcement *ex s.c.*: Caelius in Cic. *Fam.* 8.5 and 6, six months' notice of a debate on the consular provinces (51); Cic. *Fam.* 1.9.8, five weeks' notice of a debate on the *ager Campanus* (56). *Ex s.c.* embassies from provinces and *socii* had priority in February (*Fam.* 1.4.1), unless they were explicitly put off (*Att.* 1.14.5). Less formal announcements were made by consuls from time to time: M. Antonius let it be known that there would be an important debate on June 1st, 44, and Cicero was advised to stay away (*Att.* 15.5.2, with *Phil.* 2.108); Hirtius kept out of Rome in order to avoid having to debate on Antonius' proposed *s.c.* about Brutus and Cassius (*Att. ibid.*); it was to be debated on June 5th (*Att.* 15.9.1). On August 31st in the same year, it was known that the following day Antonius would propose not the *res publica infinite* but honours to Caesar, and Cicero was explicitly told that this was so (*Phil.* 1.11f.). In December 63, Cicero told those who had arrived at his house how he proposed to deal with the letters he had seized from the Allobroges (*Catil.* 3.7), and on the "immortal Nones", two days later, some Senators stayed away because they knew they were going to be asked to discuss the fate of the accomplices of Catilina, whom the Senate had decreed to have acted *contra rem publicam* (*Catil.* 4.10).

[5] Of Cicero's seventeen surviving senatorial speeches, two, *de lege agraria* 1 and *in Catilinam* 1, are of this type; so was Antonius' attack on Cicero to which *Philippic* 1 is a reply. Cf. Hirtius' and Pansa's speeches on January 1st, 43: Cic. *Phil.* 5.1.

[6] *In Catilinam* 4 re-opens a debate, and makes clear what the Senate must vote on "before nightfall" (*Catil.* 4.6), though it proposed no motion.

[7] *Post reditum in senatu* and *Philippic* 1 are clearly responses to an invitation of this sort. So is the lost speech in which Cicero proposed Pompeius' corn commission in 56 (*Att.* 4.1.6).

[8] *Philippic* 3 introduces a motion (37), so do 8 (33), 9 (15), 10 (25) and 14 (36); a series of motions in *Philippic* 5.31, 38, 53; whatever may have been the case in the later speeches, Cicero's motion in *Phil.* 3 was certainly not known or advertised in advance. *Phil.* 13 (50) and 7 (27) introduce proposals in the course of debates already under way; cf. *Prov.* 1 made in a debate whose subject was known in advance, and in which Cicero's speech was to support an already-proposed motion.

[9] Protracted debates include the restoration of Ptolemy Auletes in 56 (which was never concluded; for the variety and complexity of the proposals, Cic. *Fam.* 1.1.3.); the establishment of a court to try those charged with sacrilege at the *Bona Dea* festival of 62 lasted about two and a half months (January–March, 61) and was settled only by one party capitulating; the revision of the Asian tax-contract (*Att.* 1.18.7) lasted nearly a year. More briefly *eo die res confecta non est, eo die nihil perfectum est* (that day nothing was completed/achieved) Cic. *Q.fr.* 2.3.1 and 3; many other examples.

(*altercationes*) and complimentary speeches[10] during the discussion, nor were debates always restricted strictly to the topic announced in advance.[11]

As consul Octavian was in the chair on January 13th, 27. Unless Dio is wholly misinformed, Octavian had primed only a few of his closest associates about what he was going to say, so the majority of the Senators had come expecting to discuss the *res publica infinite*. Octavian however had written out his entire speech in advance to make sure, as Suetonius tells us, that he neither said more than he intended, nor omitted anything by accident.[12] He opened the debate, and he will have been expected to do so; we do not know what he said,[13] but we do know the results of the ensuing discussion: the first was that *ex senatus consulto* an oak-wreath (*corona querna*) was decreed to be hung above Octavian's front door;[14] the explicit statement of the *fasti* from Praeneste that this was on January 13th is preferable to the non-chronological order of *Res gestae* 34, in which the supreme unique honour, the name Augustus, is placed first,

---

[10] Cicero's *in Pisonem*, the fragmentary *in toga candida* and *in Clodium* (*et Curionem*) are written-up *altercationes*; *de haruspicum responso* and *Philippic* 12 combine self-defence with attacks on opponents; *pro Marcello* is a written-up version of what was a spontaneous and complimentary contribution to a discussion following a consular announcement; compare Cicero's account of Crassus' and his own contributions to the discussion which opened with the consul asking Pompeius' views on the court to investigate the *Bona Dea* affair (*Att.* 1.14.2–4).

[11] Cic. *Phil.* 3.13: *quamquam vos nihil aliud nisi de praesidio, ut senatum tuto consules Kalendis Ianuariis habere possint, rettulistis, tamen mihi videmini magno consilio atque optima mente potestatem nobis de tota re publica fecisse dicendi.* The implication that Cicero's extension of the field of debate was with the leave of the presiding tribunes is very clear.

[12] *Aug.* 84; for this occasion Dio 53.2.7; and cf. *id.* 11.1.

[13] The speech in Dio is generally thought an invention — certainly it cannot be put into Latin in the simple style Suetonius describes as Augustus' (*Aug.* 86). The atmosphere of hysterical amazement in the Senate may, however, be authentic. Schmitthenner 'Augustus' spanischer Feldzug' (n.1) 36, following Sattler, emphasizes the opposition, describes the settlement as a compromise, and, accepting Dio's statements about doubling the praetorians' pay (53.11.5), asks if the meeting was in fact intimidated by troops. If the answer is 'yes', the Romans played farces with straight faces superbly — better than I think credible.

[14] *Corona quern[a uti super ianuam domus imp. Caesaris] Augusti poner[etur senatus decrevit quod rem publicam] p(opulo) R(omano) rest[i]tui[t] CIL* I² 231; most accessible in E–J p.45. This, the official document, says *p. R. restituit*; *re publica restituta* exists only on a private document, the famous *elogium* (funeral monument) of 'Turia' (E–J 357). F. Millar 'Two Augustan notes' *CR* 18 (1968) 263–6 questions the validity of this document as a source for historical analysis. For the history and credentials of the *fasti* see Gagé *Res gestae* 155–160 with bibliography of discoveries since Mommsen's edition.

followed by the laurels, the oak-wreath[15] and the rest.

The oak-wreath has — with good reason — been identified with the oak-wreath bearing the legend OB CIVIS SERVATOS (for saving citizens lives) which appears on coins.[16] In *Res gestae* 34 Augustus calls it a *corona civica*. The saving of citizens' lives was the customary significance of an oak-wreath[17] (as distinct from one of laurel or ivy, etc.); there cannot be much doubt that, when the *fasti* from Praeneste associate the *corona querna* with the restoration of something to the *populus Romanus* (*rem publicam* perhaps, as in the usual supplement offered by editors, see note 14), they are referring to the same honour, and that there was only one such grant, not two.

If we are correct in supposing that a *corona querna* (with the significance of saving the citizens' lives) was voted on January 13th, Octavian must have claimed in his speech to have done something for which this would be an appropriate reward, rather than a mere imitation of Sextus Pompeius.[18]

A declaration of the end of the civil wars, and hence of the state of emergency declared at the passing of the *senatus consultum ultimum* in 43, took place in August — which can only have been August, 28 — as is stated by the *senatus consultum* quoted by Macrobius (*Sat.* 1.12.35).[19] Stopping the citizens killing one another, or subjecting them to the arbitrary treatment of civil wars or emergencies, was

[15] Dio 53.16.7f. says explicitly that the name Augustus was the last honour to be granted, but see below.

[16] The earliest coin is dated to 27: legend, obv. CAESAR COS VII CIVIBUS SERVATEIS, rev. AUGUSTUS S C which features an eagle with oak wreath and laurel trees. H. Mattingly *BMCRE* cxxiv and p.106 nos 656–8; *RIC* I² 277. "SC on this issue records the gift of the name Augustus by the Senate", Mattingly and Sydenham *RIC* I 62 n.1. OB CIVIS SERVATOS variously abbreviated is perhaps the commonest of all legends, appearing on coins of all denominations after about 19. Examples include *RIC* I² 278, 285, 302 (*aurei*), *aurei* and *denarii* from Spain *id.* 75–9, and as the normal obverse of *sestertii* from *ca* 18, *id.* p.65 etc. Further refs in E–J 19, and cf. Val. Max. 2.8.7. See also A. Bay 'The letters SC on Augustan *aes* coinage' *JRS* 62 (1972) 111–122, 114f. for their date as 18–15.

[17] Val. Max. *loc. cit.*; cf. Gellius 5.6.11; Pliny *Nat.* 16.6f. and 13 for the associated honours. Full references to ancient sources in *RE* iv, 1639f. (Fiebiger 1901).

[18] This claim might have been the source of Sextus' attested widespread popularity, see chap. 5 below.

[19] The date of the *s.c.* is uncertain, and disputed, but not relevant to this issue, since it is giving the date for the end of the civil wars only as a reason for choosing Sextilis and not September as the month to be called Augustus; September had obvious claims; the victories of Naulochus and Actium were both commemorated (E–J p.51, September 2 and 3), and Augustus' birthday (*ibid.* p.52, September 23). The declaration of the end of the civil wars is not in the *fasti* as we have them; perhaps it was felt to be best forgotten. That would argue for an early date for the *s.c.*

certainly one way of preserving lives. Though Dio says (51.2.4) "many" prominent citizens were put to death after the Battle of Actium, he records no citizen deaths after the capture of Egypt and the suicides of M. Antonius and Cleopatra and the collapse of resistance there, nor after Octavian's return to Rome in 29.

A policy of mercy (*clementia*) may also have been announced; it was an 'imperial virtue' though not a theme on Octavian/Augustus' coins,[20] and it was not widely advertised. *Clementia* was a policy for which Octavian could quote his inheritance from Caesar. Yet there were important differences, and even Caesar had found it difficult to pardon the same person more than once. Later, in *Res gestae* 3.1, Augustus declared that he spared those who asked for pardon,[21] but some groups of people, like the assassins of Caesar, never were forgiven. There were other drawbacks too: he had seen that Caesar's pardon did not appease his noble opponents (some of those who murdered him are known to have been pardoned), partly because they found the need to ask for pardon offensive,[22] as it involved an act of submission or acknowledging a superior, partly because Caesar's declaration of the policy of *clementia* was political — to put their own party's "severe punishment" of those who attacked the settlement of Sulla in a bad light (Dio 43.50.1f.). In the second place there was a credibility gap; the survivors of the civil wars cannot have forgotten so soon the merciless young triumvir who had pursued the proscribed with the most relentless energy (Suet. *Aug.* 27.1), and put to death the council of Perusia and others only fifteen years before;[23] his cold reply to their pleas "You must die" was remembered as bitterly as Antonius' relentless vendetta against Cicero.

The significance of the *corona querna* (or *corona civica*) tends to be overlooked; it imposed obligations on the person whose life had been saved towards the person who was awarded the *corona* analogous to those felt towards a *paterfamilias* or patron.[24] These include deference, if not obedience, and an obligation not to injure. This does not mean that by their vote every Senator individually declared he

[20]   *Clementia* is not in the list of reverse legends in *RIC* I² p.289 for Augustan issues.
[21]   Cf. Vell. 2.86; also the comments of Brunt and Moore 40f.
[22]   Z. Yavetz *Julius Caesar and his Public Image* (London 1983) 174f. and bibliography 249 n.6; Weinstock *Divus Julius* 233 and 237–40.
[23]   Cf. *Rom. Rev.* chap. XIV, and for Perusia Suet. *Aug.* 15; Dio 48.14; App. *B.C.* 5.48. In *Rom. Rev.* 212 Syme thinks the number of killings exaggerated.
[24]   At one time it was thought to bring the citizen saved into the *potestas* of his saviour. It also brought honour to his parent, Pliny *Nat.* 16.7f. The precedent for a *corona civica* for public services was that voted to Caesar.

felt these obligations; rather it expressed a collective recognition that what Octavian had done he had done for the good of the *res publica*; it was a vindication in short of his past actions, and an acceptance of the declaration of the end of the civil war (in August, 28, see above) and that the arbitrary acts of the triumviral era had indeed been annulled from December 31st, 28.[25] If it meant anything, this last must have included an amnesty for any of those proscribed who still survived without having been pardoned or struck off the lists of the proscribed.

The whole of the year 28 had been devoted to a wholesale dismantling of the apparatus of civil war. It embraced many fields: as censors Octavian and Agrippa reduced the size of the Senate by about 200 from about 1000 as tactfully as they could, according to Dio (52.42.1–3).[26] This means they confirmed some 800 members, a number far in excess of the 600 traditional since Sulla's day. They appointed Augustus himself as *princeps senatus*, and concluded their tenure of office with a *lustrum*, a ceremonial purification of the Roman People, the first for forty-two years.[27] We are inclined to pass this over as not significant, but contemporaries could easily be persuaded that it was very important as it meant cleansing themselves from the guilt of civil wars and complemented the other religious activity already in progress. Augustus had begun his religious programme before Actium, perhaps from the time of the *coniuratio Italiae* in 32, with the restoration of the Temple of Jupiter Feretrius,[28] and the revival of the ancient ceremony of the *fetiales* on his departure to fight Cleopatra (Dio 50.4.5).[29]

Religious regeneration and restoration of temples were pressed forward energetically after his return from the East in 29. Egyptian

[25] Octavian's own measures had been confirmed in 39 (Dio 48.34.1) and again in 29 (Dio 51.20.1); this distinguished him from the other two triumvirs (Sattler *Augustus und der Senat* (n.1) 34f.). But propaganda exhibiting deference to A. Cascellius may have been relevant. Cascellius had refused to accept the validity of the acts of the triumvirs at any time (Val. Max. 6.2.12); he was still alive, probably active, and widely respected, *RE* iii.1635 (Jors 1899).

[26] How much later propaganda is there here? We cannot tell, but should bear the possibility in mind.

[27] *R.g.* 8.2; the previous *lustrum* was in 70, well before the start of the civil wars. Purification was the principal purpose. H.J. Rose in *OCD* 626 *s.v.* lustration and refs given.

[28] Suggested by Atticus, Cicero's friend, who died in 32. For the importance of this temple, see below chap. 6 n.66, chap 7 n.15. It was so tumbledown that it had lost its roof, and Augustus lists it among the temples he built rather than restored (*R.g.* 19.2).

[29] This has been seen as evidence of his success in getting the People behind him.

rituals were prohibited within the sacred boundary of the city; temples (for the traditional Roman deities) were repaired, some by the living descendants of the builders, if there were any, the others by Octavian himself (Dio 53.2.4f).[30] 28 is the date chosen by Augustus in *Res gestae* for his repair of eighty-two temples at the request of the Senate (within the list of his buildings in *R.g.* 19–21). The magnificent marble temple of Apollo on the Palatine was opened in 28, on October 9th (E–J p.53). Apollo was said to have assisted at the victories at Naulochus and Actium, and the first celebration of the Actian games took place in 28.[31] *Religio* for the Romans was always the first business on the agenda of the *res publica*.

The political side of the *res publica* had also been overhauled in 28. From February 1st the *fasces* had been shared between the consuls in the traditional way;[32] the consuls remained in office the full twelve months — there had been *suffecti* (substitutes) every year since 41 — and at the end of his year of office Octavian took the traditional oath (*eiuratio*) swearing that he had kept the laws.[33] It is reasonable to suppose that Agrippa did the same.

Of greater importance, perhaps, was the revival of the traditional justice system in 28, epitomised by the appointment of a *praetor urbanus* (Dio 53.2.3).[34] This suggests that there was no *praetor urbanus* till Octavian appointed one, and that Rome had lacked a head of the civil law till that point, so probably also throughout the civil war period. Indeed, though we hear of various courts set up *ad hoc*, mostly to do the dirty work of the triumvirs, there is no sign of any civil jurisdiction or of the *quaestiones perpetuae* or other traditional courts, though there must have been *praefecti* at least to

---

[30] This passage is not well translated in the LCL version (vol. vi 197–9). Prefer that of I. Scott-Kilvert *Cassius Dio. The Roman History. The Reign of Augustus* (Harmondsworth 1987) 127. "Egyptian rituals" are contrasted (by the Greek *men* and *de*) with "temples, some of which ... the rest ...". For modern accounts see (e.g.) J.M. Carter *Suetonius, Divus Augustus* (Bristol 1982) 128–133; Zanker *Images* 103–110.

[31] Dio 53.1.4–6, an elaborate show with a special temporary wooden stadium and contests of gladiators (prisoners). They were repeated every four years at least to 16, n.121 to chap. 1.

[32] For shared *fasces*, Dio 53.1.1; E.S. Staveley 'The *fasces* and *imperium maius*' *Historia* 12 (1963) 458–484, esp. 478 for the importance of this.

[33] Dio 53.1.1 adds that Octavian's other acts were *more maiorum*; this hardly justifies Sattler's assertion (*Augustus und der Senat* (n.1) 34) that his *eiuratio* must mean that in the whole of 28 Octavian had made no use of extra-constitutional powers.

[34] There were also adjustments between the duties of praetors and aediles; Dio half suggests that the aediles had usurped some of the duties of the praetors.

deal out summary justice to petty criminals.[35] The choice of a *praetor urbanus*, and it is fair to assume the election of a full college of praetors for 27, was a visible claim that the mechanisms of the rule of law were being restored. This is actually claimed on a gold *aureus* which has recently appeared.[36] It bears the obverse legend IMP CAESAR DIVI F COS VI (28), the reverse LEGES ET IURA P(OPULO) R(OMANO) RESTITUIT (Imperator Caesar son of the deified (Julius) in his sixth consulship restored (their) laws and rights to the Roman People). If the coin is genuine, and this has not yet been established with absolute certainty, it confirms the idea of restoration of the normal rule of law for the *res publica*.

There might even have been the formal restoration of the citizen's right of *provocatio* (appeal to the People), even the revival of the *Lex Valeria de provocatione*, which Livy discovered was one of the first acts of the *res publica antiqua* (the primitive 'Republic') on the expulsion of the Tarquins and the vindication of the liberty of the Roman People.[37] This, though not exactly saving lives, at least proclaimed the inviolability of the *caput* of the citizens.

---

[35] Fergus Millar 'Triumvirate and Principate' *JRS* 63 (1973) 50–67 has emphasised that there is no evidence for a routine personal jurisdiction by the triumvirs in Rome and Italy, though plenty for hearing petitions and giving summary judgements on enemies. Augustus' subsequent work as judge is traced back to Caesar. *Ibid.* 52f. for appointments to magistracies, many very irregular, like the sixty-seven praetors in 36 (Dio 48.43.2); it is generally thought that they were not appointed to provide access to justice but to supply propraetors to command troops.

[36] In Switzerland. *Numismatica Ars Classica AG Auction* 25/2/92 no.400. I am indebted (and most grateful) to Joyce Reynolds for drawing my attention to the coin and to Dr Andrew Burnett of the British Museum for a photocopy of the coin and the catalogue commentary.

[37] Livy 2.8.1; rejected as a "Livian error" by R.M. Ogilvie *A Commentary on Livy, Books I–V* (Oxford 1965) 252f. Could Augustus be the cause of the error? Cf. tetradrachm (*cistophorus*) *BMCRE* i. 112 no.691 IMP CAESAR DIVI F COS VI LIBERTATIS P R VINDEX (Imperator Caesar, son of the deified (Julius) consul for the sixth time (28) Champion of the Roman People's Freedom). Attributed to the Ephesus mint by Mattingly (also *RIC* I² 476), to Bithynia (Nicomedeia) by A.M. Woodward in C.H. Sutherland and R.A.G. Carson (edd.) *Essays in Roman Coinage presented to Harold Mattingly* (Oxford 1956) 152 with refs. Cf. M. Grant *Roman Imperial Money* (London and New York 1954) 24; Syme *Rom. Rev.* 306. The reverse says PAX. Grenade *Essai* (n.2) 62f. argues that this is the more important legend. But peace was the natural (and asserted) corollary of the victories proclaimed on the dated *quinarii* ASIA RECEPTA (IMP VII) *BMCRE* i.105 nos.647–9, *denarii* AEGYPTO CAPTA (COS VI) (28 BC) *ibid.* 106 nos 650–4, *aureus* COS VII (27 BC) *ib.* no 655. Cf. also Livy 1.19.3, written before 25, R. Syme 'Livy and Augustus' *HSCPh* 64 (1959) 27–76 esp. 42. Ch. Wirszubski *Libertas as a Political Idea at Rome* (Cambridge 1950) 4f. for *libertas populi Romani* as signifying 'Republican' government; *id.* 100–106 for *libertatis p.R. vindex*.

Dio also says that the *aerarium* was restored to the public domain, with men of praetorian rank put in charge with an annual tenure. He speaks too of a cancellation of debts to the treasury and a subvention by Octavian (53.2.1 and 3). Again, in Octavian's personal life there appears a greater measure of *civilitas* (citizenlike behaviour): he opened his gardens, where his huge new Mausoleum stood, to the public;[38] he got rid of about eighty statues of himself in silver, some standing, some equestrian, some even mounted in a chariot (*Res gestae* 24.2) which he converted into golden tripods as offerings in his new Temple of Apollo, some in his own name, some in the name of those who had put up the statues.[39] Dio also reports a greatly increased corn allocation this year, at his expense, and gifts to individual Senators,[40] but neither of these appears in *Res gestae*. Some have suggested[41] that 28 is also the year and the context for his edict and oath with the hope that "he may set the *res publica* safe and sound in its place and see the fruits of this in such a manner that he may be called the author of the best state of affairs and carry with him when he died the hope that the foundations of the *res publica* which he laid (lit. shall have laid) will remain in their place". But there is no certainty that this is the date, and no weight should be put on an assumption that it is.

If this overall interpretation of the events (of 28) preceding the Ides of January, 27, is correct, we can see that putting the provinces into the hands of the Senate for the choice of governors was no more than

---

[38] Suet *Aug.* 100; for the Mausoleum itself, Strabo 5.3.8 (LCL) quoted by Zanker *Images* 72–7: "[This] interpretation of the Mausoleum as an instance of Octavian's demagoguery is very attractive ... [it] was first of all a demonstration of its patron's great power ... a monumental base for the statue of Augustus whose proportions must have been colossal ..." and after his death the site for the two bronze pillars inscribed with *Res gestae*. Zanker also reminds us that it is a warning (to us as well as contemporaries) that we must not overstate his *civilitas* (demeanour of an ordinary citizen).

[39] Cf. Suet. *Aug.* 52; Dio 53.22.3 speaks of their conversion into coinage, but *RIC* I² records no finds of silver coins from the Rome mint after 28 (cos. VI). The CIVIBUS SERVATEIS coins dated to 27 are *aurei*, and rare (*op. cit.* 277). M.H. Crawford (private communication to the author) observes "there is a hiatus in the coinage between 27 and 19". Zanker *Images* figs 69 and 70 for illustrations of what the tripods probably looked like.

[40] Dio 53.2.1f. Four times the usual ration of grain; the Senators were "impoverished" and numerous.

[41] Grenade *Essai* (n.2) 68f. is one of those who assign it to 28. Carter *Suetonius, Augustus* (n.30) 128, dates it to 17 or 16 where it also fits the context well. It has the ring of an announcement at the end of some significant episode or development. The tense of the last relative clause (future perfect) suggests that it is looking forward not backwards.

the next logical step in a process of transition to the traditional practices of the *res publica*, and the end of an era as much as the start of a new one. It was of course fraught with much larger implications than the measures so far taken, but it was not out of context or a complete bolt from the blue. The Senate's reaction of voting a *corona civica* was not inappropriate.

Nor was the second result of the debate extraordinary: Octavian's doorposts were to be publicly decorated with laurels. Augustus himself records this vote (*Res gestae* 34), and Dio associates the grant of the laurels with that of the oak-wreath (53.16.4). Dio's text says *daphnas*, and bushes of laurel appear on a number of coins, either on their own or with the *clupeus virtutis* (golden shield).[42] On other coins, however, laurel branches are shown, associated with the oak-wreath; these are not bushes, nor are they plaited into a wreath, but are shown encircling the oak-wreath and curved to fit within the rim of the coins.[43] They have been taken to represent either bushes or branches fixed in an upright position to the doorposts of his house (and presumably renewed at fairly regular intervals).

Laurels (of whatever sort) symbolized victory; victories and triumphs were much in the air in 27. Apart from Octavian's own triple triumph in 29, three triumphs were celebrated from 'his' share of the triumviral provinces in 28: C. Calvisius Sabinus from Spain (May 26th), C. Carrinas from Gaul (July 6th), L. Autronius Paetus from Africa (August 16th);[44] and victories were the appropriate counterpoint to the theme of peace.[45] Other victories had been announced: M. Licinius Crassus had caused Octavian to take a seventh imperatorial salutation in 29[46] for his victories to the North of Macedonia, M. Valerius Messalla Corvinus was winning victories

[42] For the argument that they were bushes, W.K. Lacey, *LCM* 6.4 (April 1981) 113, and 7.8 (Oct. 1982) 118; *contra* B. Curran and F. Williams, *LCM* 6.8 (Oct. 1981) 209–12. The coin evidence is in *BMCRE* i. Augustus 355–6 and plate 7 nos. 5–8 (a Spanish mint); cf. *RIC* I² plates 1 (33b) and 2 (36b) which are undoubtedly bushes though called "branches" by Sutherland. Cf. also Zanker *Images* 92f, fig. 75(a) with trees outside a door; he adds that the laurel was also Apollo's tree.

[43] *BMCRE* i. nos 134, 139, 148, 157, 165, 171, 175 etc. Plate 18 for illustrations of these and others. Cf. plate 21.8 (no 737). The laurel wreath and OB CIVES SERVATOS legend is a civil war (AD 68–9) coin, *BMCRE* i. p.289 and n.

[44] E–J p.35, from the Capitoline *fasti triumphales*; cf. the coins cited in n.37 above.

[45] Velleius 2.89.

[46] Dio 51.25.2; E–J 17 (= *ILS* 81) records Octavian as IMP VII this year, and the dedication as RE PUBLICA CONSERVATA. "Some people say" (Dio *loc. cit.*) that Crassus also was saluted as *imperator*; E–J 190 (from Athens) supports them. Syme 'Livy and Augustus' (n.37) 46 for both this point and Crassus' return (below).

in Gaul, both would triumph in 27.[47] Crassus had already returned in 28,[48] but as he claimed the *spolia opima* (he had killed a chief of the Bastarnae in battle with his own hand), research was needed to examine the validity of his claim to this antique and Romulean honour[49] — a convenient excuse no doubt, and a means of dealing with an extravagant and inconvenient claim. In addition, there were the well-advertised (if ill-starred) victories of Cornelius Gallus in Egypt and beyond its frontiers.[50] Laurels, then, symbolized great victories which Octavian claimed to have achieved, if not universal victory within the limits of the Roman world, and formed a useful prelude to a claim that the provinces were sufficiently pacified to be handed over to the Senate.[51]

To return to the Ides of January; the other act explicitly dated to them is the "return of every province to our people", as recorded by Ovid;[52] unfortunately however Ovid's text is not certain, and he puts this act on the same day as the grant of the name Augustus, stated explicitly by the *fasti* of Praeneste and Cumae to have taken place on the 16th.[53] If Ovid is right about the return of the provinces on the 13th, the Senate was given a proposal (*relatio*) to debate following

[47] Crassus on July 4th, not over the Bastarnae, but *ex Thraecia et Geteis*; Messalla on September 25th *ex Gallia* (E–J p.35).

[48] Syme *Aug. Ar.* 274 (with refs); 'Livy and Augustus' (n.37) 44–6 against Grenade *Essai* (n.2) 171.

[49] Livy 4.20.5–11, for Octavian's results; Ogilvie *Livy I–V* (n.37) 563f., with references to earlier literature, and Syme *loc. cit.* above.

[50] E–J 21 for Gallus' claims; dated April 15th, 29. Dio 53.23.5–7 (dated 26) for his disgrace and suicide; his exact offence is not clearly stated. Syme *Rom. Rev.* 309 dates it to 27.

[51] This might be what Livy *Epit.* 134 is trying to say: *rebus compositis et omnibus provinciis in certam formam redactis Augustus quoque cognominatus est.* Dio (53.13.1) says that Augustus in youthful boastfulness added that he would return his provinces also to the Senate if they were pacified sooner (than ten years time). Where did Dio find this information? It does not look like a historian's — even a rhetorician's — invention. *Cum per totum imperium populi Romani terra marique parta esset pax*, the formula for the closing of the temple of Janus, could be held to exclude foreign wars, and was evidently so held since the temple was not re-opened for Augustus' widely-anticipated expedition to Britain (Dio 53.22.5) but only for his Spanish campaign (or the war against the Salassi): Plutarch *Mor.* 322 B–C (= *de fortuna Romanorum* 9); Dio 53.26.5; cf. Orosius 6.21.1 (though he has the date wrong).

[52] *Fasti* 1.589f.: *redditaque est omnis populo provincia nostro/ et tuus Augusto nomine dictus avus. est omnis* has the support of the best MSS, Lenz (Teubner editor), J.G. Frazer and others; *immunis* was proposed by Merkel (1891), and he has convinced some historians (e.g. Gagé *Res gestae* 164). Merkel also proposed *res publica* for *provincia*, which Mommsen accepted, but later repudiated. *vestro* has MS support, but is not read.

[53] E–J p.45.

Octavian's address — the consular provinces — and it so happens that the ultimate result of the Senate's debate is that an allocation of provinces to at least one of the consuls took place.[54]

According to Dio (and here we seem to have to depend on Dio) this is precisely what happened; in his prepared speech Octavian put the provinces — which can only mean decisions on who was to govern the provinces — into the hands of the Senate.[55] They gave them straight back. Octavian's immediate reaction is unknown; his ultimate reaction was to undertake to govern Gaul, Spain and Syria probably for ten years, with the right to manage their frontier-policies (make war on and peace with the neighbouring peoples and kings).[56] The other provinces were put into the hands of the Senate to manage in the traditional way on behalf of the People by sending out members of their own order to govern them for a year at a time, the choice being controlled by the lex Pompeia which prescribed a five-year interval between a city magistracy and a proconsulate.[57] One can argue inconclusively for January 13th, 15th or 16th as the date for this ultimate solution; in favour of the 13th it can be said that Octavian was unlikely to have given no thought to the probable outcome of his speech; on the other hand some degree of hesitancy would be more democratic or 'republican'-looking, as when (for example) the consuls consulted with Pompeius about the resources he needed for his corn-commission in 56, before coming to a formal proposal;[58] an adjournment looks more attractive on the whole.

Augustus' choice of Spain, Gaul and Syria is seldom discussed. It is usually taken for granted as being no more than choosing the provinces with the largest armies. Certainly they became so, but early

[54] Whether Agrippa the other consul got a province is discussed in chap. 5.

[55] Dio 53.4.3 and 5.4, heavily underlined by Tiberius' speech as given in 56.39 (esp. 4 for the *aerarium*); but for the credentials of the latter Millar *Study of Cassius Dio* (n.1) 101. I do not believe in Dio's *cura* and *principatus* of the whole *res publica*, even in Schmitthenner's "staatsrechtlich unverbindliche Formel" ('Augustus' spanischer Feldzug' (n.1) 36, *q.v.* n.44 for references), but agree with Syme *Rom. Rev.* 313.

[56] Strabo 17.840 = 17.3.25 LCL; he says the right to make war and peace was granted for life. The 'frontiers and neighbours' of Syria were, of course, stretched to include the whole eastern frontier.

[57] Hence properly 'People's Provinces' (*provinciae populi Romani*); so Strabo *loc. cit.* Cf. F. Millar ' "Senatorial" provinces: an institutionalised ghost' *Ancient World* 20 (1989) 93–7, or 'Proconsular Provinces' since all governors held that title (Dio 53.14.2). We do not know whether the requirements of the lex Pompeia were imposed immediately or not.

[58] Cic. *Att.* 4.1.6–7 *factum est s.c. ... ut cum Pompeio ageretur ut eam rem susciperet, lexque ferretur ... Postridie ... nihil Pompeio postulanti negarunt, ille legatos cum xv postularet ... legem consules conscripserunt qua Pompeio ... potestas ... daretur.*

in 27 this may not have been the case. Augustus' annexation of Egypt had been followed by Gallus' vigorous expansionist programme in the area; his own campaigns against the tribes which disturbed the northern frontiers of Italy on the eastern flank had been followed by campaigns such as those in Thrace, from which M. Crassus had returned in 28 with extravagant claims. Africa had seen three triumphs in the last seven years; there must have been considerable numbers of troops there. There were armies in Spain and more or less continuous fighting to judge from the six triumphs since 43, and Gaul long quiescent had seen a triumph won in 28 and another pending in 27, but Syria had not been disturbed since Ventidius Bassus' triumph over the Parthians in 38, the failure of Antonius' campaigns and the triumph of Sosius over the Jews in 34; the Jews were now (hopefully) under the firm control of Herod the Great.[59] Nor did his provinces embrace the corn-producing areas; it is suggested (chap. 5) that Agrippa was given charge of this sensitive field. Nor were his provinces (in 27) the main producers of revenue, apart from Egypt, which was not mentioned.

Syme hinted (*Rom. Rev.* 326) that the choice was political, and this should be agreed. Augustus' contemporaries had heard from Cato, for example, that the root cause of the civil wars was the agreement of Pompeius, Crassus and Caesar which culminated in the decision of the meeting at Luca to divide up the Roman world by proconsulates in Spain, Gaul and Syria. The surest way of reassuring the Senators of 27 that there would not be a repetition was to put all these provinces into the control of one man, the Princeps. There were other proconsuls "responsible now to the Senate and People"[60] in military provinces — for the time being — in Africa, Macedonia and Illyricum, though only Africa saw significant military activity. By choosing the provinces he did Augustus avoided openly monopolising military power while at the same time assuring people that civil war would not recur.

Octavian's speech must have dealt with more than the provinces. There was much else in the *res publica*. Octavian had read a prepared speech to make sure he did not forget anything, and to invite the Senate to discuss the provinces was not to restore the *res publica* to them *tout court*. Dio mentions the armies, the laws and the treasury. Of these, command of the armies went with the government of the

[59] A.H.M. Jones *The Herods of Judaea* (Oxford 1967) 59–71.
[60] Syme *Aug. Ar.* 274 "... The pretext was fair, with a kind of dyarchy, though not in law or in fact". He notes that the term dyarchy "is now in discredit".

provinces by tradition; there seems no need to suppose a special or separate discussion about them. To tell the Senate that they must resume legislative responsibility was a natural result of declaring the emergency and government by edicts at an end and of restoring the praetorships. The laws (*iura*) of the Principate are dated by Tacitus to 28 (*Ann.* 3.28.2).[61]

Octavian himself had made the treasury solvent in 28, according to Dio;[62] we know that the Senate had titular responsibility for it throughout the Augustan period and after,[63] and it is not unreasonable to think that this may have been the moment when they were told to resume responsibility for it.[64] To Velleius, the venerable ancient pattern of the *res publica* was renewed when "force was restored to the laws, authority to the courts, its honourable dignity to the Senate, their traditional powers to the magistrates", and this he declared was what had happened.[65]

[61] And cf. the *aureus* noted above and n.36. A good discussion of this text in G.R. Stanton, contribution to the Festschrift for Edwin Judge *Ancient History in a Modern University* (not yet published). He points out that the striking collocation *pace et principe* means that a *princeps* is the price of peace. It is in fact almost an oxymoron. Stanton n.51 for bibliography.

[62] Dio 53.2.1; one of the occasions referred to in *R.g.* 17.1.

[63] A. Bay 'The letters SC' (n.16), esp. 119f.

[64] The treasury (*aerarium Saturni*) had always financed provincial government; to make the reorganization coincide was only natural. Cf. Bay *op. cit.* (n.63) 120, who points out that a reorganization of the *aerarium* preceded both Augustus' constitutional reorganizations. Nobody (then or now) would be foolish enough to suppose that this would exempt the Senate from having to finance the provinces (*ornare provincias*); that is why the *aerarium* never had any money. See Polybius 6.13; Mommsen *Staatsrecht* III 1136; *RE Supp.* vi 736–744 (O'Brien Moore 1935) for the norm.

[65] Velleius 2.89.3: *restituta vis legibus, iudiciis auctoritas, senatui maiestas, imperium magistratuum ad pristinum redactum modum ...; prisca illa et antiqua rei p. forma revocata. Rediit ....* This punctuation (Krause, Gagé, Woodman) should be preferred to *... modum ... Prisca ... revocata, rediit. ...* which appears to reduce *prisca ... revocata* from being the triumphant capstone to a subsidiary ablative absolute clause; but it is the reading of Halm (Teubner text) and others; some texts print the conjecture *renovata*; — "haud scio an recte" (Halm). Sattler *Augustus und der Senat* (n.1) 41 n.95 cites parallels from Cicero for *res publica* as meaning the traditional functioning of the traditional organs of state. Cf. F. Millar 'Two Augustan notes: 2. The 'Restoration of the Republic' in 27 B.C.' (n.14). In 'Triumvirate and Principate' (n.35) Millar ignores the *aerarium*; yet control of this by the Senate was the surest proof of the *maiestas senatus* in the *res publica*. The Senate cannot even have seemed to control the *aerarium* until (at least nominally) it controlled the *ornatio provinciarum* and the sending out of governors, which as Millar agrees was a power the Senate did not recover before 27. Dio's account (53.2) represents Octavian as treating the *aerarium* very much as within his own prerogative in 28, when he 'ordered' two ex-praetors to be put in charge annually. This should be seen as part of the restoration of the 'republican' norms. For a more recent interpretation of Velleius, A.J. Woodman *Velleius Paterculus: The Caesarian and Augustan Narrative 2.41–93* (Cambridge 1983) 251–4.

The *relatio* (business for discussion) then was perhaps *de provinciis consularibus* (on the provinces for the consuls), and it was introduced by a consular speech on the pacification of the Empire by victories, and the need for the Senate to resume control of the direction of its customary duties — that is all we need to assume as the formula whereby the *res publica* was restored to the Senate and Roman People. What could look more 'republican'? There was a speech of Cicero on that very topic. The alternatives are sinister, or hideous,[66] and were surely not chosen. The results of course were highly unrepublican, and probably were intended to be,[67] but until the Senate gave the provinces back appearances were what mattered.[68]

January 14th was *nefastus*, and had been so since 30. It was M. Antonius' birthday.[69] The Senate did not meet, but men could think, and talk. A short meeting could have been held on January 15th which was the festival of Carmentalia and partly not available for business. It probably was.[70] Its topic must have been the aftermath of the 13th, to hear which provinces the consuls would take, or to discuss honours, or both.

Octavian's detailed proposals, when announced, will not have taken long; they may perhaps have been accepted virtually without discussion. The Senate then turned to honours, which modern experience suggests will have taken much longer. A short day and a whole day could easily have been consumed in such an important (and delicate) debate, especially as there were rival proposals (see below).

In Dio's account the grant of the oak-wreath and laurels is

[66] One may speculate on these: *de re publica SPQR restituenda*? Surely not. It was a good *ex post facto* claim, but not a preparatory motion: *de potestate extraordinaria imp. Caesaris divi f. deponenda*? or *imperio triumvirali*? or *potestatibus*? Each gets more blatant, and improbable. And Augustus said "I am consul", Tac. *Ann.* 1.2.

[67] Nicolaus of Damascus, a contemporary writer, gave Dio grounds for his interpretation of Octavian's monarchical wishes — e.g. in Caesar's reasons for choosing Octavian as heir, F. Jacoby *FGH* ii A 416 = 90 (xxx) (120); Jane Bellemore *Nicolaus of Damascus, Life of Augustus* (Bristol 1984) 58, 128. E.T. Salmon 'Evolution' (n.2) 458.

[68] Dio reports that Octavian immediately procured a grant of double pay to those who were going to be his *cohors praetoria* (53.11.5). Dio's future tense suggests that on January 13th Octavian did not have such a *cohors*: this is natural, since one is appropriate to a proconsul, not to a consul; as triumvir, Octavian had had one, see Millar 'Triumvirate and Principate' (n.35) 59 and n.55.

[69] Dio 51.19.3 for 30; E-J p.45; the *fasti Verulani* explicitly state the reason.

[70] *Pace* Syme *Rom. Rev.* 313. The 15th, being the *Carmentalia*, was *nefastus parte* (partly unavailable for public business); this must warn us against supposing too much done.

separated from that of the name of Augustus, which is the only other honour he mentions.[71] In *Res gestae* 34 Augustus adds that the People as well as the Senate granted him a golden shield (*clupeus virtutis*).[72] But the earliest dated representation of the shield (that found at Arles) gives a text different from that of *Res gestae*,[73] Octavian's name as Augustus, and the date as 26 (consul VIII, there is no shadow of doubt about the third stroke). If the Arles shield is an exact copy of the shield in the Senate-House[74] the question of a golden shield was not debated in January 27, a new *cognomen* for Octavian will have been the sole topic debated, and the discussion was restricted to the Senate. On the other hand, if *Res gestae* is correct in associating the gift of the golden shield with 27 and the gift of the name of Augustus, the People played a part as well. Senatorial procedures might help in determining the more probable sequence of events.

In general, when the Senate proposed and the People ratified a measure, they met on successive days, though an act on the same day was not unknown; the 'republican' examples of the Senate holding a meeting after the People had finished theirs seem to be mostly after a row.[75] Two alternative programmes therefore exist. One is that on January 15th the Senate proposed the gift of the golden shield, which was ratified by the People either on the same day or the next, the 16th, whereupon the Senate re-assembled to consider their own special honour for Rome's third founder.[76] The other is that the Senate spent the whole time available on the 15th and 16th, less what was expended on the provinces, in discussing the appropriate new title for Octavian, and adjourned after ratifying the choice of Augustus; the

---

[71] 53.16.4 for the former; 16.6 for the latter.

[72] 34.2: [*et clu*]*peus* [*aureu*]*s in* [*c*]*uria Iulia positus quem mihi senatum pop*[*ulumq*]*ue Rom*[*anu*]*m dare virtutis clement*[*iaeque e*]*t iustitiae et pieta*[*tis caus*]*sa testatu*[*m*] *est pe*[*r e*]*ius clupei* [*inscription*]*em.*

[73] SPQR IMP. CAES. DIVI F. AUGUSTO COS. VIII DEDIT CLUPEUM VIRTUTIS CLEMENTIAE IUSTITIAE PIETATIS ERGA DEOS PATRIAMQUE; full text in *An. Ep.* (1952) 165. It was found at Arles in 1951: Zanker *Images* fig. 79 for an illustration; cf. Weinstock *Divus Julius* Plate 18. Coins with the legend CL(UPEUS) V(IRTUTIS), or SPQR CL V are common, from both Spanish mints, from *ca* 20, *RIC* I² 30 (p.43): 34–6, 42–8, 52, 61–2, 85–95 *aurei* and *denarii*; also with SIGNIS RECEPTIS.

[74] As argued by W. Seston 'Le *clipeus virtutis* d'Arles et la composition des *Res Gestae Divi Augusti*' *CRAI* (1954) 286–297. Zanker *Images* 95–6 dates the Roman version to 27 without considering the reason for the date in the Arles version.

[75] E.g. the rigged voting of 61, Cic. *Att.* 1.14.5; the riot at Milo's prosecution in 56 Cic. *Q.fr.* 2.3.2.

[76] For the description, Syme 'Livy and Augustus' (n.37) 55, with the evidence.

golden shield was voted by the Senate and People some time later.

The latter alternative seems better, not so much because those drawing up the *fasti* would have been less liable to miss the gift of the shield if it were granted at the same time as the other honours,[77] as because the former order of events would suggest that the *populus Romanus* was deliberately excluded from choosing and conferring the name Augustus, after having taken part in the grant of the shield. It is much more natural to think that they conferred their honour later, as the Arles version of the shield says (since it uses the name Augustus), and presumably in 26, the date on the Arles shield, which might thus commemorate the first anniversary of the gift of the name Augustus or "the restoration of the *res publica* to the Senate and People".

The virtues proclaimed, which became the stock imperial virtues,[78] are *virtus, clementia, iustitia* and *pietas* (bravery, mercy, justice, devotion to duty). It has been argued[79] that these are all derived from Caesar, and there is some evidence for precedents. Augustus' victories, however, derived from his own *virtus*, and his *corona civica* symbolized his own *clementia; iustitia* might symbolize the justice of his wars,[80] as Weinstock thinks Caesar's did, but it might also advertise the return of *ius* (law) with the ending of triumviral edicts; *pietas* may proclaim the avenging of Caesar, but the great programme of religious revival and rebuilding and the fulfilment of the promise to restore the Republic[81] is more positively commemorated in the words *erga deos patriamque* (towards gods and country) of the Arles monument.[82]

More certainty can be attained about the conferment of the name

---

[77] In E–J p.35 the omission of Octavian's second triumph on the *fasti triumphales Barberini* is a warning against over-confidence about this.

[78] M.P. Charlesworth 'The virtues of a Roman emperor' Raleigh Lecture, *Proc. Br. Acad.* 23 (1937) 105–127.

[79] Weinstock *Divus Julius* chap. xi.

[80] Another implication of the *corona civica*.

[81] The promise perhaps dates from the pamphlets published in 36 (App. *B.C.* 5.130), or to a response to Antonius' propaganda before Actium: Suet. *Aug.* 28; Dio 50.7; cf. Grenade *Essai* (n.2) 77 but pushed too far. More recently Zanker *Images* 85–92: "Self-glorification Gives Way to Religious Devotion".

[82] The opening three chapters of *Res gestae* also seem to have the imperial virtues in mind; Octavian's *virtus* liberated the *res publica* from a *factio* (1.1), to spare *veniam petentibus* was an act of *clementia* (3.1), avenging Caesar was an act of *pietas*, and pursuing the vengeance *legitimis iudiciis* one of *iustitia* (2.1). In *R.g.*, however, the order of virtues does not correspond with those on the shield; they are therefore probably in the background only.

Augustus. Romulus was proposed,[83] even favoured by Octavian according to Dio; that is incredible.[84] 'Augustus' was proposed by the ex-Antonian Munatius Plancus, it was approved by the Senate on January 16th,[85] and Augustus became Octavian's new *cognomen*;[86] the "painless and superficial transformation"[87] of the revolutionary leader was complete, but it probably took a lot of debating time to achieve.

After the drama of January 13th–16th the formulae for the choice and titles of senatorial governors of provinces had to be established. Dio duly records them (53.13–14), though there are some obvious anachronisms; the choice of Asia and Africa as consulars' provinces and the re-enactment of the *lex Pompeia* were natural corollaries, the latter being particularly instructive, since it meant that for the next five years there would be no prospect of an independent provincial command as proconsul for ambitious candidates for the consulship. Dio further records the creation of the semestral *consilium*[88] and the conduct of elections, the latter a necessary part of the restoration of the *res publica*, if it meant anything at all.[89]

Augustus' taking up his provincial command was no less political. He made first for Gaul, where his 'father' had won his greatest victories, and demonstrated the seriousness of his purpose by setting in train the repair of the *via Flaminia*, the Great North Road, placing statues of himself at either end.[90] On leaving he announced his intention to invade Britain, the scene of his 'father's' most spectacular feat when he took a Roman army across 'Ocean', the boundary of the known world, to conquer new horizons.[91] He must have left in the

---

[83] Suet. *Aug.* 7.

[84] Dio 53.16.7; Balsdon *Gnomon* (1961) (n.1) 393, and Syme 'Livy and Augustus' (n.37) 55, give reasons.

[85] Gagé *Res gestae* 145. Velleius (2.91) says "Senate and People", but *Res gestae* must be preferred. The date is in the *fasti* of Cumae and Praeneste, E–J p.45.

[86] For its progress to his regular *nomen* R. Syme 'Imperator Caesar, a study in nomenclature' *Historia* 7 (1958) 172–188.

[87] *Rom. Rev.* 313. A. Wallace-Hadrill *Augustan Rome* (Bristol 1993) 16f. for a more recent discussion.

[88] John Crook *Consilium Principis* (Cambridge 1955) 11. Since Augustus left for Gaul quite soon it would have little chance to operate in 27.

[89] Dio 53.21.6. Dio's exact use of language for once — *ho te demos kai to plethos* (*populus et plebs*) — adds confidence in a good source at this point.

[90] Dio 53.22.1f.

[91] Dio 53.22.5 and 25.2. The propaganda value of Caesar's invasion is illustrated by Octavian's advertised intention of invading Britain in 34 (Dio 49.38.2), thwarted by trouble nearer home (in Illyricum). Britain was outside the inhabited world (*oikoumenē*), Dio 60.19.2. Cf. P. Salway *Roman Britain* (Oxford 1981) 38: "The

summer, almost certainly before the triumph of M. Crassus on July 4th if an invasion of Britain that year were to be credible.[92] Since he took with him his older stepson Tiberius and his nephew Marcellus who was soon to become his son-in-law he clearly planned a prestige-winning campaign.[93]

On arriving in Gaul he 'reorganised' it, an expression modern scholars have no difficulty in recognising as meaning 'increased their taxes',[94] but administering that was left to agents, one of whom, Licinus a freedman, became notorious as a scoundrel (Dio 54.21). By diplomacy, perhaps, or intimidation he obtained embassies from the British kings which enabled him to claim that they had become 'Friends and Allies' of the Roman People, which to the Roman mind meant clients (so Strabo 4.200 = 4.5.3 LCL). In *Res gestae* 32.1 he records receiving fugitive kings from the island. Possibly their flight (or expulsion) had led to the embassies, or the threats to their expulsion, but there is no certainty. Perhaps the nearest thing to a certainty is that he had no intention of going there.[95]

His move to Spain was politically motivated too, since he spent very little time getting there; he had already reached Tarraco by January 1st, 26.[96] His purpose was to complete the conquest which had so far taken over two hundred years and seen numerous triumphs.[97] He was duly voted a triumph from there, and Janus' temple was closed, but Agrippa had to complete the job in 19. Syria was less urgent, and tangible results were required. After being dangerously ill, and conducting a political reorganisation, he moved to complete the work left him by Caesar his father, the recovery of the standards lost by Crassus, to which had been added those lost by

---

momentous fact [was] that he [Caesar] had opened up the whole possibility of conquest by demonstrating that it was possible to transport a large Roman army across the dreaded Ocean".

[92] D. Magie 'Augustus' war in Spain (26–25 BC)' *Class. Phil.* 15 (1920) 323–339, esp. 327 suggests that he did not leave till after Messalla Corvinus' triumph on September 25th, but this is surely too late if he was to appear to be going to invade Britain that year. Schmitthenner ('Augustus' spanischer Feldzug' (n.1) 48) suggests a personal hand-over from Messalla in Gaul in the summer of 27.

[93] Dio 53.26.1; for the poets' expectations A. Momigliano '*Panegyricus Messallae* and "Panegyricus Vespasiani"' *JRS* 40 (1950) 39–42.

[94] Caesar's devastations and plunderings had impoverished Gaul, so that the tribute was fixed at 40 million sesterces *per annum*, Suet. *Jul.* 25.

[95] Syme *Aug. Ar.* 383 and n.6.

[96] So Syme *Rom. Rev.* 332. The *fasti* of the Latin festival say he was "in Spain" that year. Schmitthenner 'Augustus' spanischer Feldzug' (n.1) 54–60 for the campaign.

[97] Livy 28.12.12; Horace *Carm.* 3.8.21f.

Antonius in his failed campaign. This had been the mission Caesar was going to undertake at the time of his murder. With it and the completion of his inherited tasks he ended the decade after his triumph and the campaign for which he had rallied 'All Italy' to defeat the Egyptian Queen.

The public relations aspects of the provincial division were soon revealed, as Augustus encroached steadily on the People's provinces: the peaceful Gallia Narbonensis was exchanged for the military Illyricum (Dio 54.4.1); Africa was gradually disarmed; the Alpine districts were deemed part of Gaul, not of Illyricum;[98] the military districts of Germany were added to Gaul, and Pannonia and Moesia to Illyricum, with the resultant disarming of Macedonia; client kingdoms like Galatia and Judaea were absorbed, and new provinces like Rhaetia and Noricum created. "Gaul, Spain and Syria" were and remained a political statement. Agrippa his colleague remained in Rome. Was he offered a province, and if so, what was it? A suggestion is offered in chapter 5. Certainly he continued his programme of public works for the benefit of the *populus Romanus* and was on hand when required in the crisis of 23, and to quell riots two years later.

To sum up our tentative results: after a period of careful preparation, starting in 29 and accelerating through 28, on January 13th, 27, Octavian summoned a meeting of the Senate to discuss the *res publica*. There he read a speech which recapitulated the events of 28, and claimed that peace was established and the rule of law was now restored. He added that all the provinces were peaceful too, since the Roman armies under his *auspicia* had been uniformly victorious, and then bade the Senate decide which were to be the consular provinces for the present consuls (himself and Agrippa). The Senators reacted by giving them all to him, together with an award for saving the lives of citizens and another symbolic of victory. When the Senate met again two days later Octavian said he would undertake responsibility for three provinces only, Spain, Gaul, and Syria, and the client kings and foreign peoples adjacent to their boundaries; it would be for the Senate to control the selection by lot (or *sortitio*) of the governors for the others.

---

[98] The Salassi for example seem to have been part of Illyricum during the 'protection of Italy' campaigns of 35–33, App. *Ill.* 16f., but Terentius Varro must have been a *legatus* of Augustus in his subjugation of the Salassi in 25; Strabo 4.205 = 4.6.7 LCL; Dio 53.25.3f. Momigliano (n.93) 40f. for varying interpretations of the evidence.

At one of these meetings Octavian added that the Senate should resume control of the *aerarium*, which was now solvent again, and also resume the general management of the *res publica*; this involved, as we know (and they knew) perfectly well, the functions of advising the consuls, especially in the fields of legislation and important trials, and of proposing measures for the sovereign People. The People would resume their function of confirming legislation and electing magistrates.[99] And this programme was indeed put in hand. After receiving further honours, and after the enactment of one or two consequential decisions, the newly-appointed proconsul of Gaul and Spain left for his *provincia* within six months, while his colleague continued to administer the *res publica*.

How much light is shed? Not very much, perhaps; certainly nothing very startling or new for the ancient evidence, though perhaps it suggests more clearly (what reflection shows to be clear enough anyway) that *Res gestae* 34f. is not a political or constitutional statement at all, but the capstone of Augustus' achievement. It is a statement of his two most conspicuous honours, the *cognomen* Augustus conferred by the Senate in return for his transferring the titular management of the *res publica* to the Senate and People, and the title *Pater Patriae*, conferred by Senate, *equites* and the entire Roman People for reasons unstated. The accompanying honours, symbols, and inscriptions are described under each, and in case anyone was in doubt Augustus added two things, a denial that the name Augustus gave him any constitutional power, and a statement of his age. Adding the former was a mistake.

Upon modern accounts, perhaps, more light is shed, especially on those controversial issues about the supposed powers which Octavian had to resign in order to restore the *res publica*. We find that no resignation was necessary because after all his careful planning Octavian was able to use a traditional formula — that of putting the question of the consular provinces to the Senate — to make the Senate appear to have recovered its constitutional prerogatives in the *res publica*. He thus avoided having to admit that he himself was more than consul, the only title by which he is known to have styled himself since 32.[100] And for their part the Senate also acted in a coherent way: they gave honours to Octavian of an unprecedented kind, and a *provincia* of an unprecedented magnitude, but both arose

[99] Cf. Suet. *Aug.* 40.
[100] Millar 'Triumvirate and Principate' (n.35) 58 for inscriptions using this title.

naturally out of the business put before the Senate and out of sentiment at a time when the memory of the civil wars was still vivid, and what had then been endured was felt as something to be avoided at almost any cost.

CHAPTER 4

PROTECTING THE PEOPLE *

After the end of 28, when the still unratified acts of the triumviral period were officially annulled, Octavian's legal power to manage the *res publica* rested on the consulship till mid-23, thereafter on the combination of a special proconsulate with *imperium* greater than that of other proconsuls and the *tribunicia potestas* (powers of a tribune). The former entitled him to command armies, the latter to enjoy a political position in Rome, and sustain the interests of the *plebs*.

Neither Augustus himself in *Res gestae* nor Tacitus in his account of Augustus' principate in *Annals* 1.2 mention his proconsular power explicitly, though it is implicit in the command of the state's armies, and the many celebrations of victory mentioned by Augustus (*R.g.* 4).

Augustus states that *tribunicia potestas* was conferred on him by law (*R.g.* 10.1); he does not date this, but associates the vote with the grant of sacrosanctity. Tacitus says only that he said he had it.

Dio (53.32.5) gives the details of Augustus' proconsular power as conferred in 23 — that it was superior to (*maius*)[1] that of all other proconsuls in the Empire, that it was for life, and that it did not lapse when he crossed the *pomerium* and entered the city. The 'fine print' detailed here is impressive, and suggests that at this point Dio is

* An earlier version of this study appeared in *Antichthon* 19 (1985) 57–67 under the title 'Augustus and the Senate, 23 BC'. I am grateful to the editors for permission to draw on this article, and to those who contributed to the discussion at the 22nd AULLA conference and after.

[1] Dio is using shorthand here. For the actual wording of the decree possibilities are as in Cicero *Att.* 4.1.7, discussed by J.P.V.D. Balsdon 'Roman history, 58–56 B.C.: three Ciceronian problems' *JRS* 47 (1957) 16–18, or as in Tacitus *Ann.* 2.43, as suggested by H.M. Last '*Imperium maius*: a note' *JRS* 37 (1947) 157–164, who argues for a relationship between Augustus and other proconsuls of what he calls "*maius/minus imperium* Type A". Cf. also the inscription of Tiberius' principate noted in chap. 5 below.

following a source which had access to genuine contemporary records, perhaps the minutes (*acta*) of the Senate. For the grant of *trib. pot.* however Dio's account is less satisfactory. He says that at this same meeting the Senate voted that he should be tribune for life, and adds a little later (*ibid.* 6) that this is why Augustus and his successors use the tribunician power, none of them the title of tribune. This story is unsatisfactory in itself, and contradicts Augustus' statement that he was given *trib. pot.* by law. A *senatus consultum* is not a law.

Elsewhere Dio twice records votes to Octavian of the powers and rights of tribunes: in 36, following the victory off Naulochus, when he was voted sacrosanctity for life and the right to sit with the tribunes on their bench if he wished (49.15.5f.), and in 30 following the announcement of the capture of Alexandria and the end of the war with Cleopatra, when he was voted *tribunicia potestas* along with a mass of other honours, implicitly but not explicitly by the People (51.19.6).[2] Here also Dio's account contains 'fine print', for the grant was exceptional in that (i) his *ius auxilii* (right to rescue) ran to a mile (7.5 *stadia*) beyond the *pomerium*, (ii) he was given the right to hear appeals and give judgement on them, (iii) he was empowered to adjudicate when the votes of jurors were evenly split in trials. None of the normal tribunes had these rights. Dio, it should be noted, mentions sacrosanctity and *tribunicia potestas* as separate grants, as Augustus does.

Appian (*B.C.* 5.132) and Orosius (6.18.34) both say that in 36 Octavian was voted *trib. pot.*, but as they do not agree about who voted it we might be rash to say that they used the same source (Livy has been proposed).

A number of prominent scholars, K. Fitzler and O. Seeck, A. von Premerstein and E. Kornemann for example,[3] have argued in favour of these dates, and that Octavian accepted *trib. pot.* on either or both these occasions and subsequently abandoned it. Their views were

---

[2] The last-named subject of the verbs is "The Romans at home" (Dio 51.19.1), which introduces the first of the two lists of honours reported as granted this year (30): the first list after the victory at Actium (1–3), the second after the report of Antony's death and the capture of Alexandria (4–6). The subsequent verbs are all third person plurals.

[3] Fitzler and Seek in *RE* 10 (1917) 275–381, A. von Premerstein in 'Vom Werden und Wesen des Prinzipats' *Abh. der bayer. Ak. der Wiss. phil. hist. Abt.* N.F. 15 (1937), E. Kornemann in 'Volkstribunat und Kaisertum' *Festschrift für L. Wenger* Bd. 1 (München 1944).

attacked by Hugh Last in a characteristically trenchant article,[4] and subsequent scholars like H.H. Scullard in his revision (3rd edn) of M. Cary's *History of Rome* (London 1975) 317 and 319 have sat on the fence or are dubious or even self-contradictory about the date at which *trib. pot.* was conferred,[5] and how it was activated in 23 if it was not then conferred. What follows in this chapter is a suggestion, and a reply to Last's criticism of the possibility of a grant which was accepted but not used for seven years.

To consider the background first: after his triumph in 29 Octavian had set about dismantling the apparatus of civil war and government by decree. He reconstituted the collegiality of the consulate in 28, and in January, 27, reorganised the control of the armed forces of the state by (nominally) sharing command as provincial governor with other governors who held the rank of proconsul, and were to be nominated by the Senate on behalf of the People in the traditional way. This was done, as was argued in the last chapter, by putting the traditional motion *de provinciis consularibus* (on the provinces for the consuls) to the Senate at the traditional time (mid-January). The motion had caused some consternation (Dio 53.11), as it revived memories of how the civil wars had started, but that fear was assuaged by Augustus' choosing for himself the three provinces which had formed the bases for the armies of the civil wars[6] and which gave him command of the largest armies.

If this account of the creation of Augustus' *provincia*, and the means by which he kept control of the armies, is correct (and it has never to the best of my knowledge been seriously challenged since it was first published in 1974[7]), it should be worth enquiring whether the transition from consulate to proconsulate and tribunician power can also be better understood by using an analysis based on the use of traditional procedures and the assumption that our sources know what they are talking about. This involves trying to understand how Augustus was charting his political course, and what reactions, specifically fears, he uncovered and assuaged. It is also assumed that

---

[4] 'On the *tribunicia potestas* of Augustus' *Rendiconti dell'Istituto Lombardo* 84 (1951) 93–110.

[5] E.g. A.H.M. Jones *Augustus* (London 1970) 55 who regards the powers of a tribune as being given in three instalments, in 36, 30, and 23, but omits to say how the final portion was "accorded" in 23.

[6] Chap. 3 above.

[7] 'Octavian in the senate, January, 27 BC' *JRS* 64 (1974) 176–84, which forms the basis for chap. 3 above.

the Romans were as good as we are at looking at the recent past, and as poor at foreseeing the future.

The constitution of Augustus' *provincia* in 27 was followed very shortly, probably before July 4th, the date of M. Crassus' triumph,[8] by his departure from Rome. He thus escaped from the pressures of the Senate House, while at the same time demonstrating that he was taking his provincial government seriously, and was not going to imitate Pompeius in 54 with a titular province in Spain while trying to dominate politics in the city. In his absence the Senate, if it met, met under the presidency of consuls who belonged to Augustus' political following: Agrippa for the rest of 27, Statilius Taurus in 26, one of his most stalwart partisans and now enjoying the honour of a second consulate. Statilius owned, if not exactly a private army, a cohort of slaves[9] from Germany who lived in his house and could be used to apply force in the city if it were required (though we have no evidence that it was). Outside Rome itself, in Italy, Agrippa (it is argued in chapter 5) had been given the office of prefect, a force of unknown size and the mission of establishing bases for a permanent fleet to control the seas, and in the Campus Martius he had a workforce building structures to bring some of the pleasures of the rich within the reach of ordinary people and glorify the new regime. Any attempt at a revolution or *coup d'état* was unlikely to succeed.

It must have been evident that Augustus would return from Spain sooner or later, and presumably resume the duties of consul. Announcements of a full and final victory in Spain and the closure of the Temple of Janus (dated by Dio 53.26.5 to 25), and the wedding of Julia his only child arranged for early 24 indicated that in 25 his return was imminent. In the event, he was too ill to reach the city in time for the wedding, though it went ahead with Agrippa acting the part of her father (Dio 53.27.5); as she was fourteen, it appears Augustus was in a hurry to secure descendants. If he reached Rome before the Latin Festival, held in 24 on June 13th, he was ill again then,[10] but it is unlikely that he did. Romans did not as a rule make for Rome when they were ill or convalescing; those who could afford

---

[8] *Fasti triumphales*, E–J p.35.

[9] Attested by tombstones, *ILS* 7448–9.

[10] *CIL* I² p.58 contains only the letters IVL surviving for the date. One of the three, *Kalends, Nones* or *Ides* look the most likely supplements, to judge from the entries for the adjacent years, but, plainly, there is room for almost any number of days *a.d.*, or even PR., the only impossible days being those *nefasti*. The printing of *CIL* actually suggests a gap of some 5 letters, something like PR KAL.

it moved to the hills, like modern Popes, or to the sea coast, especially
in the height of the summer. It seems a reasonable assumption that
Augustus did not enter the city till the end of the heat and the start of
autumn. Certainly, in 24 if he was too ill to go to the Alban Mount in
June, he was too ill to engage in the cut and thrust of senatorial life
and the Forum.

The consular elections for 23, held in the autumn of 24 presumably,
saw Augustus returned again with a Varro Murena who is generally
thought to have been a supporter, but he disappeared from the scene,
and from all the *fasti consulares* except the Capitoline, before
January 1st, 23. He was replaced by Cn. Calpurnius Piso, who was an
old opponent. Why Varro disappeared from all but the Capitoline
fasti has been extensively and inconclusively argued.[11] The most
commonly approved explanation is that Murena was mixed up in a
conspiracy which resulted from his taking offence at Augustus giving
evidence against his client in a trial, but for the Capitoline *fasti* alone
(the 'official' *fasti*) to have recorded the name of one condemned as a
conspirator passes my belief. Such a person would have been more
likely to have had his memory condemned and his name erased. Why
'he died' (*mortuus est*), or even 'he died while designate' (*desig. mort.
est*) which has the same number of letters as *in mag.(istratu)
damn(atus) est* (he was condemned in his magistracy) has to be a
euphemism for "he was put to death", or "condemned" (so Syme,
Aug. Ar. 388) is hard to understand, especially in a year later at least
attested as one of plague. Certainty is impossible to obtain, but the
events of the rest of the year may throw some light on the atmosphere
of the time.

Plot or no plot — and it seems much easier to understand if there
was no plot — Augustus took an old opponent as his fellow-consul in
23. Cn. Piso had been a very determined opponent of the Caesars. He
had energetically raised a force of Numidian auxiliaries to oppose
Caesar in the *Bellum Africum* ("Caesar" *Bell. Afr.* 3.1, 18.1) and
subsequently joined Brutus and Cassius in fighting the young

---

[11] Everything about this episode is controversial and the subject of what Syme has
called "an abundant and not abating bibliography" (*Aug. Ar.* 388 n.28). The
arguments of E. Badian '"Crisis theories" and the beginning of the principate' in G.
Wirth (ed.) *Romanitas–Christianitas: Untersuchungen zur Geschichte und Literatur der
römischen Kaiserzeit, Johannes Straub zum 70. Geburtstag gewidmet* (Berlin and New
York 1982) 18–41 that there was no plot in early 23 seem to me more persuasive than
versions which depend on rewriting the sources — even if they did not convince Syme
(*Aug. Ar.* 388f.). Syme however agrees that this Varro Murena and the 'conspirator'
are different people.

Octavian. After their rout at Philippi he had been granted leave to return to Rome but had sought no office until he was personally solicited by Augustus to accept the consulate offered him (in 23) (so Tacitus *Ann.* 2.43.2). Augustus thus deliberately picked a man with a history of active opposition to the party of the Caesars to be his consular colleague. Moreover the suggestion of Tacitus' account is that Piso was *suffectus* (as the Capitoline *fasti* state), nominated by the surviving consul, Augustus, for ratification by the *comitia centuriata*, not an initial choice by them. Unless there had been a total change of sentiment between 23 and 22–19 the *comitia* would not have chosen him spontaneously.

This was an extraordinary step to have taken in an atmosphere of plot and intrigue; it looks much more like a confident assertion that there was a place in the new *res publica* of Augustus for the old aristocracy, including old opponents, to attain the rank their family traditions demanded. This had to take place some time if the new *res publica* was to bear any resemblance to the old. And Piso was an ideal man to choose, for nobody could suspect him of being a stool-pigeon.

The 'plot' theory obliges its protagonists to suppose that Augustus' hand was forced; by whom? Only the Senators are possible, but to suppose that they imposed Piso on Augustus is to deny Tacitus' statement that Augustus acted *ultro* — on his own initiative. It seems better not only to believe Tacitus, but also to think that Augustus may have planned to be in Rome all year, where he could exercise control over this colleague with his *aequum imperium* (equal power) if there was a dispute, and keep his hand on the political developments he had in mind.

Steps to develop a popular front (*popularis*) programme which Augustus took before and on his return to Rome in 24 suggest that he was planning to establish an ongoing political position based on his support from the *plebs*. This was fully in tune with his inheritance from Caesar his 'father', and may also suggest that his plans were not just for a balance in the consulate between himself and an aristocrat but for a revival of the old balance of power between the consuls and the People's representatives, the tribunes. This would enable him to release the consulate to competition among those who aspired to it most passionately. The shift to tribunician power in 23 may therefore not be a sudden decision nor forced on him by opposition or plots or ill health, but the working out of a plan formed before his reappearance on the political scene in 24.

As part of a plan to appeal to the People he had promised a
donative expressly out of his own funds (*R.g.* 15.1) which was as large
as the victory donative of 29 (400 sesterces a man); as a show of
respect he got the Senate's approval before it was made public
officially (Dio 53.28.1f.). He thus compensated the *plebs* for the lack
of a donative in conjunction with the triumph which they had
probably been expecting in view of the announcements of his
completed victory in Spain.

On his arrival, in honour of his return and recovery from illness his
son-in-law Marcellus was at his request co-opted (adlected) into the
Senate *inter praetorios* (as an ex-praetor) with leave to be consul ten
years early, and become a candidate for the aedileship (naturally he
was at once elected), while his stepson, Tiberius, was given leave to
stand for all offices five years early and was immediately elected
quaestor. Both these young men were to make a *popularis* debut.
That of Marcellus is the more obvious; though adlected *inter
praetorios*, he was to be aedile. This can only be so that he could give
games, and he was given money by Augustus to present Roman
games of a splendour unparalleled perhaps since those of Julius
Caesar in 65 (and thus claim the allegiance of the *plebs* in the same
way that Caesar had done). Tiberius was to act as Augustus' own
(consul's) quaestor[12] and concern himself with corn distributions,
and with checking that the rich were not detaining in their *ergastula*
(workmen's barracks) people whom they had no right to imprison.[13]
Such people are said to have been travellers and, according to
modern English translators of Suetonius,[14] draft-dodgers. But this is
not the necessary meaning of the Latin *quos metus sacramenti ad eius
modi latebras compulisset* — those whom fear of a *sacramentum* had
driven to a place of concealment of this type. Besides the military
oath of allegiance, *sacramentum* also means (*OLD s.v.* 1) "sums of
money sworn to be paid in support of claims and forfeited in the case
of the losing party", that is, a debtor took an oath to pay his debts or
the interest on them or forfeit his property; those driven by fear of an
oath can therefore be debtors who, under threat of a worse fate —
perhaps to save their family from destitution — had been obliged to
enter a rich man's *ergastulum* and offer labour in lieu of money, and

---

[12]   E. Badian 'The quaestorship of Tiberius Nero' *Mnemosyne* 27 (1974) 160–172.
[13]   Suet. *Tib.* 8; Vell. 2.94.3f.
[14]   Suet. *loc. cit.* tr. J.C. Rolfe *Suetonius* 1 (LCL 1913) 305; Robert Graves *The
Twelve Caesars* (Harmondsworth 1957) 114; cf. Mary Johnstone du Four *Suetonius on
the Life of Tiberius* Diss. U. of Pennsylvania (Philadelphia 1941) 44f. and n.9.

were being held there contrary to the *lex Poetilia* which had (nominally) abolished the system of debt servitude (*nexum*) as long ago as 326 (or 313).[15] Or they could have taken flight to avoid being taken to court. Rescuing from imprisonment[16] fugitives from creditors who were being wrongfully detained is a much more appropriate *popularis* activity than saving draft-dodgers, especially when there is no evidence of drafts at this date, nor any apparent need for them (not that any weight can be placed on such an *argumentum ex silentio*). On the other hand, Livy's early books, with their stories of the ill-treatment of the debt bondsmen (*nexi*) by the rich,[17] provide a wholly appropriate context for *popularis* activity in aid of debtors.

In addition, Augustus himself was confirming his commitment to the *plebs* by starting distributions of corn in 23 (*R.g.* 15.1). We do not know when these started, but there were twelve, and he bought the grain himself (*ibid.*).[18] Surely he said so at the time; it is most unlikely and quite contrary to Roman practice to have made them anonymously. The evidence for *popularis* politics seems quite clear.

What Augustus had not planned for, however, was another breakdown in his health. Early in 23 he became so ill that he was convinced that he was on his deathbed. It has been suggested that this was a sham; that he was play-acting in order to achieve two ends: the first was to alarm the populace at large that they might lose him and the control he maintained over the aristocrats and the army, and thus

[15] J.A. Crook *Law and Life of Rome* (London 1967) 58–61, for voluntary slavery, 173 for 'addiction' for debt, and being sold up by *bonorum venditio*; the possibility of a poor man offering his services even in an *ergastulum* to avoid having his goods sold — and his family beggared — should not be excluded. Columella 1.3.12; J. Ramin and P. Veyne 'Droit romain et société; les hommes libres qui passent pour esclaves et l'esclavage volontaire' *Historia* 30 (1981) 486f. suppose that purging *ergastula* was a characteristic activity of a new regime, comparing Constantine (*Cod. Theod.* 5.8.1), but it was four years since the ending of the triumvirate. The sources give plenty of support to the view that there might be debtors in *ergastula*, hence possibly — perhaps probably — some unjustly so detained.

[16] If *latebras* is to be taken literally, the *ergastula* should belong to people other than the creditors; that is, the debtors had left home and were vagabonds, for whom in return for work an *ergastulum* might offer food and asylum (temporarily a man might hope) both from his creditors and from the agents of the law until the hunt for him had died down. Cf. Berlin papyrus 372 (AD 154), F.F. Abbott and A.C. Johnson *Municipal Administration in the Roman Empire* (Princeton 1926) No 175, where "travellers" are people escaping creditors etc.

[17] Especially the highly emotional and dramatic story of the veteran soldier in 2.23f. R.M. Ogilvie *A Commentary on Livy, Books I–V* (Oxford 1965) 296–8.

[18] "In my 11th consulship" (*R.g.* 15.1) ought not to mean "before my 11th consulship began", and it ought not to mean "after my 11th consulship had ended". Hence, a January start is likely.

remind them that the spectre of civil war between the followings of aristocratic factions was still alive; and the second, to give himself an excuse for giving up the consulship. While these were certainly the results of his prostration, it seems to me that the revelation of the truth that Augustus' friends, in the person of Agrippa, would not relinquish command of the legions was something that he would have preferred to avoid. And there is no other evidence that Augustus was a superb actor.

Certainly his summons to the leading citizens to attend his 'death-bed' (Dio 53.30)[19] made contemporaries think, if Dio is to be believed, that he was going to make arrangements to appoint a successor to his political position. But he did not do so; after speaking to the assembled company he handed the state papers to his consular colleague, Piso, and the seal which would authenticate dispatches to provincial governors and legionary commanders to Agrippa. Contemporaries seem to have assumed that this meant that in the event of his death Agrippa would assume command of the armies, and therefore had been appointed his heir (*heres*), since it was a basic tenet of Roman law that a *heres* inherited the *clientela* of the one to whom he was *heres*, and the army, being Augustus' troops, were part of his *clientela*. The noble Marcellus, his son-in-law, therefore was passed over.[20]

But the truth was never revealed; since Augustus recovered, his will remained sealed, and its terms unknown. But the question of who had been destined to succeed to his public position became a hot topic, so hot that Augustus was driven to the point of bringing his will into the Senate and threatening to open it and prove (which means that the Senate did not believe his denials) that he had not bequeathed his position to anyone. Dio's word for position is *archē*, position of power. This called their bluff and they did not allow him to open it. He did not deny that he had appointed an heir; that was inescapable.[21] But the claim that he had not named anyone to succeed to his *archē* amounted to an assertion that he was a magistrate not a monarch, the Senators' allegations the reverse. This story, which has the ring of truth about it, ought to have discouraged

---

[19] Dio is the source for this and the next two paragraphs.

[20] To the amazement of contemporaries — so Dio.

[21] E.g. J.A. Crook *Law and Life* (n.15) 120: "The primary function of a will was to appoint one or more heirs ... if that was not done, and not done first, the will was null and void".

modern historians from writing as if Augustus had everything under strict control. Obviously he had not.

When he recovered from his illness he went to perform the ceremonies of the Latin Festival at the Alban Mount;[22] he had reinstituted these (it is uncertain how far they had lapsed in the late 'Republic' and Civil War periods), or at least made them a significant part of the public year. At the festival, presumably after performing the rituals as consul, he 'resigned' we are told. This I understand to mean that he handed his robes of office and the command of the lictors over to his successor, L. Sestius Albinus. He will have retained a bodyguard as a proconsul's *cohors praetoria*. Sestius was also an old opponent, and had fought for Caesar's murderers ('the Republic' as they are romantically called) at Philippi (so Dio 53.32.4).

Dio says the reason he went to the Alban Mount and the shrine of *Jupiter Latiaris* was to stop him being frustrated, or perhaps hindered (the verb is *kōlūthēi* which can mean either). Consuls could be stopped from doing what they intended only by their colleague exercising his equal *imperium* or by a veto by a tribune or tribunes, which could be circumvented by a consul leaving the city. If Dio's alleged motive is correct, and Augustus knew he would be opposed by tribunes had he tried to hand over the *fasces* at the Temple of *Iuppiter Optimus Maximus* in Rome, we would have evidence that the populace, the non-senators, did not want Augustus to give up the consulate. It was made abundantly clear in the next four years that this was so. Year after year the *comitia centuriata* (which was not dominated by the lowest strata of the population) elected a member of his following and Augustus himself consul, or left a place for him; year after year Augustus, who was conveniently outside the city, declined. We simply cannot assert that Augustus was unpopular, or that his continued tenure of the consulship offended anyone except perhaps those who wanted it for themselves.[23]

---

[22] Dio 53.32.3. This (Boissevain's) text appears to be accepted by everyone. For the emendation, see Boissevain's edition.

[23] Masquerading, perhaps, as constitutional purists, to whom iterated consulships were contrary to *mores maiorum*, hence offensive, especially when there was no military crisis to cope with, as in Marius' time. On the other hand, Julius Caesar's arbitrary decision to resign in 45 had caused much resentment (Suet. *Iul.* 80.3 *et alibi*), since it meant a demeaning of the consulate in favour of the dictatorship. Cic. *Fam.* 7.30; *Att.* 14.5.2 for contemporary opinion and Shackleton Bailey's notes *Cicero, Epistulae ad Familiares II. 47–43 BC* (Cambridge 1977) 434f. and *Cicero's Letters to Atticus* Vol. VI *(Books XIV–XVI)* (Cambridge 1967) 216. The situation in 23 was quite different, however; Augustus did not have a superior magistracy — on the surface at least. *Auctoritas* is not a magistracy, and the Romans were not gifted with foresight.

Dio's account also implies that his intention to resign was planned and made public — probably in the Senate, otherwise he would hardly have known of the opposition — and that Sestius would agree to serve.[24] This implies in turn that the tenure Sestius was offered was a reasonable one, in accordance with the *mores maiorum*; almost certainly it indicates that it was the six months usually allocated when two consuls shared a year of office. In that case the date for the Latin festival was either June 30th or July 1st. PR KAL will fit the space on the stone before the word IUL, if *CIL* I² is printed accurately.

When Sestius and the other Senators returned from the Alban Mount the Senate convened, probably with Sestius in the chair[25] and without Augustus, since his *imperium proconsulare* was not yet held to be tenable within the *pomerium*. They were pleased with Augustus for resigning and choosing such a prominent opponent to succeed him as consul (Dio 53.32.4–6),[26] and were ready to pass votes to implement what they thought were his wishes for his future position.

There is no difficulty about the votes which established his *imperium proconsulare*[27] as superior to (*maius*) that of other proconsuls, as tenable for life, and remaining active within the *pomerium*, lapsing neither on crossing nor on recrossing it,[28] as Dio reports. Dio also reports that they voted him tribune for life; this is usually written off as one of Dio's errors, and Dio's muddled explanation of the consequences does not add to his credibility. But it may be true; the fact that it was not implemented does not mean that

[24] To me at least it is not credible that Sestius had not been asked publicly, and agreed to be nominated. Last's remark ('*Imperium maius*' (n.1) 105) is worth quoting: "The Romans were a civilised people and did not thrust distinctions on at any rate the more eminent of their citizens without first seeking the agreement of those it was intended to honour."

[25] It could have been Piso his colleague. It is impossible to determine whether Sestius, succeeding Augustus who had obviously held the *fasces* first, would hold them in his place, or Piso, who will have held them in June, would continue to hold them in July because he was now senior. Probability seems to me to lie with the view that Sestius took Augustus' place in this respect as in others.

[26] A statement which must be rejected by those who think that Augustus was in bad odour with the Senators all the time.

[27] As he did not resign his proconsulate, on his resignation as consul his consular *imperium* automatically became proconsular, P.A. Brunt 'C. Fabricius Tuscus and an Augustan *dilectus*' *ZPE* 13 (1974) 165.

[28] Which made it equivalent to that of the consuls, whose *provincia* was primarily the city itself, for whose protection they were responsible. This ambiguity may well be the source of the problem which was settled in 19, when it had to be decided whether Augustus' *imperium* when he crossed the *pomerium* was equal to that of the consuls or not. See chap. 6 below.

it was not voted.[29] It could have got into the record as a proposal
which passed, and the historian from whom Dio got it — or the
record itself — failed to record that it had not been rendered effective
by being accepted by Augustus. This error would also have been
compounded if there were no other record of *tribunicia potestas* being
voted in 23, as will be discussed below.

In *Res gestae* 10 Augustus states explicitly that he was given his
trib. pot. by law, that is by a vote of the People in Assembly. It is clear
that he meant what he said by comparing para. 10 with para. 6 in
which he states that the colleagues whom he asked for on five
occasions of his own initiative (*ultro .... depoposci*) he received from
the Senate (*a senatu accepi*).[30] There is plainly no mere inadvertence
in Augustus saying he got his *trib. pot.* by law (implicitly without a
previous *senatus consultum*), and for this reason alone his statement
should be taken to be correct, since those who read *Res gestae* in
Rome would have known if he were lying.[31] Dio is therefore mistaken
if he is trying to say that Augustus' *trib. pot.* was created by a vote of
the Senate in 23.

Many scholars have agreed, and the hunt for a date for the law has
ensued; in my opinion the silence of Ovid in the *Fasti* up to June 30th
must show the lack of a law before that date, if the law is to be dated
in 23. Arguments that Ovid was losing interest in his work before the
end of *Fasti* Book VI amount to no more than special pleading; how
could Ovid have omitted a festival to commemorate what had
become, by AD 4,[32] a major imperial title? For Ovid to have
continued to ignore *trib. pot.* in his *Fasti* if there was an annual
festival to commemorate its inauguration would be to display an

[29] A vote of powers to Augustus in his absence which he declined — in fact had to
beg the People not to force on him — took place the very next year when they tried to
make him dictator, an office abolished as recently as 44. The situation seems closely
parallel. He did not become dictator because he refused the offer. But the office was
voted to him none the less. The same should be possible in respect of the tribunate
which had not been abolished, even if he claimed to be ineligible as a patrician Julius.

[30] Presumably these votes of the *trib. pot.* to Augustus' colleagues were ratified by
laws of the *comitia tributa/concilium plebis*, as was necessary, so P.A. Brunt 'Lex de
Imperio Vespasiani' JRS 67 (1977) 95–116.

[31] Whether Tiberius was ever given by law an unrestricted *tribunicia potestas* after
Augustus' death is not known, but Caligula, Nero, Galba, Otho, Vitellius and
Vespasian all had *comitia tribuniciae potestatis* which were commemorated annually
when relevant, Brunt *loc. cit.* (n.30).

[32] The date *Fasti* was published, Syme *History* 34. For the importance of the title
trib. pot. by AD 4, see W.K. Lacey 'Summi fastigii vocabulum: the story of a title' JRS
69 (1979) 28–34 and chap. 7 below.

attitude to the *princeps* completely at variance with the rest of what the poet was writing. Moreover, while in exile in Tomis Ovid actually added bits to *Fasti*,[33] in honour of Tiberius. *Trib. pot.* was one of Tiberius' chief powers, the signal that he had been restored to the position of heir apparent in AD 4, and the power by which he claimed the right to ask the Senate to convene after Augustus' death to consider funeral arrangements for him (Tac. *Ann.* 1.7.3). Not to have mentioned *trib. pot.* in a revision after AD 14 becomes even more incomprehensible.

Ingenious attempts to find a date later in the year all come unstuck on the need to give Augustus' consular successor a reasonable term of office,[34] and to harmonize this with a convenient gap in the remains of all the calendars, which, though fragmentary, remain as silent on the date for a law conferring *trib. pot.* as Ovid does.

We should therefore, *pace* Last, remember the earlier votes of the People in which, by Dio's account, Augustus was given the powers of a tribune and consider how they might have been activated in 23.

When Augustus declined the vote and offer made by the Senate, should we assume that his refusal was met with a meek acquiescence? Surely not. It is surely more likely that it met with a storm of protest from those within the Senate and outside it who did not trust the old aristocracy to change their ways and look after the *plebs* while managing the *res publica*[35] as consuls. Such a storm may have been at least as vigorous as that which greeted Augustus' proposal in 27 that others might hold provinces as proconsuls and command armies, and have derived from exactly the same experiences in the past and fears for the future.

---

[33] Such as 1.533f.; Syme *History* 28f.

[34] Cf. Badian 'Crisis theories' (n.11) 34.

[35] The question whether a consul could be seen as a protector of the people has been raised. P.A. Brunt *'Laus imperii'* in P. Garnsey and C.R. Whittaker edd. *Imperialism in the Ancient World* (Cambridge 1978) 162–4, has demonstrated the popular approbation of military success, and the consequently expected popularity of victorious generals; the presence of the statues of the *triumphatores* in the Forum *Augustum* indicates the same. Julius Caesar was certainly seen as both consul and protector of the people to such an extent that later writers at least said that he had been given virtual *tribunicia potestas*. For this controversy Z. Yavetz *Plebs and Princeps* (Oxford 1969) 54 and n.4 and cf. *Julius Caesar and his Public Image* (London 1983) 56. He was never tribune. Augustus himself, by his constant stream of thanksgivings and holidays for victories won by himself and his *legati* (*R.g.* 4: 55 thanksgivings, 890 days of holidays) showed he was equally interested in enabling the people to share in his victories. The whole question has been discussed by Yavetz in his paper at Sir Ronald Syme's 80th birthday symposium, 'The *Res Gestae* and Augustus' public image', published in Millar and Segal 1–36.

Augustus would have had to respond to such protests, verbally or in writing, and certainly verbally in the Senate if they persisted. Among the questions posed (in some form or other) would be "How (*or* by what legal power) will you look after the *plebs*?" (*Quo iure plebem tuebere*?) sc. 'if you are not going to be consul'. To this the reply would have to be "By my rights as a tribune" (*tribunicio iure*). And when pressed to be tribune for life, as Dio says, his answer would be that a *tribunicium ius* was sufficient, he would be satisfied with that.

Tacitus' account seems to envisage exactly this situation, albeit in a very cryptic form. When in *Annals* 1.2 he wrote *posito triumviri nomine ... consulem se ferens et ad tuendam plebem tribunicio iure contentum* he was not describing Augustus' powers at any specific moment (as commentators have often supposed) but quoting Augustus on different occasions: "I am consul" he said at some time after the end of the triumviral period, "I am satisfied with the rights of a tribune" he said at some time, probably very shortly after July 1st, 23, when he was rejecting pressure to become tribune as Dio said the Senate voted he should be.[36]

After 28, the few coins which give Augustus any title other than CAESAR AUGUSTUS[37] call him 'consul'; compare the Arles shield (COS VIII).[38] Is Tacitus then quoting Augustus verbatim here? Sir Ronald Syme has shown beyond reasonable doubt[39] that Tacitus used the minutes (*acta*) of the Senate in the *Annals*, and quoted directly or indirectly the words of Emperors from the chair. It may be that this is the first example of this, and Tacitus gives us the key to unlock the answer to the problem of how *tribunicia potestas* was activated. Nobody 'gave' Augustus *trib. pot.* in 23, nor did Augustus 'receive' or 'take' it. He told the Senate that he already had it, and later (in *Res gestae*) recorded that he had been given it by law, as he was, in 30, or less probably 36. We do not know if anyone challenged him in 23 by asking "By what law and when were you given it", but we do know that nobody was much impressed by *trib. pot.* then or for

---

[36] For *ferens* as 'declaring' or something similar, *OLD* s.v. *fero* 34b, though this example is not cited here or anywhere else in *OLD*.

[37] E.g. the CIVIBUS SERVATEIS coins with oak-wreath and laurels (*aurei*), RIC I² 277.

[38] Chap. 3 above, n.73 for the text. The *senatus consultum* sent to Mytilene in 25, dated by Augustus' 9th consulate (E–J 307) is hardly significant; a consular date is what we would expect.

[39] *Tacitus* (1958) 278–282.

several years thereafter,[40] least of all those who attended the consular elections.

If *trib. pot.* came into existence in the unobtrusive way I have suggested, there is every reason why non-senators should not have been impressed, and every reason why Senators, even those hostile to Augustus, should not have noticed that they had created a position which might turn out to be a *summi fastigii vocabulum* (title of the supreme power).[41]

Trib. pot. was advertised on the new *aes* coinage which began to be minted either now or in 19[42] after a long break; on the *asses* it displaced the legend DIVI F[43] in conjunction with Augustus' head; on the *dupondii*[44] AUGUSTUS TRIBUNIC POTEST appears in the same style as COS VII had appeared in 27 associated with the oak-wreath awarded for saving the lives of citizens; it does not appear on the *sestertii*[45] where the legend with the same oak wreath with the addition of laurels is OB CIVIS SERVATOS. This coinage, linking as it does the three ideas of *trib. pot.*, the name Augustus and saving the lives of citizens, supports Tacitus' suggestion that Augustus took the tribune's rights as part of a *popularis* political programme. When he chose coins of denominations which had not been produced regularly in Rome since the 'Republic', but were intended to serve the needs of the traders of the city of Rome as much as the army, Augustus may have been trying to draw attention to something not well known — *trib. pot.* — as much as to make more widely known something already well known through the passage of a law (the process of advertisement for *tres nundinae* (3 market days), senatorial

---

[40] Lacey '*Summi fastigii vocabulum*' (n.32) for example, and chap. 7 below, Jones *SRGL* 12. Whether Agrippa in 18 and 13 or Tiberius in 6 were seen at the time as more than guardians of Augustus' adopted sons is uncertain, but in AD 4 *trib. pot.* was added to adoption to mark out Tiberius as destined successor without doubt.

[41] And every reason for ancient historians less perceptive and vigilant than Tacitus to have thought that such an important power must have been conferred in 23. Since they could find no trace of a law, because there wasn't one, they reported the *senatus consultum* which was passed but aborted by Augustus' refusal to accept it, without realising that it had been made irrelevant. And modern historians have followed their example, writing that *trib. pot.* was conferred in 23. This example of Tacitus' perception is not noticed by Syme in *Tacitus* chapter XXII.

[42] The date (23 or about 19) has been much disputed among numismatists; see chap. 7 below.

[43] *BMCRE* i. p.28: two coins not in the British Museum collection. Cf. *BMCRE* i.137, 138, 143–6, 153–6, 161–4, 169–70, 174 etc.

[44] *BMCRE* i. 135–6, 141–2, 150–1, 158–60, 166–8, 173, 176–7 etc.

[45] *BMCRE* i. 134, 139, 140, 147–9, 157, 165, 171–2, 175 etc.

debate, *contiones* (public addresses), *comitia* (formal vote)) for the benefit of those who had seen the law's passage. For the bronze currency was primarily the civil not the military coinage, even if soldiers (as might have been expected) got it in their petty transactions.

But to revert to the Senate; whether Augustus said *tribunicio iure* or *tribunicia potestate* is not particularly important. In dialogue, *iure* is more likely in that the question is more likely to have been *quo iure?* than *qua potestate?* For a title, however, *tribunicia potestate* is clearly normal Latin usage if one may judge from Cicero, who couples *aliqua potestate* with *magistratu* in *Tusc.* 1.74, *potestate* with *imperio* in *Ver.* 3.122, *imperia, potestates, legationes* together in *Leg.* 3.3.9 etc. *Ius* seems not to be used quite in this way, though it is coupled with *consulis imperium* in *Phil.* 4.9.

What is significant, however, is that (according to Tacitus) Augustus said he was content with it. *Contentum* is not a natural way to describe a man in the act of receiving an honour or a position he has not got but which he desires in order to make good some prerogatives he is surrendering. It is a natural word for a man who is protesting against attempts to give him what he does not want, or to give him more than he wants. This is known to have happened often enough in the months following Augustus' resignation from the consulate, but, as I have shown above, there is every possibility that it could also have happened in the aftermath of his resignation, when those who did not want him to resign were protesting at it, or being too enthusiastic in rectifying his powers.

If *contentum* is not a quotation of Augustus' own words, why is it there? Tacitus is not being ironical here, the irony (or sarcasm) comes later in the paragraph, as is Tacitus' wont, as he explains the reasons for Augustus getting away with his deceptions. *Contentum* in fact is the tell-tale word, and though the evidence does not admit of certainty, an analysis on these lines at least does no violence to the evidence we possess; it enables Dio to be accepted as making a series of accurate statements, and explains some of the evidence other explanations ignore, dismiss, leave unexplained, or require special pleading to substantiate.

To sum up: Augustus in 23 resigned the consulate and when he was challenged said that a tribune's rights were all he needed to protect the people; so the so-called 'Second Settlement' came about. No contemporary noticed that a new imperial formula had been devised (unless Augustus himself did); Augustus' sleight of hand completely escaped the compilers of the calendars, and no festival remained because there was no specific day on which to commemorate the birth of *trib. pot.* Since *trib. pot.* was not at first seen to be of major significance, and was not from the start a means for dating regnal years, the reply to those who, like Hugh Last, have enquired why he started counting from 23 when he had had a tribune's rights since 36 or 30 or 29 is that a *trib. pot.* era was made to begin only when it was convenient and required, and not before: ancient communities had no difficulties and few scruples about starting new eras.[46] From 32 to 23 Augustus' consulates provided an era, a new one was not needed till that based on his consulates ran out, then it got one. In 23 it would have been wasteful — and contrary to ancient practice — to have back-dated the start of the *trib. pot.* era to 30 (or 29 or 36) when the period already had an era dated by Augustus' consulates. Besides, before 23 it would have been very un-Republican (and quite contrary to the traditions of early Roman history as reported by Livy, which show the plebeian tribunate as a counter-balancing element to the patrician-dominated consulship) to have advertised an unbroken series of tenures of *trib. pot.* co-existing with an unbroken series of consulships. It would thus have been very inappropriate both to the period when Augustus was a triumphant military leader,[47] and to the period when the *res publica* had been re-established, nominally under the direction of the Senate.[48] It became appropriate when Augustus shifted his political stance to the *popularis* programme traditional to the party of the Caesars. And this *popularis* stance may also explain why we find Augustus unpopular with the Senate in late 23 and early 22 though his surrender of the consulate to Sestius earlier had earned him warm praise. Senators even plotted to kill him, or so it was officially reported. He would not have been the first *popularis* leader to suffer that fate.

[46] E.J. Bickerman *Chronology of the Ancient World* (London 1968) 70–77. Whatever we may make of Dio's dating of Augustus' regnal years from Actium, there was never an official era starting from Actium in Rome.

[47] *Dux* as Syme puts it, *Rom. Rev.* XXI.

[48] When the *dux* wanted to become *princeps, Rom. Rev.* 313. For his acceptance as *princeps* see chap. 6 below.

CHAPTER 5

AGRIPPA'S *PROVINCIA*

The historiographical method traditionally used by ancient historians is to gather all the available evidence surviving on a question, sift it, weigh it, test it for its veracity, and draw conclusions, of which some become self-evident in themselves, others can be thought to be proved sufficient for acceptance by their coherence with other related bits of evidence and the context. There are, however, some questions where the evidence is inadequate to prove to the satisfaction of every scholar where the truth lies, so that the question (especially if it is a useful teaching exercise) becomes one of endless argument and entrenched doctrines. There are also some questions for which there is no direct evidence at all, so that this deductive method fails entirely, and scholars either do not discuss the question if it is not vital or present theories which satisfy only their authors, while the rest of the world says "non liquet", or, like Syme, "dubitation persists".

This study offers an alternative method of approach to such a question; it is based on the method of enquiry adopted by mathematicians, scientists and philosophers among others, the inductive method. This involves starting with a hypothesis, then testing it to see if it is supported by what we know of the context and produces consequences which do not conflict with the rest of the picture, so far as we can reconstruct it. The question for discussion is 'What was Agrippa's position at the end of his two-year consulate (28–27)'? The hypothesis offered is that he received a command, in a large naval *provincia* with powers analogous to those set up by the *lex Gabinia* of 67. Certainty will not be achieved, but my hope is that those who are not persuaded will be stimulated into putting forward another hypothesis which fits the context better, and demonstrating its superiority. That is how much science progresses.

First, the context. For the latter part of 27 Agrippa was in charge of the *res publica*, holding the *fasces* alone, since his colleague Augustus had set out for Gaul (and perhaps Britain) at an unknown date. Pretty certainly Augustus will not have been in the city on July 4th, the day of the triumph of M. Crassus, who had claimed the *spolia opima* but had been denied them. He might have set out before this date, or absented himself from the triumph possibly on the grounds of ill health and set out later, but not much later since on any analysis he must have planned, and be seen to have planned, to reach Gaul before autumn set in. Agrippa had therefore been in charge of the *res publica* for three months at least, perhaps as many as six, at the end of a consulate which had lasted two years and seen the restoration of government by the consuls using the Senate as their *consilium* (at least that was the appearance presented). Are we now to think that the carefully constructed 'restoration' was immediately demolished when Agrippa assumed what Roddaz[1] has called "some temporary, ill-defined power [*pouvoir* — Roddaz does not attempt to define whether it was *imperium* or *potestas*] resting on no specific office or function. He was merely the representative of the absent consul Augustus."? Did the government, in short, revert to the days of the triumvirate or at least to before the Ides of January 27, with Agrippa playing the part of Maecenas? This seems to me at least an unlikely scenario; it would be a singularly inept politician who proclaimed freedom from a civil war emergency and immediately reinstated a civil war exercise of power. Augustus was not an inept politician.

Under the 'Republic' (so-called), consuls normally went to a *provincia* for at least a year, most who wanted to stayed longer. There were exceptions for the unwilling. A change in the third consulship of Cn. Pompeius created a gap in the tenure of consulship and proconsulship, but as this obviously sowed the seeds of civil war it was hardly a promising precedent. The alternative to a *provincia* was to become *privatus*, as Cicero for example did in 62.

To judge the probability of Agrippa becoming *privatus* in 26, his position needs to be considered: he had fought with and for Octavian throughout the civil wars;[2] he had helped to mould, or perhaps remould, public opinion from hostility to Octavian to support for

---

[1] J.-M. Roddaz *Marcus Agrippa* (Rome 1984) 231, the most recent biography of Agrippa known to me.

[2] Stressed by Zanker *Images* 71, *q.v.* for Agrippa's popularity-seeking at the time. There is a question how far Agrippa was deliberately campaigning against the memory of Sextus Pompeius, and trying to supplant him as the popular hero. If he were, it would cohere with what came later.

him by the enormous volume of public works he had undertaken on his behalf for the benefit of the *plebs* in Rome. For this, though *consularis* already, he had taken the relatively humble office of aedile. He had not acted as *privatus*. That is not to say he could not have carried out public works as *privatus* — many *triumphatores* did[3] — but Agrippa had not done so in the past. Nor was he a humble man: he had accepted exceptional or unique honours twice, or three times, if we include the two-year consulate. Shedding all legal power and carrying on with public works does not at first sight seem a very likely thing for him to have done.

Could anyone be a proconsul without a *provincia* in which to exercise his *imperium*? A.H.M. Jones did not think so,[4] and his arguments seem persuasive for Augustus. Hence even more so for Agrippa. The question therefore 'What *provincia* did he have, and for how long?' seems to be a real, and important one.

Agrippa was the most prominent man in Rome in January, 26. Apart from his own achievements, he had become a member of Augustus' family by marriage to his niece Marcella. During his consulate he had been engaged in a renewed building campaign, erecting buildings for the benefit of the city populace, thereby presumably earning more popularity.[5] The *Saepta*, begun by Julius Caesar and continued by M. Lepidus, were completed with marble embellishments, annexed by the Caesars as *Saepta Julia* and opened in 26 by Agrippa (Dio 53.23.1). The place where the *populus Romanus* met to vote in the *comitia* in the Campus Martius was a focus of civic life. Its completion was followed by the construction of the *Diribitorium*,[6] which was also for the comfort of the People in political action — to have their votes counted under a roof so large it ranked as one of the wonders of the world (Plin. *Nat.* 16.201; 36.102).

Simultaneously, the aqueduct bringing the *Aqua Virgo* to this part of the city was under construction,[7] and on adjacent privately owned

---

[3] Statilius Taurus (e.g.) was at this time building an amphitheatre, following his triumph in 34; it was dedicated in 29 (Dio 51.23.1); cf. Zanker *Images* 70f. C. Sosius, a supporter of Antonius, also triumphed in 34 and rebuilt a temple to Apollo *in Circo*, *op. cit.* 66–8, *alibi*.

[4] 'The *imperium* of Augustus' *SRGL* 3–17.

[5] Horace *Sat.* 2.2.185 quoted by Zanker *Images* 71.

[6] Completed in 7, and given to the People by Augustus as Agrippa's heir, along with the *Campus Agrippae*; in 26, the land was still *solum privatum* (Dio 55.8.3).

[7] The work was completed in 19 (Dio 54.11.7). It supplied water to the Baths of Agrippa and flowed thence no doubt to the lake (*Stagnum Agrippae*) and via the stream *Euripus* to the Tiber (Zanker *Images* 141, plan 140; Roddaz *Agrippa* (n.1) 254f.).

land Agrippa was building a complex: a Basilica of Neptune to commemorate his victories at sea (Dio 53.27.1), a remarkable painting of the Argonauts (which Roddaz[8] thinks was in a portico along one side of the *Saepta*), a *laconicum*, or vapour bath, as the first part of the Baths of Agrippa, the first great public baths in Rome. Next to these, the Pantheon was under construction. Originally intended as a shrine for ruler-worship — it is anachronistic to call it an *Augusteum*, as that name dates from 27, the building from before Actium — it became a shrine stating the claims of the Caesars to rule, as the statues of Mars father of Romulus, Venus divine ancestress of the Caesars, and the divine Julius, stood in the inner shrine; those of Augustus himself and Agrippa in the ante-chamber.[9]

This whole complex, it has been argued,[10] designed alike for the business of the *res publica* and for pleasure, was intended to create a new centre of civic life in the Campus Martius, and glorify the house of the Caesars, perhaps at the expense of the Pompeii, whose complex of buildings there had been a conspicuous example of the competitive building of the 'republican' nobles.[11] This new complex, to glorify the house of the Caesars, lay between the Theatre of Pompeius and the city and probably obscured it at least partly from a distant prospect. Imitating and outdoing the achievements of the Pompeii was a significant part of Agrippa's self-representation, pretty certainly with the connivance and approval of Augustus himself.

The buildings appear to have been built on land which had come into Agrippa's possession as a result of the confiscation of Antonius' property after his death; Antonius had obtained it at an auction held by Caesar on his return from the East in 46, an episode on which Cicero offered one of his finest scornful tirades (*Phil.* 2.64–73).

Agrippa was without question the leading admiral of the day. He had been awarded extraordinary honours; the first was the golden *corona navalis*, or *corona rostrata*, according to Pliny (*Nat.* 16.7f.) an honour originally inferior in prestige but superior in value to the *corona civica* and awarded to the soldier who first boarded an enemy

---

[8]   Roddaz *Agrippa* (n.1) 260, so Zanker *Images* 143.

[9]   Dio 53.27.3; seen by Zanker *Images* 141 as part of Octavian/Augustus' retreat from Hellenistic ruler-cult traditions. For Venus and Mars as standing for the Caesars and Rome *Images* 195–201.

[10]   Roddaz *Agrippa* (n.1) 273; cf. 253, and the plan 254f. Zanker stresses the 'recreational' aspects of the works, creating a sort of "villa for the common people" *Images* 141.

[11]   N. Purcell 'Atrium libertatis' *PBSR* 61 (1993) 125f. and refs.

ship, but converted by Cn. Pompeius into an honour for officers when he awarded it to M. Varro for distinguished service in the war against the pirates in 67. Agrippa was the only other such recipient when Octavian awarded it to him as a reward for his victories off Naulochus in 36 which had destroyed the forces of Sextus Pompeius. In *Res gestae* Augustus dismisses Sextus as a "pirate",[12] and certainly this battle put an end to the interruption of the food supply and the critical shortages in the years before 36 which had caused distress and discontent in the city (Dio 48.31 etc.). Not that Sextus had been blamed at the time; it was the triumvirs against whom the demonstrations were made (App. *B.C.* 5.67f.). In 40 Sextus had been enormously popular, perhaps because he had had no part in the proscriptions; he had in fact claimed to have saved the lives of citizens (which he symbolised on his coins by an oak wreath,[13] to be annexed by Augustus in 27), and to have avenged[14] his father (murdered after his defeat at Pharsalus) and brother (killed at Munda), by adopting the name PIUS[15] which he used with his father's cognomen MAGNUS (The Great). He also claimed to have been saluted *Imperator* twice (IMP ITER on coins), and added the office granted him by the Senate of Supervisor (*praefectus*) of the fleet and coast.[16]

Agrippa's other — and unique — honour was the dark blue pennant or flag which he was awarded after the victory at Actium. Dark blue was Neptune's colour. Sextus Pompeius, who had claimed to be Neptune's son (App. *B.C.* 5.100)[17] because as Dio says (48.19.2)

---

[12] But this was written, or at least published, some forty years later. Less than twenty years after the great wave of popularity Sextus had enjoyed at the time of the Treaty of Misenum, it might have been necessary to supplant him as a benefactor in the minds of the *plebs* rather than simply to dismiss him as an outlaw.

[13] E.g. on the golden *aurei* with the portrait of Sextus himself, H.A. Grueber *BMCRR* II.561f. (Sicily 13) and III. pl. 120, 9 and 10; M.H. Crawford *Roman Republican Coinage* (Cambridge 1974) 511 no.1. For the claim to divine paternity, see the NEPTUNI coins of Q. Nasidius, BMCRR II.564 and n. on 562; cf. Dio 48.19. The claim was to enable him to compete with Octavian, the *Divi filius*.

[14] By his defeats of the generals sent against him by the dictator and later the triumvirs, especially in his sea victory over Q. Salvidienus Rufus in 42.

[15] Clearly rivalling the claim of "*pietas* towards his parent" which Octavian was claiming as his excuse for civil war. His father's portrait appears frequently on Sextus' coins, as does Neptune's (Crawford *Roman Republican Coinage* (n.13) 511) along with a range of naval symbols, ships and the lighthouse at Messana.

[16] PRAEF(ECTUS) CLAS(SIS) ET ORAE MARIT(IMAE) EX SC., an interesting, and recent precedent for a naval command, and Sextus did not have *imperium proconsulare*.

[17] Cf. the legend NEPTUNI with his father's head, found on *denarii*.

"his father had once ruled the whole sea", had assumed a dark blue Greek cloak (*chlamys*) in place of the Roman purple cloak of the *imperator* (*id.* 48.48.5). If Agrippa's pennant was intended to claim Sextus' place as ruler of Neptune's waves — and it is hard not to see this as the image projected — was it intended to be entirely retrospective? Does it mean that Agrippa had retired from command at sea? There is no evidence that this was so. On the contrary, there is evidence (Hor. *Carm.* 4.5.19; Suet. *Aug.* 98.2) that contemporaries thought of the Augustan regime making the seas safe for commerce, and from Tacitus (*Ann.* 4.5) that the imperial fleets based at Ravenna and Misenum were built under Augustus.[18] Building bases at these sites and commandeering materials for them and the ships cannot possibly have been done without *imperium*. No source reveals who held it, but nobody seems more likely than Agrippa,[19] the regime's leading admiral and Augustus' closest political ally.

Mos maiorum (following precedents) was the most potent justification for any step in Roman political life. As Agrippa was annexing the position of the Pompeii in the Campus Martius, presenting himself as the one responsible for suppressing piracy and protector of the city's food supply, and providing buildings for the comfort and convenience of the *populus*, he might have drawn a political precedent or precedents also from the Pompeii in respect of his *provincia*. They were ready enough to hand: Cn. Pompeius (Pompey), the *popularis* politician who turned into the 'defender of the Republic' and gave his name to the party of those who opposed the Caesars, had had a series of commands which fitted the bill. First his command against the pirates under the *lex Gabinia* of 67, then his corn-gathering commission some ten years later in 56, and his command in Spain the following year, gave all that was wanted. Under the *lex Gabinia* Pompeius' *provincia* embraced the whole Mediterranean basin, all islands, all coasts, including that of Italy, up to fifty miles from the sea for three years; it empowered him to build a

---

[18] C.G. Starr *The Roman Imperial Navy* (New York 1960) 18: "the chief standing duty of the Misene fleet as a police force was the maintenance of peace in the Tyrrhenian Sea". That is to say, preventing piracy on the main sea routes leading to Rome.

[19] "General supervision", Starr *Navy* (n.18) 13; "The organisation of the navy and construction of the stations at Ravenna and Misenum owed much to Agrippa's experience" M. Reinhold *Marcus Agrippa. A Biography* (Geneva, New York 1933) 74. Contra Roddaz *Agrippa* (n.1) 182f: "Agrippa did not have time"; he denies that *ILS* 2817 is dated as early as 27, prefers a date of 20–10. There is a question of how far Agrippa had to be personally present supervising each or any of his public works.

fleet, levy troops, draw on the treasury (*aerarium*) and the funds of the provincial *publicani* (tax-gatherers). Whether his *imperium* was equal (*aequum*) or superior (*maius*) to that of other proconsuls has been debated at length,[20] but his later commands certainly carried *imperium maius*.[21] These also provided other precedents, such as his five-year tenure for the corn commission of 56 and the proconsulate in Spain in 55 without restriction on numbers of troops, and the right to make peace and war at his own discretion.[22]

The hypothesis that Agrippa had powers modelled on those conferred on Cn. Pompeius by the *lex Gabinia* cannot be proved by direct evidence. No historian records it. But their silence is explicable. In the first place, no historian records who organised the Roman Imperial navy, built the ships and established the bases and dockyards which kept the Mediterranean Sea free of pirates for more than 200 years, and thus kept the grain flowing to Rome to feed the population. In the second place, the Romans themselves had never taken much interest in their fleets, and traditionally naval commands were seldom sought by consuls and other senators — a possible reason being that there was likely to be less booty to be won in such commands. In the third place, historians who were expected to entertain as well as inform their readers may have found that routine patrolling of the seas did not capture the imagination, and was not easy to make interesting. So, when naval commands did not carry as much prestige or power as military ones, or stir the interest of the governing class, they were usually left to those below the rank of Senator, and did not get the attention they merited. And this continued to be the case under the empire.[23]

Dio, of course, ought to have recorded Agrippa's command if he had one, but at this point he appears to be following a source which stresses Agrippa's "moderation", and avoidance of the limelight and positions of power (53.23.3f.; 27.4; 32.1; 54.11.6). This however is

---

[20] R. Seager *Pompey. A Political Biography* (Oxford 1979) 33, 35, with bibliography.

[21] Seager *Pompey* (n.20) 42f. for *lex Manilia* in 66.

[22] Seager *Pompey* (n.20) 110f., 130.

[23] The fact that the imperial fleets were usually commanded by *equites* may in fact illustrate their importance rather than their insignificance. The Praetorian Guard, the most powerful force in the city, was also commanded by *equites*, as were the *vigiles*. Interruptions to the city's food supplies might be more serious for the Emperor's position — and would certainly be for his popularity — than the defeat of legions in Germany or elsewhere on the frontiers. And naval, or at least marine, troops saw fit to exercise pressure during the civil wars of AD 69–70. Cf. Starr *Navy* (n.18) 20, 23 for the presence of contingents from the Misenum and Ravenna fleets in Rome.

clearly a distortion of the truth. Agrippa's acceptance of extraordinary honours is not the mark of a self-effacing, modest person,
and in this period in particular his buildings were reminding people
of these honours with their naval flavour (Basilica of Neptune,
Painting of the Argonauts); besides, the Baths of Agrippa bore his
own name and his statue soon stood in the ante-chamber of the
Pantheon along with that of Augustus, whether or not the pediment
above the entrance declared him to be the builder.[24] Dio's source may
at least be suspected of failing to reveal the whole truth about
Agrippa's *provincia* in precisely the same way, and for precisely the
same reason, that Augustus omitted his *imperium proconsulare* in *Res
gestae* — that the exercise of *imperium* within the city in peace-time
by people other than the annual magistrates was a denial of the *mores
maiorum*.

How could this silence occur? Deliberate falsification is possible,
but an alternative possibility is that Agrippa had an inconspicuous-
sounding post to conceal the reality of a far-reaching *imperium*.
Again, the Pompeii provide the necessary precedent: *Praefectus
classis et orae maritimae* (Supervisor of the fleet and the coastal
lands) was a title conferred on Sextus Pompeius by the Senate.[25]
What could be more appropriate? We can see that it was in effect a
powerful proconsulate, the equivalent at sea of the vast *provincia* on
land given to Augustus, but contemporaries, accustomed as they
were to ignoring the navy, might well have accepted it as of no great
significance and have simply been grateful for the assurance that the
city's food supply was being protected. Such a post coheres well also
with Agrippa's avoidance of the normal honours of the tradition-
bound nobility.

When was the position created? The obvious date is in January, 27,
when the Senate was thrown into confusion by Augustus' (or rather
Octavian's) address putting the provinces into the Senate's hands
(Dio 53.11f. whatever we think of Dio's speech). A prospective
prefecture of the fleet and coasts to guard the grain supply would
very easily escape the attention of any but a vigilant and perceptive
recorder. Certainly any *provincia* could hardly have been created
without discussion with Augustus who was in Spain at the end of the

---

[24] As it does today: M. AGRIPPA COS III FECIT (M. Agrippa consul 3 times
built (lit. made) [this]) is one of Rome's most pleasing inscriptions, eloquent in its
simplicity. The text might however belong to the Hadrianic restoration and not be that
of the original building.
[25] For the text of the coin see n.16.

year. And our sources' failure to mention Agrippa in their account of the events of January is curious; it must be thought unlikely that no consideration was given to his future at that time, or before Augustus left him in charge of the *res publica* in the summer. For the alternatives are that he was either to become *privatus* or be voted some position outside the frame of the newly re-established *res publica*, keeping *imperium* but without a *provincia*, contrary to the *mores maiorum*.

It might be worth looking at the corollaries to these courses of events to see if an alternative credible scenario emerges. First, if he became *privatus*, when Augustus returned from Spain to what he thought was his deathbed in 23, he put into the hands of a *privatus* the seal for authenticating proconsular documents, subsequently sending him to the East with a command (for which the grant of *imperium* is no better attested than a *provincia* in 26), which Dio's source alleged to be a quasi-banishment to stop him quarrelling with Marcellus (Dio 53.32.1). While Agrippa was holding this post Maecenas is said to have told Augustus after the death of Marcellus that he had made Agrippa so mighty that he must make him his son-in-law or kill him (Dio 54.6.5). A right to issue orders to the legions and their commanders without *imperium* followed by an unattested grant of *imperium* to create a great command for which there was no pressing need[26] simply to get him out of the city, but which made him so mighty that nobody could rival him as Julia's next husband, seems a somewhat illogical course of events, too odd to be credible.

Alternatively if Agrippa retained *imperium* and had a position outside the constitution, and remained in Rome and Italy (as he would without a specific *provincia* to go to), he would be in a position dominating the consul of 26, Augustus' colleague. This was T. Statilius Taurus, another very prominent member of the Caesarian party, *consularis* already, *triumphator*, thrice hailed *Imperator* by his legions (*ILS* 893; Syme *Rom. Rev.* 325). We would have to assume that Taurus assented to the prospect of a great but undefined power looming over his management of the *res publica* in a period in which Augustus was trying to show how constitutional his regime was. This also seems an unlikely scenario, especially when Taurus himself had an extra-legal force in Rome, a bodyguard of German slaves (*ILS* 7448–9). There is no evidence to suggest that he used them in public life, to try for example to stop the electoral riots either in 26 or later.

---

[26] For no particular activity *CAH* X^2 84f.

Nor was he held to have failed in his duty, since some ten years later he is found in the post of *praefectus urbi* when Augustus went overseas again in 16, the first person to have held this post for any length of time.[27] Plainly he was no cipher, nor incompetent. He had already governed provinces (Syme *Rom. Rev.* 325), but apparently did not take one after his consulate of 26. He might have held the view as expressed by Syme (*op. cit.* 327): "Consulars who had governed vast provinces as proconsuls, who had fought wars under their own auspices and celebrated triumphs would consider it no great honour to serve as legates".

The consul of 25, M. Junius Silanus, was a much slighter figure. A successful trimmer, he had joined the Caesarian party before the final struggle; he had no known military or civil distinction. Syme describes his selection as consul 'baffling' (*Aug. Ar.* 33). After his consulate he may have governed Asia during the period of Agrippa's oversight of the East (Jos. *A.J.* 16.168), but the identification has been challenged (Syme *Aug. Ar.* 191 and n.27).

The choice of C. Norbanus Flaccus as consul for 24 is more easily explained. He had been a loyal member of the Caesarian faction for many years. After his consulate he simply vanishes (Syme *Aug. Ar.* 33). Death is the most likely explanation. Dio's account (53.13f.) says that the *lex Pompeia* of 52 was enforced (a five-year gap between city magistracy and province) for proconsuls, but this did not apply to the *legati Augusti pro praetore* governing the Emperor's provinces. The choices of Taurus, Silanus and Norbanus as consuls were clearly not to provide Augustus with needed *legati*. Nor can we say that there was yet established any 'principle' of whether an ex-consul should be given a province. In this period appearances in Rome itself were perhaps paramount.

To return to Agrippa himself. In 23 he was in Rome. He was present at Augustus' 'death-bed' scene, and there received Augustus' signet ring. What his legal status at the time was is unknown, but it can be suggested that if he had a naval commission of the type suggested in this study he was able, on Pompeian precedents, to be there without forfeiting his *imperium*.

After Augustus' recovery popular report spoke of friction between

---

[27] This means that twice Taurus was left in charge of the city by Augustus when he went to his *provincia*: as consul in 26, as *praefectus urbi* in 16. Can this be pure coincidence, or is it evidence that Augustus had a high opinion of Taurus? Surely, the latter. It also provides a neat example of an encroachment on the prerogatives of the magistrates noted by Tacitus *Ann.* 1.2.

Agrippa and Marcellus,[28] in consequence of which Agrippa left Rome, pretty certainly before the Roman games in September given by Marcellus. It is always assumed that he was given a proconsulate, but in the sources he is never called proconsul. When he returned to Rome in 13, Josephus (*A.J.* 16.86) describes him as returning from a ten-year *dioikesis* — that is management or administration, usually with financial implications[29] — "of the affairs of Asia". Certainly he was not proconsul of the province of Asia, since we know the names of several of the proconsuls of Asia in the ten years between 23 and 13. 'Asia' however can be used for all the lands of the old Seleucid kingdom, which had stretched westwards from Syria to the Aegean Sea, embracing all the Roman provinces East of the Hellespont.[30] Dio (53.32.1) says he was 'sent' to Syria (which was the only 'imperial' province East of the Hellespont at this date), but he did not go there, he went to Lesbos and sent *legati* (which as has been pointed out means that he had *imperium* and was not a *legatus* of Augustus).[31] It is not at all inconceivable that Dio in fact means the same as Josephus, and that Syria or its coast was indeed part of his command.[32] In an earlier passage (*A.J.* 15.350) Josephus says that Agrippa was sent as *diadochos* (deputy or successor) to Augustus of "the parts beyond the Ionian Sea" — that is, of the empire East of the Greek peninsula. Expressed in nautical and not territorial terms, this looks like a naval command.[33]

Whatever his title, he went to Lesbos (so Dio *loc. cit.*), which was part of the province of Asia, a fact which has caused much discussion of his possible relationship with the governors of Asia. But the point of going to Lesbos is that Mytilene was an ideal naval base for overseeing the sea-routes of the Aegean which all vessels travelling from Syria and Asia crossed on the way to Rome, and the Hellespont itself, a key waterway, and always liable to piracy as ships waited for

---

[28] Dio 53.31.4–32.1; *q.v.* for Agrippa's great (and richly deserved) popularity among the *plebs*.

[29] *LSJ s.v. dioikesis*; the cognate *dioikētēs = procurator* and not *proconsul* in Strabo (17.3.25) and Plutarch (*Ant.* 67), passages quoted.

[30] *OLD s.v. Asia*, and cf. *id. s.v. Asiaticus*; "of the affairs of Asia" translates *tōn epi tēs Asiās*. Cf. the silver ASIA RECEPTA *quinarii* produced in Italy in large numbers at this time (*ca* 29–26), to claim the recovery of the eastern provinces given away by M. Antonius. *RIC* I² p.31 and 276 (p.61).

[31] Reinhold *Agrippa* (n.19) 168.

[32] But he was not the proconsul of Syria. Augustus was. Nor was he a *legatus Augusti* (see last note). The case for a naval command on the coast here is strong.

[33] *tōn peran Iōniou*. Note the masculine/neuter form. That is, the Ionian sea not the land of Ionia.

a wind to enable them to negotiate the straits into the Black Sea.[34] The prevailing northerly wind also meant that from Lesbos commanders would more often than not be able to set sail at short notice. It is worth noting that Lesbos was where Germanicus first based himself forty years later when he was given charge of the East (Tacitus *Ann.* 2.43).

The simplest explanation of what our sources say is that Agrippa had his prefecture of the fleet and coasts renewed, perhaps for ten years, perhaps to make a total of ten years, this time in the eastern half of the Roman world.

Things changed however; Marcellus died, and this was a good reason for Agrippa to stay in Lesbos, since the question of Julia's new husband was of importance to him in the light of his dispute with Marcellus, and whether her new husband would be compatible with him. Maecenas saw the point; he told Augustus that there was no alternative to Agrippa as her new husband unless he was prepared to get rid of him, put him to death that is.[35] The result was that Augustus moved to Sicily in 22, where he met Agrippa. At their conference they exchanged spheres of responsibility: Augustus took over the East with a view to recovering the standards, Agrippa went to the West,[36] to Rome for his marriage and to see that the consuls for 20 were elected, establish law and order in the city if he could, and deal with the problems in Gaul and Spain. Which he did. As has been suggested, if he was still holding his prefecture of the fleet and the coasts, this was all within his sphere of activity, though there might be an instance of encroachment here — a not quite explicit equalisation of his *imperium* to that of Augustus.

This might be what the well-known papyrus,[37] universally agreed

---

[34] In this region piracy can be traced back as far as the fifth century (Plut. *Per.* 19); it resurfaced in the fourth (Dem. 23.166). It reappeared in fact whenever the naval powers of the day weakened or were at war. Ships waiting for a favourable breeze were always vulnerable (H.A. Ormerod *Piracy in the Ancient World* (Liverpool 1924) *passim*).

[35] Dio 54.6.5.

[36] Whether this means that he was formally or informally made a co-princeps has been debated. See Syme's criticism of Kornemann's *Doppelprinzipat* in *Rom. Rev.* 345 n.4. It seems to me more likely that he was still *praefectus* of the navy and coasts, but in practice nobody dared to tell him when he was more than fifty miles from the sea. So he did what he did in Augustus' provinces with Augustus' support, but recognised as being *suis auspiciis*. Syme *loc. cit.* and 346 ... "Agrippa is rather to be regarded as the deputy leader of the Caesarian party".

[37] First edited by L. Koenen 'Die "laudatio funebris" des Augustus für Agrippa auf einem neuen Papyrus' *ZPE* 5 (1970) 217–83, *q.v.* for the text.

to be a Greek translation of Augustus' laudation of Agrippa, is saying, when Augustus goes on from recounting Agrippa's grants of *trib. pot.* to say (addressing Agrippa) that "it was enacted by law that into whatever province the business of the *res publica* sent you, nobody's *exousia* [*imperium* or *potestas*?] should be greater than yours". Though this is undated, and modern scholars have discussed at length whether it means from 23, 18 or 13 and whether "nobody" includes Augustus or not,[38] the papyrus does not exclude the possibility that he did have such a position under a prefecture, and that the law by which he got this *imperium* was that which derived from his consulate, and was a *lex curiata*. Augustus in a funeral *laudatio* did not need to present a strictly legal case. Once again, the fact that we cannot find in the sources a record of Agrippa being given a command may mean that there was no new act, just an extension of the old authority, exactly like Augustus' own *imperium*, given for life and not renewed because there was no need, and not renewing it avoided embarrassment — which would be even more likely to occur with Agrippa since he was unpopular with the Senators (Dio 54.29.6; cf. Syme *Rom. Rev.* 344).

An appropriate formula for a command for Agrippa has recently been found in a Latin inscription[39] setting out the *imperium* of Cn. Piso, dated AD 17 by Tacitus (*Ann.* 2.43), when he was sent as special commissioner to co-operate with Germanicus in the eastern provinces (though they failed to co-operate and clashed violently). Piso is given "*imperium* superior to (*maius*) that of the proconsul of any province he enters, save that the *imperium* of the Princeps is greater in all matters". Tacitus omits this. Was this formulation an innovation? Not very likely, in view of Tiberius' well-attested unwillingness to innovate. Precedents should be Augustan. Whether for Agrippa or for the field marshals who took over after Agrippa's death is guesswork, but it is a reasonable development from a naval command with powers based on the precedents in the *lex Gabinia*. There is also an interesting development in the advance from "nobody's *imperium* is superior (*maius*) to yours" to "your *imperium* is superior to that of every proconsul save that of the Princeps." A good example of encroachment, perhaps.

---

[38] An excellent summary of the main views in B. Levick *Tiberius the Politician* (London 1976) 233 n.6.

[39] Information Mr Nicholas Purcell. I am grateful to him and to Dr Werner Eck for allowing me access to the draft publication forthcoming.

If our hypothesis is correct, one notorious problem disappears: our sources contain no record of any resistance to Agrippa when he was restoring some measure of order to the city in 21 (Dio 54.6.6), and no record of his having been given any grant of *imperium* or other power with which to do it. He was simply sent by Augustus from Sicily, or so we are told, in a period in which Augustus had stepped down from the consulate, refused to be made dictator to deal with the food crisis, claimed no more than *tribunicia potestas* for the protection of the people, and could have come himself had Agrippa not had sufficient power to deal with the situation in the Campus Martius, the site for the elections (and outside the *pomerium*).[40]

With powers of the sort suggested here, Rome outside the *pomerium* was within the ambit of his command, but in any case another Pompeian precedent was available: after the passing of the *lex Trebonia* Pompeius was nominally proconsul of Spain but actually in the city trying to maintain order. Moreover when Agrippa left Rome for Gaul and Spain in 20, he was a colleague rather than *legatus* of Augustus since, when he finished pacifying Spain in 19, Augustus proposed that he should be awarded a triumph. Triumphs — at least in recent times — had been awarded only to those who were *suis auspiciis*, never to *legati*. If he were *suis auspiciis*, when did he become so if he was not still retaining the *auspicia* he had got as consul?[41] A final point: Agrippa's position was redefined in 18. Why? In 18 Augustus' own *provincia* had to be renewed or discontinued, but did Agrippa's — unless his command had also been for ten years or two periods of five years from 27? Can it be pure coincidence that Agrippa now, if not before, became Augustus' colleague in *imperium maius*? His *trib. pot.* also was conferred for the same period as Augustus' provincial tenure.

Various explanations exist: Augustus needed a colleague to preside at the Secular Games if Lepidus was not going to be invited, Augustus was planning to adopt his grandson as Gaius Caesar whatever the sex of the child Julia was carrying etc., but the most

---

[40] All Agrippa's buildings of this period are outside the *pomerium*, hence not, technically, *domi*. The granaries which are the corollary to securing the arrival of the grain ships, the *Horrea Agrippiana*, are within the city proper, but they belong to the period 20–10, that is, after 23, perhaps after 18; so Roddaz *Agrippa* (n.1) 294–5. Is this a mere coincidence?

[41] Florus (2.33.51) distinguishes Agrippa from his two predecessors, Antistius and Furnius, who are called *legati* while Agrippa is not.

natural one is surely that the tenure of Agrippa's previous *provincia* was coming to an end at the end of the year.[42]

To sum up: no evidence compels us to accept that Agrippa was given a *provincia* in 26, but the hypothesis that he was, that his title was *praefectus classis et orae maritimae*, and that his powers and sphere of competence were modelled on those granted to Cn. Pompeius in 67 by the *lex Gabinia* fits the context, accords with Agrippa's own predilection for positions and honours, and accounts for a number of problems, almost all of which can be explained away by scholarly ingenuity or written off as inexplicable. A simple solution is often better, however, and silence is really the only objection. Is that compelling? It is not usually thought to be so, and in this case the silence itself is not hard to explain.

The hypothesis can perhaps stand until a more convincing one is produced.

---

[42] Josephus, however, thought that Agrippa's command did not end before 13, when he returned to Rome "after it" (*A.J.* 16.86). See also Reinhold *Agrippa* (n.19) 168.

CHAPTER 6

THE BEGINNING OF THE PRINCIPATE *

When did the Principate begin? We must define our terms. Dio (51.1.1f.) says it began on the day of the Battle of Actium (2nd September, 31).[1] After this there could — at least for a time — be no serious challenge to Octavian/Augustus' military power, and Rome was destined to revert to rule by one man (i.e. become a monarchy).[2] So it may seem with the advantage of hindsight. But this criterion will not suffice. By it the older Caesar would have established a principate on the day of the Battle of Munda. But he did not. He went a different way, to a lifelong dictatorship which did not meet with the acceptance of even his friends and protégés so that they murdered him — the ultimate failure.

In 31, it was far from certain that after the fighting was over Caesar's heir, who had shown himself not at all merciful towards those who had opposed him,[3] would find a solution to the problem of his own position which was less autocratic and more acceptable. Moreover we have learned from Sir Ronald Syme to remember that every form of government, whatever its title, depends for its stability and durability on the ruler(s) winning the co-operation of an oligarchy of executives. And the Principate lasted a hundred years in the hands of Augustus' dynasty, and more later. So, the Principate, it

* The basic thesis of this chapter was put forward in *Classicum* 23 [IX.2] (1983) 30–35. I am grateful to the Editor for permission to use the material therein.

[1] Cf. Andrew Wallace-Hadrill *Augustan Rome* (Bristol 1993) 10. The year 31 is also chosen by many writers and editors of series, e.g. the Methuen series, as a point at which to divide 'Republic' from 'Empire'.

[2] So Tacitus *Ann.* 1.1; on a long view the 'Republic' was an interlude between periods of monarchical rule.

[3] In comparison with the older Caesar, for whom *clementia* (mercy) was an often repeated theme (see for example Cicero *pro Marcello*); the appearance of *clementia* as one of the virtues of Augustus on the golden shield in the Senate House must have prompted some ironical (at least) comments.

will be argued in this chapter, cannot be said to begin till the Princeps had won the acceptance which Tacitus describes as when 'every one put aside [claims to] equality and looked to the instructions of the Princeps'.[4]

Later (when he wrote *Res gestae*) Augustus claimed that all the closures of Janus' temple took place while he was Princeps (*me principe*, *R.g.* 13). This suggests that with the advantage of hindsight he thought the Principate was in existence in 29, but it must be very doubtful if at the time he did. Though he had had the oath of Italy behind him, and seven hundred Senators in his forces for the Actium campaign (*R.g.* 25.3) he was still only a military leader, *dux* as Syme (*Rom. Rev.* Chapter XXI) put it, and the poets agreed. He was not even regarded as the only military leader by Cornelius Gallus for example or M. Crassus, the one making huge claims for successes on Egypt's southern frontier, the other about to make a claim to the almost unheard-of honour, the *spolia opima* from his campaigns in Thrace.

Other dates can be briefly considered. February 1st 28, when the appearance of normal (that is consular) government returned with the rotation of the *fasces* between the consuls in the traditional way — but this was no more than a first step.[5] The closing ceremony (*lustrum*) of the census of 28, when Augustus became *princeps senatus*, as was only proper for the consular with the largest number of tenures of office — but *princeps senatus* was not Princeps.[6] The 'Republic' had always had a *princeps senatus* when it was functioning properly; it had *principes viri*, it could be thought, only when military men were exercising non- or supra-legal power (*potentia*) through resources and patronage superior to that of other nobles in order to control political life.[7] Rome had never yet had one Princeps, not even Caesar, because he used the military office of dictator on which to base his rule.

January 1st 27, the day following the annulment of all the illegal acts of the triumvirate from December 31st 28, is stressed by Dio

---

[4] *Omnes exuta aequalitate iussa principis aspectare*, *Ann.* 1.4.

[5] The two-year consulate of Augustus and Agrippa and Augustus' continuing tenure remained symbolic of the powers of civil-war generals.

[6] Brunt and Moore 49, comm. on 7.2. And the *lustrum*, while ceremonially purifying the Roman People and separating them from the rest of the world, had no constitutional significance. R.M. Ogilvie '*Lustrum condere*' *JRS* 51 (1961) 31–39.

[7] Syme *Rom. Rev.* 387: "The *principes* of the dying Republic behaved like dynasts, not as magistrates or servants of the state".

(53.2.5), but the significance of this day is overshadowed by the events of the Ides which followed. On January 13th 27, Octavian bade the Senate resume all its ancient functions, including allocating provinces to the consuls, thus appointing the future commanders of the armies.[8] There followed the so-called 'First Settlement' in which the legal powers of Augustus, as he now became, were (besides his *auctoritas* or mana which was supra-legal) founded on an annual consulate and a huge *provincia* consisting of Spain, Gaul and Syria. This is the date which Dio says (53.19.2–6) marks the start of government by decisions made in private, which is the antithesis of *res publica*, open government as it is called today. It is also the date at which Syme, in one of his memorable phrases, says that Octavian went through "a painless and superficial transformation" from Dux to Princeps (*Rom. Rev.* 313, and the opening of Chapter XXII).

A fifth date, the one perhaps most commonly favoured, is on or about July 1st 23. And there are good reasons; with Augustus no longer consul the consulate ceased to be in fact the most important position in the state, even if it remained so in theory; the consuls still performed their ancient functions, though their morning *salutatio* ceased to be the place where the affairs of state were discussed and the Senate's business planned. The private meetings between Augustus and his *amici* became an alternative forum, and one better informed about the resources available for implementing any policy discussed. In provincial government too the direction of policies and the sort of management decisions and judicial authority which proconsuls had always exercised now came under the explicitly superior *imperium* of Augustus instead of the less explicitly superior *imperium* of a consul.[9] With his mana (*auctoritas*) to back it his *tribunicia potestas* created a new centre of power outside the ancient constitutional offices which was to become the monopoly of the Princeps and the mark of his intended successor — what Tacitus calls the *summi fastigii vocabulum*.[10]

    [8] Chap. 3 above, and cf. W.K. Lacey 'Octavian in the senate, January 27 B.C.' *JRS* 64 (1974) 176–184.

    [9] Syme *Rom. Rev.* 330: a consul's *imperium* was superior to that of a proconsul, but its superiority was "vague and traditional" rather than explicit. It should also be borne in mind that in the 'Republic' proconsuls were apt to have armies under their command which owed their loyalty to the proconsul, while the consuls had no mobilised forces at their disposal.

    [10] "The name for the highest pinnacle of power". For the process by which this came about, see chap. 7 and W.K. Lacey *'Summi fastigii vocabulum*: the story of a title' *JRS* 69 (1979) 28–34.

But perhaps what most appeals to the scholarly mind is the fact that Augustus' nomenclature — the façade of his *res publica* it might be called — was now settled. *Tribunicia potestas* and *imperium proconsulare* became and remained the official powers of the Princeps. But is the façade the truth? Tacitus did not think so; for him 23 was the springboard from which Augustus progressed to take over the prerogatives of the Senate, magistrates and laws (*Ann.* 1.2). More important still, the 'Settlement' of 23 failed to gain the approval of the governed,[11] so that this date fails to meet one of our criteria.

Another possible date is in AD 14, when the powers of Augustus were transferred to Tiberius by the renewal of the oath of support taken to Octavian (as he then was in 32).[12] The oath was spontaneous (in Tacitus' account), Tiberius was not present and the initiative came from the consuls. But in truth this merely shows that Augustus' constitutional arrangements had by now won the assent of the Senate, and their oath should be seen as expressing their wish to continue the leadership of a Princeps in a Principate which already existed. Shortly after this, the ending of the People's part in the consular elections should be seen as the legal termination of the institutions of the 'Republic' rather than the start of the Principate.[13]

Can Tacitus' view be ascertained? Not explicitly before AD 14, of which he wrote *ruere in servitium consules, patres, eques* (the consuls, Senators and Equestrian Order rushed headlong into servitude, *Ann.* 1.7); but he made no attempt to date the starting point of the Principate.

On the other hand, in *Annals* 1.2 after his account of Augustus' assumption of *trib. pot.* he adds a clause *ubi militem donis, populum annona, cunctos dulcedine otii pellexit* (when he [sc. Augustus] had won over the troops with gifts, the People with a food supply, everyone at large with the pleasant experience of a life at peace) before continuing his account of the process of encroachment by which Augustus drew into his own hands the functions of the government. The clause does not follow chronologically the evolution of the titles; it runs parallel, giving an account of the means which he used to gain acceptance and his springboard for taking over.

---

[11] Demonstrated in detail by A.H.M. Jones 'The *imperium* of Augustus' *SRGL* 3–17 (= *JRS* 41 (1951) 112–119).

[12] *In verba Tiberi Caesaris iuravere*, Tac. *Ann.* 1.7.

[13] So Syme *Tacitus* 369.

His generosity to his troops whether as Octavian or Augustus is not in doubt; their abundant coinage shows that all the commanders of the revolution paid their troops well. He had also looked after his discharged veterans: in *Res gestae* 3.3 he claims to have rewarded all 300,000 discharged veterans with farms or cash. Though this figure is thought to include all troops till his death, the year 30 is later picked out as one of the two in which he bought land for discharged soldiers' farms — the first and only commander in living memory to have done so, or so he claims (*R.g.* 16). At this time (in 29) he also gave a cash donative out of the booty (from Egypt) to each of the soldiers already settled in colonies (*R.g.* 15.3). Dio also records colonies and lands given to discharged veterans at the end of campaigns in 26 (53.25.5) and 25 (53.26.1), in Spain at Emerita (Merida) and in the Alps at Augusta Praetoria (Aosta) respectively. By 23 the soldiers must have been sure that they would be looked after at the end of their service with gifts of money or farms or both.[14]

It must be uncertain whether by *annona* Tacitus meant securing the regular supply of grain-ships, with sufficient storage and points of sale for the distribution of the city's food supply,[15] or grain for the continuing doles for the *plebs*. Perhaps both, but the use of *populum* should mean the city's population as a whole.[16] The victory at Naulochus had been an important success for this, and if the hypothesis in chapter 5 is correct Agrippa had been securing the seas ever since his consulate ended in December 27. In *Res gestae*, Augustus' first reference to assistance in this area is the twelve distributions of free grain in 23 (*R.g.* 15.1), the next chronologically his ending the crisis at the end of that year or early 22 (*id.* 5.2). His systematic supplementation did not start till 18 (*id.* 18).

More problematic is the reference to the pleasant experience of a life in peace-time, *otium*. *Otium* obviously included the end of civil wars, and arbitrary rule, but that ended long before 23. But is that all it meant? *Otium* might have the meaning Cicero gives it in his *Pro Sestio* of 56,[17] civil peace, freedom from rioting and the disturbances at elections and meetings endemic in the 'Republic' from 59, if not

---

[14] The interpretation of R.H. Martin, quoted by F.R.D. Goodyear *The Annals of Tacitus* (Cambridge 1972) vol. I 104 n.2.

[15] So H. Furneaux *The Annals of Tacitus Books I–VI* (2nd edn, Oxford 1896) 181 (n. *ad loc.*).

[16] Goodyear *loc. cit.* (n.14) for bibliography on the *annona*, mostly later than 23.

[17] W.K. Lacey 'Cicero *Pro Sestio* 96–143' *CQ* 12 (1962) 67–71. For a more general discussion, C. Wirszubski 'Cicero's *cum dignitate otium*' *JRS* 44 (1954) 1–13.

from the first consulate of Sulla and the Social War thirty years
before that. None are recorded during Augustus' consulates from 31
to 23, but electoral riots resumed after his resignation in 23, and came
to an end in 19 for twenty-five years.[18] 19 also marked the end of the
career of Egnatius Rufus, suppressed by the consul C. Sentius
Saturninus (though the hand behind Sentius is usually thought (and
by Tacitus *Ann.* 1.10) to have been that of Augustus). But at the time
Sentius might have got the blame; he did not see the year out, and was
replaced by another military man, M. Vinicius (Syme *Rom. Rev.* 372).

Tacitus' verb *pellexit*, which as so often gives colour to the
sentence, perhaps merits a note. "Seduced" is favoured by Michael
Grant (Penguin) and by others,[19] to convey a pejorative moral
overtone (though this may be old-fashioned these days). *OLD*,
however, offers a broader and different range of meanings. For
example Cicero (*de Orat.* 1.243) "You won (*pellexisti*) the majority of
the votes by your wit (*sale tuo*) and charm (*lepore*) and exquisite jokes
(*facetiis politissimis*)".[20] Pleasure for the person(s) won over seems
clearly combined with the attainment of his ends by the person
winning. *Otium* to a war-weary generation was a consummation
devoutly to be wished, and an important element in the acceptance of
Augustus' settlements.

From several points of view therefore the year 19 deserves
somewhat closer scrutiny than it has usually received, especially with
the above assessment of Tacitus in mind. The events of the year
enabled Augustus to vindicate his claim to sole leadership in the two
fields in which he had claimed to lead, and also to gain from the
Senators the acceptance of his (hitherto perhaps unspoken) claim to
enjoy in the city an *imperium* as proconsul equal to that of the
consuls, and in consequence remain in the city and engage personally
in the management of the *res publica* as part of the leadership in the
Senate rather than in the role traditional to tribunes as what we now

[18] Syme *Rom. Rev.* 372: riots occurred (Dio 55.34.2) in AD 7 when Augustus
sought to withdraw from participation in the elections, that is, when he ceased
canvassing personally for the candidates of his choice.

[19] M. Grant *Tacitus, The Annals of Imperial Rome* (Harmondsworth 1971) 32; cf.
D.R. Dudley (1966) quoted by K. Chisholm and J. Ferguson *The Augustan Age* (Open
University: Oxford 1981); 'enticed' M. Reinhold *The Golden Age of Augustus* (Toronto
and Sarasota 1978) 11, N.P. Millar *Tacitus Annals Book I* (London 1959) 101;
'conciliated' J. Jackson LCL (1948); 'won over' Church and Broadribb (1869).

[20] Cf. Cic. *Clu.* 13. Goodyear (n.14) on *Ann.* 1.2 points out that *otium* can also have
pejorative overtones. With both *otium* and *pellexit* perhaps Tacitus is challenging his
readers to decide which way to interpret his account.

call 'opposition'.

In his rise to the position of Princeps Augustus, or Octavian as we call him at this period, had pursued the leadership of the party of Caesar (as he admitted (*R.g.* 2) and Tacitus (*Ann.* 1.2) clearly saw), which Caesar himself had based on his military following and on the patronage of the *plebs*. How universal this patronage was intended to be has been discussed by scholars,[21] and the provisions of Caesar's will appear to be clear evidence that he at least thought of the whole of the *plebs* as having a claim on his munificence. Those who accepted the proffered legacy counted themselves as his *amici* (supporters) or at least clients. Accepting a legacy was a formal act in Roman society and law,[22] and acceptance involved establishing a relationship with the *heres* (heir) or *heredes* (heirs) from whose inheritance the legacy was seen as being taken.[23] And Caesar's heir's assumption of the burden of paying the legacies showed that he was claiming the adherents of his father as his own.

His claim to military leadership had the same starting-point, except that even in 44 Caesar's troops did not embrace the whole of the legionary forces of the Roman world, and there were other independent proconsuls governing provinces and commanding armies. Nor did the troops of Augustus until 19, because there were still proconsuls campaigning with independent commands (*suis auspiciis*) and holding triumphs until L. Cornelius Balbus held the last non-imperial triumph (on March 27th, from Africa). The previous one, that of L. Sempronius Atratinus, on October 12th 21, had also been from Africa. The *fasti triumphales* show how completely the army had been taken out of politics in ten years. It was a steady process leading from Octavian's own triple triumph in 29 through the driving of Cornelius Gallus to suicide to punish his attempted rivalry with his leader, to the steadily dwindling stream of triumphs as those holding independent commands before 27 came home: there were three in 28, two in 27, one of whom was that of M. Crassus who had been defrauded of his claim to *spolia opima* and forced to wait a year for his triumph from Thrace and the Getae,[24]

---

[21] See e.g. Z. Yavetz *Julius Caesar and his Public Image* (London 1983) 165–8, stressing his consistent appeal to the People.

[22] Alan Watson *Roman Private Law around 200 B.C.* (Edinburgh 1971) 108; J.A. Crook *Law and Life of Rome* (London 1967) 125 *et alibi*.

[23] E.g. W.W. Buckland *A Textbook of Roman Law* (3rd edn, revd by P. Stein, Cambridge 1963) 334.

[24] Syme *Rom. Rev.* 308–9. For Gallus' inscription E–J 21.

one in 26 awarded to Sextus Appuleius, the proconsul in Spain who was relieved by Augustus himself. He was the last non-imperial *triumphator* from the provinces allotted to Augustus in 27.

Moreover, when Augustus refused to hold a triumph to celebrate his return after his Parthian 'victory' of 20, though he took an imperatorial salutation, and when Agrippa refused to triumph over Spain at what was proclaimed as (and actually turned out to be) its final subjugation, despite the fact that the honour was proposed by Augustus himself (Dio 54.11.6), it became evident that the right to hold a triumph as the apex of a public career was not to be as easily achieved as it had been in the late 'Republic' and the triumviral era. Contemporaries of course could not foresee the future, but in 19 the precedent set by Augustus in 25-4 (when he was ill at the time he returned from Spain) of receiving a salutation as *Imperator* but not triumphing became well established; henceforth salutations, with thanksgivings to the gods and days of holidays (*R.g.* 4), were to take the place of triumphs. And with rivalry for triumphs removed, one of the incentives for seeking military commands, especially for commands of troops *suis auspiciis*, was also quietly removed from the scene. 19 was the end of an era for the commanders of the legions. It removed equality of status (*aequalitas* as Tacitus put it) from this sphere of the *res publica*.

The 'victory' over Parthia set the capstone on Augustus' pursuit of Caesar's heritage. At the time of his assassination Caesar had been going to avenge the defeat of Crassus at the disastrous battle of Carrhae in 53, and it had been envisaged that he might be away for several years, which was why the consular elections and provincial allocations had been arranged in advance.[25] After Caesar's murder M. Antonius had attempted to vindicate his claim to succeed to Caesar's military position by undertaking this mission. His campaign was reputedly based on Caesar's plans,[26] and its failure had been perhaps the most important downward turn in the course of his career, as it was crucial in upsetting the balance of power between him and Octavian, and gave Octavian the chance to cheat him, which of course he took.[27] Augustus, however, pursued this part of his heritage with the same patient and devious resolve with which he had

[25] M. Gelzer *Caesar, Politician and Statesman* (E.T. Oxford 1968) 309; Syme *Rom. Rev.* 55.

[26] Syme *Rom. Rev.* 263.

[27] Syme *Rom. Rev.* 265.

pursued his more overtly political aims.

When he became proconsul of Syria in 27 he apparently took no great interest in the province, leaving its government in the hands of partisans he believed to be loyal, since it is uncertain whether the Varro who was governing Syria in 24 was the consul elected for 23, the 'conspirator' Varro Murena, or someone else. In 27, his first thoughts had been for the scene of his 'father's' great victories in Gaul and Britain, and, to publicise the fact in Rome, the *via Flaminia* had been repaired in anticipation, and Augustus' statue placed at the crossing of the Tiber (Dio 53.22.2). This suggests that the move to Gaul in 27 was the higher priority, undertaken with political motives as much as military imperatives in mind. Dio implies — and we ought to believe him — that Augustus said he was going to invade Britain, but did not do so for two reasons: (a) the Britons appeared to be going to negotiate;[28] and (b) Gaul was still very poorly organised, and in need of a census.

This probably means that Gaul had recovered from the devastation of Caesar's campaigns and was ready to have its tax-assessments revised and probably increased from 40 million sesterces.[29] How long Augustus remained in Gaul is unknown, but the conquest of Britain was much in the air at the time.[30] Horace (e.g.) in *Carm.* 1.21.15; 3.5.3f. links the conquests of Britons and Persians explicitly; in *Carm.* 1.35.29f. Caesar is about to go to Britain, plainly not as a timid tourist like Horace in *Odes* 3.4.33. Both Strabo (4.200 = 4.5.3 LCL) and Tacitus (*Agr.* 13) know of embassies and kings seeking friendly alliance (*amicitia*) (which to the Roman mind was equivalent to their becoming clients), while Augustus himself (*R.g.* 32) names two kings to whom he gave asylum. He had, however, to go to Spain, on whose conquest Velleius concentrates his praises (2.90).[31] What Velleius says should reflect the official line, avoiding the admission that Augustus had done little for the inheritance of Caesar in Britain and Gaul and magnifying his achievements in Spain which were celebrated at the time by the closing of Janus' temple in 26, and an imperatorial salutation in 25, and gifts to the *plebs*.

---

[28] Accepting, as all modern editors seem to do, the emendation of Cobet, changing the aorist tense of the MS of Dio 53.22.5 to a future.

[29] Suet. *Jul.* 25; Holmes *Architect* II 5.

[30] Dio 53.25.2; Syme *Rom. Rev.* 331f.

[31] Vell. 2.90; the campaigns of Augustus, Carisius and Agrippa, 26–19, completed a conquest begun in 218. Spain had seen many triumphs in the last years of the 'Republic'. Cf. R. Syme 'The Spanish War of Augustus' *AJPh* 55 (1934) 293–317.

Gaul, then, and Britain were advertised as settled before the political settlement of 23; Parthia (and Syria) had to wait for Augustus' personal attention till after that settlement. Settling the account with Parthia began actively in 23 when envoys from the Parthian King (Phraates) were in Rome, along with his rival Tiridates who had been defeated seven years earlier and had been given asylum in Syria by Octavian (Dio 51.18.3). According to Dio, Augustus brought Tiridates and Phraates' envoys before the Senate (53.33), who referred the question back to him.[32] Augustus decided to satisfy neither party; on the one hand he continued Tiridates' asylum, but refused to assist him to gain the Parthian throne, on the other he sent Phraates back the son whom he had been holding as an honoured hostage, and demanded in exchange the return of the prisoners and standards lost by Crassus and M. Antonius.[33]

But Augustus was in no hurry to secure them. When he left Rome at the end of 23 he first went no further than Campania perhaps,[34] from where he returned to deal with the crisis provoked by shortages of food which led to demands for him to be dictator and his acceptance of the management of the supply of grain (*cura annonae*) (*R.g.* 5). He remained in Rome much of 22 (see below). Thereafter he did little more than keep out of sight of the Senate and People, moving around Sicily and Greece, where he paid off a few old scores (Dio 54.7.2). He reached Samos probably late in 21. On the way, or perhaps in Sicily, he met Agrippa, who had been sent to the East in 23, perhaps with a great commission.[35] His marriage to the now

[32] The protocol should be noted: the governor of Syria (Augustus) referred Tiridates and the Parthian King's envoys to the Senate; the Senate invited Augustus to make the decision about whether or not to accede to Tiridates' request. Did the Senators feel they did not have enough information about the resources (financial and military) available or did they lack the confidence to try to direct policy? And was the debate embarrassing? — if for example the Senators complained that they had not been given the information they needed? Dio's account is too brief for any judgement to be attempted.

[33] In the defeats at Carrhae in 53 and Antonius' disastrous campaign of 35. This is a nice example of Augustus' patient approach to problems, waiting as he did for an opportunity to secure what he really wanted.

[34] Th. Mommsen *R.g.* 2nd edn 24; S. Jameson '22 or 23?' *Historia* 18 (1969) 223.

[35] L. Koenen 'Die "laudatio funebris" der Augustus für Agrippa auf einem neuen Papyrus (P. Colon. inv. Nr. 4701)' *ZPE* 5 (1970) 217–283 and E.W. Gray 'The *imperium* of M. Agrippa' *ZPE* 6 (1970) 227–238 on the character of Agrippa's powers (whether *imperium* or *potestas*, and whether *maius* (superior) or *aequum* (equal) to that of the other proconsuls in the eastern provinces), and the extent of his *provincia*. See chap. 5, and discussion of the nature of this command in J.-M. Roddaz *Marcus Agrippa* (Rome 1984) 344 and n.24.

widowed Julia was arranged, and Agrippa undertook two commissions: to restore order in Rome and see to the election of consuls for 20, then to complete the conquest of Spain (Dio 54.6.4–6 and 11).

In 20 Augustus still did not hasten to Syria. After his winter in Samos (21–20), he toured Asia and Bithynia doing nothing that has been recorded except punishing the Cyzicenes for having flogged and executed Roman citizens (Dio 54.7.6). He thus took over two years from the end of 23 to reach his own province of Syria. It was his arrival there (or so we are told by Dio, 54.8.1f.) which prompted King Phraates to carry out the bargain he had made in 23 (Dio 53.33.2 above) and return the prisoners taken from Crassus and Antonius, apart from a few who lay low, not wishing repatriation according to Dio (54.8), and — of greater propaganda importance — the standards lost in these defeats.

This success was extensively publicised (the evidence is abundant on the coins)[36] — so extensively that modern commentators have tended to react by discounting it, and have not seen its full importance, which was that it completed Augustus' military obligations as Caesar's heir. Now, apart from the office of *Pontifex Maximus*, Augustus had fully entered on Caesar's inheritance. He was prepared to wait for that post, despite a vote in Caesar's lifetime that it should pass to his son (Dio 44.5.3),[37] and an offer to transfer it to him (*R.g.* 10.2).[38] It was a good opportunity to advertise his modesty at little or no cost, and at the same time his respect for the *mores maiorum* — the tenure of the office of *Pontifex Maximus* was for life. And he did not hasten home to celebrate the 'victory' over Parthia.

According to Dio he made some rearrangements among the client kingdoms on the frontiers of Syria and returned to winter again in Samos (20–19), leaving Tiberius to establish Tigranes as King of Armenia (Dio 54.9.4f.). In Samos he received embassies from kings of the East,[39] and he received others in Athens, to which he travelled

---

[36] In the SIGNIS RECEPTIS (and variations) issues, *RIC* I², 41, 58, 60, 80–7, 131–7 etc., and MARTI ULTORI (and variations) *id* 68–73, 103–6, etc., and by implication other issues showing the *clupeus virtutis*.

[37] One of Caesar's many breaches of the *mores maiorum*; the post had never been heritable.

[38] Probably in 36, when Lepidus was deposed as triumvir. The offer was made by the People, the traditional electors.

[39] Augustus' reception of these envoys in Samos and Athens (both cities under the jurisdiction of other proconsuls) and establishment of relations of *amicitia* with them expressed the reality of his control of foreign policy. Perhaps the Senate's actions in 23

in 19 to be made an initiate at the Eleusinian mysteries which were held out of season for him — in the spring presumably instead of the usual date in September.[40] He was plainly in no hurry to return to Rome to celebrate a triumph, though his settlement with Parthia in 19 marked the end of an era on the eastern frontier.

19 also marked the end of an era in the political sphere. From the outset of his career Augustus had pushed on with the policy of popular leadership he had inherited from Caesar.[41] He had committed his patrimony and borrowed from friends to pay Caesar's legacies[42] which established him as *patronus* of those who accepted them. He claimed to have fought for Italy both against the 'pirate' Sextus Pompeius who was starving the *plebs* by cutting off the food supplies, and against the Orient represented by Cleopatra and Antonius. The People had responded with honours of all sorts after Naulochus in 36[43] and Actium and the capture of Alexandria in 31 and 30. The two victories were followed by tangible rewards in the shape of buildings for amenity and providing work in the aedileship of Agrippa in 33, his own religious revival and temple building and restoration from 28, and Agrippa's work in and after his joint consulship (28–25); the *plebs* had had a cash bonus after the victory over Egypt (a *congiarium* of 400 sesterces)[44] but it was in 24 and 23 that Augustus had lavished gifts on them most liberally; another *congiarium* in 24 of 400 sesterces per man out of his own estate, twelve distributions of grain in 23, paid for out of his own pocket, and shows at and before the Roman games at which he assisted his son-in-law, C. Marcellus, to make unprecedented benefactions like shade for the Forum throughout the season of intense heat. In the eyes of conservative senators this must have looked like populist unreliability[45] and a deliberate copying of Caesar, which would naturally arouse their dislike and suspicion. The suspicion was confirmed perhaps by Augustus' resignation from the consulship in the middle

---

(n.32 above) showed their unwillingness to act in foreign affairs, but it was entirely contrary to the *mores maiorum*, under which all such alliances had to be ratified by the Senate in Rome. *R.g.* 31 and 32.3 for Augustus' own account.

[40] From 15 Boedromion, H.W. Parke *Festivals of the Athenians* (London 1977) 59.

[41] For a full treatment see Z. Yavetz *Plebs and Princeps* (Oxford 1969) esp. chap. 3.

[42] 300 sesterces per man, *R.g.* 15.1.

[43] Dio 49.15, Yavetz *Plebs* (n.41) 89. It meant the end of civil wars, or so the current propaganda said.

[44] Explicitly from the spoils (*ex manibiis*) *R.g.* 15.1.

[45] Or 'populist lack of principles' (*levitas popularis*); cf. Yavetz *Plebs* (n.41) 51–3. The phrase was a catchword.

of the year and his adoption of a populist stance with the promotion
of his tribune's rights to an important place in his constitutional
position. They were to protect the *plebs* — or so he said.[46] Yet this,
the so-called 'Second Settlement' of 23, did not please either the *plebs*
or the Senate; indeed it seems to have polarised opinion.

The choice of Cn. Calpurnius Piso to succeed Varro Murena as
Augustus' fellow-consul can be interpreted as an assurance that the
consulate could again be available to the noble families after almost a
decade in which only Augustus' *amici* had been allowed to share it
with him.[47] The choice of L. Sestius Albinus to succeed himself,
probably from July 1st, had been favourably received by the
Senators,[48] but the implications of his new status as people's
champion were not well received either inside the Senate or outside it.
On the other hand he knew that there would be opposition if he tried
to hand over the *fasces* at the Temple of *Iuppiter Optimus Maximus* in
Rome; indeed it might be strong enough to stop him; he decided to do
so at the Temple of Jupiter Latiaris at Alba during the Latin Festival.
On the other hand, defending the *plebs* (sc. against the noble families)
aroused ancient and deeply-rooted antagonisms going back perhaps
a hundred years to Tiberius Gracchus' enlistment of the *plebs* to
support his policy-initiatives.[49] The games of Marcellus reminded
Senators of the political debut of Julius Caesar.[50]

Discontent was fanned by events over which neither Augustus nor
the Senate had any control — the weather, which brought an autumn
of floods, a winter of plague and a failure in the city's food supply.
The *plebs* naturally contrasted the twelve distributions of grain in
Augustus' consulate with his successor's and the new consuls' (of 22)
failure to secure sufficient food for the people. The weather and
disease are often seen as 'acts of god', and were easily interpreted as
showing the gods' anger that the *auspicia* were no longer with
Augustus. In their fury the *plebs* threatened the Senators' lives[51] if
they did not restore the *auspicia* to Augustus as perpetual (perhaps

---

[46] See chap. 4 above. The implication that they needed protection (from the Senate
presumably) was unwelcome, if traditional.

[47] For Piso's longstanding opposition to the Caesars, Tac. *Ann.* 2.43.2, and see
chap. 4 above.

[48] Dio 53.32.4. Dio emphasises Sestius' history as an opponent.

[49] Gracchus remained a hero in the propaganda of the 'popular' party, and a
symbol of senatorial oppression. Cf. Yavetz *Plebs* (n.41) 41.

[50] Suet. *Jul.* 10f.; Gelzer *Caesar* (n.25) 37f.

[51] Dio (54.1.3) says they threatened to burn down the Senate House over their
heads.

third) consul or dictator to deal with the food crisis, and the agitation forced Augustus to return to the city.

The Senate's reluctance is understandable; it was galling (to say the least) to have the consulate restored to them and then be asked to institute a magistrate superior to the consuls either in mana (*auctoritas*) or rank. That did not mean that they had to agree to Augustus' takeover of the food supply graciously. As he solved it in a few days — or so he declared in *Res gestae* (5.2) — the suspicion lurks that the shortage may have been politically manipulated, not necessarily by Augustus himself.[52] But there is no evidence.

Dislike of Augustus was apparent throughout the trial of M. Primus which took place at this time, and its aftermath. Primus had alleged instructions from Augustus or Marcellus his son-in-law as an excuse for his aggressions. When Augustus appeared in court to deny these allegations he was spoken to in an insulting manner by Primus' counsel (Dio 54.3.3); a number of jurors gave their votes in such a way that they indicated their opinion that Augustus had lied in court (*ibid.* 4). Those who subsequently voted for the acquittal of Varro Murena and Fannius Caepio when they were charged with plotting to kill Augustus (*ibid.* 6) indicated that they thought the accusations untrue. Can we believe that Maecenas' brother-in-law could have been arraigned without very good evidence? I think not. Fannius Caepio's father's protest against his son's death while in flight was reminiscent of — and surely meant to be reminiscent of — the proscriptions some twenty years previously.[53] Possibly this is why Augustus retaliated by allowing the killing of the 'plotters' to be celebrated as if it were a victory. Since, by Dio's account,[54] Augustus was criticised for failing to stop the celebration, not for promoting it, it was his friends who got the Senate or People to vote for it.

Rumours are signs of disquiet. There were many around at this time, or so Dio alleges. When Agrippa was given a great command in the eastern Mediterranean, described by Josephus (probably

---

[52] Certainly he might have anticipated the grain-shortage, and taken preliminary steps to deal with it, remembering the riots of 40–39, but he could hardly have foreseen the weather and the plague. He might also have foreseen that the *plebs* might not take his resignation lying down. Could he have foreseen the strength of their opposition?

[53] Dio 54.3.7. Fannius manumitted a slave who had stood by his son, but punished one who had not by parading him through the Forum with a placard round his neck and then crucifying him.

[54] 54.3.8. His word is *perieide*; 'to look on without regarding, allow, suffer' LSJ *s.v. perioraō*.

incorrectly) as a ten-year proconsulate of Asia,[55] he was alleged to have been 'banished' from Rome because of enmity with Marcellus, Augustus' son-in-law. This enmity was said to have been caused by Augustus' action in handing his signet-ring to Agrippa when he thought he was on his deathbed earlier in the year. The truth was perhaps otherwise; Maecenas, one of Augustus' most intimate advisers, is said to have told Augustus after Marcellus' death that he had made Agrippa so mighty that he must either make him his son-in-law or kill him (Dio 54.6.4–6); this is odd for a man in a sort of exile.

A second rumour, that Livia had caused Marcellus' death (Dio 53.38.4f.) because he had been promoted above her son Tiberius, seems equally good evidence of ill-will. Tiberius was in fact promoted again in 19, received Agrippa's daughter in marriage, and Drusus his brother was given the same advancement in public life as Tiberius had had.

When Augustus solved the food-crisis in 22 the People's Assembly voted that he should be censor for life (Dio 54.2.1), a vote not recorded by Augustus in *Res gestae*, though the names of the two censors he appointed are attested by the *fasti Colotiani* (E–J p.36). Augustus' response was to nominate two nobles, whose tenure began with an accident[56] — to Roman eyes a mark of the gods' displeasure. Augustus interfered in their work in a number of matters, and the *lustrum* (ceremonial closing of the census) was not completed.

The People's demand for a census is noteworthy; one censorial activity was to revise the Senate's roll, which of course gave an opportunity to remove unsatisfactory members; another (traditionally) was to curb luxury and extravagance and punish with the *nota* (black mark) those guilty of these and other 'immoral' activities. It was of course the rich, especially Senators, whose lifestyle would come under such scrutiny. Popular agitation for Augustus to undertake a census should indicate a wish by the non-Senators for him to come down on the Senators.

Dio (54.2.3f.) records reductions in the extravagance of public feasts, which at a time of food-shortages may have been causing resentment; more significantly however (*ibid.*), he prevented future bids for popular favour by aediles' lavish games and shows, and by

---

[55] See chap. 5.

[56] The platform on which they were to take their seats collapsed. This seems to have destroyed their authority.

exhibitions of gladiators; the annual games in future would be presented by praetors, more senior magistrates funded by the state. Competitive rivalry was forbidden, and gladiatorial shows would in future require a licence from the Senate. He also made dealing with fires the responsibility of the magistrates (aediles), to whom he assigned a labour force of 600 slaves. This may well have been a takeover of the force created by Egnatius Rufus;[57] the takeover may have prompted Egnatius' decision to run for the consulate two years later. (See below.)

Activities of this sort will have kept Augustus in Rome for most of 22; certainly he was there for the dedication of the temple of Jupiter Tonans on the Capitoline Hill on September 1st (Dio 54.4.2; E–J p.51). This temple too caused gossip, and allegations that he was making competition for the state's great temple of *Iuppiter Optimus Maximus* on the summit with cults of his own. It is almost certain that he left the city before the consular elections for 21, since these ended in a stalemate after the election of Augustus' supporter M. Lollius, and Augustus' own refusal to accept nomination (Dio 54.6.2). Riots ensued,[58] and the city was so disturbed that even after Agrippa arrived no *praefectus urbi* could be elected for the Latin Festival. Perhaps without taking the office Agrippa took charge on the strength of his existing prefecture (chap. 5) and managed affairs himself. No trouble is recorded at the consular elections for 20, after which Agrippa left for Spain and his campaign there.

Dio's source for 54.6, esp. 4, has much to say about Augustus' irritation at not being able to leave the Senators to manage the city and political life without him, but he resolutely kept out of sight in the eastern half of the Empire, as noted above. What is most significant about this perhaps is that he toured provinces being governed by proconsuls,[59] and exercised his *imperium*, thus demonstrating that he could and would use his superior authority if he wanted. His actual measures were of minor importance, though some, like the rewards to Sparta for having sheltered Livia when she was a refugee, were reminders that even old favours could be repaid, and others, like the punishment of Athens for favouring Antonius,

---

[57] Vell. 2.91: Egnatius' force was of his own slaves.

[58] Cf. Jones '*Imperium* of Augustus' (n.11) *SRGL* 12 for a summary without names.

[59] Described in older works as 'Senatorial' provinces; more properly 'People's' provinces. So Fergus Millar '"Senatorial" provinces: an institutionalised ghost' *Ancient World* 20 (1989) 93–7.

that choosing the wrong party might not be soon forgotten (Dio 54.7.1–4).

It may be that he was merely filling in time waiting for his diplomatic pressure on the Parthian king to work; he was also probably present in Pergamum while the new temple to Rome and Augustus was close to completion, if not completely finished and dedicated by early 19.[60] He may also have been teaching the Senators the uncomfortable lesson that they had lost the power to manage the *res publica*, and that without the help of Augustus their dreams of a consulate were not likely to come true. This becomes clear if we analyse the consulates between Augustus' resignation and his return to the city in 19.

Under Augustus' supervision, probably in fact on his nomination in 23, two old enemies became *consul suffectus* (replacements); and for 22, when he was present at the election (in 23), the noble Marcellus Aeserninus and the ex-Pompeian L. Arruntius were elected; in 22, when Augustus was not present at the election for 21, a *novus homo* among Augustus' generals was successful,[61] while the *comitia* kept the other place for Augustus (Dio 54.6.1f.). When he declined, riots ensued, neither noble would yield, Augustus refused to nominate either, so that the eventually successful candidate[62] emerged with little credit. Agrippa supervised the election for 20, held in 21; a relative of Augustus' and another military *novus homo* were chosen.[63] In 20, the election for 19 produced the same stalemate as that for 21: a *novus homo* of Augustus' following, C. Sentius Saturninus, was elected; the other place was again kept for Augustus. This time, when Sentius' consulate had begun, Egnatius Rufus offered himself for the vacant place; he had gained a great following by organising a fire brigade and making boastful claims about his preservation of the city; this was perhaps in 26–5, when according to Dio (53.24.4–6) he became praetor. Sentius refused to accept him as a candidate. Riots ensued. Egnatius was arrested and suppressed (Velleius 2.92). The charge was plotting to kill Augustus. The truth probably was that he was threatening to rival Augustus as the

---

[60] By deduction from the coins: silver *cistophori* inscribed COM(MUNE) ASIAE with a hexastyle temple inscribed ROM ET AUGUST (*RIC* I² 505–6 and plate 9) are dated TR PO IV (rare) or TR PO V (common), that is 20–19 or 19–18. These should date the temple to just before Augustus left Asia for Italy in mid-19.

[61] M. Lollius.

[62] Q. Aemilius Lepidus.

[63] M. Appuleius, son of Augustus' half-sister, with P. Silius Nerva.

champion of the *plebs*. But this was of course not mentioned. With the advantage of hindsight Tacitus listed Egnatius as one of the victims of Augustus' "bloodstained peace" (*Ann.* 1.10.4).[64] But are we to think that many Senators disapproved of his suppression? I for one doubt it, especially when the result was that Augustus was willing to nominate as consul a noble, Q. Lucretius Vespillo, when representatives went to Greece to meet him.[65] A noble aspiring to a consulate did not have to be very acute to note that with Augustus he might succeed, without him he would not.

Egnatius was also a symptom of another unpleasant fact; the *plebs* were now not afraid of expressing their opinion, and of rioting at election-time in particular, and the Senate was incapable of stopping them. In riots the *plebs* might get split heads, but it was the rich whose property was endangered. Few Senators perhaps wanted to return to the days when the followers of rival *principes* fought in the streets. *Otium* (peace at home) depended on Augustus. We should not be surprised that they chose peace and promotion in Augustus' *res publica*, as Tacitus says.

In 19 Augustus left Greece and travelled to Italy, where he took up residence in Campania, probably at his villa at Nola. It was midsummer and probably hot, and the 'haste' of Dio (54.10.2 *fin.*) began after his meeting the embassy, to prevent further embarrassing honours. Augustus was in no hurry to get to Rome to triumph.

It has been shown (in chapter 1) how important a man's reception when he returned to the city had always been. Augustus' reception was unprecedented, as he points out in *Res gestae* (12). When the Senate voted to send Lucretius, the consul Augustus had nominated, with praetors, tribunes (to represent the *plebs*) and leading citizens (*principes viri*) on a journey of several days into Campania they were making a statement. It is to be assumed that the envoys had a brief to negotiate with Augustus about the future. A triumph must have been discussed, but there is no trace of it in the literary sources.[66] Instead,

---

[64] Listed with the noble Varro, and the still more noble Iullus Antonius. To Tacitus therefore Augustus was responsible but at the time Sentius might have got the blame; certainly he was not allowed to complete his year as consul. M. Vinicius replaced him as *suffectus* later in the year. But this might have been simply for Vinicius' sake, to qualify him for the high commands he subsequently held, as did Sentius, or as a prelude to a new policy of annual consulates for nobles.

[65] Two men, each with two lictors, not to be confused with the embassy to Campania of *R.g.* 12, so Dio 54.10.2, not as *CAH* X² 90f.

[66] Dio (54.10.3) records "many honours of all sorts" being voted, not explicitly a triumph, but says that Augustus refused all the votes except that of the altar to *Fortuna*

permanent memorials were to be put up: in the Forum his triumphal arch commemorating Actium was to be made a triple arch to commemorate the Parthian victory, and to adorn it panels were to be carved containing the names of consuls and those who had held triumphs ever since Romulus;[67] it was part of Augustus' policy of building up the Romans' pride in their history and those who had made Rome great.

A greater honour perhaps was to have been summoned home by the deputation; this set him on a par with Camillus, described in Livy as *parens patriae conditorque alter urbis* (his country's parent, and second founder of the city), called to return to save the city not from a foreign foe as Camillus had done but from self-destruction. In Livy's account (5.51–4) the programme Camillus put forward is so redolent with Augustus' ideas that it is hard to believe that it is pure coincidence, and the parallel with Camillus fits very well here.[68]

The second monument which Augustus focuses on in his account is the altar to *Fortuna Redux* (Fortune who brings home), to be erected outside the prestigious *Porta Capena*, with an annual festival to celebrate the day of his return, called *Augustalia* after him.[69] It was to be a major one, since not only *Pontifices* but the Vestal Virgins, guardians of Rome's sacred hearth, were to take part. There were other honours too, but we are not given details. Dio records (54.10.4)

Redux, and goes on to add that he returned by night, thus escaping a reception, which receives no note in *R.g.* 12. This means that the *ovatio* of Dio 54.8.3 is an error of Dio's even if it was voted, and not the first grant of *ornamenta triumphalia* proposed in *CAH* X² 90f. Cassiodorus *Chronica* in 19 mentions 'a golden crown and a chariot'; the latter has been identified (C.H.V. Sutherland *Roman History and Coinage 44 B.C.–A.D. 69* (Oxford and New York 1987) 16) in the 'empty triumphal chariot' coins (*RIC* I² 114ff.) dedicated to Augustus by the *SPQR*. They show a tetrastyle domed temple like that on some of the MARTI ULTORI issues (*RIC* I² 68 etc.). This temple was built on the Capitol by Augustus' order perhaps to emulate that of Jupiter Feretrius (Dio 54.8.3), where traditionally Romulus' *spolia opima* were housed. The message of the juxtaposition can hardly have been unintended. Cf. Zanker *Images* 186f.

[67] Cf. Wallace-Hadrill *Augustan Rome* (n.1) 18. For the triple arch *RIC* I² 131 (an *aureus* of *ca* 18–17), photo plate 3. This coin adds that citizens were also recovered.

[68] R.M. Ogilvie *A Commentary on Livy I–V* (Oxford 1965) 4 places book 5 before Timagenes' quarrel with Augustus, book 9 after it; the quarrel took place probably in or before 25.

[69] October 12th, E–J p.53. The name is variously reported: *ludi Augustales* according to the textual tradition of Tacitus (*Ann.* 1.15 and 54) and the calendar of Philocalus (E–J p.53); the day and the festival are called *Augustalia* in *R.g.* 11.2 (Greek text) and Dio 54.34.2. The altar was dedicated on December 15th (E–J p.54). It is rather unusual for the celebration to be held on a day other than that of the dedication. The *fasti* from Cumae actually note a thanksgiving (*supplicatio*) in December (E–J *loc. cit.*).

that Augustus actually arrived at night to escape a formal reception, though Suetonius[70] says he usually travelled by night when he could, to avoid the heat of the day. The promotions of his stepsons took place the next day (Dio *loc. cit.*). Our sources do not say what the *plebs* received, if anything; a cash distribution (*congiarium*) would surely have received notice. They may have been content with no more than a festival to enjoy, and the assurance that their champion was back in Rome.[71] There may have been promises about their food supply, since Augustus records (*R.g.* 18) that he undertook to supplement it on a regular basis the next year (18).

Whether Augustus' *imperium* was in fact now altered in any way is not to my mind very material; on the whole Brunt's explanation[72] seems to me the most satisfactory — that is, that the right to have twelve, that is consular, *fasces* carried before him in the city and a curule chair between the consuls in the Senate House were the outward and visible symbols of the fact that the *imperium* Augustus had (and had had from 23) was actually consular, or to be more exact equal to that of the consuls. To some perhaps this was an admission of something they had not understood, or had not wanted to understand, or even did not believe they had done when they voted him *imperium* not limited in time or area in 23, but now had to accept in the interest of satisfying the *plebs* and maintaining order in the city. To others it may merely have confirmed what they had always thought they had done, and they were glad now to see it made explicit and no longer a question of dispute and interpretation.

It may also be worth asking what, if anything, the Senators got in return. It may be no mere coincidence that the names of noble families now appear on the consular *fasti* with some regularity, and that tenures are now for the full twelve months except in the case of deaths. This may well be their gain from the negotiations. Augustus had perhaps a sufficient supply of ex-consuls not of noble birth to fill the posts in his provinces and command armies as *legati* and was able to allow the noble families to satisfy their honour. It would explain

[70] *Aug.* 82.

[71] Dio 54.10.5 comments on the difference in their behaviour when Augustus was in Rome and when he was not, although he attributes their quietness to fear — or perhaps awe; the verb is *phoboumenoi*. Yet the contrast between this return, when the *plebs* received nothing tangible, and the returns from victories in 29 and 24, is very striking. There seems no ready explanation, unless there was a feeling that his cultivation of the *plebs* had gone far enough.

[72] P.A. Brunt 'Roman constitutional problems' *CR* 12 (1962) 70–73.

the substantial measure of co-operation Augustus won for almost fifteen years, which Tacitus scornfully expressed as "led ... nobles to promotion to wealth and offices in proportion to their readiness to serve", and made them "prefer the safety of the new order to the dangers of the old" (*Ann.* 1.2.1).[73]

This welcome from the Senate was the springboard from which Augustus launched his crusade for a new society. Declining the post of supreme curator of morals in 19 and again in 18, he initiated a new revision of the Senate's roll at which he attempted to persuade the Senate to purge their own "unworthy" (unreliable?) members, proposed the Julian Laws on adultery and parenthood, had the provinces he had been allocated renewed, and brought forward the hitherto little recognised *tribunicia potestas* as a sort of magistracy with numbered tenures, and used it as a means for proposing legislation.

19 has also been identified by some numismatists as the year in which the new range of base metal coins with the legends AUGUSTUS, TRIBUNICIA POTESTAS, and OB CIVES SERVATOS began to be minted.[74] The moment would certainly be as appropriate as 23 for this.

In the whole context of 19, Augustus' return home and the altar and festival of *Fortuna Redux* with its sacrifices and annual commemoration has a strong claim to mark the beginning of the Principate in the terms in which it was defined at the start of this chapter,[75] since it marks the moment when Augustus successfully came to terms with the nobles of the Senate. Certainly his position was never the same again, as he now felt strong enough to remain in Rome for over two years. By the time he set out again for his provinces in the West he had acquired by adoption two sons to inherit the name and the fortune of the house of the Caesars; and the opening of a new era had been celebrated in the Secular Games and the mission of Rome in Virgil's *Aeneid*, published posthumously in 19. By then, 16, the Principate was well under way, and equality of

---

[73] *cum ... (ceteri nobilium) quanto quis servitio promptior opibus et honoribus extollerentur, ac ... tuta et praesentia quam vetera et periculosa mallent.* "Readiness to serve" translates the strong word *servitio*, which could be rendered "a life of slavery", except that the Romans knew what slavery really meant, and Tacitus knew that the nobles lost their independence, not their liberty. Even the most resentful noble knew he was not a slave.

[74] The coins are listed in nn.43–45 to chap. 4, bibliography in n.7 to chap. 7.

[75] Cf. A.H.M. Jones *Augustus* (2nd edn London 1970), whose chapter 5 'The Principate' begins in 19.

standing (*aequalitas* as Tacitus put it) was certainly a thing of the past. And the Senate's acceptance of the destruction of that equality can be laid at the door of those who voted for that embassy to Campania in 19.

Perhaps the whole episode of Augustus' return in 19 suggests that one of the reasons for his success was that he deliberately avoided the clearcut and explicit and preferred cautiously to allow political developments to occur, exploiting those which turned out to his advantage. If this be so, dating the beginning of the Principate to the formulating of its formal institutions is neat, but mistaken. The Principate began when it was recognised as such. On the date this occurred opinions will differ, but the Senate collectively recognized it in 19.

CHAPTER 7

TRIBUNICIA POTESTAS:
THE PATH TO *SUMMI FASTIGII VOCABULUM**

Tacitus (*Ann.* 3.56) described tribunician power (*tribunicia potestas, trib. pot.* hereafter) as the title of the highest pinnacle (sc. of power) in the Roman world (*summi fastigii vocabulum*), and Augustus counted his years of *trib. pot.* from 23. So much may be stated with confidence and without dispute. In 23 however *trib. pot.* was introduced quietly, so quietly that the exact date of the law by which it was conferred (if it was conferred in 23) is unknown;[1] and the title itself made so little impact on contemporary opinion that the reaction of the common people of Rome, for whose protection according to Tacitus Augustus said he took the power,[2] was negative — so negative that they spent

---

* This study originally appeared in *JRS* 69 (1979) 28–34 under the title '*Summi fastigii vocabulum*: the story of a title'. Research published since that date, particularly on the coinage, and the publication of C.H.V. Sutherland *Roman Imperial Coinage* Vol. I (2nd edn London 1984) (abbreviated as *RIC* I²), *id. Roman History and Coinage* (n.4 below), and R.A.G. Carson *Coins of the Roman Empire* (n.1 below), have caused me to revise my previous conclusions about the evidence of the coins for the early days of *trib. pot.*

[1] In *Res gestae* Augustus insisted that *trib. pot.* was bestowed on him by law (10.1). Th. Mommsen *Römisches Staatsrecht* (1887) II.2 747 n.3 selected 26 June as the commencement date; G.E.F. Chilver 'Augustus and the Roman constitution 1939–1950' *Historia* 1 (1950) 411 and 433f. and Syme *Rom. Rev.* (1939) 336 selected July 1st. Other scholars, H. Stuart Jones in *CAH* X 140, H.H. Scullard *From the Gracchi to Nero* (3rd edn London 1970) 221, A.H.M. Jones *SRGL* 9f. and *Augustus* (2nd edn London 1970) 55, E.T. Salmon 'The evolution of Augustus' principate' *Historia* 5 (1956) 456–78, and many more, evade the issue by silence or by phrases like 'half way through the year'. C.H.V. Sutherland, N. Olçay and K.E. Merrington *The Cistophori of Augustus* (London 1970) (= *Cistophori*) 34–6 have recently supported Mommsen. Since 1979 Sutherland in *RIC* I² p.21 and Andrew Wallace-Hadrill *Augustan Rome* (Bristol 1993) 34, have described *trib. pot.* as 'accepted' or 'invented'. A few scholars, e.g. M.P. Charlesworth, *The Roman Empire* (Oxford 1951) 8f., M. Grant *From Imperium to Auctoritas* (Cambridge 1946) 449f., and R.A.G. Carson *Coins of the Roman Empire* (London and New York 1990) (= *CRE*) 1 carefully avoid saying that *trib. pot.* was conferred in 23. In chap. 4 above it is argued that they are right.

[2] *Ad tuendam plebem* Tac. *Ann.* 1.2. For the negative reaction Jones *SRGL* 12 and chap. 6 above.

much of the next five years trying to re-elect Augustus to the consulate which he had resigned at or about the time that the era of *trib. pot.* began. We must conclude that the conferment of *trib. pot.* (if there was any ceremony at all in 23) was not made the subject of a great celebration designed to win popular acclaim for this new institution (if it was a new one), nor was it immediately advertised widely as a new formula for the government of the Roman world.

Coins are generally held to be an important, if not the most important, medium for the self-representation the issuers wished to disseminate to the people at large — at least of those still available to us; *graffiti* on walls, in the Roman world not the preserve of the illiterate and the vandal, are all lost even when official. Coin design appears to have been a special concern of Augustus as a means of putting over what his government wanted people to think. His own new name, for example, had immediately supplemented or supplanted in whole or in part IMP CAESAR or CAESAR DIVI F which had been his previous designation on the coins.[3] In 23, however, *trib. pot.* seems to have been used at once only in Spain, and only on the *aes* (base metal) coinage[4] issued by P. Carisius who had succeeded Augustus in command there. Augustus' head appears on the obverse, and Carisius is styled '*legatus* of Augustus' on the reverse (*RIC* I[2] 11–25). The contemporary gold and silver coins style Carisius *legatus pro praetore* (lieutenant general in praetor's rank) (variously abbreviated), without any mention of *trib. pot.* on the reverse; the obverse is Augustus' head and the legend IMP CAESAR AUGUST(US). It is assumed that these were to pay the troops, and provide currency for the new colony at Emerita.

---

[3] E.g. *RIC* I[2] 277, AUGUSTUS on the reverse of CAESAR COS VII CIVIBUS SERVATEIS, dated explicitly to 27. Cf. the undated *cistophori, id.* 487–94, attributed by Sutherland to 27–6, and 477–9, dated more tentatively to 25.

[4] *Aes* coinage is the expression customarily used to describe the token base metal coinage (silver *denarii* and gold *aurei* were both worth their weight as bullion). The values were inherited from the 'Republic': the copper *as* was the basic unit, *dupondii* (2 *asses*) and *sestertii* (4 *asses*) were minted in an alloy known as orichalcum which differs in colour, being paler. The *quadrans* or quarter *as* was a copper coin. For a very clear account, Carson *CRE* (n.1) 5; cf. C.H.V. Sutherland *Roman History and Coinage 44 B.C.–A.D. 69* (Oxford and New York 1987) (= *RHC*) table facing p.xii. The *aes* coinage also differed from the gold and silver in that the designs were unchanging, as was natural for a coinage designed to meet the needs of small change in a largely illiterate society. Some features indeed — the presence of a portrait on the *asses*, but not on any other value, for example — carried on the 'Republican' conventions: C.H.V. Sutherland *The Emperor and the Coinage* (London 1976) 12 and *RIC* I[2] 12f. The gold and silver coins however offer a wide range of design and legend illustrating contemporary issues for the troops and the more influential classes.

It used to be generally believed that the gold and silver coinage enjoyed wide circulation in the Roman world (certainly it was legal tender everywhere)[5] whereas *aes* coinage circulated only locally, but C.H.V. Sutherland in *RIC* I[2] has identified five imperial mints besides Rome whose *aes* coinage circulated widely.[6] These do not include the mint of Emerita, which produced Carisius' coins, so it is probably true to say that the introduction of *trib. pot.* on *aes* coins there does not suggest a wish to advertise the new title widely in the Roman world, let alone in the city of Rome itself for the use of the *plebs*.

The date at which the Augustan *aes* coinage was first issued from the mint in Rome has been disputed among historians and numismatists. Opinion has been divided between 23 and about 19;[7] the evidence on which a choice should be made is clearly set out in *RIC* I[2] pp.31–34 and it is not conclusive, though recent opinion among numismatists writing in English has moved to support the later date. Historians who think that Augustus must have spread the news of *trib. pot.* when it was first used naturally prefer 23,[8] but if this is so, the publicity was a failure (see chap. 6 above, for example), since the *plebs* were interested only in Augustus being elected or appointed to offices carrying the traditional power of *imperium*. It can also be argued that between 23 and 19 Augustus had very little time for a publicity campaign. Moreover, in 23–2 he was showing his interest in the *plebs* by other means, including the Roman games he financed for

---

[5] Sutherland *RHC* (n.4) 30, citing Epictetus *Dissert.* 3.3.3.

[6] *RIC* I[2] p.5f.: Lugdunum and Nemausus in Gaul, Ephesus and Pergamum in Asia, Antioch in Syria. Cf. Carson *loc. cit.* (n.4).

[7] Mattingly *BMCRE* i, xcivf. argued for 23, supported by A.M. Burnett 'The authority to coin' *Num. Chron.* 137 (1977) 46–52, E–J 19, Clive Foss *Roman Historical Coins* (London 1990) 47. K. Kraft 'Zur Datierung der römischen Münzmeisterprägung unter Augustus' *Mainzer Zeitschrift* 46/7 (1951/2) 28–35 argued for 19, supported by A. Bay 'The letters SC on Augustan *aes* coinage' *JRS* 62 (1972) 111–122, and most recent numismatists who write in English, Carson *CRE* (n.1) 6, J.P.C. Kent *Roman Coins* (London 1978) 19, Sutherland *RHC* (n.4) 34 but *id. Emperor* (n.4) 12 proposed *ca* 23 for *aes* coins, *ca* 19 for gold and silver. New arguments in support of 23 in A. Wallace-Hadrill 'Image and authority in the coinage of Augustus' *JRS* 76 (1986) 66–87.

[8] And it is natural, perhaps, to suppose that one reason for Augustus to change the management of the treasury from *praefecti* (who were nominated officials, not necessarily senators) to praetors, who were elected, and senators of some seniority, in 23 (Dio 53.32.2) was to begin the production of a new coinage bearing the names of the senatorial *iiiviri a a a f f* (see next para.). But a plan to start coining in 23 need not have been fulfilled; unexpected events like Augustus' illness and later the appalling autumn weather, plague and the crisis in the food supply could easily have upset calculations, and the relations between Augustus and the Senate. See chap. 6 above.

Marcellus, taking control of the city's food supply, and measures he took in association with the censorship of Munatius Plancus and Paulus Aemilius Lepidus. Besides, he was not on good terms with the Senate for much of the time (chap. 6 above), and was not in Rome at all after the opening of the temple of Jupiter Tonans, but in the eastern provinces, negotiating for the return of the standards lost by M. Crassus and M. Antonius, planning the neutralising of Armenia as a client kingdom, and attending to the problems of the southern border of Syria, with its wild tribes and the ambitions of the Jewish king Herod, whom he found a useful agent for patrolling some of the wilder districts.[9] He (Augustus) was also inaugurating the temple to Rome and Augustus in Pergamum for the *Commune Asiae* (League of cities of Asia), which was commemorated on coins (*RIC* I² 505–6, the latter an abundant issue).

The year 19 also seems appropriate because the Rome mint coinage represents a meeting of interests between Augustus and the Senate. The issues are dated by the names of the Senatorial moneyers (*iiiviri monetales* or *a a a f f (auro argento aere flando feriundo)*) and include SC as the major feature of their design on many. The meaning of SC has also been much debated, but the view of Sutherland,[10] that the bullion for striking the coins was issued from the Treasury on the authority of the Senate with the approval and perhaps on the prompting or proposal of Augustus himself, seems to me most satisfactory, not merely because it reflects the mood of compromise prevailing in 19, but also because the letters SC disappear from the gold and silver coinage after very few years, when the imperial mint moved to Lugdunum in Gaul where the Senate had no say in the management of the supply of bullion. This coheres with the general process of encroachment which Tacitus saw.

Yet even on this *aes* coinage *trib. pot.* is far from the only, even the dominant, theme. Much greater prominence is in fact given to the oak wreath voted to Augustus in 27 for saving the citizens' lives. The legend OB CIVES SERVATOS, often abbreviated, is the principal design of the *sestertii* from the same year that TRIBUNIC POTEST becomes the major feature of the *dupondii*. Moreover, this theme, unlike *trib. pot.*, is also used (as OB CS or OCS) — and in an oak

---

[9] A.H.M. Jones *The Herods of Judaea* (Oxford 1967) 62–71.
[10] Sutherland *RHC* (n.4) 35–38 with refs, *id. Emperor* (n.4) 11–22 for a more extended discussion of the various views.

wreath — on gold issues (*aurei*).[11] The oak wreath encircles Augustus' head on a number of other designs, all of *aurei*.[12] *Trib. pot.* does not appear on *aurei*.

Trib. pot. became a chronographic instrument, and years began to be numbered by Augustus' years of *trib. pot.* in the same way as the Hellenistic monarchs had numbered the years of their rule.[13] This tradition may have been why Augustus was slow to start the numeration of the years of his *trib. pot.* in Rome, but it became so well accepted (and indeed was so much more convenient than numbering the years by the frequently rather ephemeral consuls of the year) that in AD 22 (Tac. *Ann.* 3.57) it was proposed that the year of *trib. pot.* become the official title for a year. Tiberius' traditionalist and conservative preferences made him reject the proposal, despite the fact that by then imperial communications with the provinces, *civitates* and other bodies were normally dated by *trib. pot.* (see further below).

Numbering years of *trib. pot.* began in Asia, where the *Commune Asiae* needed an era following their reorganisation as a League for the worship of Roma and Augustus.[14] Silver coins of a traditional weight (the so-called *cistophori*, tetradrachms valued at 3 *denarii*), were issued with Augustus' head on the obverse and IMP IX TR PO IV or V (20–19 and 19–18 respectively). The reverse sides celebrate the new temple (*RIC* I² 505–6), and Augustus' Parthian victory, either in the small temple of Mars Ultor on the Capitol[15] (*id.* 507) or

---

[11] Examples include *RIC* I² 278, 312, dedicated to Augustus (AUGUSTO), the obverse heads being of Liber and Honos respectively, 285 (including also laurel branches).

[12] Oak-wreathed heads on *RIC* I² 293, 298, 308, 316, 409, 411, all *aurei*, legend CAESAR AUGUSTUS.

[13] A.S. Hunt and C.C. Edgar *Select Papyri* II (LCL 1956) no. 327 (= Pap. Oxy. 1453) for a new era, "the first year of Caesar" as following the "22nd and 7th year" sc. of Cleopatra. It began on 1 Thoth (August 30th) 30. Cf. E–J 116, 118.

[14] The old provincial era had petered out with the start of the civil wars in 49 (*CIL* I², p.762f.), D. Magie *Roman Rule in Asia Minor* (Princeton 1950) 257f., 1131 n.63. The various communities had a multiplicity of eras, *id.* index *s.v.* eras, but the *Commune Asiae* proud of its new temple needed one. Hence most exceptionally the issue of coins dated both by years of *trib. pot.* and by salutations as *Imperator* (IMP IX) to serve the army and wealthy traders.

[15] Zanker *Images* 186–7; Mars Ultor was a little domed temple right next to Jupiter Feretrius and Jupiter Tonans, of which Augustus had restored the one and built the other: "In the temple of Jupiter Feretrius stood the *spolia opima* of Romulus and Marcellus, which now received competition in the recaptured standards. The significance of all this was well understood" (*id.* 187). L. Richardson *A New Topographical Dictionary of Ancient Rome* (Baltimore 1992) 245 has doubted its existence, arguing that Horace *Carm.* 4.15 meant Jupiter Capitolinus not Rome in the

in the triumphal arch SPR SIGNIS RECEPTIS (*id.* 508–10). TR PO V with COM ASIAE or MART ULTO are copious issues, classed by *RIC* as 'Common'. The TR PO IV coins are however much less common, there being none at all with the MART ULTO reverse; this should indicate a date at the end of the *trib. pot.* IV year (20 – June 19) for the start of the series.[16] The series resumes, probably the next year, with a variety of types commemorating the recovery of the standards and the occupation of Armenia (*RIC* I² 511–526). But *trib. pot.* years are not repeated. This may suggest that these coins were minted for those interested in neither Augustus' powers to serve the *plebs* nor the temple in Pergamum — the troops in the East.

With this in mind, we may ask 'which was the more important, the IMP IX, taken for the Parthian success, or TR PO?' We may think the TR PO because we know what happened later, but for the army the salutation they helped to win, and perhaps acclaimed in person, is likely to have appealed more. We may add that one of the Armenia coins (albeit a rare one) includes IMP VIIII (*RIC* I² 518).

On Rome mint issues, *trib. pot.* became a chronographic feature only very briefly on the gold and silver coins of Mescinius, Vinicius and Antistius in 16 (who appear to have coined no *aes*); they include *trib. pot.* VII (17–16) and VIII or IIX (16–15) on a number of very elaborate designs commemorating the Secular games (*RIC* I² 350, 354–5), vows for Augustus' safe return (*id.* 351–3, 356), money for road-building (*id.* 360) and vows for Augustus' health (*id.* 369), the last a gold coin. In these examples gold and silver coins with the *trib. pot.* legend do not seem to have the primary intention of serving the needs of the petty traders of the capital, or indeed the *plebs*.

In the previous year coins dated *trib. pot.* VI (*aurei*) were minted in Spain in the last year before the western mint moved to Lugdunum in Gaul; the reverse themes are various, but the dated *trib. pot.* coins all have military successes (the return of the standards etc.) commemorated. They were presumably minted to pay troops.

---

words *Iovi* ... *nostro*. But see further below chap. 9, and R. Hannah (Otago University) 'The temple of Mars Ultor on the Capitol in Rome' (paper as yet unpublished which I have been privileged to see).

[16] K.E. Merrington *Cistophori* (n.1) 76–84 reports 41 triumphal arch coins, two with TR PO IV, 67 ROMA ET AUGUSTUS coins, four with TR PO IV, 59 Mars Ultor temple, none with TR PO IV. Sutherland *op. cit.* 36 comments on the "not very successful TR PO IV style" compared with the "initially brilliant large head TR PO V style". Note also the lack of consistency in abbreviating *trib. pot.* (TR PO on the obverse, but TR POT on some triumphal arch coins, also the aberrant SPR for SPQR; *RIC* I² 508–510 etc.).

The slow emergence of numbered tenures of *trib. pot.* is equally evident from the inscriptions. Dessau (*ILS*) records two in which the omission of *trib. pot.* is most surprising if it was always Augustus' intention to use 23 as the start of an era. The first is on the inscription put up by L. Appuleius (*cos.* 20) at Tridentum on Augustus' orders. It must be dated between 23 and 20 since Appuleius does not designate himself 'consul' — or even 'consul designate' — only '*legatus* of Augustus' (like Carisius in Spain), and fails to mention the number of years of the latter's *trib. pot.*[17] The second is even more surprising, since it is a very important document for the locality, and must also be dated between 23 and 20. On it the first colonists at Aosta (Augusta Praetoria) speak of Augustus as COS. XI, IMP. VI . . (with a break of not more than two letters), TRIBUNIC. POT ... Augustus became Imp. VIIII in 20 on the occasion of the Parthian 'victory'.[18]

No number appears on the consular *fasti Capitolini* (*CIL* I² p.28) for 22, a year in which Augustus' *trib. pot.* is entered below the names of the consuls; but since on no occasion is the first year of *trib. pot.* entered as *trib. pot. I* for any other emperor (just as *cos I* is never used for consuls), this is not significant. The names of the consuls are recorded for 21, so that if *trib. pot.* was recorded for that year, it followed their names and did not precede them. The stone is broken off after the consuls' names, so whether or not *trib. pot.* was ever numbered is not known.

Trib. pot. first appears to be brought into active use in the context of the social legislation of 18. In *Res gestae* 6 Augustus claimed that the laws he then passed by his *trib. pot.* were in response to public demand (though they were resisted) and to counter proposals that he should become *curator legum et morum summa potestate solus* (sole guardian of laws and manners with supreme power).[19] We may believe, if we wish, that Augustus encouraged his friends in this agitation, but it is a fact that the steps which Augustus took in the *leges Iuliae* of 18 had the result (whether intended or not, and it is hard to believe that the result was not intended) of curbing the ability of the rich to dispose of their property with complete freedom and to

---

[17] *ILS* 86 (= E–J 58). If it were the first year of *trib. pot.* we should not expect a numbered tenure.

[18] *ILS* 6753 (= E–J 338). Cf. T.D. Barnes 'The victories of Augustus' *JRS* 64 (1974) 21f. with refs.

[19] *R.g.* 6; the Latin text is missing, but the Greek version is certain, lacking no more than a letter or two. Suet. *Aug.* 34 for the resistance.

enjoy the advantages of their position without assuming some of the responsibilities of public life (which in ancient thought always included the procreation of children both to maintain the religious cults of the families and to keep up the man-power needed by the state to sustain its activities).

Was it because such legislation was inappropriate for a consul that Augustus acted through his *trib. pot.* at this period rather than arranging for the consuls to introduce the measures through the Senate? Or was it to demonstrate (especially to his supporters) that his *trib. pot.* was not just an empty title, but that it could be used to curb the ostentation and extravagance of the rich, which can scarcely have failed to give offence to the impoverished masses of the *plebs*?[20] Here perhaps is a glimpse of the People's protector.

This year (18) was also important in the evolution of *trib. pot.,* for Augustus got the Senate to grant it to Agrippa who was now Augustus' son-in-law and father of his only grandchild, Gaius Caesar. As is well known, Agrippa's *trib. pot.* differed from that of Augustus in two important ways: it was bestowed by the Senate[21] and not by a law of the People, and it was not annual and perpetual but for five years only. This senatorial grant made *trib. pot.* look much more closely comparable to the normal magistracies, for which a collegiate tenure and a specified duration were normal. Consequently, numeration of tenures as for an iterated magistracy would appear quite normal,[22] and less like the monarchical appearance of years of rule Augustus might have wanted to avoid previously.

Dio remarked in a generalizing passage (53.17.9) that holders of *trib. pot.* were to be free from any kind of insult whatsoever. The only explicitly recorded use of *trib. pot.* for self-defence in a context of this kind is Tiberius' punishment of a man who abused him while he was in Rhodes (Suet. *Tib.* 11.3). Tiberius' conservative attitude however

---

[20] Z. Yavetz *Plebs and Princeps* (Oxford 1969) 53f. *et alibi.* Compare their demand for a censorship in 22 (chap. 4 above).

[21] *Res gestae* 6.2; cf. the fragment of Augustus' funeral laudation for Agrippa, *P. Colon.* 4701 (L. Koenen 'Die "laudatio funebris" des Augustus für Agrippa auf einem neuen Papyrus' *ZPE* 5 (1970) 217–83, discussed in chap. 5 above).

[22] But this must not make us call *trib. pot.* a magistracy; Augustus does not (*R.g.* 6.2), he calls it a *potestas* (power). Magistracies were obtained by vote of the People; except for Augustus' own, all grants of *trib. pot.* were made by the Senate, and under Augustus at least there is no evidence that the grants were confirmed by a vote of the *comitia.* For numeration, compare the priesthoods; these were important and brought prestige, but as they were appointments for life, with tenures not iterated or renewed, never do holders of priesthoods of any sort enumerate their years of office.

makes it unlikely that he had no precedent. It may be that either accusations of plotting mentioned by Dio in 18 (54.15.1–3) or the abuse which formed the chief charge against Aemilius Aelianus of Cordoba, who "vilified Caesar" in a period described by Suetonius as in Tiberius' youth (*Aug.* 51) came under this heading.[23] When did Tiberius' youth end? Certainly, it might be supposed, before he became consul (13) or Augustus' son-in-law (11). The episode therefore should belong to 22, or to the period 19–16, which were the only periods after 23 when Augustus was in Rome before he went abroad again to Gaul in 16; perhaps most probably to 18 when Augustus was introducing his controversial social legislation.

In 17 Augustus and Agrippa jointly celebrated the Secular Games as *magistri collegii XV virorum sacrorum faciendorum* (chief officers of the College of Fifteen responsible for sacrifices). In the *senatus consultum* decreeing who might attend the games they are described as *tribunicia potestate* (no number given), but throughout the *acta* (minutes) this title is omitted (as are all others).[24] In this year Agrippa's second son was born, and Augustus adopted both boys as C. and L. Caesar, an event commemorated on *denarii*, possibly of 13, the year when Agrippa's *trib. pot.* was renewed and Augustus made his next triumphant return to the city.[25] But *trib. pot.* is not explicitly mentioned in these contexts.

Inscriptions with numbered tenures of *trib. pot.* begin to appear on milestones in Italy from 17–16. Two on *via Appia* are dated TRIB. POT. VII, two on *via Salaria* TRIB. POT. VIII; the repairs were undertaken EX SC and should be connected with the coins of L. Vinicius.[26]

---

[23] If there were condemnations they escaped the notice of Tacitus, both in *Ann.* 1.10.4 (Augustus' "bloodstained peace") and in *Ann.* 1.72.2f. (his sketch on the history of *maiestas* (treason) trials).

[24] Texts E–J 30–2; Dessau *ILS* 5050 for the *acta* (minutes).

[25] *RIC* I² 404–5 (rare); though two of the moneyers exhibit portraits of Agrippa there is no mention of his *trib. pot.* on any coins, but all are either *denarii* or *aurei. R.g.* 12.2 for Augustus' return on this occasion; cf. E–J 36, no mention of *trib. pot.* See also chap. 1 above for his return.

[26] *CIL* IX 5986 and 5989 (= X 6914 and 6917) from *via Appia, CIL* IX 5943 and 5950 (= *ILS* 5815) from *via Salaria* (cf. *id.* 5954 from *via Salaria, trib. pot.* XII), *CIL* X 6903 and 6904, *cos* XI and *cos* XIII, *trib. pot.* unnumbered, *via Latina* (the end of 6904 is broken). For the coins, *RIC* I² 360–2, dated TR POT VII and VIII and without *trib. pot.* The reverse legend is SPQR/IMP CAE/QUOD V/M S EX/EA P Q IS/AD A DE in 6 lines, read by Sutherland (*loc. cit.*) as *quod viae munitae sunt ex ea pecunia quam is ad aerarium detulit* (the Senate and Roman People (to) Imperator Caesar because roads were built with the money he paid into the treasury). Cf. the contemporary Spanish *aurei* and *denarii, RIC* I² 140–4.

When Agrippa died and Tiberius was elevated first to the position of Julia's husband, then to a triumph and a second consulate (7) and to a five-year tenure of *trib. pot.* (6), though there seems no special commemoration on the coinage it seemed that this was intended to be the title of the intended guardian of the heritage of the Caesars, and this impression was perhaps confirmed when Tiberius' *trib. pot.* was not renewed when he retired to Rhodes, and Augustus started to promote the claims and careers of his 'sons', who had the title of *principes iuventutis* (leaders of the officer-cadets) instead.

However, executive action was now being regularly dated by years of *trib. pot.*, as on the Cyrene edicts (7–6 and 4) and the letter to Cnidos of 6.[27] Although not everyone used *trib. pot.* dates in their correspondence, this period probably saw the beginning of what became standard practice for letters from the Emperor.[28] But, with the exception of the *quinarii* (see below), the coins do not mention numbered tenures of *trib. pot.* at all. The Lugdunum *aurei* and *denarii* (gold and silver) use Augustus' imperatorial salutations until the start of the very large promotional (and perhaps later commemorative) issues for Gaius and Lucius Caesar, *consules designati principes iuventutis* (consuls designate, leaders of the cadets).[29] The 'altar' series *aes* entitle Augustus CAESAR PONT MAX on the obverse until 2, when the legend changes to DIVI F PATER PATRIAE.[30] *Aes* from the Roman mint consisted of bronze *quadrantes* only without either portrait or titles of Augustus from *ca* 9–8 till it closed, apparently, for a time, except for the exceptional 'Victory' *aes* coins dated by Mattingly to 7 and two groups of *asses* modelled on them. The heavy 'Victory' *aes* consists of pieces with Augustus' head laureate (unparalleled on Roman *aes*) and the legend PONT MAX TRIB POT unnumbered (also unparalleled). This legend is retained on *asses* of a more normal weight with the normal bare head of Augustus issued by the 'Victory' *aes* moneyers and one other college, usually assumed to be their successors. The large coins should probably be classed as medallions or pseudo-medallions, but

[27] E–J 311, 312, and perhaps 314.
[28] But not for *senatus consulta*: e.g. E–J 278 (the aqueducts), 311.5 (Cyrene edicts). Proconsuls also used their own names and titles, E–J 313; cf. Germanicus' edicts, E–J 320. The consular date for 1 appears at Nysa ad Maeandrum in Asia, E–J 316, an era dated from 6/5 in the oath of the Paphlagonians of 3, E–J 315; for the Egyptian era under Augustus n.13 above.
[29] Augustus is DIVI F IMP X, XI, XII, or XIIII; hence 15–8. For C. Caesar, *RIC* I[2] 198f., C. and L. Caesar *id.* 205–212.
[30] The reverse is the altar to Rome and Augustus ROM ET AUG *RIC* I[2] 229–233.

there is no real explanation for this sudden issue of *asses* with *trib. pot.* (unnumbered) linked to *pont. max.*[31] The only historical event which may be relevant seems to be Tiberius' triumph and the conferment of *trib. pot.* on him in 6, but it is hard to see any explicit reference to him on the coins themselves.[32]

Trib. pot. (and numbered) appears otherwise only on the tiny gold *quinarii* of which a series runs from IMP XII and TRIB POT XIII (11–10) to XXXI (AD 8–9) with a largish gap between 7–6 (TRIB POT XVII) and AD 1–2 (TRIB POT XXIIII) (*RIC* I² pp.53–6). The rarity of these pieces may suggest that these too were were not normal currency, but were for gifts, produced in small quantities for selected officials in the administration, and recording Augustus' regnal years for commemorative purposes.[33] But with the switch from IMP XII to TRIB POT XIII, the chronographic use of *trib. pot.* has become very clear, as it also is on the *fasti consulares*, of which two large surviving fragments show Augustus' TRIB. POT. XXIIII as a preface to the names of the consuls for the year,[34] and thereafter annually. And *trib. pot.* was not used for the next round of social legislation; all the later social laws bear the names of the consuls who introduced them into the Senate.[35]

The promotion of Augustus' 'sons' and Tiberius' withdrawal to Rhodes had thrown *trib. pot.* into the shade except as a chronographic instrument, but after AD 4 when succession through

[31] *RIC* I² 426, 429, 433 etc., footnote to p.75. For the criteria for pseudo-medallions, J.M.C. Toynbee *Roman Medallions* (New York 1944) 24f. Cf. chap. 1 above for Tiberius' triumph in 7.

[32] The lack of a portrait of Tiberius on the coins may be due to his dislike of such distinctions, B. Levick *Tiberius the Politician* (London 1976) 38.

[33] M. von Bahrfeldt *Die römische Goldmünzenprägung während der Republik und unter Augustus* (Halle 1923) 160f. splits the coins into two groups: (i) the earliest two issues, with Augustus' head bare and with the Victory on the reverse with her hands either buried in or holding a fold of her dress, and with the legend IMP XII or TRIB POT XIII, and (ii) the later issues with Augustus' head wreathed, and the Victory on the reverse holding something whose character is not clear till the TRIB POT XXX issue when it is clearly a fillet, or wreath, as it continues to be on Tiberius' early *quinarii*. Bahrfeldt also says that group ii were Rome mint coins, not Lugdunum; if he is right, this would much strengthen the view that they formed some of the gifts alluded to by Suet. (*Aug.* 75). A point in favour of their being special issues is their great rarity. Bahrfeldt lists the known specimens as: IMP XII 4, TR POT XIII 2, XV 1, XVI 2, XVII 8, XXIIII 1, XXVII 7, XXVIIII 3, XXX 12. Sutherland *RIC* I² adds XXV (214) and XXXI (218) and lists all under Lugdunum. On the other hand, the Victory reverse is the common way of advertising a 'half' value issue, as on the silver *quinarii* (half *denarii*).

[34] *CIL* I² p. 29, P. Vinicius and P. Alfenus Varus (AD 2).

[35] *Leges Fufia Caninia* (AD 2), *Aelia Sentia* (AD 4), *Papia Poppaea* (AD 9).

principes iuventutis could no longer be envisaged Augustus not merely adopted Tiberius but returned to a *trib. pot.* formula, though this was not at once advertised on the coins. Tiberius' imperatorial salutations V (AD 8–10) and VII (AD 12) (and very rarely VI) (AD 11) (*RIC* I² 242–3) appear on the Lugdunum *aes*,[36] but it is only at the reopening of the Rome mint in AD 10–11 that he has the combined titles IMP V PONTIFEX ... TR POT XII, and Augustus the following year IMP XX ... TR POT XXXIII (*RIC* I² 469–71).

When Tiberius, clearly instituted as heir apparent after the banishment of Agrippa Postumus, was given *trib. pot.* for the third time,[37] it was probably *sine die*;[38] and though it was not widely commemorated at the time, it was the power he used politically to convene the Senate, inform them of Augustus' death, and invite them to arrange his funeral.[39]

Augustus left *Res gestae* behind him; in it he mentioned his *trib. pot.* six times. It has been claimed that these six mentions of *trib. pot.* in *Res gestae*, against none of *imperium proconsulare maius*, show that Augustus laid much more stress on his *trib. pot.* But this impression may be misleading for his period of leadership as a whole. Over the years, the Senators who offered triumphs and twenty-one times voted the title of *Imperator*, with fifty-five *supplicationes* (formal thanksgivings to the gods) and eight hundred and ninety days of holidays as thanksgivings for victories (twenty-nine whole months!), and the People who joined them in celebrating, cannot have supposed that these victories were won without *imperium*, nor that laureate heads on coins and celebrations for *signa recepta* (recovery of the standards) and temples like that to Mars Ultor and triumphal statues were not in honour of an *imperator*. It would be much more true to say that the results of Augustus' proconsulate were frequently, if not constantly, before their eyes.[40] By contrast,

---

[36] *RIC* I² 235–248 TI CAESAR AUGUSTI F IMPERATOR, head bare or laureate.

[37] The date is uncertain. Tiberius was voted *trib. pot.* three times (*R.g.* 6.2), since Agrippa was voted *trib. pot.* twice. The *Fasti Capitolini* (*CIL* I² p. 29) show that his tenure was continuous from AD 4, but whether it was then renewed for five years (Suet. *Tib.* 16 — not 3 as in LCL) and again in AD 9 (nowhere recorded), or for ten years (Dio 55.13.2) with a renewal in AD 13 for an unstated period (Dio 56.28.1), is uncertain. See next note.

[38] Tacitus *Ann.* 3.56 nowhere suggests that the *trib. pot.* proposed for Drusus was unprecedented in any way, nor that it was limited in time. This strongly suggests an Augustan precedent.

[39] Tac. *Ann.* 1.7.3 and 8.1.

[40] He even used *Imperator* as a *praenomen*, and regularly on the precious metal coins.

benefactions by a holder of *trib. pot.* occurred more seldom; after the *frumentationes* (distributions of food grains) of 23–2 (or however long they went on), they were only sporadic; donatives were given in 12 when Augustus became *Pontifex Maximus*, and again in 5 and 2 to celebrate his sons' coming of age. These donatives coincide rather exactly with the promotion of Augustus and his family,[41] and seem to have little to do with proclamations of popular leadership and tenures of *trib. pot.*

Of the mentions of *trib. pot.* in *Res gestae*, the first need be no more than a mere date (4.4) along with consul XIII, at the end of his triumphal honours and the start of the list of honours he refused. The second terminates this list (6.2) with a brief statement that he did what the Senate wanted by means of his *trib. pot.*, and is followed by the remark that he received a colleague in *trib. pot.* five times. This latter sentence fits awkwardly and rather incongruously into its context and looks like an addition.

The actual conferment of *trib. pot.* is sandwiched insignificantly (along with the inclusion of his name in the hymn of the *Salii*) between two extended and elaborate accounts of honours; of these, the former (*R.g.* 9.1–2) is of vows and prayers decreed by the Senate for his health and safety, celebrated first in the games of 28 (Dio 53.1.4, so Gagé, edn of *R.g.*, n. on 9.1), and later repeated in Rome and elsewhere; the latter is his election as *Pontifex Maximus* (*R.g.* 10.2) traced from his refusal in 36 till his eventual election in 12, a dated and emphasised account, the first of the three exceptional honours so recorded. But *trib. pot.* and sacrosanctity, dated by our other sources to 36 or 30 (see chap. 4 above), and the Salian hymn are flatly recorded. The chronological confusion (for the Salian hymn is dated by Dio to 30 (51.20.1)) should cause surprise. Augustus does not break chronological sequences in *Res gestae* except to start new topics. Perhaps sacrosanctity and *trib. pot.* begin a section on popular votes for his protection and divine support beginning in 36 and building up to his election as *Pontifex Maximus*. In any event it is given no political part.[42] Dating by *trib. pot.* is restricted to chapter 15, the chapter devoted to Augustus' gifts of cash and grain to the *plebs*; here *trib. pot.* is used on its own once, and once in conjunction with a consular date; the other five dates are to his own consulates.

[41] Brunt and Moore 58.

[42] If the entry about the *Salii*, which is the only 'divine' honour recorded in *R.g.*, is a later insertion (L.R. Taylor *The Divinity of the Roman Emperor* (Middletown, Conn. 1931) 151, 236), the chronological norm would be preserved.

Outside chapter 15 all dates are consular. Thus, even in *Res gestae*, *trib. pot.* does not play a conspicuous role, though it seems very plausible to connect at least one addition to the text with a growing consciousness of the value of *trib. pot.* as a quasi-magistracy reserved for the emperor and his chosen successor — which of course was what Tacitus meant by *summi fastigii vocabulum*.

Tiberius, of course, followed Augustan precedents. His coin legends combine numbered tenures of *trib. pot.* with numbered imperatorial salutations, and the issues are sporadic. The continuous series is of *quinarii*, like the Augustan all very rare, and like them perhaps merely recording, for the benefit of the administration (or perhaps the army), the passage of the years.[43] If *trib. pot.* had ever been seriously intended for the purpose of protecting the plebs that purpose was now well on the wane.

In AD 22 the debate on Drusus' *trib. pot.* is the context for the proposal that years of *trib. pot.* should become the official system for dating.[44] Though this was declined, and the names of the often unimportant consuls were retained for ceremonial purposes, imperial communications with the provinces continued to be dated by years of *trib. pot.* When Drusus was granted *trib. pot.* he was designated heir apparent, and in the following year, when his twin sons were born, bronze *asses* from the Roman mint duly appeared with the legend DRUSUS CAESAR TI AUGUSTI F DIVI AUG N(epos) PONT(ifex) TR POT II (or TR POT ITER), and many show on the reverse *cornucopiae* containing the twins.[45] That *trib. pot.* was *summi fastigii vocabulum* was by now undoubtedly true, but the manner in which it became so casts much light on the Augustan principate.

Trib. pot. was presented on its inauguration as an office for the protection of the *plebs* in 23; after about four years it was found to be useful as a convenient method of dating documents (including coins) where a new era was required. In 18 it underwent a major development, when it was used as an instrument for introducing legislation and for distinguishing Agrippa as Augustus' partner in imperial power; the convenient dating-system thus turned into the means for expressing an imperial era, and an imperial position.

---

[43] The *quinarii* run from AD 15–16 to AD 36–7, though there are gaps. It may be significant that military diplomas, where complete, all have full imperial titles and numbered *trib. pot.*; the only exception in the first century is from Vespasian's first year. As with a magistracy, he did not include a number in his first year of tenure.

[44] Tac. *Ann.* 3.57.

[45] *RIC* I² Tiberius 42 and plate 11.

The hiatus in collegiate tenures after Agrippa's death, whether caused by Tiberius' reluctance to accept *trib. pot.* or Augustus' reluctance to choose between Tiberius and his brother, followed by Tiberius' acceptance of *trib. pot.* and subsequent retirement to Rhodes, and the new formula for designating successors represented by the title *princeps/principes iuventutis* inaugurated in 5, converted *trib. pot.* back again for a time into Augustus' personal honour (like his *auctoritas* and the *praenomen* (forename) *Imperator*). However, on the death of C. Caesar *trib. pot.* was brought to the fore again, and from now (AD 4) its progress became inevitable as the formula for designating the emperor's chosen successor to his civil position, as the *imperium proconsulare maius* represented succession to his military power, and the prospective promotion of his son (by adoption or otherwise) to the headship of his family and the patronage that went with it. And the existence of an imperial era was emphatically, and repeatedly, asserted.

CHAPTER 8

AUGUSTUS AND THE RELIGION
OF THE FAMILY *

E.L. Harrison[1] has remarked that according to the "fundamental principles of Roman religion ... the gods are either favourable or hostile; there is no grey area in between"; the latter was expressed by the idea of gods' anger — *ira deorum*, the former by peace — *pax deorum*.[2] *Ira deorum* required special, even extreme, acts of sacrifice or worship to assuage the anger; *pax deorum* was maintained by keeping up the regular festivals, sacrifices and prayers, that is, by the proper observance of *religio* (cult and ritual).

It is well enough known that in public religion Augustus cultivated, if he did not activate, the view that the civil wars were the gods' punishment for the Romans' past neglect of the gods,[3] and that the early years after Actium were a time of extensive construction and restoration of shrines and festivals by Augustus himself, by Agrippa (who advertised his collaboration with Augustus), by his kinsfolk — Octavia his sister for example — and by certain noble families who restored buildings which their ancestors had erected.[4] All this was encapsulated and publicised in the great festival of the *ludi saeculares* (Secular Games) in 17, which were celebrated not by *Pontifex Maximus*, but by Augustus himself and Agrippa, taking the lead as members of the *xv viri sacris faciundis* (College of Fifteen responsible for sacrifices) and holders of *trib. pot.* as recorded on the inscription that has survived.[5]

---

* This study was presented at a seminar in the University of Alberta, Edmonton. I am grateful to Professor Fishwick and his staff for comments and discussion.

[1] 'The tragedy of Dido' *Echos du Monde Classique* 33.1 (n.s. 8) (1989) 1-21, 12.

[2] It has been suggested that *pax deorum* was an Augustan innovation, but *pax Iovis* is Plautine (*Am.* 1127); for other examples *OLD s.v. pax* 2.

[3] Most clearly in Hor. *Carm.* 3.6.1–20. For earlier ages, Livy *passim*.

[4] *R.g.* 19; cf. Suet. *Aug.* 29; Vell. 2.89.4; Tac. *Ann.* 3.72. Cf. Dio 49.42.2 (before the battle of Actium).

[5] E-J 30.

In this study I hope to show that Augustus was no less interested, and successful, in using Caesarian precedents to harness the private religious cults of the Romans of the city to support the regime. The process was a slow one, and culminated in his salutation as *Pater Patriae* (Father of his Country) in 2 which made him no longer just *patronus* of the Roman People but their *paterfamilias* (Father (and head) of the family).

Pax deorum, maintaining the favour and support of their gods, had as its primary objective the preservation of the state against rival or hostile states. This meant success in war, and the war-gods had their due place in the state religion. Individual families were equally involved in this, since the defence of the state included defence of their own lives and of their families from rape and enslavement[6] (the normal consequences of being conquered in war). The Roman state also sought the support of its gods in providing enough food for its citizens; many of the state religious festivals were concerned with success in agricultural and pastoral farming activities.[7] Equally the protection of his own family from starvation was an absolute priority[8] for the individual citizen, along with providing shelter and procuring children — *heredes* — to support the family in the old age of their parents, provide for its future and so keep up the honours due to the family cult, which included the dead, and thus obtain their support also.

For these reasons the state and the families worshipped the same gods. They are discussed in turn.

First, Vesta. Families and the state each had a cult of Vesta. The

---

[6] Their success in empire-building might be thought to have removed the Romans' fear of foreign domination, but the sheer panic after the defeat at Arausio in 106, and the hysterical reaction to the conspiracy of Catilina in 63, show that their confidence was in fact rather shaky. The fear appeared again in AD 6 at the time of the Pannonian revolt, and in AD 9 after Varus' disaster. In the area of religion the citizens' reactions had been reflected in the worship of Marius' *Genius* by private citizens in their homes after he had ended the German menace at Vercellae in 101: offerings of food and wine were made, Plut. *Mar.* 27.5; Val. Max. 8.15.7. Weinstock *Divus Julius* 295 for other examples. In the political arena their reaction had been the repeated election of Marius as consul and the enrolment of the *capite censi* (landless poor) in the legions.

[7] Ov. *Fast. passim*; see also below and nn.26, 35–7, 57, 63.

[8] For religious honours to magistrates who provided supplies of food, Weinstock *Divus Julius* 293f.; P. Garnsey 'Famine in Rome' in Peter Garnsey and C.R. Whittaker *Trade and Famine in Classical Antiquity* (Cambridge 1983) 56 n.1 for bibliography. Starvation was a present menace during the civil war, *ibid.* 58–61 *et alibi*; but the need for adequate supplies of grain, and their distribution, subsidised or free, as a means of winning political support is a recurring issue in the late 'republican' period.

state cult of Vesta is well enough known, though its uniqueness is not often stressed:

1. Vesta received cult every day; her hearth was always alight — as was the family's Vesta. Other deities did not; their altars were normally unlit except at times of festival.
2. Vesta's place of worship was an *aedes* (shrine), not a *templum* (temple) consecrated by augurs. (She was in fact not unique in this, but unusual for a major cult.)
3. She was worshipped inside the shrine at a hearth (*focus*), not outside it on an altar (*ara*); i.e. on ground level, not at waist height or higher.
4. There was no image in the inner shrine, just a burning hearth.
5. Vesta's priests were female and full-time, and not male and part-time;[9] the Vestal Virgins were dedicated to her service for thirty years, not public men rewarded with a priesthood for life for public services or noble birth.[10]
6. Vestal Virgins had to deny their sexuality; male priests did not.
7. They were mostly young (being chosen between six and ten years old — before puberty), so were still under forty when they were eligible to withdraw from office, though not all did. Priests were mostly quite elderly, though some *nobiles* were chosen while still quite young. But never before puberty.
8. Vestal Virgins were selected by the *Pontifex Maximus*; priests were elected by the People — at least in theory.

Vesta was in a sense Rome's most special deity; she was of the soil of the place — of Roma that is, who being of the soil was female; as Ovid put it:[11] "Vesta and the earth are the same thing; beneath each lies a perpetual fire; the earth and the hearth stand for one's own *sedes*." *Sedes* is hard to translate; "home", Frazer's translation, is much too

---

[9] Mary Beard 'The sexual status of Vestal Virgins' *JRS* 70 (1980) 12–27 for the "ambiguity" of the Vestal Virgins being an important element in their role as mediators with the gods.

[10] *Flamen Dialis* was an exception; his position was 'ambiguous' too (cf. Beard 'Sexual status' (n.9) esp. 18) since he was a *civis optimo iure* (full citizen) but exempt from the *munus* (duty) of military service. Also he was chosen when young, or could be. Julius Caesar was not more than fifteen when he was chosen to follow Cornelius Merula when he died in 87, but was still only *destinatus* (intended to succeed) in 82 when Sulla occupied Rome and dismissed him (Suet. *Jul.* 1.1). *Flamen Dialis* could also be an exception to the norms 7 and 8 outlined below.

[11] *Fast.* 6.267f. Cf. W.K. Lacey '*Patria potestas*' in B. Rawson (ed.) *The Family in Ancient Rome. New Perspectives* (London 1986) 125.

weak for our day, in which every land agent offers "homes" for sale.
Rather *sedes* is the place where a person belongs by right, especially
by descent or long time occupation. The Maori expression *turanga
waewae* expresses it exactly. A person cannot move or change the
earth of their *sedes*.

The Romans knew that they could not move Rome's Vesta from
her position in the Forum, for then it would not be the Vesta of Rome
any more. This point is made most clearly in the speech of Camillus
in Livy 5.52. Here Vesta, Jupiter Capitolinus, Mars the father of
Romulus, and Quirinus are the gods of the very site of Rome.[12]

Vesta's hearth in the Forum was traditionally the hearth of
Numa's palace, brought there forty years after the city's foundation
(*ab urbe condita*) (Ov. *Fasti* 6.257–60), when Rome was created out of
the community of the Palatine founded by Romulus, and the
community of the Quirinal the people of Quirinus. Its fire came from
Alba Longa,[13] and in Vesta's shrine were housed the city's *Penates*,
which, since tradition said they came from Troy carried by Anchises
who was carried by Aeneas, cannot have been large or heavy objects.

Ogilvie has argued that this speech of Camillus is pure fiction,
Ciceronian in style, an appeal for the defence of the constitution as
Livy knew it with its traditions and ceremonies, for the customs of
grandeur and above all for the preservation of the city of Rome.[14] "It
is not propaganda for Augustus" says Ogilvie; maybe so, but Livy
said what Augustus wanted about the uniqueness of Rome and the
impossibility of Roman rule being based anywhere but at Rome — at
Alexandria for example — and Camillus was the second founder of
Rome[15] and perhaps Augustus' model initially.[16]

The goddess Roma or *Dea Roma* had her dwelling in Rome too.
She is interesting, as she appears not to have had much early history,
perhaps because the *nobiles* of the 'Republic' (and the common

[12] The three deities served by one of the *flamines maiores* (senior specially
designated priests); cf. Cic. *Att.* 7.11.3 *non est in parietibus res publica at in aris et focis*,
"the *res publica* does not have its being in house walls but in altars and (burning)
hearths". The hearths were the Vesta of the city, and the Vestas of the families.

[13] In another tradition, not accepted by Virgil, it came from Troy. The hearth was
extinguished then lit afresh annually on March 1st, the old New Year's Day, or at least
the ashes were raked out and the flame given new impetus on an ash-free hearth. On
March 1st the laurel branches of the *flamines* were also renewed and so were those at
the *Regia* as well as at Vesta's shrine. Ov. *Fast.* 3.137–40.

[14] *A Commentary on Livy, Books I–V* (Oxford 1965) 741–50, esp. 744–7, the part on
religio.

[15] Explicitly in Livy 5.49.7.

[16] Syme *Rom. Rev.* 305f. All Augustan writers spoke of the *nefas* (sin) of a capital
city anywhere but in Rome.

peasants too) thought more about the spirits of the lands from which they got their wealth — and food. They got no food from the Forum; they got political power and leadership there which was the sphere of male gods like Jupiter and Mars. But Roma was promoted by Augustus — or appears to have been. This is significant because it was an assertion that the Romans were the people of Roma, had a single shared home for worship with a hearth, and in their *Pontifex Maximus* a single chief priest as it were of a single family whose hearth lay in the bosom of Rome.[17]

And Roma also became the focus of loyalty cults; in the Western provinces in association with Augustus, originally Augustus himself but later the Emperor for the time being. "In Augustus' hands, *Dea Roma* became the embodiment of imperial Rome."[18]

Vesta was closely linked with the other family gods: *Lares, Penates, Genius* of *paterfamilias* and *Di Manes*. All these gods were felt to be important; "the *sacra privata* (private cult practices) were the Romans' real religion, the cults that really mattered"[19] because they touched them most deeply as the gods who watched over their families, nurturing and nourishing them, and especially those who did not live in the city itself. Romans practised the family cult every day, or some did; its main essentials were fundamentally Roman and native — especially the cults of *Lares* and *Penates* — and were as old as the civil institutions of the families themselves. In this sphere of religion the Roman state consisted of family units each under the priesthood of its own *paterfamilias*.[20] The private cults supported the state, and the maintenance of the *sacra* and cults contributed to the survival and welfare of the families, hence of the state.[21] It was the particular contribution of the family of the Caesars to use their own family cult to unite the community in a single cult, with their own family cult assimilating that of the state.

Some of the city's *Di Penates* (those known as the Trojan *Penates*) were kept in Vesta's shrine, possibly within the inmost part since the *penus* is the inmost part of a thing,[22] though the *Penates* also had a

---

[17] See further below.
[18] D. Fishwick *The Imperial Cult in the Latin West* (Leiden 1987), 1.1.52. For earlier cults of Rome in the East, Weinstock *Divus Julius* 403.
[19] Inga Mantell *Roman Household Religion* (unpublished PhD Thesis, Edinburgh 1979) 217.
[20] Mantell 218f.
[21] Mantell 220.
[22] Serv. on Virg. *A.* 3.12 for the emperor's sacrifice before the *Di Penates* before leaving for his provinces. He was leaving the "family".

shrine on the Velia.[23] It is uncertain exactly what the *Di Penates* of Vesta's shrine consisted of;[24] there was the *Palladium* (statue of Pallas (Athene)), and the gods that Anchises brought out of Troy.[25] That the *Penates* also were gods of the storehouse is a traditional view though there is very little hard evidence to support this. Yet it is not likely that such an important element in the life of a family, and especially a peasant family, should not have had some deity to protect it.[26] Certainly *Lares* and *Penates* were the gods that a family had always worshipped, and were felt to matter to the state.

This is attested by the laws concerning adoptions. Briefly, these provided that to adopt a man not in his father's *potestas* (legal supervision) — i.e. who was *suo iure* (independent) — required the assent of the ancient *comitia curiata* (assembly of *curiae*) meeting under *Pontifex Maximus*.[27] The reason was that the person being adopted had to renounce his ancestral religious rites[28] (*sacra*), and if the adoption resulted in these rites having nobody to maintain them the gods would be offended so that the adoption would not be approved. The state was officially opposed to the neglect of any cult; it would incur the anger of the gods concerned. We do not know what happened to the *Penates* of a family which became extinct, or those which were absorbed because they had only female heirs and did not adopt a male *heres*. Females transferred their participation in

[23] For the temple of the *Lares* which Augustus built on the highest part of the *via sacra*, see further below.

[24] Mantell *Household Religion* (n.19) 23. There was confusion and uncertainty even in antiquity; they may be simply the *numina* (spirits) of the *penus*, *ibid*. 20f. Cf. Cic. *N.D.* 2.68, to whom *penus* is *omne quo vescuntur homines* (any foodstuff), but Arnobius 3.40 for the wide range of opinion in late antiquity.

[25] Saved by the *Pontifex Maximus* L. Metellus from a fire in 241, Cic. *Scaur.* 48; Ov. *Fast.* 6.443-54. Ovid says it is uncertain how they got to Rome (*Fast.* 6.433-6). For Metellus cf. Mantell *Household Religion* (n.19) 20.

[26] Other evidence of the *Penates*' connexion with food (e.g.) Cic. *Har.* 57; *Ver.* 2.4.48; Virg. *A.* 5.62f, Plin. *Nat.* 28.27, though none actually mentions storage of food. Many modern scholars state flatly (without reference) that the *Penates* guarded the store. Cf. also Jane Chance Nitzche *The Genius Figure in Antiquity and the Middle Ages* (New York 1975) 7.

[27] Strictly speaking this was not adoption (*adoptio*) but *adrogatio* (Gaius I.99; Gell. 5.19), but Cicero (e.g.) in attacking the adoption of Clodius by Fonteius uses the word *adoptio*; R.G. Nisbet *M. Tulli Ciceronis de Domo sua* (Oxford 1939) 97 (comm. on 34-8) suggests that this adoption was no more than a means of effecting a *transitio in plebem* (passage into plebeian status), and there was no *detestatio sacrorum* (abjuration of family cults). Cicero certainly pretends there was (*Dom.* 35), but he may be misrepresenting the situation.

[28] *detestatio sacrorum*.

religion to their marital families[29] whether or not they transferred their property by marrying *cum manu*.

It has been asserted that a family's *Lares* were the deceased ancestors,[30] and this is quoted by Arnobius (3.41) as having the authority of Varro. The *Lares* then should have played a prominent part in festivals of the dead, like the *Lemuria* and *Parentalia*, but they did not; on the other hand they played a part in the feast of the kinsmen, the *Caristia*, which followed the *Parentalia*. In art the *Lares* always appear as jolly young males which is quite inappropriate for severe old ancestors, and slaves joined in the worship of the *Lares* which would also be inappropriate for ancestors.[31]

The *Lar familiaris* (often singular)[32] promoted the material welfare of a family; in art the *Lar* is associated with the hearth, the table, meals, drink-offerings, the *cornucopia* of fertility and abundance, and with hospitality, but not with a fixed place. The *Lares* accompanied a family to a new place.[33] This was natural; if the *Lar familiaris* was the spirit of the family it must be concerned that the family should survive, i.e. have enough to eat.[34] This may be confirmed by the song of the Arval Brethren[35] *enos Lases iuvate* (aid us, *Lares*); the Arvals were concerned with the procurement of the harvest, the family's foodstuffs for the year.[36] A family's *Lar* was the guardian spirit of the house, stayed in it, was rarely removed from it unless the family moved to a new house; it was concerned to bring prosperity, hence to a peasant good crops of grain, good vegetable

---

[29] In the case of the childless, the *Genius* of the *paterfamilias* might be held to be at fault, though childlessness was normally blamed on the women.

[30] E.g. by Weinstock *Divus Julius* 292; so J.G. Frazer *The Fasti of Ovid* (London 1929) II 469–73 with full discussion.

[31] *Lemuria* Ov. *Fast.* 5.419–46; *Parentalia id.* 2.533–70; *Caristia id.* 2.617–38.

[32] Though Ovid (*Fast.* 2.615f.) calls the *Lares* twins; J. Ferguson *The Religions of the Roman Empire* (London 1970) 68, thinks that *Lar familiaris* was brought into the house from the land around.

[33] Mantell *Household Religion* (n.19) 41f.

[34] This perhaps was why Cicero (*Leg.* 2.19) established "abiding places for the *Lares*" in the countryside.

[35] The text surviving on an inscription is of the imperial era (AD 218), but *Lases* appears to be an ancient form, so *OLD s.v. Lar*.

[36] The shrine of the Arvals' rites was five miles outside the city; their rite was similar to, if not identical with, that of the *Ambarvalia*, which was both public and private, Scullard *Festivals* 124f. When the shrine was damaged, the *Lares* and their mother were among the many deities propitiated, as was Vesta (Ferguson *Religions* (n.32) 75).

garden, good reproduction among the animals.[37] In the country too there were *Lares Compitales* (*Lares* of the crossroads shrines) who guarded the paths which must often have marked boundaries in country districts. Boundaries were always of great importance, and the annual festival of *Terminalia* celebrating the agreement of neighbours on their common boundary marks was an important one[38] — perhaps hard for us to grasp in an age of post and wire fences.

The city also had *Lares*; were they functionally different? Probably not. They are difficult to pin down though. Ovid (*Fasti* 5.129–46) knew of a very ancient shrine of the *Lares Praestites* presiding over the city walls;[39] Augustus built (*feci*, not rebuilt, *refeci*) a shrine of the *Lares* at the top of the *via sacra* (*in summa via sacra*); the index to *CIL* VI lists twenty-one shrines of the *Lares Augusti* attested by inscriptions; there were also *Lares* in the vestibule or *atrium* added to the front of Augustus' house on the Palatine when he became *Pontifex Maximus*. Coarelli has suggested that the *sacellum* (small shrine) on the right of the entry to the *atrium Vestae* is the ancient shrine of the *Lares Praestites* converted to be the shrine of the *Lares Compitales* of the *vicus Vestae* (the district (or ward) of Vesta), and the original site of *CIL* VI 30960. When the cult of the *Lares Compitales* became fully developed, the shrine built by Augustus at the top of the *via sacra* might also have been converted into one of these.[40]

Of the other cults of the families, the *Di Manes* had two festivals, *Parentalia* and *Lemuria*.[41] The state did not have *Di Manes*, but by

---

[37] Mantell *Household Religion* (n.19) 35. Cf. Tib. 1.1, esp. 24. Cato *R.R.* 143 for the concern of the (slave) *vilica* (bailiff) of an estate for the *Lar*, daily cleaning the shrine and offering a garland each Kalends, Nones and Ides and on festivals.

[38] Ov. *Fast.* 2. 639–84, esp. 661–4. Scullard *Festivals* 79f. for the importance of *termini*.

[39] The text of Ov. *Fast.* 5.131, naming the founder, is disputed. See Frazer *Fasti* (n.30) IV 12f. n. on line 131. Var. *L.L.* 5.74 for a temple to the *Lares* founded by Titus Tatius; Ovid *ibid.* for the *Lares*' function of watching over houses — "like dogs", including night duty. The images were so old as to be unrecognisable. Wissowa's allegation that Ovid was merely too lazy to go and look at them in Augustus' new temple is criticised by Frazer *op. cit.* IV 338.

[40] F. Coarelli *Il Foro Romano Periodo Antico* (Rome 1983) 265–70, reviving a suggestion of F. Lanciani (1882). Cf. L.R. Taylor *The Divinity of the Roman Emperor* (Middletown, Conn. 1931) 190 n.17 for Huelsen's suggestion that *CIL* VI 30954 came from Augustus' shrine *in summa sacra via*. But as it was found in the Forum and has a statue-niche it seems more probable that it was always in a shrine of the *Lares Compitales*.

[41] Ov. *Fast.* 2.533–70 and 5.419–44.

setting aside days for these family occasions it showed due respect, and the very severe law against desecrating tombs shows a similar concern that the dead should not be antagonised.[42]

The cult of the *Genius* (spirit) of *paterfamilias* was also — naturally — under-developed for the state. It is unknown when the cult of the *Genius* of the state came into being.[43] It appears in the Second Punic War after the disaster at Cannae.[44] A festival of the *Genius publicus* took place on the Capitol on October 9th,[45] too late in the year for Ovid's *Fasti*; so we know nothing of it. The *Genius populi Romani* appears at the end of the 'Republic',[46] but this was perhaps a vain attempt to secure loyalty to the *res publica*, and the cult never developed before the imperial period.[47]

The state also possessed other sacred, or magic, elements of the family and its home. It had its home territory bounded by the *pomerium*;[48] within it the Roman people was *domi*; no arms were carried except when an emergency had been declared, the *fasces* did not include the axe, the tribunes of the people curbed the *imperium* of the magistrates by their *potestas*; no foreign religions were worshipped there or had their temples within its bounds,[49] nor were the

---

[42] *SEG* 8.13 = *FIRA* 1.69, though it is disputed whether the rule is general or a ruling on a particular case. Paulus *Sent.* 1.21 (= *FIRA* 2.334f.) is of later date but quite explicitly general.

[43] Weinstock *Divus Julius* 205f.

[44] Livy 21.62.9; probably a non-Roman cult act, Taylor *Divinity* (n.40) 47, n.42; Weinstock *loc. cit.* (n.43).

[45] Weinstock *Divus Julius* 206; Scullard *Festivals* 191.

[46] Dio 47.2.3 and 50.8.2. Taylor *loc. cit.* (n.44) thinks the cult may derive from Sulla along with the other cults worshipped on October 9th. For earlier coins showing a *Genius*, Weinstock *loc. cit.* (n.45), but this *Genius* could represent a *Genius publicus*.

[47] For the abundance of this art form in Britain, Joan Alcock in M. Henig and A. King (edd.) *Pagan Gods and Shrines of the Roman Empire* (Oxford 1986) 122; a *cornucopia* and *patera* (shallow bowl for libations) are characteristic accompaniments, and on intaglios, *id.* 125.

[48] For the original *pomerium*, H. Last in *CAH* VII (Cambridge 1928) 359; it was subsequently extended, certainly by Servius Tullius (Livy 1.44) and Sulla (Gell. 13.14), who was the last to do so before Claudius (Sen. *Brev. Vit.* 13.8). Dio 43.50.1 for Caesar's interest in it, and 55.6.6 for Augustus'; cf. Tac. *Ann.* 12.23 *fin.* The silence of *Res gestae* and *Lex de imperio Vespasiani* (Dessau *ILS* 244) 14–16, added to that of Gellius and Seneca, has made most commentators think Tacitus mistaken; so Syme *Tacitus* 378, 514, 705, if somewhat obscurely.

[49] The prohibition on carrying arms within the *pomerium* lapsed in the imperial period for the Emperor's *cohors praetoria* (bodyguard). But Campus Martius (dedicated to the War God) remained outside it. Foreign cults did not obtain a toehold within the *pomerium* till Caracalla's rule. Before that, only Isis in Campus Martius had a shrine within the wider boundaries of the city (under Gaius Caligula). For earlier resistance even to Greek gods within the *pomerium*, F. Altheim *A History of Roman Religion* (E.T. London 1938) 243f.

dead buried within it.[50] In addition to its gates,[51] the city also had its door, though only a ceremonial one, since it is far from certain that the temple of Janus ever stood on the line of the *pomerium*. Augustus was interested in this temple and its ceremonial closure on three separate occasions during his principate, though it is likely that the reassurance of peace was more relevant to his purpose than the reminder that the Roman people's doorway was a part of their inheritance as a family.[52]

Family religion involved daily acts of worship; families kept their hearth burning continuously like the Vesta of the state. It was thought to be very unlucky to let the fire go out and it was made to blaze up on specially propitious occasions.[53] Originally the family hearth was the kitchen fire and so it always remained in the houses of the less well-off, especially peasants in the country. But as houses of the richer classes got grander, and the family left the kitchen to the slaves — and of course in *insulae* (apartment or tenement blocks) — it became a portable brazier or even a portable altar. On the walls of Pompeii and in Roman houses on Delos stone altars are painted blazing brightly. According to Plautus (*Aul.* 23–5) a pious girl offered prayer daily with incense and garlands; the first act of a bride the morning after her wedding was to sacrifice at her husband's hearth.[54]

Roman dinners were also occasions for an act of worship when part of the meal was offered at the hearth, and to the *Lares* and *Penates* of whom the former were often brought in to share at the table.[55] This was ongoing daily religious observance and each family had its own cult. Its persistence and popularity may be illustrated from Pompeii where shrines to the household deities are very

---

[50] Though there were exceptions, even after the XII Tables were passed (N. Purcell 'Tomb and suburb' *Bayerische Akad. der Wiss. Phil. Hist. Klasse, Abh.* N.F. 96 (1987) 27), and earlier burials were not exhumed.

[51] For deities of gates, Portunus (e.g.) carried a key; he also guarded harbours, hence his temple in Forum Boarium, rebuilt in Sulla's day. Gates also had *numen*, whether or not they were on the line of the *pomerium*, *Porta Capena* particularly so. Cicero used it for his triumphant return in 57 (*Sest.* 131; *Att.* 4.1.5 by implication) and possibly on 31 August, 44 (*Phil.* 2.76), and Augustus in 19 (*R.g.* 11.1). On these occasions the reception was formal. The road to it led through one of the city's most prestigious suburbs and splendid approaches, Purcell *Tomb and suburb* (n.50) 28f.

[52] Much emphasis in *R.g.* 13; it had only ever been closed twice previously.

[53] Mantell *Household Religion* (n.19) 18f. citing Virg. *A.* 1.704 and T.E. Page, *Aeneid of Virgil Books I–VI* (London 1910) 202, n. on 703; *G.*4.384f.; Mart. 3.58.23; Juv. 12.91f.

[54] J.P.V.D. Balsdon *Roman Women* (London 1962) 185.

[55] Between the *cena* and *secundae mensae* even at Trimalchio's depraved feast, Petr. *Cena* 60.

common, often painted on the walls where there is no actual site for offerings. 292 houses contain a shrine, 61 have 2, 11 have 3, 4 have 4, one even 6. When Pompeii was overwhelmed, a number, their offering table no more than a projecting tile, had offerings on them. Evidently a reasonable proportion of the population took this family religion seriously.[56] And this is not surprising since it was natural to gain the assistance of the gods of the family for its preservation, that is, for securing enough food and preserving it from harvest to harvest. To repeat Garnsey's remark (above, n.8), "The first concern of the inhabitants of the ancient world was how to feed themselves and their dependents", and for this the aid of the family gods was enlisted.[57]

The continuity of the family was held to lie in the procreative power of *paterfamilias*.[58] This was his *Genius*, which was worshipped especially on his birthday, an occasion which was a celebration for the whole family. Deceased ancestors were also worshipped on their birthdays, and prayers were made for the future happiness and fortune of other family members too.[59]

The birthday of Roma the goddess of the city was celebrated at the *Parilia*, April 21st.[60] Notable features were that no animal sacrifice took place (nor was there any on individuals' birthdays). Nor were there circus games either till 45 when they were added to the *Parilia* by Caesar in his own honour. This is stressed by both S. Weinstock and L.R. Taylor as being a claim to be a founder of the city, and as an important precedent for Augustus.[61] The account of Ovid mentions

[56] Mantell *Household Religion* (n.19) 59f. Were the Pompeiani, a mixture of Greeks and ex-soldiers, more or less devoted than others to the Roman household deities? It might be rash to suppose they were more so.

[57] Ferguson *Religions* (n.32) 69 "Family life and agriculture were of predominant importance ... The evidence for this kind of religion extends from republican times to St. Augustine. ... It was a relevant religion; it dealt with the things that matter in life and revealed a desire to be right with the powers behind the universe in life's central concerns." Sacrifices of food in an agricultural society represent gifts of *pecunia*; C. Bailey *Phases in the Religion of Ancient Rome* (Westport, Conn. 1932) 77; Gordon J. Laing *Survivals of Roman Religion* (New York 1931) 162.

[58] Children were the other essential for the family, to protect the family and feed the parents in old age, rear the next generation and keep alive the cult of the ancestors.

[59] For Sulpicia's birthday Tib 3.12 (= 4.6) esp. 15; for his wife's Ov. *Tr.* 5.5. esp. 1–12; for Virgil's, Plin. *Ep.* 3.7.3; for gifts Mart. 10.24, 29, 87; Ov. *Ars* 1.417–430.

[60] Ov. *Fast.* 4.721–862; Cic. *Div.* 2.47.98. Scullard *Festivals* 103–5. However, it is hard to believe that games were celebrated in 45, since they could hardly be organised in one day; Weinstock thinks (*Divus Julius* 184) that the announcement of the victory may have been manipulated so as to arrive the day before the Parilia. If so, there could have been time for preparations before that.

[61] Weinstock *Divus Julius* 184–6; Taylor *Divinity* (n.40) 65.

the transfer of the Romans' *Lares* to their new homes on the city's birthday, and attributes a foundation prayer to Romulus who prayed to Jupiter, Mars and Mother Vesta from whose shrine the fire to start the festival was taken.[62]

The Romans' religious calendar assumed that they were an agricultural people, and Ovid's *Fasti* is full of festivals of the countryside and of agricultural pursuits.[63] Families also worshipped the deities of their country residences, as country houses also had their *sacra*,[64] and their garden had its Priapus.[65] Sophisticated Romans attended country festivals.[66] In virtually every landscape painting which has survived there is a shrine as part of the picture, often more than one shrine.[67] Many of these shrines were nameless;[68] some places were felt to have a deity as *numen* (divine power) could be felt;[69] in others dedications were put up to "the *Genius* of the/this place".[70]

Within families the priest was *paterfamilias*, who was head of this as of all other parts of the family and its life. The whole family worshipped the *Genius* of *paterfamilias* on his birthday, when offerings might also be made by clients. A man could even make offerings to his own *Genius*.[71] Like the families, the state also had its religious head. By the late 'Republic' this had become *Pontifex Maximus*, who had his official residence in the *Domus Publica* next to

[62] *Fast.* 4.801–6, 827f., 731f.

[63] *Terminalia Fast.* 2.639–84, *Robigalia* 4.905–42, *Cerealia* 4.393 and 679–712, *Fordicidia* 4.629–72, *Parilia* 4.721–862 (see n.60 above), sacrifices like that to Faunus 2.193, feasts not on the normal *fasti* because they were movable like *Sementiva* (sowing festival) 1.658–96. Add *Consualia* on August 21st, Altheim *History* (n.49) 196f., Scullard *Festivals* 177, *q.v.* also for *Opsiconsivia* 181, *Meditrinalia* 192, etc.

[64] Cic. *leg.* 2.8; Cato *Agr.* 2; Pliny's villa however (*Ep.* 2.17) seems to lack a shrine of any sort. These shrines were ancestral. For a grave whose honour will bless a family Mart. 10.61; for the many gods of Martial's *parvum agellum* (croft) Mart. 10.92; cf. Tib. 1.1 etc..

[65] To ward off birds and thieves Virg. *G.* 4.110f.; Maecenas' gardens in Rome had a Priapus too, Hor. *S.* 1.8.

[66] Ov. *Am.* 3.13; Prop. 2.19.13–16; Tib. 2.1 etc.

[67] Ferguson *Religions* (n.32) 67 and 254 n.67 for sources.

[68] Virg. *A.* 8.351f.; Ov. *Am.* 3.1.1–3; Virg. *Ecl.* 1.6f., 52; 7.24; 8.64f; Lucan 3.399–405. Serv. *ad Virg. Geo.* 1.302 *nullus locus sine Genio*.

[69] Ov. *Fast.* 3.295f.

[70] Dessau *ILS* 3646–3657, sometimes linked with other deities such as Fortuna. Inscriptions come from Rome, Italy, Pannonia and Britain, a province in which they seem specially common; Alcock in Henig and King (n.47) 116–18.

[71] Mantell *Household Religion* (n.19) 105–9, 113–20, Taylor *Divinity* (n.40) 204, especially on birthdays; and women to their *Juno*, e.g. Nitzche *Genius Figure* (n.26) 10f.; Dessau *ILS* 3644 to her husband's *Genius* and her own *Juno*.

the *atrium Vestae*, where the Vestals lived.[72] He presided, as the king had once done, over the sacred assembly (*comitia calata*); he was responsible for the cult of Vesta and had the persons — not the property — of the Vestals in his *potestas*.[73] In religious matters his position gave him the power in the state which *paterfamilias* had in the family.

Julius Caesar was the first *Pontifex Maximus* we know of who had exploited the position for political purposes (successfully), especially after the civil wars.[74] In 44, after the Senate had honoured him with the title '*Parens Patriae*' it was provided that men should take oaths by Caesar's *Genius*,[75] just as family members did by the *Genius* of their *paterfamilias*. It was also voted that this office of *Pontifex Maximus* should become hereditary, and be passed on to his son.[76] These decrees imply that in the religious sphere Caesar had, as *Pontifex Maximus*, made himself the equivalent of the *paterfamilias* of a family, as his office of dictator had given him regal power in the political field.

When the young Octavius claimed his heritage to Caesar's property as his *heres* he declined to assert a claim to his religious leadership of the state by seeking the position of *Pontifex Maximus*. He later acquiesced in Lepidus' occupation of this office and made a virtue — at least in *Res gestae* — of not having ousted him from it "though the people offered it to me because my father had had it".[77] But Lepidus was in fact very convenient to Augustus. As he lived in exile in Circeii he could not exercise the functions of *Pontifex Maximus* in Rome and broke the tradition that *Pontifex Maximus* must live in the *Domus Publica*. By his absence Lepidus also created a convenient vacuum in the state's religious life, which Augustus was both able and willing to fill. By the time that Lepidus died the people

[72] In the heart of the city near where the Sacred Way enters the Forum.

[73] Lacey '*Patria potestas*' (n.11) 126–8.

[74] He had been *Pont. Max.* since 63; there is no evidence that either his own or his contemporaries' attitudes were affected by this election. Perhaps the overt bribery which is the principal topic of Suetonius' account (*Jul.* 13) undermined his mana. Cf. Plut. *Caes.* 7 etc.

[75] Dio 44.6.1. Dio's word for *Genius* is *tychē*.

[76] Dio 44.5.3. He says explicitly *huion* (son) — should he beget or even adopt one — not *klēronomon* (= *heredem* or heir) as stated in most history books. LSJ cite no example of *huios* = *heres*.

[77] *R.g.* 10.2, though the Greek version of the text takes *quod* as relative ("which my father had had"). Dio 54.15.8 for the repeated offers; the first is recorded in 36 after Lepidus' humiliation, Dio 49.15.3. If Dio is reporting Octavian's words he took his stand as upholder of tradition (or law).

were not only willing but anxious that Augustus should take over the position.[78] He was thus enabled to unite the cults of the state as a family with those of his own family, with himself being the head of both.

To try to trace the steps of Augustus' rise to hegemony in the religious sphere:

1.   Two decrees passed in 29 when Octavian had still not returned to Rome after his victory at Actium:

(a) That his *Genius* should receive an offering at every banquet, public and private (presumably as benefactor). This was a drink offering, and we know that it happened. Horace says so (*Carm.* 4.5.33–40), though the date of the poem is about 13. The vote however linked Octavian with the Vesta, *Lares* and *Penates* of each family, as well as those of the state.[79]

(b) Sacrifices were to be made to his *Genius* — i.e. offerings not necessarily in the context of a meal. These seem however to have remained private till 12, when Augustus became *Pontifex Maximus*.[80]

The significance of these votes is that Augustus' personal welfare was seen as part of the welfare of each family and citizen as well as of the state, and since families made similar offerings to the *Genius* of their *paterfamilias*, Augustus was made his equal in cult.

2.   In 19 Augustus' return to the city was commemorated by the *Augustalia*.[81] This celebration was not at first as important as it became when the festival was assimilated into the *Compitalia*. See below.

3.   In 17, when Augustus and Agrippa were conducting the sacrifices at the Secular Games, the state prayers included "me, my house and my household" with "the Roman people, the *Quirites* and the Board of Fifteen" as those for whom the favour of the gods was

---

[78] Lepidus died in 13; the *comitia* (electoral assembly) for Augustus' election took place on March 6th, 12. Why the delay? Was it to assemble the crowd, stressed by Augustus, or to enable the new shrine at the entrance to his house shared by Augustus and the city to be built? The latter may have been the real reason.

[79] The link is especially clear in the offering of incense to the *Di generis*, food to the *Lares*, and the libation to Augustus at the *Caristia*. Ov. *Fast.* 2.617–38, but this ritual may not have begun before 2 as suggested perhaps by *Patriae Pater* in line 637.

[80] Dio 51.19.7. For the significance Taylor *Divinity* (n.40) 151f., "The ceremony in a sense recognised Augustus as the father of the Roman state." Taylor *loc. cit.* for the sacrifices.

[81] *R.g.* 11; Dio 54.10.3.

being sought.[82]

4. At some time unknown, but before 13, games were given on Augustus' birthday, the day on which the *Genius* of *paterfamilias* was specially worshipped. These were unusual in that they extended over two days, though a birthday actually involved only one. By adding a second day to these games, Augustus' birthday was made comparable to the city's after Caesar had added the extra day to the *Parilia* in honour of his victory at Munda in 45.[83] Dio writes as if the games and slaughter of wild beasts and the dinner to the Senate in 13 were on the occasion of Augustus' birthday, but they were also celebrating his return and the opening of the Theatre of Marcellus, and, of course, the vowing of the *Ara Pacis Augustae* (Dio 54.26.2).

5. In 12 he became *Pontifex Maximus*. His measures on this occasion were very significant, and perhaps only made possible by the vacuum left by Lepidus as noted above. As *Pontifex Maximus* he ought to have moved from his house on the Palatine Hill to the *Domus Publica*, but he did not do so.[84] A fragment of Dio (54.27.3) suggests that the Senate discussed the question of his residence, but whether or not there was a *senatus consultum* to prompt or approve his action,[85] he turned the *Domus Publica* over to the Vestal Virgins, thus giving them no doubt welcome extra space, and made part of his own house a public place. This took the form of an *atrium*[86] with a Vesta and a shrine of the *Lares*; there were *Penates* too, apparently, and a *palladium* like the original which had come from Troy. The new building was dedicated on April 28th; if it is April 28th, 12, Augustus' need for time to prepare for his election can be appreciated. The effect of this shrine was that, as Taylor remarks, "Augustus was

---

[82] Dessau *ILS* 5050 line 99 *mihi, domo, familiae*.

[83] Dio 43.42.3; n.60 above. The games were certainly held in 44 (Cic. *Att.* 14.14.1, 19.3) but had ceased before Ovid wrote *Fasti*. The *Parilia* like other birthdays traditionally involved no blood-sacrifice.

[84] For Augustus himself the *Domus Publica* would have brought inconvenience; perhaps the site — in the low-lying Forum area (L. Richardson *A New Topographical Dictionary of Ancient Rome* (Baltimore 1992) 133 *s.v. Regia*) — would have been detrimental to his health. More significantly his *cohors praetoria* within the *pomerium* would be much more obtrusive there than in the complex of buildings on the Palatine Hill.

[85] And Ovid *Fast.* 4.949f. suggests there was. He also suggests that this *atrium* may have had the entrance wreathed with the oak leaves of the *corona civica*, and decorated with the olive bushes, and thus would have formed the official entrance to Augustus' house. Recently it has been identified. Ovid writes as if the whole complex can be regarded as a single dwelling, belonging to Apollo, Vesta and Augustus.

[86] Or perhaps more of a *vestibulum* (entrance court) as the archaeological remains suggest; T.P. Wiseman *Death of an Emperor* (Exeter 1991) appx.

making his private household worship an official cult of the state".[87]
And this, of course made his *Genius* an even more appropriate
subject for worship.

It was perhaps not before 12 that people started taking oaths by the
Genius of Augustus.[88] People had always sworn by the *Genius* of their
paterfamilias, as they had by Jupiter and the *Di Penates*, and slaves by
the *Genius* of their *dominus* (master).[89]

After 12, celebrations of Augustus' birthday became fully public
occasions, and annual, and open to all, even the unmarried (Dio
54.30.15). From 11, beast hunts were held almost every year (Dio
54.34.2) by one of the praetors whether there had been a *senatus
consultum* or not. If Dio is to be taken literally, such shows needed
authorisation as they were not part of the regular calendar, but the
praetors in office or one of them volunteered to give the show and the
act was tacitly at least approved. Horse races became an official part
of the calendar in 8 (Dio 55.6.6).

Suetonius (*Aug.* 57) adds that though the sincerity of the Senate's
decrees might be doubted, the *equites* always celebrated his birthday
for two days on their own initiative and by agreement. But he gives
no date from which this began.

The year 12 also marked the start of the reorganisation of the
administration of the city. Caesar had registered the city-dwellers
vicatim — by *vici* (streets) — for their free distributions of food (Suet.
Jul. 41.3). Augustus adopted these *vici*, and added new ones for
additional administrative purposes such as policing and firefighting,
and divided the whole city into fourteen *regiones* (districts). Each
regio had a stated number of *vici* in it;[90] a number of these *vici* have
recorded their date of foundation on inscriptions; none is earlier than
12, nor later than 7; from this we should conclude that the
reorganisation fell in this period, and that the administration of each
vicus began when it was organised. Each *vicus* had its own

---

[87] Taylor *Divinity* (n.40) 184.

[88] *Id.* 191 n.19. The date of Horace *Ep.* 2.1.16 is crucial, especially with the reading
numen, but there is no objective criterion for putting it before rather than after early 12.

[89] *Di Penates* depend on reading *Zeu, patrioi kai theoi* in App. *B.C.* 2.145. Antonius
was gesturing towards the Capitol. The alternative, *Zeu patrie, kai theoi*, leaves Jupiter
with an unwanted epithet and *theoi* undefined.

[90] *Notitia Regionum Urbis XIV*, a fourth-century document which lists the
principal buildings of each *regio*, the number of *vici*, *insulae* (apartment blocks),
crossroad shrines etc; the even numbered *regiones* also state the cohort of the night
watch (*vigiles*) responsible for patrolling the district.

vicomagistri (officers); all we know of were citizens of humble origins so far as we can judge from the epigraphic records.[91]

Within the city the cross-roads (*compita*) had always existed, and there had been shrines of the *Lares* at them. It would be unwise to claim that every crossroad in 'republican' Rome had had its shrine, but some certainly had, since the *Compitalia* festival had a long history even within the city.[92] Under Augustus' reorganisation the two *Lares* of the *compita* were given a third figure in their shrines, the *Genius Augusti*, in the form of the old country god *Liber Pater*, the god of fertility and abundance.[93] Augustus gave orders that offerings of spring and summer flowers should be made at these shrines,[94] but the *plebs* must have enjoyed more the feast of the *Compitalia*, held shortly after midwinter, at which fattened pigs were sacrificed at the *compita* (Prop. 4.1.23) accompanied by much merrymaking. This feast had been abolished in the city, along with the *collegia*, in 64,[95] and, though it had been revived by P. Clodius and his friends in 58 for political reasons, the history of the *collegia*, and of the *Compitalia* festival thereafter, is unknown until Caesar abolished all the *collegia* except the ancient ones in his reforms.[96] The revival of the *Compitalia*

---

[91] Dessau *ILS* 6073, *q.v.* (p.489) for a list of other inscriptions put up by *magistri*. 3090 is of particular interest: it is a prayer for the welfare of Augustus, the Senate, Roman People and *gentes*, offered to the Capitoline Triad, Sun, Moon, Apollo, Diana, Fortuna, . . . nae, Ops, Isis, Pi . . . and the Fates, and is dated AD 1. If the first gap can be supplemented by Anno], though this seems to be one letter too long, it would firmly link the food-supply of the *vicus* with the state's divinities; but in any case, Ops, mother of Vesta and Ceres, refers to abundance of food. She had a chapel in the *Regia* (Ov. *Fast.* 6.285 and Frazer *ad loc* IV.195). *Salus Semonia* was later added to the bottom . line. This addition refers to days of holiday, cf. Macrob. *Sat.* 1.16.8 associating *Salus* and *Semonia* with dedicating a day to rest from work.

[92] Scullard *Festivals* 58–60. Primarily a rural festival, attributed to Servius Tullius not Numa. Servius had organised the people into tribes and centuries (traditionally). Some centuries were of technical personnel, hence perhaps the origin of these *collegia*. They were perhaps the 'ancient' ones not abolished by Caesar (Suet. *Jul.* 42.3). Gell. 10.24.3 for the festival's antiquity. Cato *R.R.* 5.3 and 57 for rural associations, but the use of slave *ministri* (Cato *loc. cit.* and Dion. Hal. 4.14.3) matches ill with the *census*, which excluded free *capite censi* (the poor, lit. 'counted by the head') from the *classes*; naturally, also the slaves.

[93] *Lares Compitales* associated with boundaries Livy 4.30.7–11; Ov. *Fast.* 5.143–6; for the identification with *Liber Pater* Taylor *Divinity* (n.40) 185. Such statues were not unprecedented. Marius Gratidianus (e.g.) was given statues and libations in all *vici* for suppressing the debased currency, Weinstock *Divus Julius* 295, Taylor *loc. cit.* n.11.

[94] Suet. *Aug.* 31.4; Prop. 4.3.57.

[95] The generally accepted date, Cic. *Pis.* 8, though the consuls' names are different in the MSS (R.G.M. Nisbet *Cicero, in Pisonem* (Oxford 1961) 65, also in Ascon. p.7 Clark) commenting on the passage.

[96] n.92 above; cf. Suet. *Jul.* 42; *Compitalia* were certainly being celebrated in the countryside in 59 (Cic. *Att.* 2.3.4) and 50 (*id.* 7.7.3). Suet. *Aug.* 31 certainly suggests

in the city must have been extremely popular, and the festival was very long lasting.[97]

During this period too there also occurred (in 11) the first major celebration of the *Augustalia*, which were held on the anniversary of Augustus' return to the city in 19.[98] This means that *Augustales* had also been chosen by then. They also, as far as epigraphic evidence goes, were people of humble, even servile birth. Augustus was thus by these two institutions cleverly linking the common people to himself in a very personal way. It is legitimate to wonder why the *Augustalia* were not held for the first seven years after the inauguration of the feast to commemorate Augustus' return, but there seems no convincing explanation; the best perhaps, is that there was no means of choosing *Augustales* till the registration of the people by *vici* (*vicatim*) was well in hand, but against this there is the valid objection that there must have been some means of identifying those eligible for the corn distributions which went on during this period — and before it.

The calendar now contained a number of regular festivals for the common people and their magistrates: the winter *Compitalia*, the spring and summer flower festivals, *Augustalia* on October 12th, and probably the festival of the Guardian *Lares* on May 1st, which Ovid connects with the *Lares Compitales* (*Fasti* 5.129–146), with the comment (*ibid.* 147f.) that he must leave his account of Augustus in that context till August — which received its new name in this period also, in 8 according to Dio (55.6.6).

As *Liber Pater* in the shrines of the *vici*, Augustus' *Genius* was worshipped as the giver of food. This had always been an important part of his public image: *Res gestae* records the *frumentationes* of 23 (15.1), the *cura annonae* in 22 (5.2), and the general supplementation of the state's resources whenever there was need from 18.[99] We should not, surely, assume that these supplements were given without publicity? And it was, as we have seen, the general function of the family's *Lares* and *Penates* to see that the family was fed.

It was perhaps this linkage with the family's protecting deities

---

that Augustus revived the festival in the city. Cf. Alan Wardman *Religion and Statecraft among the Romans* (London 1982) 96. The date is unknown but 7, with the completion of the reorganization of the *regiones*, seems at least possible if not the most probable date, Dio 55.8.7.

[97] Shrines listed by Pliny *Nat.* 3.66, and in the *Notitia* (n.90 above).

[98] October 12th, E–J p.53; Dio 54.10 and 54.34.2, celebrated in 11 *ex s.c.*

[99] Cf. Suet. *Aug.* 41 for a general account.

which stimulated the common people to think of Augustus as their *paterfamilias*, and it appears that they had started to use this appellation before Valerius Messalla took the critical step in the Senate on February 5th, 2, when he proposed that the title *Pater Patriae* be conferred on him. In Suetonius' account (*Aug.* 58) they had sent an embassy to Antium when Augustus was out of the city to make the offer, and they had demonstrated at games on his return to Rome. Perhaps this was the occasion on which the *equites*, who formed an identifiable group at the games, had made their salutation.[100] But there is no certainty.

This title was rightly seen by Augustus himself as the capstone of his achievement (*R.g.* 35), and its timing — in 2 — is of great interest. Since Agrippa's death in 12 Augustus had been steadily promoting his own family. In 2 he had taken the consulate for the thirteenth time in order to introduce his younger son Lucius to public life. On February 5th he was also about to open at last the magnificent temple of Mars Ultor in the Forum Augustum with its commemorative colonnades and his own triumphal four-horse chariot in the foreground;[101] the animals must have started to arrive for the games, and excavation of the site on the Tiber bank for the seabattle must have begun. These things must all have been visible, and the subject of conversation. And the Forum Augustum was a great dynastic statement, glorifying the Julian family.[102]

Nor must the role and position of Livia be neglected.[103] Her public role had begun as early as the civil war period, with the grant to her and to Octavia of the *sacrosanctitas* of the tribunes, and the freedom from *tutela* (tutelage) which gave her financial independence. Her position in the *ordo matronarum* (honourable ranks of matrons) had been confirmed by the grant of the *ius trium liberorum* (rights granted to parents of three) (Dio 55.2.5); as this grant conveyed only the legal

---

[100] Ov. *Fast.* 2.127–49. Cf. Weinstock *Divus Julius* 200–5. Possible chronologies in W.K. Lacey '2 B.C. and Julia's adultery' *Antichthon* 14 (1980) 131–3. Cf. chap. 9 below.

[101] The Forum of Augustus was in use before Mars Ultor was dedicated, Suet. *Aug.* 29.

[102] Lacey, '2 B.C.' (n.100). By serving as a new, perhaps now the principal, access from the crowded *Suburra* to the centres of political and religious life in the old and new Forums, Senate House and Capitol, it complemented the new splendid approach from the North, by the repaired *via Flaminia*, or from the Tiber through the Campus Martius, now dominated by Augustan monuments, the sundial, the *Ara Pacis Augustae*, the Mausoleum; Strabo 5.3.8; Purcell 'Tomb and suburb' (n.50) 26–7.

[103] For what follows, Nicholas Purcell 'Livia and the womanhood of Rome' *PCPhS* 32 (1986) 78–105.

independence (freedom from *tutela*) which she already enjoyed, its purpose must have been only to enhance her *dignitas*. Livia had exercised patronage,[104] and restored temples of the goddesses especially worshipped by women;[105] her son Tiberius had joined her in dedicating the *Porticus Liviae* in 7 (Dio 55.8.2).[106]

The period of the military successes of her sons (12–7), saw other public acts by her: she gave dinners to the *matronae* in 9 and 7 to complement those given by Tiberius to celebrate his ovation and triumph (Dio 55.2.4 and 8.2); on the former occasion at least she was joined by her daughter-in-law Julia who was still Tiberius' wife. But the records available to Dio did not say where the dinners took place; they cannot have been part of the public record. In 9 two statues were voted to console her for the death of her son Drusus (Dio 55.2.5), but after Tiberius' departure for Rhodes she disappears from Dio's record. We must however remember that in this period Dio is represented only by Xiphilinus' and Zonaras' abridgements. Following Augustus' receipt of the title *Pater Patriae* however, and even more after the deaths of Gaius and Lucius Caesar, her public *persona* was greatly enhanced, as she is portrayed in the favourable tradition as exhibiting the ideal traits of the classical Roman matron (*matrona*).[107]

With the opening of the temple of Mars Ultor, the cult of Augustus' *Genius* passed into the hands of the *pontifices*,[108] though this did not bring to an end the cult at the *compita* or the celebrations of the *Augustales*. Later developments did, however, elevate Augustus from the status of *Pater Patriae*, with his *Genius* being worshipped by everyone among their family gods, to the status of a divine being. The institution of a blood-sacrifice to his spiritual power (*numen*) was the crucial step which raised him above the normal rank of *paterfamilias*. As Fishwick has expressed it:[109] "To pay cult to the *numen Augusti* was to ascribe to the human emperor the quintessential property of a god." This was reinforced as the custom grew up of sacrificing bulls,

---

[104] E.g. at Samos, J.M. Reynolds in *Aphrodisias and Rome* (London 1982) 105; Purcell 'Livia' (n.103) 87 and 102 n.55.

[105] *Fortuna Muliebris* and *Bona Dea Subsaxana* with Ovid's comment on imitating Augustus (*Fast.* 5.157f.), and perhaps others; Purcell 'Livia' (n.103) 88.

[106] The colonnade of Livia had a Temple of Concord in the centre, surrounded by a colonnade.

[107] So Purcell *loc. cit.* (n.105).

[108] Taylor *Divinity* (n.40) 204.

[109] D. Fishwick '*Numina Augustorum*' *CQ* 20 (1970) 191; cf. Taylor *Divinity* (n.40) 192.

the symbol of Jupiter, king of the gods, with obvious life force in its procreative power. But even at great cult centres such as the *Ara numinis Augusti* at Narbo founded in AD 11, the priests at the sacrifice on Augustus' birthday were three *equites* and three freedmen[110] — citizens like the *Augustales* of comparatively humble birth.

The progress of Augustus' rise to the position of *Pater Patriae* is at least as interesting as the results and the consequences,[111] which it is not the business of this study to pursue. It reveals Augustus working in the religious field as cautiously and gradually as he did in the political. The precedents lay in Julius Caesar's position, but Augustus proceeded much more carefully. The public and private prayers for his health were quite different from worship — indeed if there were need for prayers for his safety it implied that he was mortal and not a god; the worship of his *Genius*, long private and not public, was modelled on the family traditions of all Romans. The great leap forward was at the point that he became *Pontifex Maximus*, the post which he had long waited to assume. This post enabled him to fill a vacuum which he had partially filled before as patron and benefactor,[112] but was now able to exploit by associating the cults of the common people with those of his own family. He thus brought to the forefront the usually latent idea of the Roman People as a single family with all the gods of a Roman family. Consequently his formal nomination as the head of that family was both long anticipated and prepared for, and perhaps made to seem little more than an acceptance of the *status quo*. It reflects the fact that by this time Augustus felt politically secure, so that his potential *patria potestas* need not cause political ructions.

In this he might have been mistaken; the exposure of Julia in the same year with its challenge to the claims of the young Caesars[113] was a warning that not all were happy to accept this development in the leadership of the state.

---

[110] E–J 100; Taylor *Divinity* (n.40) 282.

[111] For families, cf. the assumptions revealed by Tacitus *Ann.* 1.73. *Cultores Augusti* in every household equate Augustus to the *dominus* — or *paterfamilias* — as a recipient of cult. Statues in parks and oaths by his *numen* reflect the public aspects.

[112] For the connexion between Augustus as *Pater* and as ideal benefactor T.R. Stevenson 'The ideal benefactor and the father analogy in Greek and Roman thought' *CQ* 42 (1992) 421–36.

[113] The conclusion of the paper '2 B.C.' (n.100) 141f. not as given by Syme *Aug. Ar.* 92 n.70.

CHAPTER 9

THE SUCCESSION TO AUGUSTUS *

Modern historians of Rome have expended much care and ingenuity in discussing the constitutional basis for the Augustan Principate. Ancient historians had a much simpler view — it was a monarchy. And they were right, even if it was a monarchy within a constitution so that as monarch Augustus contrived to govern with the consent (and support in many cases) of the traditional governing classes without constantly having to invoke the reserve powers of a monarch whose will is ultimately sovereign.

In his preparations for the succession to himself too — for the method by which power is transmitted is perhaps the surest touchstone for evaluating the true nature of any political organization — Augustus can be seen as recognising his Principate as a monarchy, though not of the modern British or Danish type in which hereditary claims are the sole determinant. Augustus' successor had also to be accepted as the leader of the Caesarian party, and to be able to secure the loyalty of the following of that party, especially the army and the common people of Rome, of whom the Caesars claimed to be the patrons and protectors. Any intended successor thus had to be introduced to them and win a following among them.

And contemporaries were not deceived, for it was precisely at the points in his Principate at which Augustus arranged for the accelerated promotion of the members of his own family to positions in which they could start to win a personal following of their own (in terms of patronage and *gratia* (favour)) among the army and common people of Rome that Augustus met with damaging opposition. These points are 23, 6 and 2. The purpose of this study is to argue that the 'revelation' of Julia's adultery in 2 was provoked by

* This study derives from '2 BC and Julia's adultery', published in *Antichthon* 14 (1980) 127–142. I am grateful for permission to use the material in this version.

a realisation of the implications of Augustus' dynastic claims, and must be seen in that light, and not in the light either of shocked morality or of political intrigue.

When Augustus Caesar stood for the consulship of 2 people must have known what to expect — at least in general terms. They must have been sure that there would be no repetition of the unfortunate episode of 6 when the *comitia centuriata* (electoral assembly) had been prompted to elect the fourteen-year old Gaius Caesar to be Augustus' colleague in 5.[1] This election (they must have recalled) had resulted in a compromise whereby the still entirely inexperienced youth would have a five-year apprenticeship in the Senate before his consulate at the age of twenty,[2] and there had followed a serious rift between Augustus and his son-in-law, Tiberius, which had resulted in the latter's withdrawal from public life to Rhodes.[3] Gaius Caesar, however, had been proclaimed *princeps iuventutis* (leader of the cadets) and, to celebrate this, gold and silver coins had been produced in substantial quantities with a new reverse type showing C. Caesar galloping on horse-back, with the legend C CAES AUGUS F.[4] The foundations of a position of leadership in the army

---

[1] The hand behind the *comitia* is unknown, and ancient historians disagree. Dio (55.9) cites Augustus' protest in a prayer that circumstances should never arise to make it necessary for anyone under the age of twenty to become consul, as had once happened to him, and his pronouncements, which implicitly criticized Gaius for inexperience and lack of judgment; Tacitus says Augustus was hypocritical, and passionately wanted what was granted (*Ann.* 1.3.2) — a statement not wholly incompatible with what Dio says.

[2] The Roman educational curriculum should not be forgotten. Boys in the *toga praetexta* (boy's robe) did not participate in public life, but on donning the *toga virilis* young nobles started their apprenticeship in public life by attending their elder relatives when they were engaged in public business, whether as magistrate or acting as part of a *consilium* (council) political or judicial, formal or informal. The honour of attending the Senate proclaimed that the Senate was Augustus' *consilium*.

[3] B.M. Levick *Tiberius the Politician* (London 1976) 38f.

[4] "Gaius Caesar son of Augustus". Gaius holds sword and shield; in the background an eagle and military standards. The obverse is AUGUSTUS DIVI F as on the previous IMP XII issues and the IMP XIIII issues which are dielinked with this one; *RIC* I² p.54. *Aurei, denarii* and a *denarius* type in copper are all known, but there are no varieties in legend or type. Since the issue is an abundant one and was produced over only a short period, it is likely that it should be connected with the large-scale demobilizations of 4, 3 and 2 in which the troops' rewards were paid in cash (*R.g.* 16.2). For the coins cf. *BMCRE* i, Augustus 498–503. It is possible, however, that the issue should be dated earlier, to 8, to commemorate Gaius' first participation in the exercises of the *equites* (presumably in the *lusus Troiae*) ('Troy Game') on which occasion Dio says there was a cash distribution to the soldiers (55.6.4). The soldiers are undefined, though the implications of Dio's account are that they were Tiberius' troops on the Rhine frontier. But the demobilizations of 7 and 6 are also possible reasons for a large issue of new coins.

were clearly being laid.

Lucius Caesar appears not to have been promoted before being given the *toga virilis* (man's robe — i.e. active citizenship) in 2 except perhaps in the unique *sestertius*-type coin described by Mattingly as 'of beautiful style and fabric' on which the obverse is CAESAR AUGUSTUS, while the reverse shows two young Caesars facing each other with the legend C CAESAR AUGUST F L CAESAR AUGUST F.[5] He had, however, at least drawn attention to himself by going to the theatre alone, without an attendant, on one occasion,[6] and had the reputation of being no more amenable to his father's discipline than his brother was. Even so, public opinion may have been less than fully prepared for the dynastic claims of 2.[7] It may be helpful to consider these in detail.

Augustus took as his colleague in 2 the son of Livia's confidante Urgulania.[8] M. Plautius Silvanus held the office for six months only, it appears, since Augustus' colleague on August 1st was L. Caninius Gallus.[9] Augustus' plans for the year were designed to cover the first six months or so, and when the year began, it must have been clear that Augustus had great celebrations in mind. Work must have been started on the basin for the sea-fight across the Tiber,[10] and the conduit to tap the *aqua Alsietina* for the basin must also have been

[5] "C. Caesar son of Augustus, L. Caesar son of Augustus". One specimen is known; it is in Paris. The obverse is CAESAR AUGUSTUS, which means that it should be earlier than 2, before Augustus became *Pater Patriae*. *BMCRE* i p.119 for description and note by Mattingly, who suggests a date of about 5. But it may not be genuine; it appears not to be listed in *RIC* I².

[6] Dio 55.9.1 under the dateline 6.

[7] Much of what follows starts from Sir Ronald Syme's paper 'The crisis of 2 B.C.' *SBAW* 7 (1974) 3–34, to whom many references are due, and much guidance despite the differences in interpretation which are here presented.

[8] *RE* Supp. IX (1961) 1868–9 (Hanslik); Tac. *Ann.* 2.34; 4.21f.; Syme *Rom. Rev.* 385 n.4 for her influence with Livia.

[9] Caninius' father was consul in 37 and a partisan of Antonius (so Syme *Rom. Rev.* 200). He was Augustus' colleague when Mars Ultor was opened (Velleius 2.100.2). The traditional date of the dedication (August 1st) was questioned by C.J. Simpson 'The date of the dedication of the temple of Mars Ultor' *JRS* 67 (1977) 91–4. He proposed May 12th, as given by Ovid in *Fast.* 5.550–98 and the *fasti* from Cumae, but he has not convinced other scholars, e.g. Syme *History* 31f.; cf. discussion in Gagé *Res Gestae* 175f. It seems very unlikely that Urgulania's son would have had a very brief consulate.

[10] The length and width of the excavation are given by Augustus (*R.g.* 23) as 1800 x 1200 square feet; he does not give the depth, but it cannot have been less than about 10 feet to float the fully-manned warships; thus 2,400,000 cubic yards of soil were moved (less any hollows provided by nature).

under way.[11] The work on the *Circus Flaminius* to make it watertight to at least a shallow depth need not have taken so long, but in view of the size of the Circus cannot have been insignificant.[12] Some time before the shows too the animals must have started to arrive. Two hundred and sixty lions and thirty-six crocodiles at least had to be assembled and housed;[13] some of them, or at least news of them, must have started to arrive quite early in the year, for Augustus will hardly have failed to whet the popular appetite by not announcing in advance that there would be special shows,[14] and it is scarcely credible that he did not specify the occasion on which he, as consul, would give the shows — at the opening of the new temple of Mars Ultor.[15]

This temple, and the Forum Augustum in which it stood, must have been known to be nearing completion, and the *plebs* will also have been able to anticipate that this year there would be another donative, either of food-grains (a *frumentatio*) or of a cash distribution (*congiarium*), as there had been in each of Augustus' last two consulates.[16] There was every reason for the *plebs* to look forward to the year in pleasurable anticipation.

There can thus be little surprise that a popular demand could be engineered that Augustus should be formally granted a title that he had already heard used informally — that of *Pater Patriae*,[17] which had been formally bestowed only on his adopted father Julius Caesar, and on Romulus.[18] Augustus, of course, was ready; he was

---

[11] Frontinus *Aqueducts* 1.22 suggests that the conduit was new, and built specifically to flood the basin, which must therefore have been finished before the conduit, and sufficiently long before August 1st for the conduit to fill the basin constructed. As the water was not potable it had no connexion with the public water supply for the citizens' use.

[12] Its exact dimensions are unknown, but it had been used to hold meetings of the people, *RE* III (1899) 2580f. (Pollack), and gave its name to one of the *regiones* of the city.

[13] Dio 55.10.7f.; are we to suppose these were the only animals hunted on this occasion, or were these the *pièce de résistance*? Gladiators are also mentioned by Dio, but no other animals.

[14] As happened under the 'Republic'; Milo's games in 53 were announced in advance (for example), Cicero *Q.fr.* 3.8.6; 3.9.2; Caesar advertised his intended benefactions by putting on displays of the things he intended to put on show at his games (Suet. *Jul.* 10).

[15] The Forum Augustum was open already (Suet. *Aug.* 29.1).

[16] *R.g.* 15.1f.; in 23 twelve *frumentationes* (distributions of food), in 5 a *congiarium* of 240 sesterces per man.

[17] Dio 55.10.10.

[18] Certainly bestowed on Caesar (Dio 44.4.4; M. Gelzer *Caesar, Politician and Statesman* (E.T. Oxford 1968) 315; but *parens* in Cic. *Phil.* 2.31 and 13.23); dubious for

conveniently out of the city (as he was when he resigned the consulship in 23) so that he could meet an embassy, and decline the offer in such a way as to stimulate the reiteration of the demand — which duly took place, according to Suetonius,[19] as Augustus was taking his place at shows (*spectacula*).

This statement raises problems; the *fasti* record the date on which the Senate voted Augustus the title *Pater Patriae* as February 5th,[20] but there were no regular *ludi* with *spectacula* (games with shows) before February 5th.[21] February 5th itself may be a date not without significance; it was the day of the annual sacrifice at the temple of *Concordia* on the Capitol,[22] the very temple which Tiberius, Augustus' self-exiled son-in-law, had undertaken to restore in his own name and that of his brother Drusus to commemorate his triumph at the opening of his consulate in 7, and to which he had ostentatiously dispatched a statue of Vesta which he had compelled the Parians to sell him as he proceeded to his retirement in Rhodes.[23] The day was in consequence *parte nefas* (partly unlawful for public business). There are neither *ludi* (games) nor *spectacula* (shows) regularly associated with this day either, but according to Suetonius the people were awaiting Augustus in the place for the *spectacula*, having garlanded themselves with laurel wreaths in advance; the demonstration must therefore have been pre-arranged on a day for which *spectacula* had

---

Romulus, who is called by Livy only *parens patriae* (1.16), R.M. Ogilvie *A Commentary on Livy, Books I–V* (Oxford 1965) 86 (note on 1.16.3); this title echoes the ancient formula for invoking the dead ancestors at the *Parentalia*. Similarly Camillus (Liv. 5.49.7) and Cicero (*Pis.* 6) had been hailed *parens patriae* — but not *pater patriae*. *Pater patriae* is a much more significant title, containing as it does the juridical and religious overtones of *pater familias*, and lacking the commemorative tone of the *Parentalia* noted by Ogilvie (above). But see T.R. Stevenson 'The ideal benefactor and the father analogy in Greek and Roman thought' *CQ* 42 (1992) 421–436. He believes that Cicero was hailed *pater patriae*.

[19] *Aug.* 58.

[20] E–J p.47, the isolated fragment of *fasti Praenestini*. February 5th (the Nones) was a normal day for a meeting of the Senate.

[21] Neither the *fasti Praenestini* nor the *fasti Caeritani* mention LUDI (shows) at the *Agonalia* or the *Carmentalia*, which took place on January 9th, 11th and 15th; their silence should be significant since they do record LUDI at the *ludi Megalenses* and the *ludi Florae* (for example), *CIL* 1² pp.212, 231–6 etc. Though it must be admitted that the *fasti Praenestini* are broken up on January 9th and 11th, there does not seem room for a note on *ludi*.

[22] *fasti Praenestini CIL* 1² p.233.

[23] Dio 55.8.1f. and 55.9.6. For the political message implicit in these actions, Levick *Tiberius* (n.3) 36f. and 'Tiberius' retirement to Rhodes in 6 B.C.' *Latomus* 31 (1972) 779–813, esp. 803–5.

been announced in advance. It cannot have been an unpremeditated outburst.[24]

The scene in the Senate House was also pre-arranged, if Suetonius' account is accurate (*Aug.* 58), and the verbatim quotations he gives from the speeches make it hard not to accept that he was using authentic documents. The Senate did not have a formal *relatio* (notice of motion) before it, Suetonius says, but all gave place to Valerius Messalla; that is, the consul Plautius (who would be in the chair in republican tradition in February) asked Messalla for his *sententia* (expression of opinion). In his speech Messalla explicitly linked Augustus' family with the public weal in proposing the title *Pater Patriae*,[25] and the quotation from Augustus' reply carefully denies the dynastic implications of Messalla's words[26] as he prayed that he might retain the Senate's consensus till his life's end — a sentiment appropriate indeed on the day of the sacrifice to *Concordia*, in whose temple Cicero had been hailed *Parens Patriae* very shortly after Augustus' birth some sixty years before (though on that occasion there had been a somewhat hysterical[27] acclamation, unlike the solemn, almost religious occasion Suetonius describes).

However, Augustus himself (*R.g.* 35) and Ovid (*Fasti* 2.128) agree that the *ordo equester* (*equites* — Knights) played a part as well. The question must be asked: what part? At some time this year they welcomed Lucius Caesar as *princeps iuventutis*; this is unlikely to have taken place before he was given his *toga virilis*. The normal date for this ceremony was the festival of the *Liberalia* on March 17th.[28] A possible date (after March 17th) is the periodical review of the *equites* mentioned by Suetonius (*Aug.* 38.3), for which the expected date

---

[24] No *ludi* of any sort appear on the *fasti* for this date (*CIL* 1² p.223, *fasti Maffeiani*), and Cicero's diary of the events of early 56 (*Q.fr.* 2.3.1) passes over this day in total silence. But, under the 'Republic', February was the month for receiving embassies, and not for games. And in any case the weather could not be relied on to be fine at this time of year. Rather the reverse.

[25] Messalla, according to Suetonius, wished blessings on the house of Augustus and added "For in doing so we feel that we are praying for everlasting good fortune for the *res publica* and joy for this city", or perhaps "for this order"; there is a lacuna in the MSS. which modern editors seem to fill with *urbi*; *ordini*, however, which dates at least from Torrentius in 1578, seems at least as appropriate on a senatorial occasion.

[26] Not Ovid, however, who explicitly demonstrates that Augustus was greater than Romulus — *Fast.* 2.133–44. For the relevance of Romulus, see below. Suetonius informs us that Augustus had tears in his eyes; they can hardly have been of surprised delight!

[27] And not unanimous, as Stevenson points out, 'Ideal Benefactor' (n.18) 421.

[28] Ov. *Fast.* 3.771–88; Scullard *Festivals* 92.

would be sometime in March, the ancient month of the muster at the beginning of the year. But if this gathering of the *equites* was the occasion for their hailing Augustus *Pater Patriae*, Suetonius is incorrect in saying that the salutation by the *equites* took place at a show (*spectaculo*).

On the whole, it might seem a more satisfactory account of the evidence to suppose that both Suetonius and Augustus (in *R.g.* 35) have telescoped the course of events; that is, there was an acclamation on a day of a show, for which the senators and *equites* sitting apart in their privileged positions had garlanded themselves in advance with laurel wreaths and they and the *plebs* welcomed Augustus as he arrived at the venue with shouts of *Pater Patriae*, and it was this salutation that Augustus thought fit to record in *Res gestae*, not the solemn occasion in the Senate House, though it was the latter that was recorded in the *fasti*. But the acclamation at the show was after, not before, the senatorial occasion.

The decree(s) or vote(s) of the People that the words *Pater Patriae* should be added to certain inscriptions will then have taken place on one or more other occasions. Two of the sites chosen for these inscriptions (the entrance-porch of Augustus' house and in the *curia Julia*) recalled the 'restoration of the *res publica*' and the gift of the name Augustus in 27, but the inscription on the base of the four-horse chariot in the Forum Augustum would appropriately be associated with the completion of the forum when the temple of Mars Ultor was at last ready to be opened. It thus appears evident that the *Pater Patriae* celebrations were prolonged and were intended to remind people of the occasion when Augustus "put the management of the *res publica* back into the Senate's hands" a quarter of a century before.

One possible order of events is:

 (i) an embassy sent to Antium by vote of the people some time before February 5th;

 (ii) a face-to-face salutation by Valerius Messalla in the Senate on February 5th;

(iii) a demonstration by the *equites*, or more probably by Senators, *equites* and *plebs* at a spectacle — possibly one of those connected with the *ludi Martiales* on May 12th or the opening of the Forum Augustum;

(iv) votes (no doubt following debates) on where and how this new honour should be recorded.

The disadvantage of this order of events is that it contradicts

Suetonius' account. He places the events in the order (i), (iii), (ii), (iv). If his order of events is to be retained, the agitation before February 5th must have started in 3 — perhaps after Augustus' election as consul for 2 was announced — stimulated by the popular hopes of benefactions during 2, as noted above. In this event the 'spectacle' at which the demonstration occurred was not one of those given in the spring, but one of those normally held in the (European) autumn of 3. But the celebrations were nonetheless prolonged and lasted several months.

Arguments based on Suetonius' order of reporting events, however, are not generally regarded as soundly based, and it may be better to retain the order of events suggested above. These celebrations will thus have gone on into August (when the temple of Mars Ultor was opened), and have included the *Liberalia* on March 17th, when Lucius Caesar was presented with his *toga virilis* by his father Augustus as noted above. There must have been a festival on this occasion too, though we do not know what the form will have been in 2; Ovid speaks of games at an earlier date, and the calendars of the later Empire show games too, but Ovid mentions none in this period.[29] This might, however, have been the occasion for the cash distribution of 600 sesterces to each man of the *plebs* on the roll of those eligible to receive the grain dole (*R.g.* 15.4), the same sum as that given in Gaius Caesar's name three years before.[30]

The celebrations which were to crown this year of achievements led up to the opening of the Forum Augustum and the dedication of the temple of Mars Ultor on August 1st. They began on May 12th with the *ludi Martiales*, celebrated for the first time in 2 (*R.g.* 22.2) and commemorating the recovery of the standards from the Parthians in 20.[31] These included lion hunts and a gladiatorial show in the *Saepta Julia*, but no stage performances because these were unsuited to the war god (Ov. *Fast.* 5.597f.). These were followed at a date unknown by a sea battle, the fleets being manned by gladiators;

[29] Ov. *Fast.* 3.785 in fact suggests that the *ludi* that had once taken place on this day had been transferred to the Cerealia on April 19th. The calendars of Philocalus and Silvius (*CIL* I² pp.260, 261, 312) list *ludi* in the *Circus Maximus* on this day. J.G. Frazer *The Fasti of Ovid* (London 1929) III 140 (commentary on line 785) argues that games on March 17th must have been added after, perhaps long after, Ovid wrote *Fasti*.

[30] The date would have been appropriate, with the association of *Liber Pater* (the old god of abundance) with the *Liberalia*; the time of year was suitable too as spring was the season when food was most expensive.

[31] To be given by the consuls annually, which illustrates the great prestige attached, as does the fact that they were established by law (Gagé *Res Gestae* 121).

Augustus devotes a whole chapter of *Res gestae* to this (23), and Velleius' language (2.100.2) suggests that it was intended to evoke a memory of Caesar's show forty-four years before, the last naval battle which had been staged. Crocodile hunts followed in the flooded *Circus Flaminius*.[32]

The temple of Mars Ultor and the colonnades of the Forum Augustum were designed to represent the glory and fortunes of the Julian family as united with those of the Roman state. The temple itself commemorated the avenging of Julius Caesar, Augustus' divine father, and the avenging of the defeats of Rome by the Parthians.[33] Temples had been vowed for both, though it is certain that the site eventually chosen was not the site envisaged at the time they were vowed.[34] In 42 there can have been no question of anything like a Forum Augustum. Even in 19/18 it is an open question whether the new small temple to Mars Ultor on the Capitol was meant to be a permanent or a temporary home for the standards recovered from the Parthians. Siting it next to Jupiter Feretrius, the ancient temple which Augustus had rebuilt and which housed the *spolia opima*, and commemorating it on the coins, seem not quite appropriate for a temporary structure.[35] Nor is it certain that Augustus always intended that his new forum should be the setting for a temple to Mars; he gave out (Suet. *Aug.* 29) that a new forum was needed for additional space for judicial work and purchased land privately. The forum was of irregular shape because he was unwilling to expropriate landowners who were unwilling to sell.

The evidence on the whole seems to suggest that Augustus' plans developed, and that the decision to build a splendid monument to the military glories of the Romans and the Julian family indicates an advance in his self-representation which was surely dynastic in

---

[32] This order of events is that given by Dio 55.10.7f. He adds that the fleets were called 'Athenians' and 'Persians', and the 'Athenians' won. Syme 'Crisis' (n.7) 15 adds the point that this symbolised the victory of the West over the East. Cf. Ov. *Ars* 1.171f., Syme *History* 31f., and for Velleius A.J. Woodman *Velleius Paterculus, The Tiberian Narrative (2.94–131)* (Cambridge 1977) 120.

[33] *R.g.* 21.1 says it was built from spoils (*ex manibiis*); this was perhaps an unfortunate claim since, if the spoils came from Philippi, they came from Romans; we can trace no claim earlier than 2 to have won large amounts of booty from the Parthians.

[34] In the heat of the moment it is most unlikely that he had any specific site in mind. And nothing happened for twenty years.

[35] For the significance of the site, Zanker *Images* 186f., and cf. above chap. 7 and n.15.

intent. Ovid certainly made clear in *Ars* 1.177–228 the connexions between the new temple, the Parthian enemy and the prospects of the dynasty.[36] The connexion was natural enough since the avenging of Crassus was Caesar's intended mission in 44 at the time of his assassination, and to recover the lost standards was to complete Caesar's self-allotted task. Dio's account of the decrees governing the uses of this temple (55.10.2–4) makes it plain that it was to become the shrine of Rome's military endeavours. Apart from the transfer of the standards from the temple on the Capitol it was decreed that all future captured standards should be deposited there, *triumphatores* should dedicate their sceptre and crown there after their triumphal procession, commanders were to set out from there (after sacrificing of course), the Senate was to meet there to vote triumphs, the temple was to be the focus for the recruitment of the *iuventus* (cadets), and the censorial nail was to be driven into the posts of this temple instead of that of *Iuppiter Optimus Maximus*.[37]

The elaboration of the Forum Augustum calls for attention.[38] Everything was of the most splendid in design and rich in decoration; the massive wall screening the Forum from the *Suburra*, together with the steep monumental marble-faced steps which led into the Forum from the entrance arches on that side show plainly that it was not designed with a view to providing a new site for *Suburra* merchants; the costly coloured marble slabs covering the whole floor area were clearly not designed to take wheeled traffic, and the porticoes flanking either side, standing as they are three steps above floor-level, were equally unsuitable for booths and stalls. The back walls of the porticoes and *exedrae* (open bays) had a variegated marble facing interspersed with half-columns and niches for statues between them, and horizontal decorative bands of yellowish Greek marble; the porticoes themselves had gabled roofs, and were two-storied with rows of caryatids (decorative, not structural) all along

---

[36] This is a contemporary document, Syme *History* 8f. Cf. Ov. *Fast.* 5.545–98, esp. 563–6; for their date Syme *History* chap. 2.

[37] Roman traditionalism did not omit the fact that the object of the census was originally, and primarily, to assess the state's military resources in men and materials. Dio also relates that the temple was to be elevated to the same status of honour as those of Jupiter Capitolinus and Apollo, in that senators were to be permitted to contract to be responsible for its care and to supply horses for chariot-races presumably at the *ludi Martiales* or the games on August 1st to commemorate the temple's dedication; Dio 60.5.3 for horse-races that day, Gagé *Res Gestae* 175f.

[38] P. Zanker *Forum Augustum. Das Bildprogramm* (Tübingen 1968), which is the source of most of this account, supplemented by personal observation. For Zanker's more recent interpretation, *Images* 193–215, *q.v.* fig. 66 for a model.

the upper storey, and heads of divinities decorating the marble facings between the caryatids. On the temple itself the tufa podium had a rich marble facing; the carving of the capitals of the pillars with their carefully worked acanthus-leaves and Pegasus heads and wings are of a very high standard of workmanship; the soffits between the peristyle and the temple proper are of extreme beauty and fineness; the pillars of the *cella* (sanctuary) and its flanking pilasters are set on high bases and had bronze statues between them. It was, in short, a Hellenistic temple precinct rather than a Roman forum in the sense that a forum was the centre of a city's life.

Within the temple the cult statue of Mars was huge (Ov. *Fast.* 5.553), bearded and armed;[39] beside him stood Venus (Ov. *Tr.* 2.296), fully clothed with a small child at her skirts, and a third figure usually said to be Julius Caesar.[40] These too will have had to be more than life-size to balance Mars. The doors were adorned with weapons and arms captured from various enemies,[41] and the standards recovered from Parthia were in a shrine within along with other trophies.[42]

Yet it was more than a military shrine; it was also a shrine of the Augustan peace[43] and of the Julian family. The pediment is thought to be pictured on the panel of Claudius' *ara pietatis Augustae* now in the Villa Medici in Rome.[44] The figure of Mars Ultor is shown in the centre, but without breastplate or shield, and his sword is sheathed; he wears only a civilian cloak and a helmet of modest proportions. On his right stands Venus with a cupid on her shoulder; on his left *Fortuna* (Fortune) with rudder and cornucopia.[45] Beyond Venus is Romulus seated on a stool dressed as a shepherd with a crook; *Dea Roma* is seated beyond *Fortuna*, on a pile of arms, with helmet, spear and shield. The corners of the pediment were occupied by Father Tiber next to *Dea Roma* and *Mons Palatinus* next to Romulus, and

---

[39] Mars Ultor was usually bearded, Zanker *Forum* (n.38) 18 and plates 46, 47, 49; cf. *Images* figs 151, 155, Gagé *Res Gestae* 115f.

[40] The child is an Eros and carries a toy sword. The cult statues in this temple are thought to be represented in the group from Malga in the Algiers museum. Zanker *Forum* (n.38), Gagé *Res Gestae, q.v.* both for references to earlier studies.

[41] Ov. *Fast.* 5.561f.

[42] *R.g.* 21.2, 29.2 etc.

[43] Even the huge Mars in the shrine has a *corona civica* on his shield (Zanker *Forum* (n.38) plate 47).

[44] M. Cagiano de Azevedo *Le antichità di villa Medici* (Rome 1951) inv. no. 3, pictures in Zanker *Forum* (n.38) plates 45, 46; *Images* fig. 86.

[45] For Caesar's connexions with shrines to *Fortuna*, the goddess of successful generals, Weinstock *Divus Julius* 112–16.

above the pediment stood victories with wings outstretched.

Works of art were gathered from far and wide to adorn the temple and the Forum: two paintings by Apelles, one depicting Castor and Pollux with Victory and Alexander the Great, the other War with his hands tied behind his back and Alexander in triumph,[46] an ivory Apollo, and perhaps a very valuable Diana and an ancient Athena Alea from Tegea.[47]

The Forum was calculated to provoke wonder — it still does, even in its present ruined state.[48] The overall design had a second and equally important purpose: it was a dynastic statement by Augustus, identifying the destiny of Rome with that of the Julian family. Augustus' own name appeared on the architrave below the pediment, located on the axis of the two *exedrae* which open out of the flanking colonnades; it is thus the focal point of the whole architectural concept. On the pediment Mars as the ancestor of the Roman people through Romulus is partnered by Venus, the foundress of the Julian line through Aeneas;[49] Romulus and Aeneas face one another from the centres of the *exedrae* across the top step of the podium and the front of the temple. Bearing the *spolia opima* Romulus headed the parade of statues of the *triumphatores* each with his name on an ornamental plinth and his achievements inscribed on a slab attached to the base on which his statue stood,[50] on the other side stood Aeneas carrying Anchises and the family gods from Troy at the head of 'many an ancestor of the Julian line' — Ovid unfortunately does not specify, but Tacitus mentions the Alban kings

[46] Pliny *Nat.* 35.93f.; which might be the picture Servius had in mind in his comment on Virg. *A.* 1.294.

[47] Zanker *Forum* (n.38) 23f., *q.v.* for sources. There must have been a Vulcan too, Ov. *Tr.* 2.296. Traces of the presence of bronze statues have also been discovered. Perhaps all the *Di Consentes* were represented.

[48] Frazer *Fasti* (n.29) IV.63 "the temple and its surroundings were designed to be the outward and visible symbols of the military glories of Rome"; and cf. Zanker *Forum* (n.38) 21 and Rekonstruktionsplan (Falttafel A).

[49] The association of Mars and Venus as the parents of the Roman People and the Julian family had already been made both in the Pantheon and in the *Ara Pacis Augustae*.

[50] For Romulus as the *exemplum virtutis* and Aeneas as the *exemplum pietatis* Zanker *Images* 201-3. Augustus' edict in dedicating the statues of the *triumphatores* (Suet. *Aug.* 31.5) proclaimed that the life (sc. of each of them) was to be the standard by which he desired to be weighed by the citizens as long as he lived, and by which he trusted that the *principes* of future ages should also be weighed by them. The implication that there would be *principes* in future generations is clear, and in its context surely dynastic.

as being counted as Julian ancestors.[51] The dynastic claims implicit in this complex are unmistakable, and blatant. So were the claims for the future — at least as seen by Ovid, for the message of the title of the *principes iuventutis* was that presently they would become *principes* of the elders as well.[52]

Nor was the Senate backward in taking the hint. They voted a most beautiful dedication (which still stands in the *Foro Romano*) to Lucius Caesar AUGUSTI F. DIVI N. PRINCIPI IUVENTUTIS COS. DESIGN. CUM ESSET ANN[OS] NAT[US] XIIII AUG[URI] (*CIL* VI.36908); a similar but more elaborate dedication to Gaius Caesar had already been erected (now restored as *CIL* VI.36893).[53] And the message was hammered home by the new coinage, both the normal issues and the commemorative medallions of which one has been preserved,[54] with their legends: (obverse) CAESAR AUGUSTUS DIVI F PATER PATRIAE; (reverse) C. L. CAESARES AUGUSTI F COS. DESIG PRINC IUVENT.

But in all this show Augustus went too far, and he provoked a reaction[55] (as he had also done in 23), which naturally took the form of an attack on his family, this time through Julia, the mother of the *principes iuventutis*. Our sources say that she was convicted of adultery, publicly denounced by her father in a letter to the Senate, and banished to an island.[56] Her alleged paramours were punished,

---

[51] *CIL* 1² 186–197. Cf. *Notizie degli scavi* ser. 6, 9 (1936) 455ff. For Ovid's description *Fast.* 5.563–6; Tac. *Ann.* 4.9.2 for the Alban Kings.

[52] Ov. *Ars* 1.171–228, esp. 194; the whole passage presages a new campaign and triumph against the East (Syme 'Crisis' (n.7) 15f.). Syme also suggests that the poem was reissued at this date with the new passage in it rather than now published for the first time. This suggestion seems most attractive, since the republication of an offensive poem with new material — even if laudatory — on the *principes iuventutis* might aggravate the offence in the light of the Julia affair that followed.

[53] "Son of Augustus grandson of a god *princeps iuventutis*, consul designate when he was 14 years old, Augur". The dedication to Gaius Caesar was by the Senate and People and declares that Gaius was "the first person (PR[I]MUS OM[NIUM]) to have been elected consul at the age of 14".

[54] *RIC* I² 205. G. Corini, *Annali dell'istituto italiano di numismatica* 15 (1968) 49ff., for the controversy as to its genuineness. Mr T.R. Volk, of the Fitzwilliam Museum, who has handled it and the undoubtedly genuine medallion of AD 2, found in Pompeii (*RIC* I² 204) agrees that he can see no reason why it should not be genuine. The coins of this type are far the most numerous of all Augustan issues found in the West, and the numerous varieties indicate a long period of issue.

[55] Velleius 2.100.2f. certainly implies that the Julia affair was later in the year than the celebrations. Dio (here Xiphilinus) implies the same, 55.10.12; cf *RE* X.1 (1917) 902 (Fitzler).

[56] Pandateria, Tac. *Ann.* 1.53; Velleius 2.100.3 alleges that she committed every sort of offence against the moral code in the belief that her position put her above the law.

mostly by exile, though Iullus Antonius the ringleader killed himself when charged with *maiestas* (treason). But, as Tacitus pointed out, seducing the princeps' daughter was hardly *maiestas*, and the spontaneous departure of Julia's mother Scribonia, recorded by Velleius (2.100.5) and Dio (55.10.14), challenged the charge of adultery.

Most modern writers have scented palace intrigue, plans to supplant Tiberius as guardian of Julia's children and as Julia's husband, perhaps even to dispose of Augustus himself. But two weaknesses of this line of approach are evident: first that it assumes that C. and L. Caesar would be amenable to guardianship now that they were no longer of an age that required a guardian, when their behaviour while they were still in the *toga praetexta* was such as to make this unlikely;[57] and second that the conspirators condemned were, comparatively speaking, lightweights[58] — they had aristocratic names, but they did not carry the influence with the army or the common people, the bastions of the Caesarian party, necessary for them to take over. And is it conceivable that a decision by anyone other than Augustus himself could dispatch a centurion to Rhodes with orders to dispose of Tiberius? And what of Livia? Could Tiberius be disposed of without disposing of Livia, or Livia without disposing of Augustus himself? And what of the military men in the wings, kinsmen like Domitius Ahenobarbus, to whom Syme has drawn attention,[59] or it might be added M. Lollius or Sulpicius Quirinius? Disposing of Augustus himself was out of the question, a speculation, and certainly a later fabrication.[60] A political plot against Augustus, and hence a purely political explanation of the charge of *maiestas*, simply will not do, despite the authority of its

---

[57] See the stories in Dio 55.9; Syme *History* 195 for the view that it was Julia's plain duty to organize a council of regency.

[58] Syme 'Crisis' (n.7) 26: "the recorded names do not quite add up to a comprehensive faction"; but *id. History* 195 "the five *nobiles* are a faction, not a society coterie", *Rom. Rev.* 427 "a formidable faction".

[59] 'Crisis' (n.7) *loc. cit.* (n.58); cf. *History* 195, to whom he adds Fabius Maximus who either had governed Tarraconensis or was still doing so, and L. Aemilius Paullus who was Julia's nephew, and about to marry the younger Julia, his first cousin.

[60] Syme 'Crisis' (n.7) 24, and despite the fact that the suggestion was known to the Elder Pliny (*Nat.* 7.149). Though some people may have wanted to assassinate Augustus these cannot have included Julia, whose whole position depended on his being alive. As a parricide, how could she or any new husband she took hope to win the loyalty of the legions? The consequences of Caesar's murder cannot have been completely forgotten, especially in the year of the opening of the temple of Mars Ultor.

proponents.[61]

An alternative interpretation which starts from the ancient evidence should perhaps not be too hastily dismissed. This evidence contains at least two strands: one, reported in its fullest and most lurid form by Seneca (*Ben.* 6.32), speaks of revellings in the Forum, garlands for the statue of Marsyas and sexual orgies on the *rostra*; the other, reported by Tacitus (*Ann.* 1.53.3),[62] is that Julia had been committing acts of adultery from the time of her marriage to Agrippa — and was now at last exposed. The Senecan tradition reappears in Pliny and Dio,[63] the Tacitean in Macrobius.[64] None of these authors reveals the name of the contemporary source, though the letter in which Augustus denounced Julia to the Senate must have been extant, and it was seen by Pliny, who notes that it mentioned the garlanding of Marsyas' statue on more than one occasion.[65]

It seems most improbable (to me at least) that Augustus' letter mentioned incidents that nobody had ever heard of,[66] and almost equally improbable that if the Senators had heard of these revels at all they had not heard of them in their fullest and most titillating details. It would therefore follow that the repeated honours paid to the statue of Marsyas (with or without orgies on the *rostra*)[67] had

---

[61] E. Groag and Syme for example. Nor will the view hold water that it was Livia's machinations in Tiberius' interest that brought Julia down since, as Syme (e.g.) has pointed out, Julia's fall led to no improvement in Tiberius' position in Rhodes. It actually made it worse, since Julia's exile automatically extinguished her marriage to him, and thus broke his connexion with the Julian family (Suet. *Tib.* 11–13; Levick *Tiberius* (n.3) 44f. and refs), which had been the subject of so much glorification this very year. While Gaius and Lucius Caesar were in the *toga praetexta* Tiberius might have been designated their guardian, but after they had put on the *toga virilis* Tiberius had no chance of withstanding their claims to Augustus' heritage as *sui heredes* except as Julia's guardian (or *tutor*) or as *coheres* with Gaius and Lucius Caesar (Suet. *Claud.* 1.5); Suetonius' silence here suggests that Tiberius had not. Nor could he have been adopted, since siblings — even by adoption — could not marry (Gaius *Inst.* 1.61; Levick 'Tiberius' retirement' (n.23) 782 n.2). Anyway, it was only the known estrangement between Augustus and Tiberius which made it possible for Julia to complain to Augustus about him (Tac. *Ann.* 1.53.3), and ask for a new husband.

[62] Tacitus explicitly names Sempronius Gracchus in this context, uses a rare and striking word (*temeraverat*, *Ann.* 1.53.3), and comments on his long period of favour — he was *pervicax adulter* (persistent adulterer) (*ibid.*) and still inciting her against Tiberius. Nowhere does Tacitus mention political plots (so Syme *History* 197).

[63] Pliny *Nat.* 21.9; Dio 55.10.12.

[64] Macrobius *Sat.* 2.5.9.

[65] *Nat.* 21.9: *filia divi Augusti cuius luxuria noctibus coronatum Marsuam litterae illius dei gemunt.*

[66] The notion that Julia was denounced privately by Livia or anyone else is rightly discounted by Syme *History* 194.

[67] These should certainly be accepted with great caution. It might be suggested that those who loved watching *pantomimi* (mime artists) might be prompted to try

caused a scandal which had prompted demands for a public enquiry — possibly even in the Senate House.[68] Augustus' hand was thus forced; to prevent a public enquiry into Julia's past life, Augustus had to use his *patria potestas* and punish his daughter under the law which bore his own name, the *lex Iulia de adulteriis coercendis*, which prescribed relegation to an island as the penalty for adultery.[69] His letter to the Senate was the act of a *pater familias* communicating with his *consilium*. The more titillating the public account he gave of Julia's orgies, the more likely it was that attention would focus on them and not on her past, of which Augustus may in fact have been ignorant up to that time, as Seneca suggests (*Ben.* 6.32.2). The whole story may indeed have come out in the private enquiry which Augustus conducted, at which slaves were tortured to procure evidence — or fabricate it (Macrobius *Sat.* 1.11.17). If he were genuinely surprised at what was being said about Julia, his anger, which is stressed in the traditions of Seneca and Dio,[70] is easily understandable.

Moreover, to hush up the past was more important to Augustus than to save his daughter in the present, since in the context of 2 the other web of stories was more damaging. Julia's long career as an adulteress was common knowledge in her own circle, as one specimen of her wit quoted by Macrobius (*Sat.* 2.5.9) makes clear: "On one occasion her intimates wondered why her children were so like Agrippa; she replied, 'I never take a pilot on board except when I have a full ship'."[71] In other words, though she admitted she was

---

imitating them when in their cups, and to use the *rostra* as their stage. Sexual acts certainly appear to have been part of the repertoire of the *pantomimi*, and some sort of play-acting of a shocking sort on the *rostra* could easily be blown up into a full-scale orgy such as Seneca describes (*loc. cit.*).

[68] But not necessarily there; there are many other ways in which it could have been revealed to Augustus that the rumours about Julia were public property.

[69] The title of the law is in fact dubious: *Acta divi Augusti* ed. S. Riccobono *et al.* (Roma: Regia Academia Italica 1945) 1.112, Velleius 2.100, and cf. for the normal nature of the punishment of relegation to an island, Paul. *Sent.* 2.26.14 = *FIRA* 2.352; *Acta divi Augusti* 1.126, *q.v.* for the capital penalty of the *Institutes* (4.18.4) and earlier rulings to this effect.

[70] Sen. *Ben.* 6.32; Dio 55.10.12 and 14; Syme *History* 193.

[71] *Numquam enim nisi nave plena tollo vectorem*. The remarks, as reported, can only have been made at a party, and Julia's circle at least must have been very frank about her sexual activities. What is interesting about Julia's reply though is the present tense — *tollo*; she had not been pregnant for eight years at least. It might be thought that the nasty letters about Tiberius, said to have been written by Gracchus, and her requests to Augustus for a new husband were in fact prompted by sexual frustration. There is no record of her having become pregnant at any time after her separation from Tiberius and she was not old enough to have reached her menopause.

promiscuous at the period of time when her children were conceived, she said she had sexual relations with men other than Agrippa only when pregnant.

This allegation — that Julia's sons were, or could have been, bastards because of her promiscuity — was much more damaging to Augustus' plans than tales about her current revels in the Forum. Unless we are to believe that the celebrations Augustus organised in 2 represent a sudden urge for overt self-glorification, those celebrations were intended to establish clearly and unequivocally the claim of the Julian family to a hereditary principate to which the heirs of the Father of his Country were destined to succeed.

If anyone asked Cassius' famous question *cui bono?* (whose gain?) with reference to these celebrations, the answer must have been "Augustus' sons, C. and L. Caesar, the *principes iuventutis*". And if in the friendly intimacy of Julia's circle the question of their paternity was openly raised, it is likely that the same question was also raised in unfriendly circles, among those who did not wish to subscribe to the claims of the Julian house. And in these circles, even if they were powerless to act against Augustus, they could mock; mockery indeed would be the natural reaction of the salt-loving Romans to the pretensions of bastards[72] — or to be more precise, of children born in promiscuous intercourse — to succeed to Augustus' inheritance. If this is so, Augustus' dynastic plans had at least come under suspicion, and at worst had been made a laughing-stock if it was widely being said that nobody knew for sure who the fathers of the *principes iuventutis* were. Hence another cause for Augustus' anger, if Julia had made him a laughing-stock; this he could never forgive, and never did.[73]

Anger is as much a natural reaction to discovering what people

---

[72] For such children, Gaius *Inst.* 1.64; Ulpian 4.2. They were known as *spurii*, were never in *patria potestas* and had succession-rights only to their mother, *RE* IIIA (1929) 1889f. *s.v. spurius* (E. Weiss): cf. W.W. Buckland *A Textbook of Roman Law* (3rd edn Cambridge 1963) 105 n.2. The possibility of *spurii* being adopted, e.g. by their mother's father, and becoming *sui heredes* to an adoptive father seems never to have been considered by the lawyers, but as *spurii* were always *sui iuris* the full ceremony of *adrogatio* would be needed. Consequently, if Gaius and Lucius Caesar were indeed *spurii*, they could not have been legally adopted by Augustus under the formula of *adoptio*, which is the one he will surely have used on the assumption that they were legitimate.

[73] Stressed by Suetonius (*Aug.* 65.3), whose version of the causes of her banishment is comparatively colourless, but like the others contains no hint of political intrigue. He reports that there was a number of petitions to restore her — to which Augustus did not accede (*ibid.*).

were saying as a result of Julia's parties as it is to discovering that she was promiscuous. In other words it is suggested that what Augustus discovered was not her manner of life (which he was perfectly well aware of)[74] but what people were saying about her children as a result of her manner of life in the past. And Augustus could defend her sons (who were now his sons) by punishing her for gross immorality in 2, an accusation which would (he might have hoped) — especially if it were accompanied by titillating details about orgies — succeed in focussing attention on that charge, which did not affect the legitimacy of her children, rather than on her long career as an adulteress, which did. And by and large he succeeded, especially if Velleius (2.100) reports the official story, which is all about depravity in 2 and not about the parentage of her children.[75]

It was the more perceptive Tacitus who saw that it was Julia's longstanding relationship with Sempronius Gracchus that was worth recalling, and stressing,[76] and the fact that Iullus Antonius was put to death and did not kill himself as Velleius states (loc. cit.). Iullus was put to death for aspiring to the Principate, or so we are told by Xiphilinus' abridgement of Dio;[77] on the account given here this is perfectly possible, for, if Augustus' sons' claims were laughed out of court, Augustus' nephew by marriage might well be thought the leading candidate for succession to his uncle, especially if he married Julia.[78] To do so would heal the last wounds of civil war (it might be argued), and there was no doubt about his parentage.

Scribonia might protest that the charges as laid were untrue by voluntarily accompanying her daughter into exile (Vell. 2.100.5) — though we do not know which charges she denied — but Augustus'

---

[74] Macrobius Sat. 2.5.3.

[75] Velleius' story is of course not coherent. He speaks of Augustus' clementia (mercy) towards Iullus Antonius; this may be purely literary, through modelling Augustus on Caesar (Woodman Velleius, Tiberian Narrative (n.32) 120, and other modern commentators have agreed). Augustus was indeed clement if Julia's circle had been plotting a coup d'état, and he put to death only Iullus, but if their actual offences were no more than laughing at Augustus' claims, revelling, and (possibly) adultery with Julia, and the official line was that Augustus was punishing a clique of adulterers, then he merely enforced the normal provisions of the adultery law, except in Iullus' case. Woodman, however, thinks (123) that Augustus' clementia lay in his having allowed Iullus a distinguished public career. If he is right then Tacitus' irony (Ann. 3.24.2) takes additional point.

[76] Ann. 1.53.3, and see n.62 above. Cf. Syme History 196.

[77] 55.10.15; Syme History 194 n.7, who points out that Xiphilinus states that others besides Iullus were put to death.

[78] He had literary talents too, as Syme points out (History 196), which might make him a congenial husband.

plans for the Principate were saved, and the *principes iuventutis*
(Julia's children) pursued their planned paths[79] until death destroyed
Augustus' hopes. And the coinage, the most abundant by far of all
the Augustan issues,[80] continued to glorify the next generation of
principes in the Julian house.

To sum up: the issues in 2 were on the one hand a dynastic claim by
Augustus of the right of the Julian family to a hereditary Principate,
and on the other resistance by some of the leading *nobiles* to these
claims, a resistance which took the form of laughing at Augustus'
dynastic claims as being made for children born of promiscuous
intercourse.[81] Indeed, for the ruling class as a whole perhaps there
was a real crisis. Their attitude to Augustus himself may have been
one of ambivalent acceptance, as Tacitus saw (*Ann.* 1.2); many men
of ambition could see no good reason for not seeking honours and
wealth in the domain traditional to their class (or to the class to which
they aspired), and while Augustus lived even those who cherished the
nobiles' traditions of independence in political life might opt for
coexistence with his leadership. But collaborating with Augustus was
quite different from accepting an overtly monarchical succession to
power by youths who had to their credit none of the achievements
which qualified a man to be *auctor publici consilii* (initiator of public
policy) simply because Augustus had named them as his sons and
heirs. This, it is suggested, was the real issue in 2. Julia's revellings
were important only because they created a scandal which Augustus
could not hush up or ignore, and her promiscuity was important only
because her reputation gave those who wished to resist Augustus'
plans an opportunity to subvert her (and his) sons' claims to rule.
Augustus, who appears to have cared more about the future of C.

[79] Gaius' career was to include a new campaign against Parthia, for which the
Temple of Janus was solemnly opened in 1 BC (Syme *History* 10) or perhaps 2 (above
n.146 to chap. 1); his journey to it enabled him to avoid the embarrassment of holding
his consulate in person in AD 1 (so Syme *loc. cit.*). Certainly his progress reveals a lack
of urgency for the campaign.

[80] It has been remarked (by Mr Volk to the author) that this issue marks the end of
the inventive period of the Augustan coinage. After 2 the types become standardized
and stereotyped, the only new idea being the introduction of Tiberius into the few new
issues made after his return from Rhodes. It can be compared with the coinages of the
Hellenistic kingdoms when compared with the rich variety of the Roman 'Republic'
with its annually changing colleges of moneyers each with their own ideas and themes.

[81] It is true that their adoption by Augustus (if it was legal, see n.72 above) had
made them members of the Julian house, and that their facial resemblance to Agrippa
was an answer to allegations about their paternity, but considerations of that sort have
never prevented the mockery of tongues no sharper than those of the Romans.

and L. Caesar than about anything else (Suet. *Aug.* 64),[82] could only divert attention from past promiscuity to present scandals and at the same time vindicate his own position as guardian and upholder of the moral code. Julia's adultery was the real issue in 2, but not because it was, as it was alleged to be, a recent straying from the path of virtue by the 38-year-old princess. Political implications were present, of course, but they were secondary and more relevant to the prospects of Julia's children than to those of her husband at the time.

---

[82] Cf. *Rom. Rev.* 427: "[Augustus'] ambition was the unhindered succession to the throne of Gaius and Lucius."

CHAPTER 10

ENCROACHMENT AND SERVILE FLATTERY (*ADULATIO*)

The background

Tacitus (*Ann.* 1.2) described Augustus after his settlement as "gradually encroaching, drawing the functions of the Senate, magistrates and the laws into his own hands". To assess this account, it may be well to go back to 29, when Augustus (*Imperator Caesar divi filius* as he then was called) returned from Egypt to triumph, distribute largesse in quantities hitherto unknown to troops, veterans in colonies and citizens of the capital, dedicate the great temple to his divine parent in the Forum and the altar of Victory in the Senate House and celebrate the anniversaries of his victories at Naulochus and Actium (August 13th — September 3rd). He had, as he said in *Res gestae* 34, everything in his power (*rerum omnium potitus*).

He spent the next fifteen months in dismantling the legacy of the civil wars: he restored the collegiate character of the consulate in February, 28, followed this up with a censorship which, though we focus on the number removed from the list, ratified the membership of the rest whatever their past political affiliation, and ceremonially gave the Senate and People a clean start symbolised by the *lustrum*. The treasury was restored to the public domain when ex-praetors chosen by the Senate were put in charge of it (Dio 53.2);[1] replacing whom? *Praefecti* perhaps chosen by the triumvirs (or one of them), but pretty certainly not Senators either elected to the post or nominated by the Senate. The legal system was reinstated by the appointment of its head, an urban praetor, and the abolition of all the unratified acts of the triumvirs at the end of the year. The rule of

---

[1] Replaced in 23 by praetors in their year of office chosen by lot (Dio 53.32.2). Tacitus *Ann.* 13.28–9 records no change till Claudius' time, but his comments "the lot kept falling on unsuitable men" and as a result the arrangement "did not last long" are odd for one which lasted (on this account) for 78 years.

law was restored.[2]

The final step was to invite the Senate to nominate the army commanders by selecting the provinces to be allocated to the consuls,[3] a decree which would traditionally be followed by one nominating the praetors to draw lots for the others in the pre-civil war fashion. This step represented the final dismantling of the apparatus of civil war (in which the triumvirs had had their nominees given *imperium* by titular office as praetors or consuls, then military or provincial commands at their own discretion). Whether this was or was not the restoration of the public business (*res publica*) to the traditional managers the Senate and People can be, and has been, debated. But the power to direct control of the areas of the public business which had given rise to the civil wars was formally offered to the Senate. No wonder the Senators were horrified and were happy enough when the Caesar took charge of the three provinces from which the civil wars had been generated.

Augustus, as he now became, went overseas within six months and took no part in senatorial debate or life till late in 24.[4] Nine months after that and after a serious illness he withdrew still further from public office by resigning the consulate and saying that all he needed to protect the common people, the *plebs* his clients, were the powers of a tribune.

Resistance this time was more serious and prolonged and did not come only from Senators. Events over which neither he nor the Senate had any control, the weather and an outbreak of plague, brought demands that he should be invested with overriding dictatorial powers to meet the people's needs for food (which he did without accepting new powers), then to discipline the wealthy classes (to which he contributed by naming censors, both nobles, and by enactments of his own during the censorship); then for four years they elected him to the consulate every time he or Agrippa was not present to resist them.[5]

The process of encroachment thus comes out of a background of withdrawals from offices and refusals to accept offices; it must also be borne in mind that it is at least possible that some of the apparent

---

[2] So Velleius (2.89.3) ... *restituta vis legibus, iudiciis auctoritas* ... and the recently marketed *aureus* LEGES ET IURA P R RESTITUIT (if it is genuine), see chap. 3 n.36.
[3] See chap. 3.
[4] In time for the consular elections, chap. 4.
[5] See chap. 6.

encroachments may have got their initiatives not from Augustus but from those who preferred him to be in charge rather than the nobles of the Senatorial families. The different areas of the state's activity must also be distinguished: Augustus refrained from holding public office except very rarely, but was able to make up for any apparent shortage of consequent executive powers by the device of pro-consular *imperium* equal to that of the consuls,[6] which enabled him to enforce his decisions if he were challenged, and of *tribunicia potestas*, which enabled him to introduce business to the Senate or popular assembly when he wished. In consequence, the public business he drew into his own hands and many of the measures he took after 19 when the encroachment process got under way were executive, and we do not usually know whether the initiative came from Augustus himself, his *amici* (or advisers) or others.

Honours

Honours seem to have been thrust upon Augustus rather than sought. This was certainly the case in 19 (see chapter 2) and the other occasions on which he returned to the city, his election to the position of *Pontifex Maximus* (*R.g.* 10.2) and the gift of the supreme honour of *Pater Patriae* (*R.g.* 35). The election of his grandson Gaius to the consulate was contrary to his wishes,[7] and the public expressions of grief at his death and that of his brother Lucius can be assumed to have been spontaneous.[8] On the other hand, we do not know how far Augustus was prompted in his successive promotions of Tiberius. Crook argues, very persuasively, that Augustus, 'implacable' and 'indefatigable' in the path of duty, was responsible (*CAH* X[2] 105ff.), and accepted the consequences for Agrippa Postumus. But it was the creation of a 'divine family' which was his major encroachment, *id.* 94.

The army

One area in which there was never any retreat from sole charge was control of the armies, and with it, direction of provincial and foreign policy. He had had this in 31, and it is likely that few wanted him to share it. Yet on the first occasion after 27 when envoys from Parthia

---

[6] From 19, see chap. 6.

[7] Dio 55.9.2, though Tacitus (*Ann.* 1.3.2) says his opposition was hypocritical and he passionately wanted it.

[8] E.g. the inscriptions from Pisa, *ILS* 139, 140 = E–J 68, 69.

came to Rome, Augustus referred them to the Senate. The Senate referred them back to him for negotiations (Dio 53.33.1f.). This might be seen as a precedent enabling him to conduct future negotiations without reference to the Senate. Certainly he received envoys in Samos (at least),[9] and established client kings and links of *amicitia* with peoples to the East of the empire while he was in the East between 22 and 19. Dio does not say whether these negotiations were reported to Rome or not, though in a generalising passage (53.21.6) he mentions the Senate as continuing to receive embassies and negotiate. *Res gestae* (31f.) may suggest that the Indian embassies of Dio (*loc. cit.*) were not reported, but this section of *Res gestae* mingles *me*, *nostrum* (our), and "the Roman People" without careful discrimination.[10]

Augustus never, so far as we know, proposed that anyone should command an army after 19 save as his own lieutenant or colleague, nor that any troops should be recruited by or take an oath of allegiance to anyone else. This was, and must have been seen as, the best guarantee against any revival of civil war — which was what the vast majority of the population wanted. In this field there was no encroachment, just the maintenance of the *status quo*, a monopoly of control.

Staffing the provinces and maintaining the officer cadres for the armies put an enormous number of appointments into Augustus' hands, at many levels. Many of these must have been made on the recommendation of or even directly by deputies who had his ear, and the growth of this group into what was in effect a court which did not so much encroach on as swamp all previous networks of influence and patronage was inevitable.[11]

Finance

Continuing command of the armies imposed responsibility for their

---

[9] Dio 54.9.7f. He also speaks of an Indian envoy in Athens, but it is not clear whether he travelled there with Augustus or met with him there, *ibid.* 9f.

[10] He received them as *dux* (commander in the field); the next sentence speaks of "our" *amicitia* (friendship). In *id.* 32.1 fugitives came "to me", in 32.2 hostages were sent "to me" to seek "our" *amicitia*. 32.3 speaks of the *fides* of the *p.R.* and ties of *amicitia* "when I was *princeps*" (*me principe*). Cf. *id.* 30, the Dacians' army was defeated *meis auspiciis*, and later *exercitus meus* compelled submission. If there is any distinction, it is between those in the field, him and his army, and the diplomatic organs of the *res publica*.

[11] So A. Wallace-Hadrill *Augustan Rome* (Bristol 1993) 30f.

recruitment, pay and discharge after service. Financing them was, as it had been before the civil wars, the chief expenditure of the *res publica*. It was expressed as the *ornatio* of the provinces — paying that is for their government, the greater the number of troops the greater the *ornatio* (and profit). What was not spent on the army and navy was spent on feeding the population of Rome — the so-called 'corn dole', public works (much neglected) and religious buildings, festivals and shows, though much of this was left to private enterprise. Before and during the civil wars much of the public revenue also disappeared into the pockets of the governing class through excessive allowances, the profits of patronage and office and bribery. We have Tacitus' word for it (*Ann.* 1.2.2) that this diminished under Augustus. Whether this curtailment of the profits of the nobles should be included as an encroachment on the *res publica* may be debated.

Of the disbursements from the *aerarium* (treasury), nominally at least under the control of Senators since 28, Augustus must have been the chief recipient since the provinces under his control contained most of the armies which had to be paid. Even if he got an enormous revenue from Egypt (Vell. 2.39.2),[12] and it was a general principle that provinces should pay the cost of their governmental staff,[13] some were certainly too poor and too expensive in terms of troops required (like Pannonia/Moesia). The *aerarium* seems to have been chronically short of funds, and Augustus claims to have subvented it four times from his own vast resources (*R.g.* 17.1). He thus took a great interest in it.

In 13 when Augustus standardised the conditions of service in the legions (Dio 54.25.5f.), he converted the entitlement of a farm on discharge into a monetary payment. This pleased landowners, we are told, particularly those in Italy with the assurance that their lands would not again be liable to confiscation for veterans, as had happened in the civil wars from Sulla's time. Those who were given lands thereafter were settled in colonies in conquered territories in

---

[12] Vell. 2.39.2; this was as much as Caesar got from Gaul, which (*loc. cit.*) brought in as much as the rest of the empire. Augustus deposited his surplus from Egypt in the *aerarium* (*loc. cit.*), which gave him a very good reason for being concerned about it. A.H.M. Jones *Augustus* (London 1970) 120f. supposes this to be the source from which the armies and other activities under his charge will have been funded.

[13] The clear implication of Cic. *Man.* 14, and this is why poorer areas where possible were left to client kings. Jones *loc. cit.* (n.12) for a hypothetical reconstruction of how the system worked, but he does not distinguish the funding of the armies from that of the administration of the provinces.

areas derisorily called by a leading mutineer in AD 14 "marshy swamps and barren mountains" (Tac. *Ann.* 1.17.3). This was an improvement on what had gone before rather than an encroachment on the *res publica*.

The next major development in army pay and conditions did encroach on the pockets of the Romans themselves. This was the establishment of the *aerarium militare* in AD 6 to pay the gratuities of the troops on discharge (Dio 55.24.9). This treasury always remained outside the management of the Senate, though the Senators had to pay their contributions when liable to the taxes which fed it. Naturally they resented these, though Augustus sweetened the pill by promising a special grant to start it off (*R.g.* 17.2), and an annual contribution (Dio 55.25.3). Augustus negotiated and invited Senators to make alternative suggestions, but eventually introduced his own ideas, 'experimentally' in the first place although he made them permanent some seven years later, in AD 13, meeting objections with much more distasteful proposals (Dio 56.28.4–6). This was un-doubtedly an encroachment on their previous tax-free status, and on the Senate's control of finance. But the process of imposition illustrates, perhaps, the caution which characterised Augustus' methods: the policy was determined, the Senate invited to discuss ways and means and make suggestions, implementation was decided 'experimentally' to soothe feelings, and, after a few years habituation, made to appear less objectionable than the alternative.

Coinage

The evidence of the coinage is that for a time, perhaps from 19, the traditional officers of the mint, the *iiiviri a a a f f*, put their own names on the coins issued under their direction in Rome as agents of the Senate which decided on how much metal there was to be available for turning into coinage.[14] Most of the silver and gold for the precious metal currency, which had real rather than token value, was not brought to Rome however but to mints in the areas where it was needed for paying the troops.[15] This was more convenient and more sensible and represented no change at least from the civil war period, during which the combatants coined enormous quantities of bullion

[14] Sutherland *RIC* I² p.3, and cf. chap. 7 above.
[15] Ephesus and Pergamum 28–18 BC, *RIC* I² 476–526, including one issue of *aes*; Carisius' coinage in Spain *id.* 1–10, also *aes*, and "uncertain mints" issues, *id.* 26–153 (19–16 BC), Lugdunum from 15 BC *id.* 162–277.

for their troops as they moved. But it represented an encroachment on the arrangements before the civil wars, when there was no standing army and a monopoly of coining by the *aerarium*.

After 13 the *iiiviri a a a f f* minted no more gold or silver coins with their names on them; after 5, by which time there seems to have been four of them, they ceased to put their names on any coins they minted. A large issue of *aes* (bronze token) coinage was made in AD 10–12 in the names of Augustus or Tiberius dated by their years of *trib. pot.* There is no information as to why these developments took place, whether the *iiiviri* voluntarily gave up the privilege of putting their names on the coins, or whether it was taken away from them.

Censorial functions

In *Res gestae* 8 Augustus mentions three *lectiones* (revisions of the roll) of the Senate (undated) and three censuses dated to 28, 8 and AD 14.[16] In addition he gives (in *R.g.* 6) three occasions on which he was voted sole curator of laws and morals with supreme power (19, 18 and 11), but he "never accepted any position inconsistent with the *mores maiorum*" (tradition). This has been interpreted as meaning he took the censorial powers mentioned by Dio as being granted for five years in 19 and 12 (54.10.5 and 54.30.1).[17] The administrative measures he took to bring home to the Senators their responsibilities encroached upon their *libertas* (independence). The right to stay away from meetings as a criticism of the consul was traditional[18] (and

---

[16] Whether the three *lectiones* were or were not part of the censuses has been disputed. *R.g.* dates the censuses as 28, 8 and AD 14. Dio mentions three *lectiones* in the course of his work: in 13 (54.26.3), in 11 (54.35.1) and AD 4 (55.13.3). These are usually thought to be additional to the censuses but the sources are mutually contradictory, Brunt and Moore 50f. The difficulty and danger of this task is shown by Augustus' decision to wear a breastplate under his toga on at least one occasion while doing it, bearing a sword (Suet. *Aug.* 35.1) and with a strong bodyguard of his friends (*ibid.*). This has been associated both with the census of 28 and with the purge of 18, which he began, perhaps with Agrippa (Dio 54.12–15), and converted into an elaborate system of co-option, but it failed. The *lectio* of AD 4, using a system of selection, seems to have succeeded (Dio 55.13.3–6). The failure to complete in 18, and the completion in AD 4, may explain why Dio does not include the former, but does include the latter among Augustus' *lectiones*.

[17] Note that the *fasti Venusini* (*CIL* IX 422) mention *censoria potestas*.

[18] At times ostentatious, as for example Cicero absenting himself on September 1st, 44, W.K. Lacey *Cicero and the End of the Roman Republic* (London 1978) 150, Elizabeth Rawson *Cicero: a Portrait* (London 1975) 271, and most other authors on this period. Staying away was also a ploy to prevent consuls presenting business which required a *frequens senatus* (well-attended meeting), as happened to Caesar in the later months of 59, and to M. Antonius in 44.

many examples can be found in the correspondence of Cicero for example), and so was the right of the consul to fine absentees, though we do not hear of instances of this happening. We do not know if the absenteeism which Augustus met with was in criticism of his management of business, or of the importance or relevance of the business or of him as Princeps, but senatorial life certainly became less attractive for some. Augustus used the traditional coercive measures of fines, and increased them in 17 (Dio 54.18.3) and again in 9 (Dio 55.3.2) and on the latter occasion he took steps to enforce the payment of unpaid fines (*ibid.* 3). He also deprived men of the excuses that they did not know of the meeting nor that their presence was expected, by publishing a list of the two meetings a month which they were required to attend and for which other business was to be suspended, and another list of the names of those required to attend, annually revised, also the number of those required to make a quorum for the different classes of business (cf. Suet. *Aug.* 35.3).

These rules certainly altered the status of Senator from one of unfettered privilege to one of privilege matched by obligations to the *res publica*, and Augustus' encroachments in this area may be his response to a growing lack of co-operation with his unrelenting demands, prompted, perhaps, by the *leges Iuliae* of 18; see also Crook *CAH* X² 94ff.

Some Senators might have been unwilling to attend meetings. Other men of senatorial wealth were unwilling to become Senators at all. The poet Ovid is an example; his refusal to enter on a senatorial career was a refusal to rise in standing, as his family was equestrian not senatorial. But some wanted to drop out of the senatorial order altogether and used the excuse of poverty, an excuse made more plausible by Augustus' raising the qualification to a million sesterces in 13 (Dio 54.26.3) from 400,000 (54.17.3); Suetonius' figures are to 1,200,000 from 800,000 (*Aug.* 41.1). And to us too it must seem plausible that those who did not win offices and were deprived of their traditional sources of income from the profits of patronage and power did become impoverished. Others are reported as rich enough but unwilling. For example, on returning to Rome in 13 Augustus compelled those under thirty-five years of age who had the financial means to enrol.

This year too there was a shortage of candidates for the tribunate, which had lost popularity as there were now no powers (Dio 54.30.2). Before Augustus' return an interim measure was passed whereby the requisite number were recruited by lot from among the ex-quaestors

under the age of forty (Dio 54.26.7). Augustus took the interim step
of making each of the magistrates nominate one man from outside
the Senate with the necessary financial standing and put his name to
the assembly for election, on the understanding that after his year of
office he could either revert to the standing of *eques* or remain a
Senator. We are not told how many took each option.

This was one way of recruiting new Senators. A more important
way of recruiting new blood was taken in Augustus' absence. This
was through the vigintivirate[19] (Dio 54.26.5-7), through which
citizens of sufficient wealth could gain access to the Senate whatever
their place of birth. This was a much better way — gaining volunteers
— and seems to have been effective, as the problems did not recur (at
least in the evidence we have); it was not Augustus' initiative
however, as Dio stresses.

Resistance to performing the duties of Senators is also evident in
Dio's record (in 11, 54.36.1) that the tribunes and aediles had been
negligent in carrying out their function of supervision of the public
records.

In regard to the moral aspects of his social legislation, Augustus
claimed (*Res gestae* 6.2) that the *leges Iuliae* of 18 were in response to
the expressed wishes of the Senate. It has (with some justice) been
doubted whether the Senators really wanted the freedom to manage
their own lives compromised in the ways in which it was; this does not
mean that they did not assent to the proposition that something
should be done about the loosening of the traditional norms in
society. After all, the nobles' own champion Sulla as well as Caesar
had legislated in this area, and Cicero might well not have been the
only one to support Caesar, as he did in *Pro Marcello*.[20] But it is clear
that the *leges Iuliae* as passed provoked opposition, though it took
over a quarter of a century before the amending legislation, the *lex
Papia Poppaea* of AD 9, was enacted.[21] We should assume that this
law was not passed in the teeth of opposition from Augustus, but it

[19] The college of 20: 3 *tresviri capitales*, responsible for executions (not "criminal
trials" as in LCL); 3 *tresviri a a a f f*, or *monetales* (mint officials); 4 *quattuorviri viis in
urbe purgandis* (responsible for street-cleaning); 10 *decemviri stlitibus iudicandis*
(presidents of the centumviral courts before which many, if not most, civil cases in
Rome were argued). Cf. Suet. *Aug.* 36.

[20] Esp. section 23.

[21] Dio attributes the opposition to the *equites* (56.1.2), introducing a long speech
on this topic (*id.* 56.2-9). Cf. Suet. *Aug.* 34. Tacitus' comment (*Ann.* 3.28.3f.) is not that
the rules were made more rigid but that informers (the means for enforcing them) were
encouraged.

represented some withdrawal from his previous more rigid stance.[22] Laws to control the numbers of slaves emancipated by their masters were also passed by consuls a little earlier, Fufius and Caninius in 2 and Aelius and Sentius in AD 4. These too encroached on the freedom men had had in respect of their families, but the laws were not Augustus' own, and perhaps were enacted with the assent of most of the Senate.

Elections

Elections continued to be seriously contested. These have been discussed by E.S. Staveley.[23] Augustus quickly abandoned his idea of having the votes from his friends in the Senates of the Italian colonies given a place in the *comitia* in Rome. Laws against electoral bribery mean that competition for some offices was keen. But such laws were not innovations; they had existed, even if they were not enforced, before the civil wars. And if they were disliked (for which there is no evidence) they were hard to argue against even if they encroached on the Senators' independence in managing their income.[24] The introduction of the pre-electoral college in memory of his 'sons' known from the *Tabula Hebana*[25] had the effective result of making the traditional voting in the *comitia* almost a foregone conclusion. This did not alienate sympathy for Augustus however, since two years later, when he sought to withdraw from the elections on account of his age and the strain of the personal canvass he had been in the habit of making, there were riots; Augustus was compelled to nominate the magistrates for the year AD 7, and from then on to publish a list of those whom he favoured.[26] These riots indicated that the exercise of

[22] Amendments were also made to the *lex Voconia*, easing the rules governing women's rights in succession.

[23] *Greek and Roman Voting and Elections* (London 1972) chap. 12.

[24] *Lex Iulia de ambitu* (of 18) must show there was bribery, and that in turn shows competition for office, and that the elections under Augustus were not foregone conclusions. In AD 8 Dio mentions candidates having to give surety for their conduct, which they would forfeit if they were found to have used bribes, which also suggests that bribery was alleged. In this context we have to remember that giving gifts to the members of your own tribe was not bribery either under the 'Republic' or under Augustus. He 'always' gave gifts to the two tribes to which he was affiliated, *Fabia* by adoption by Caesar, *Scaptia* by birth, Suet. *Aug.* 40.2.

[25] *Lex Valeria Cornelia*; there is a very extensive bibliography on this law, but it does not affect this point. Text in E–J² (1976) 94a. For the college's duration, Syme *Tacitus* 756–60 (Appx 67). He thinks it quite short-lived.

[26] Following the riots, Dio 55.34.2. Dio does no more than imply that Augustus was asked to state his preferences. But it is probable.

the traditional *commendatio* of leading Senators was expected of him, and no doubt very welcome to those he favoured.

Political life

While Augustus continued into old age the social custom of a morning *salutatio* (levée) open to all, in his house (Suet. *Aug.* 53.2), these occasions can hardly have taken place daily, but when they did take place they must have usurped the place of the consuls' *salutatio* which Senators had attended first thing in the morning in the time of the 'Republic' with or without an invitation to discuss public affairs and prepare the business of the Senate. This open type of forum for discussing public business was replaced by a 'committee'[27] to preprocess senatorial business in Augustus' house. The significance of this for encroachment on the *res publica* is twofold: **(1)** it was a closed group of advisers, even if its membership changed every six months; only those magistrates and Senators who drew the lots could attend, and **(2)** it met in Augustus' house whether or not he was consul, and usually he was not. It was thus more like the cabinet of a ruler than the *consilium* of *amici* (council of supporters) of the 'republican' magistrate. Crook has suggested[28] that even this body did not initiate policies; it may only have scrutinised them and acted as a sounding-board, to enable Augustus to gauge the probable reception proposals might receive in the Senate. Policies were more probably initiated by a (to us) more shadowy body of *amici* who met in private, as coteries of nobles had always done, on social occasions, rather than at the open meetings, *salutationes*, before the Senate met. Cicero, for example, used to find out from Atticus what went on at such gatherings; the presence of non-senators at these was no innovation. We cannot trace the steps by which this 'committee' came into being, nor the dates,[29] though by 4 it had been formally constituted and recognised as having a place in

[27] J.A. Crook *Consilium Principis* (Cambridge 1955) chap. 2.

[28] Crook *Consilium Principis* 11. He sees them as the seed from which the *consilium principis* of later emperors grew. *Amici* included non-senators; we can name Maecenas without hesitation.

[29] But obviously some time when he was in Rome for a protracted period. These were not frequent before 13. Fergus Millar 'State and subject: the impact of monarchy' in Millar and Segal 43 has calculated that in the eighteen years from Actium he was in Rome for about 7 years. After 13 (when he reached the age of 50) he was rarely away, especially after Tiberius' triumph in 7.

the political life of the state.[30]

Self-glorification

Republican *nobiles* had glorified their families by erecting buildings.[31] This continued under Augustus, especially at the beginning of his Principate. He actually encouraged others to build and repair public works (Suet. *Aug.* 29.4f.) and helped some of them (Dio 54.24.2f.), though his own works and those of Agrippa far outshone them in magnificence. Spoils are said to have been one source of their funds,[32] and all the people listed by Suetonius (except Agrippa) were *triumphatores*.[33] But triumphs disappeared from the scene after 19, except for the imperial family, so that a near monopoly in building was created. Families which had already erected buildings may have been like the Pompeii, who under Tiberius could not afford to repair the theatre which bore the family name. Those who could petitioned the Senate for leave to do so.[34] But this was under Tiberius.

Games and spectacles, traditionally a means for aspiring politicians to win public attention, and so used by the Caesars, were brought under supervision, which was another encroachment on the independence of the Senators. Dio's account is dated to 22 (54.2.3–4), but he must be reporting developments over time. Augustus abolished some public banquets and reduced others to a more modest scale; he reduced the opportunities for competition among aspiring or ambitious younger men and the scope for rivalry in winning popular favour by putting the public festivals in charge of the praetors (quite senior magistrates) who were provided with funds from the treasury, and no member of a college was allowed to

[30] Crook *Consilium Principis* (n.27) for the *s.c. Calvisianum* from the fifth edict of Cyrene. See also Suet. *Aug.* 35.3–37 for other cases of encroachment.

[31] Zanker *Images* 18–25, noting that political strife since the time of the Gracchi had inhibited proper planning and construction of buildings for the *plebs* to use, and had encouraged politically motivated expressions of success, like Opimius' restoration of the temple of *Concordia* or Sulla's temple of *Iuppiter Optimus Maximus*, while allowing the old cult shrines to decay — giving Octavian his chance to build for the people and the old divinities.

[32] Tac. *Ann.* 3.72.1.

[33] Cf. Vell. 2.89.4, J.M. Carter *Suetonius, Divus Augustus* (Bristol 1982) 132 (comm. on 29.5) for a list. Balbus, the last *triumphator* outside the Julian family, dedicated his theatre in 13. The exception was Agrippa who never triumphed, for reasons unknown (a suggestion in chap. 2), but erected public buildings, especially for the *plebs*.

[34] Tac. *Ann.* 3.72.2.

outspend his colleagues, or put on a gladiatorial show without the leave of the Senate. As Wallace-Hadrill remarks[35] "so long as he (Augustus) refused to allow others independent power-bases in popular citizen support and military triumph, the ambitious must necessarily look towards him ...". That is, he encroached on others' independence in this area too, by reserving for himself the more spectacular performances. These he gave on occasions when he wanted to commend his family members to the general public, as in 2 at the opening of the temple of Mars Ultor and the Forum which bore his own name.[36]

Encroachments on the laws

In the sphere of the law Augustus claimed (*Res gestae* 8.5) that he introduced legislation which revived traditional practices, but he also encroached on the prerogatives of the courts and other magistrates with legal powers. In this latter sphere he frequently sat as a judge of the first instance in civil and (rarely) in criminal cases, presumably by virtue of his proconsular *imperium*.[37] Though traditional this jurisdiction seems to have occurred only very rarely in the late 'Republic'. He must also have had the right (and responsibility) to act as a court of appeal from the rulings of those who were his *legati* in the provinces, who will have had to hear cases affecting Roman citizens and communities (*civitates*). Such jurisdiction was only proper for the proconsul of the province, but it encroached on the independence of those who hitherto had been responsible for dispensing justice and could only be appealed against by prosecution in the *quaestiones perpetuae* in Rome, where the provincials chance of gaining redress was not good — as Tacitus remarks in *Annals* 1.2.2. We do not know when such appeals began, nor whether they were begun on the initiative of Augustus or the *legati* or the litigants, but it seems quite probable that the process started without any *senatus consultum* or law, but simply because the *legati* were *legati* and not the final authority. However, in A.H.M. Jones' judgement "His system of courts of appeal was by far the most important change Augustus made", and "the facility of appeal must have remedied

---

[35] Wallace-Hadrill *Augustan Rome* (n.11) 30. Cf. Zanker's emphasis (*Images* 20) on the Senate's prevention of the building of recreational centres which the *plebs* might use for expressing themselves.

[36] See chap. 9.

[37] From 19. So Jones *Augustus* (n.12) chap. 11.

many injustices and reversed many erroneous decisions".[38] This verdict implies a low view of the legal competence of the governors of Augustus' provinces, and their neglect to take legal experts with them (perhaps they were not encouraged to do so), and a favourable one of the skill of Augustus and his legal advisers. If Jones is right, it is no wonder that the provinces approved of the Principate as Tacitus said.

Another innovation which had a long life was the introduction of the city prefect's court for dealing with petty crime;[39] by Nero's time it had taken over much of the work of the *iudicia publica* of the *res publica*. Here again there is encroachment, since the city prefect was appointed by the Princeps, and was not an officer elected by the People. On the other hand, Augustus upheld the principle for which the Senators had fought hard in the late 'Republic', that Senators should be tried by their peers. Under his successor this had terrible results, but they were hardly Augustus' fault.

Religion

Religio, the traditional round of observances, was part of the *res publica*; indeed matters of *religio* had priority in the Senate. After Actium, or more exactly after the young Caesar's return from Egypt and his triumph, *religio* was one of his first concerns, with the massive programme of restoration and reconstruction of ancient temples, and the revival of old cults and priesthoods as an atonement for the civil wars. He lavished enormous sums of money on the great temple of *Iuppiter Optimus Maximus*, though the sums stated by Suetonius in his account are impossibly large.[40]

Later, however, a subtle change took place as the cults favoured by Augustus encroached on Jupiter's: those of Apollo, whom he regarded as his personal champion and guardian; Mars, the father of Romulus, and hence of the Roman People; and Venus, the divine ancestor of the deified Julius and Augustus himself. We need not doubt that elements of the state cult of Jupiter went on, the prayers at the beginning of the year, and the first meeting of the year being held in his temple;[41] but the Sibylline books were transferred to the temple

[38] *Augustus* 129f.
[39] Tacitus *Ann.* 6.11.2 stresses the maintenance of law and order as the principal reason for the appointment.
[40] Suet. *Aug.* 30.2. The figures are impossible because they exceed the total of the sums Augustus says he gave away (*R.g.* 21.2), Brunt and Moore 63 (note *ad loc.*).
[41] Alan Wardman *Religion and Statecraft among the Romans* (London 1982) 4, 11.

of Apollo on the Palatine, and after the opening of the temple of
Mars Ultor in the Forum Augustum in 2 virtually all military
business conducted in Rome was moved there from Jupiter's temple.
It is true that Jupiter still granted *imperium* to magistrates and to
proconsuls when they set out, and presided over the ceremony of the
auspicia,[42] but except for the imperial family these no longer had any
military significance, as they alone campaigned *suis auspiciis* (under
their own *auspicia*) and carried their victory laurels to Jupiter's
temple in a curule triumph (after 19). By making it more exclusive,
Augustus sidelined the temple and cult. Augustus was also criticised
for erecting another temple to Jupiter on the Capitol — that of
Jupiter Tonans — to commemorate his escape from a lightning strike
when in Spain in 26/5, which was criticised for diverting worshippers
from the great temple on the summit of the hill.[43] We do not know
how justified this was.

The temple of Apollo however became more and more central to
the day-to-day life of the *res publica*. Augustus said the site was
indicated to him by a stroke of lightning[44] (though lightning was
properly in the sphere of Jupiter). Apollo had associations with his
victories at Naulochus and Actium; the temple was dedicated on
October 9th, 28, significantly the year in which the *res publica* was
being reinstituted, and received custody of the Sibylline books.[45] In
its situation next to Augustus' own house it was made a virtual part
of the *Palatium* when he was made *Pontifex Maximus* in 12, being
linked to it by a portico which had a shrine of Augustus' family gods
in it.[46] Meetings of the Senate took place there in Augustus' old age,
and under Tiberius we find the portico being described as both *in
Palatio* and *ad Apollinis* (in the Palace and at Apollo's temple) and
being used for the drafting committee of a *senatus consultum*.[47]

The great temple to Divine Julius stood in the Forum on the site
where he was cremated; it was dedicated as part of the triumphal
celebrations in 29 (August 18th), and adorned with *rostra* (ships'

---

[42] J.S. Richardson '*Imperium romanum*: empire and the language of power' *JRS* 81
(1991) 1–9.

[43] To Jupiter Tonans, Suet. *Aug.* 29.1; dedicated in 22, Dio 54.4.2; on September
1st, E–J p.51; illustrated on a series of coins of about 19, *RIC* I² p.46.

[44] Suet. *Aug.* 29.3, and cf. Brunt and Moore 63 (n. on 21.2).

[45] It also had libraries attached to it, the best in Rome, which fact must also have
prompted interest in it and visits to it among the literate members of the population.

[46] See chap. 8.

[47] Explicit in the 'Piso decree', to be published shortly by Prof. Dr W. Eck. I am
grateful for the privilege of sighting a draft.

prows) from the navy defeated at Actium (Dio 51.22). But it seems to have been little used in public life. This is not surprising, as Augustus gradually played down his inheritance from the dictator.

By contrast, the cults of Mars and Venus, linked in Greek myth in the humorous story[48] of their being caught *in flagranti delicto* committing adultery, but in Augustan publicity as the founders of the Roman race (Mars being father of Romulus and Venus mother of Aeneas and ancestress of the Julian family), were much favoured. They received early honours in the Pantheon when Agrippa converted it into a shrine to the Julian dynasty when it was opened in the Campus Martius in 26. The association was repeated on the *Ara Pacis Augustae*[49] and carried much further in the great temple to Mars Ultor in which the avenging of Caesar was associated with the triumphs of the Roman People and the Julian line — and with Augustus himself, since his name was carved on the architrave and on ground level in front where the words *Pater Patriae* were added below the inscription on the victory chariot.[50]

The temple of Mars Ultor also took over custody of the standards recovered from the Parthians which had previously been housed on the Capitol in the small temple sited significantly next to that of Jupiter Feretrius where all *spolia opima* were housed — and which Augustus himself had caused to be rebuilt.[51]

Augustus' use of the traditional family cults has been treated in chapter 8 above.

His dynasty

Roman tradition dictated that Augustus' family should play a leading part in his *res publica*. Families, each under its own *paterfamilias*, had always been linked with one another in a maze of marriage relationships, hereditary obligations earned by good turns, help in elections and in promoting the careers of family members, friends and retainers (clients). Leading families had always been

---

[48] *Odyssey* 8.266–366. For Roman precedents, Weinstock *Divus Julius* 128f.
[49] Zanker *Images* 201–3.
[50] *R.g.* 35. The Senate had voted the triumphal chariot.
[51] See chap. 7, esp. n.15. The date of the temple is unknown; it was suggested to Octavian by Atticus who died in 32; it was then roofless, and Augustus includes it in a list of the temples he built rather than repaired (*R.g.* 19). The 'evidence' of the linen corslet of Cornelius Cossus (Livy 4.20) and the obvious addition of this section to Livy's text indicate an early date. Zanker *Images* 103 implies a belief that Octavian acted promptly on Atticus' advice.

cultivated by those without a voice in the Senate but who wanted their voices to be heard in the *res publica*. A man's family dictated where he started in public life, as a future Senator, an *eques*, a *domi nobilis* (magnate at home, i.e. in one of the *municipia* (self governing towns) of Italy), or a member of the *plebs*.

Of no one was this more true than of Augustus himself, who as the young C. Octavius owed his whole position to his testamentary adoption by Julius Caesar. Once he accepted that legacy he became *paterfamilias* to the house of the Caesars and was entitled to seek the support of all who had regarded the dictator as their patron and defender. He also took on the responsibility of seeing to the continuation of the Julian family, by procreation or adoption. When he failed to procreate more than one daughter, Julia, the issue of who would be the next head of the Julian family became, after Actium, not just an academic question, but a matter of vital importance to the state,[52] since the heir or heirs would inherit the status of *patronus* to the whole of the army and the *plebs*, because the whole army had taken the oath of obedience to him. This also was no innovation; Roman armies had always sworn to serve and obey their commander, not the *res publica*.

It was not within Augustus' power, and certainly not in his interest, to change this situation and make the armies the forces of the *res publica* or the Senate or one of the gods of the Roman pantheon. He made no attempt to do so, but recognised that it was necessary to have an heir to the Julian house by adoption, who would be able to command the loyalty of the army and the consent of the civil population, *plebs* and Senate alike. In the crisis of 23, when he thought he was going to die, he recognised that the only person who could command the loyalty of the troops was Agrippa, whether or not he was named in his will as heir. However, his heir was and remained unknown because his will remained sealed.

The death of his first son-in-law Marcellus in 23 made Augustus choose Agrippa to be his new son-in-law despite his lack of pedigree (or possibly because of it) and the difference in age, and to raise up grandchildren for the Caesars. This he did, and Augustus adopted the two eldest boys as Gaius and Lucius Caesar. The family now had *heredes sui* (heirs by right). Agrippa became guardian to the family

---

[52] Even before Actium he must have made a will and named an heir, but it probably did not matter much since the Caesarian armies would surely have deserted to M. Antonius' banner had Octavian been killed or died.

and was given an appropriate place in political life, as partner in tribunician power and proconsular *imperium*. When he died in 12 (he was only about fifty), Livia's sons became the guardians of Augustus' children. Tiberius became the third husband of the widow Julia, now aged about twenty-five. Augustus sent the brothers to win honours in the army, and this they did, though Drusus died on service.

When Tiberius for reasons unknown to us withdrew his services Augustus brought forward his young sons; Gaius was fourteen. Whatever the Senate thought about it we do not know, but the electoral assembly chose Gaius Caesar as consul at the age of fourteen. There was plainly no need to force him onto the Roman People.[53] Augustus modified the vote, but introduced him to the Senate's business with a view to a consulate at the age of nineteen, in AD 1. He never held office in Rome, however, as he was sent with a strong body of advisers to win military honours in the East, but was wounded and died without returning to Rome. Lucius Caesar, for whom similar honours had been obtained, had previously died outside the city. Augustus now reverted to Tiberius in preference to his remaining grandson or the husbands of his grand-daughters, and made him heir to the house of the Caesars by adoption. We do not know if this had the support of the Senate and People or the army. At all events they acquiesced and Tiberius and his nephew Germanicus were sent to win military laurels, which they did, though not perhaps as decisively as Augustus, or they, would have wished. And the Senate acquiesced in the transfer of power in AD 14, swearing to support him (Tac. *Ann.* 1.7.2), on the initiative of the consuls of the year, before he had reached Rome from Augustus' deathbed.

The news of Augustus' death prompted a mutiny on the northern frontiers, but it came to nothing because the commanders refused to support the discontented troops, who appear in fact not to have had any alternative Princeps in mind. The truth was that the Romans had a choice between a family dynasty and civil war, unless Augustus took the risk of opening the door to the choice of others. The wisdom of not doing so may be seen in the fact that his thoroughly unsatisfactory successors kept the Principate in the family of the Caesars for fifty-five years, and they lost it only when it became apparent that Nero was not going to provide a successor in the family. The family-orientated traditions of Rome ensured that a family succession was necessary.

---

[53] Above and nn.7 and 8.

Adulatio

Tacitus saw *adulatio* (servile flattery) as the aspect of the Principate he found most distasteful. Certainly Domitian's megalomania and fear of challenges produced an upsurge in what may have been endemic, but Tacitus was perhaps naive in not recognising that toadying was inherent in the Roman system of patronage and clientship. Before the civil wars there was at least a suspicion of toadying within the retinues of the *principes viri*, and we must admit doubt about the purity of the motives of tribunes who proposed great commands for their leaders — Gabinius and Manilius for example in 67 and 66 or Trebonius in 55.

In Augustus' case we simply do not know how many, if any, of the magistracies and other offices he was offered and refused were in fact sponsored by men trying to win favour, or even following a hint that the nominations were wanted so that they could be declined.[54] We can be reasonably sure from his reactions at the time that the dictatorship offered him in 22 was unwelcome, and so was the reception planned for 19, because he avoided it by arriving at night. Moreover his habit of arriving and departing at night thereafter, already noted above (chap. 1), must indicate that he was less willing to receive public demonstrations of support than others to offer them.

Augustus had a very acute sense of what went too far,[55] but we never get into his inner counsels; if he revealed his opinions in his autobiography (and this is perhaps not very probable) it would not reach beyond 25. The records of the meetings of his inner circle of advisers, if they were ever put into writing, have naturally not been preserved. He also knew, apparently instinctively, how far he had to go to satisfy popular expectations; a good example is the way he regularly attended the shows the common people enjoyed so much, and joined in their enjoyment, his behaviour in this being compared favourably with that of Julius Caesar (Suet. *Aug.* 45) and of his

---

[54] Showers of honours began in the triumviral period. Lists in Dio after the victories at Naulochus, Actium and the fall of Alexandria. After 29, a list of honours declined is in *R.g.* 4–6, 10; most are datable between 23 and 19. See A. Wallace-Hadrill '*Civilis princeps*: between citizen and king' *JRS* 72 (1982) 32–48 for the view that *recusatio* was a basic, even indispensable and distinctive feature of the Roman monarchical style. Only an autocrat refuses, *nobiles* had always grabbed as many honours as possible. This trend may be most easily seen by those with the advantage of hindsight.

[55] Cf. Z. Yavetz 'The personality of Augustus' in Raaflaub and Toher *BRE* 1–41.

successor Tiberius (*id. Tib.* 47). The high level of support Augustus enjoyed from the common people can also be illustrated by their unwillingness to allow him to withdraw from the electoral processes in AD 7, despite the passing of the *lex Valeria Cornelia* two years previously which had reduced the elections to more or less a formality (n.25). His attempt to withdraw may be an example of his becoming more out of touch; so perhaps was his treatment of Julia, which raised objections and petitions to restore her. In this affair we know that he regretted the loss of the counsel of Agrippa and Maecenas,[56] and the lack of outspoken but trusted advisers may be one of the invisible problems of the last decade of his life.[57]

It should not surprise us if an ageing ruler after many years in control lost some of his ability and perhaps willingness to detect place-seekers and private agendas among those who surrounded him, and also if he became more intolerant of dissent. This phenomenon is common enough in our century when leaders who have led their people out of civil war or colonial status regularly become more dictatorial, and opposition becomes treason.

There are clear signs that Augustus became more eager to be represented favourably by the men of letters: he pressed Horace to resume writing poetry in lyric metres and to produce *Odes* Book IV. Though some of the poems are in similar vein to those of the first three books, there are others on public themes, in particular poems 4 and 14, which we are told were written at Augustus' behest,[58] to commemorate the victories of Tiberius and Drusus his brother.[59] Livy was persuaded to resume his History from the victory at Actium, the point he had reached in Book 133, where he originally stopped, and to continue as far as the death of Drusus in 9 before his own death. The summaries of the epitomator give no idea of the quality of this part of his work.[60] Ovid, the spokesman for those who rejected the boring life of a Senator, spent listening to debates on

[56] Seneca *Ben.* 6.32.2–4: "None of this would have happened to me had Agrippa or Maecenas been alive."

[57] Neither Agrippa nor Maecenas was a member of the old aristocracy, hence it may be suggested that they had an independence in viewpoint, and one different from that he encountered in most of the Senators.

[58] In the *Vita* attributed to Suetonius.

[59] In the Alpine region, between about 15 and 13.

[60] But it is unlikely that they were 'Pompeian' like the account of the late 'Republic'. They are regarded as an "epilogue" by Syme *History* 2, not begun till the resolution of the question of the succession in AD 4 after a period of retirement, *q.v.* for refs. to earlier work in *HSCPh* 64 (1959).

matters of less than crucial importance and undertaking periods of service outside Italy as staff-officers or civilian administrators, in favour of the excitements of sexual adventures in the capital,[61] compromised his independence by adding laudatory passages to the *Ars Amatoria* and turning to antiquities in the *Fasti*, the work he tired of and did not complete. *Fasti* also contains passages designed to please the regime. After his exile to Tomis on the Black Sea coast Ovid was not gagged, however, and was able to appeal to people prominent in public life by name without compromising them (so far as we can judge).[62]

In *History in Ovid*[63] Sir Ronald Syme has detailed a considerable undercurrent of writing of various kinds hostile to Augustus and Tiberius. These include a T. Labienus, whose works were burned by decree of the Senate, and Cassius Severus, the first person to be charged with treason (*maiestas minuta*) for his writings (Tac. *Ann.* 1.72.3). He was tried and banished to Crete (*id.* 4.21.3) in AD 8, the same year that Ovid was sent to Tomis. Augustus' censorship however seems not to have been severe, nor the prosecution of authors frequent.

When Tacitus refers to the falling off in the writing of distinguished history (*Ann.* 1.1.2) he implies that this began under and not after Augustus,[64] and in quoting an example of *adulatio* in the year AD 16 Tacitus says he mentions it to show that *adulatio* was deeply rooted and longstanding (*Ann.* 2.32.2). Yet a scrutiny of Dio in the last years of Augustus shows him using sources not uncritical for example of the campaigns during the Pannonian revolt (55.29.4, 30.5f., 32.3f.; 56.11–16); piracy and revolts in the provinces are mentioned (55.28.1f.) and resistance to the levies of troops to replace those lost in the disaster of Varus in AD 9 (56.23.2). Dio also records disturbances among the common people over the food shortages in

---

[61] Mockingly interpreted as harder than military service, *Am.* 1.9; cf. 2.9; 2.12. Reminders of the original association in legend of Mars and Venus were also perhaps unwelcome; see (e.g.) *Am.* 1.9.39f., and the oppositions of 1.8.29f., 41f. Proverbial for passion in *Am.* 2.5.27f.

[62] Including Livia, appealed to 3 times in the *Epistulae*, Syme *History* 226, and for other names *id.* 228.

[63] 212–4. Syme sees the punishment of Cassius as indicating that freedom of speech was now "curbed and subverted under pretext of social harmony".

[64] Syme (*History* 110) brackets Cremutius Cordus with Livy among those who succumbed to *adulatio* at the end of Augustus' principate. Cf. Syme *Tacitus* 337f. on Cremutius' trial, Tac. *Ann.* 4.34f.

AD 6 which led to bread rationing and other measures to conserve supplies (55.26f.), and the riots at the elections in AD 7 (55.34.2). The banishment of Julia provoked dissent (55.13.1), and his account of the campaigns of Tiberius in Book 56 has been seen as unfriendly to him. We cannot name Dio's sources, and the writers may not have been contemporary, but the material must have had some contemporary origin.[65]

Suetonius also relates anecdotes showing that Augustus did not always have a docile Senate, but met with criticism and opposition to his face which resulted in exasperation and loss of self-control (*Aug.* 54). Suetonius also cites examples of his making efforts not to be aloof and superior (53.3) but, as he fails to date any of the episodes he recounts, no change or development in attitude can be proved. Our sources also mention opposition to the financing of the *aerarium militare*, and criticism of the *leges Iuliae* and the agitation which caused them to be modified, also of the *lex Voconia* regulating the capacity of women to inherit. We should not be too hasty to assume that the style and tone of Velleius Paterculus were typical of Augustus' principate. His monograph was published to commemorate the consulate of Vinicius in AD 30, Tiberius' sixteenth year.

The troubles over the succession to Augustus must also have prompted a feeling that caution was required in forming political alliances, and an anxiety to please or make up for false choices. Even the decisive leads given by Augustus in promoting then demoting and finally restoring Tiberius as guardian to the successors then as successor-designate to the family of the Caesars could not eliminate rivalries and factions. There were also those who, like Tiberius, harboured resentments, and others, over-enthusiastic supporters of the *principes iuventutis*,[66] who used Tiberius' period of demotion to humiliate him, and suffered, sooner or later.[67] On the other side, after AD 4 Tiberius probably found as many place-seekers around him as genuine supporters.[68] It cannot be without significance that when he

---

[65] For a list Syme *History* 108–110.

[66] Their supporters and the friends of Julia are seen, by B. Levick for example (*Tiberius the Politician* (London 1976) 42), as standing for an alliance between the *Princeps* and *plebs* against the austere and oligarchic programme of Tiberius.

[67] M. Lollius, the most bitter opponent of Tiberius recorded, had already committed suicide, Syme *Rom. Rev.* 428, but Archelaus of Cappadocia was deprived of his kingdom (Tac. *Ann.* 2.42.2f.) and the exiled Julia was treated more harshly and her lover Sempronius Gracchus put to death when he became Princeps (Tac. *Ann.* 1.53).

[68] Levick *Tiberius* (n.66) 52–4.

became Princeps in AD 14 he had already acquired an unerring eye for flatterers and hypocrites of all sorts. He could hardly have got that except through experience, and he had had little of that in the Senate since his praetorship in 16.[69]

But the prevalence of *adulatio* should not be exaggerated. There were men of integrity in the Senate, respected by both Augustus and Tiberius, and some rose to the top and had very successful careers.[70] It has been suggested[71] that Augustus became estranged from educated opinion in the last decade of his principate, but there was never any chance of a successful plot or coup d'état, and he died in his bed with his last words addressed to Livia his wife.[72]

[69] Syme *Tacitus* 427.

[70] L. Calpurnius Piso for example, who was consul in 1 and prefect of the city under Tiberius, praised not only by Velleius (2.98) but also by Tacitus (*Ann.* 6.10.3) at his death. *Id.* 3.68 for an instance of tactful independence, and cf. Syme *Aug. Ar.* X, M. Lepidus, praised for opposition to *adulatio* in Tac. *Ann.* 4.20.2, and at his death, *id.* 6.27.4, and Cocceius Nerva, *Ann.* 6.26.1f.

[71] Syme *History* 198. That is, the estrangement should be dated to the death of Gaius Caesar in AD 4 and the establishment of Tiberius as successor-designate. But this date may be too late, and the estrangement may go back a further five years, to the punishment of Julia in 2 and the promotion of Gaius Caesar to the command of the armies of the East. We know of popular demand at least for Julia's recall, and Gaius' appointment can not have impressed more educated people. Cf. Suet. *Aug.* 65.3 and chap. 9 above.

[72] Suet. *Aug.* 99.1.

BIBLIOGRAPHY

A select list of the works consulted (apart from those already listed in the abbreviations), from which I have profited to a greater or lesser extent. Books or articles (apart from those in the list of abbreviations) are cited in full on their first appearance in each chapter, and in a shorter form for the remainder of that chapter, with reference back to the note where they were first mentioned. Many, but not all, of the works cited are also listed below.

Abbott, F.F. and Johnson, A.C. *Municipal Administration in the Roman Empire*. Princeton U.P. 1926.

Adcock, F.E. 'The interpretation of *Res Gestae Divi Augusti* 34.1' *CQ* 1 (1951) 130–35.

Altheim, F. *A History of Roman Religion*. E.T. by H. Mattingly, London 1938.

Badian, E. 'The quaestorship of Tiberius Nero' *Mnemosyne* 27 (1974) 160–72.

— '"Crisis theories" and the beginning of the principate' in G. Wirth (ed.) *Romanitas–Christianitas. Untersuchungen zur Geschichte und Literatur der römischen Kaiserzeit, Johannes Straub zum 70. Geburtstag gewidmet*. Berlin and New York 1982, 18–41.

Bahrfeldt M. von, *Die römische Goldmünzenprägung während der Republik und unter Augustus*. Halle: A Riechmann 1923.

Bailey, C. *Phases in the Religion of Ancient Rome*. Westport, Conn.: Greenwood Press 1932.

Balsdon, J.P.V.D. 'Roman history, 58–56 B.C.: three Ciceronian problems' *JRS* 47 (1957) 15–20.

— *Roman Women. Their History and Habits*. London: Bodley Head 1962 (repr. New York: Barnes and Noble 1983).

Barnes, T.D. 'The victories of Augustus' *JRS* 64 (1974) 21–6.

Bay, Aase 'The letters SC on Augustan *aes* coinage' *JRS* 62 (1972) 111–22.

Beard, Mary 'The sexual status of Vestal Virgins' *JRS* 70 (1980) 12–27.

Bellemore, Jane *Nicolaus of Damascus, Life of Augustus*. Bristol: B.C.P. 1984.

Brunt, P.A. 'Roman constitutional problems' *CR* 12 (1962) 70–73. (Review of A.H.M. Jones *SRGL*)

— 'C. Fabricius Tuscus and an Augustan dilectus' *ZPE* 13 (1974) 161–85.

— 'The Roman mob' in M.I. Finley (ed.) *Studies in Ancient Society*. London: Routledge and Kegan Paul 1974. 74–102. (reprinted from *Past and Present* 35 (1966)).

— '*Lex de Imperio Vespasiani*' *JRS* 67 (1977) 95–116.

— '*Laus Imperii*' in P. Garnsey and C.R. Whittaker (edd.) *Imperialism in the Ancient World*. Cambridge 1978. 159–91.

Buckland, W.W. *A Textbook of Roman Law*. 3rd edn, Cambridge 1963.

Carson, R.A.G. *Coins of the Roman Empire*. London and New York: Routledge 1990.

Carson, R.A.G. and Sutherland, C.H.V. *Essays in Roman Coinage presented to Harold Mattingly*. Oxford 1956.

Carter, John M. *The Battle of Actium. The Rise and Triumph of Augustus Caesar*. London: Hamish Hamilton 1970.

— (ed.) *Suetonius, Divus Augustus*. Bristol: B.C.P. 1982.

Charlesworth, M.P. 'The virtues of a Roman emperor: propaganda and the creation of belief'. Raleigh Lecture. *PBA* 23 (1937) 105-27.

— *The Roman Empire*. London: Oxford U.P. (1951) 1968.

Chilver, G.E.F. 'Augustus and the Roman constitution 1939-50' *Historia* 1 (1950) 408-35.

Coarelli, F. *Il foro romano* Vol. I. Roma: Quasar 1983.

Crawford, M.H. *Roman Republican Coinage*. Cambridge 1974.

Crook, J.A. *Consilium Principis: Imperial Councils and Counsellors from Augustus to Diocletian*. Cambridge 1955.

— *Law and Life of Rome*. London: Thames and Hudson 1967.

D'Arms, J.H. *Romans on the Bay of Naples*. Cambridge, Mass.: Harvard U.P. 1970.

Eck, Werner 'Senatorial self-representation: developments in the Augustan period' in Millar and Segal (1984) 129-67.

Ferguson, J. *The Religions of the Roman Empire*. London: Thames and Hudson 1970.

Finley, M.I. (ed.) *Studies in Ancient Society*. London: Routledge and Kegan Paul 1974.

Fishwick, D. '*Numina Augustorum*' *CQ* 20 (1970) 191.

— *The Imperial Cult in the Latin West*. Leiden and New York: Brill 1987.

Fraenkel, E. *Horace*. Oxford 1957.

Frazer, J.G. *The Fasti of Ovid*. (6 vols) London: Macmillan 1929.

Furneaux, H. *The Annals of Tacitus* Vol. I *Books I-VI*. 2nd edn Oxford 1896.

Garnsey, P. and Whittaker, C.R. (edd.) *Imperialism in the Ancient World*. Cambridge 1978.

— (edd.) *Trade and Famine in Classical Antiquity*. Cambridge Philological Society Supplement 8. Cambridge 1983.

Gelzer, M. *Caesar, Politician and Statesman*. E.T. Oxford: Blackwell 1968.

Goodyear, F.R.D. *The Annals of Tacitus Books 1-6* Vol. I *Annals 1,1-54* Cambridge 1972.

Gordon, Richard *et al.* 'Roman inscriptions 1986-90' *JRS* 83 (1993) 131-58.

Grant, M. *From Imperium to Auctoritas. A Historical Study of Aes Coinage in the Roman Empire 49 B.C. - A.D. 14*. Cambridge 1946 (2nd edn 1969).

— *Roman Imperial Money*. London and New York: Nelson 1954.

Gray, E.W. 'The *imperium* of M. Agrippa, a note on P. Colon. inv. no. 4701' *ZPE* 6 (1970) 227-38.

Grenade, P. *Essai sur les origines du Principat*. Paris: De Boccard 1961.

Griffin, J. *Latin Poets and Roman Life*. London: Duckworth 1985.

Henig M. and King A. (edd.) *Pagan Gods and Shrines of the Roman Empire*. Oxford: Oxford U. Committee for Archaeology 1986.

Holland, G.D. *Returning to the City in the Late Republic*. Unpublished Research Essay for the M.A. Degree. U. of Auckland 1986.

Horsfall, N.M. *Cornelius Nepos: A Selection*. Oxford and New York: Oxford U.P. 1989.

Hunt, A.S. and Edgar, C.C. *Select Papyri* II. LCL London: Heinemann and Cambridge, Mass.: Harvard U.P. 1956.

Jones, A.H.M. *The Herods of Judaea*. Oxford 1938, repr. Oxford 1967.

— *A History of Rome through the Fifth Century* 2 vols. London: Macmillan 1968, 1970.

— *Augustus*. 2nd edn London: Chatto and Windus 1970.

Jory, E.J. 'The literary evidence for the beginnings of Imperial pantomime' *BICS* 28 (1981) 147–61.

Kent, J.P.C. *Roman Coins*. London: Thames and Hudson 1978.

Koenen, L. 'Die "laudatio funebris" des Augustus für Agrippa auf einem neuen Papyrus (P. Colon. inv. Nr. 4701)' *ZPE* 5 (1970) 217–83.

Lacey, W.K. 'Cicero *Pro Sestio* 96–143' *CQ* 12 (1962) 67–71.

— 'Octavian in the senate, January 27 B.C.' *JRS* 64 (1974) 176–84.

— *Cicero and the End of the Roman Republic*. London: Hodder and Stoughton 1978.

— '*Summi fastigii vocabulum*: the story of a title' *JRS* 69 (1979) 28–34.

— '2 B.C. and Julia's adultery' *Antichthon* 14 (1980) 127–42.

— '*Patria potestas*' in B. Rawson (ed.) *The Family in Ancient Rome. New Perspectives*. London: Croom Helm 1986. 121–44.

Laing, G.J. *Survivals of Roman Religion*. London: Harrap n.d. and New York: Longmans Green 1931.

Last, H.M. '*Imperium maius*: a note' *JRS* 37 (1947) 157–64.

— 'On the *tribunicia potestas* of Augustus' *Rendiconti dell'Istituto Lombardo di scienze e lettere* 84 (1951) 93–110.

Levick, B. 'Tiberius' retirement to Rhodes in 6 B.C.' *Latomus* 31 (1972) 779–813.

— *Tiberius the Politician*. London: Thames and Hudson 1976.

Magie, D. 'Augustus' war in Spain (26–25 B.C.)' *CPh* 15 (1920) 323–39.

— *Roman Rule in Asia Minor to the End of the Third Century after Christ*. 2 vols. Princeton U.P. 1950.

Mantell, Inga *Roman Household Religion*. Unpublished PhD thesis. Edinburgh 1979

Millar, F. *A Study of Cassius Dio*. Oxford 1964.

— 'Two Augustan notes' *CR* 18 (1968) 263–6.

— 'Triumvirate and Principate' *JRS* 63 (1973) 50–67.

— ' "Senatorial" provinces: an institutionalised ghost' *Ancient World* 20 (1989) 93–7.

Momigliano, A. *'Panegyricus Messallae* and "Panegyricus Vespasiani": two references to Britain' *JRS* 40 (1950) 39–42.

— *Augustus* in *OCD*, 149–51.

Mommsen, Th. *Römisches Staatsrecht*. 3. Auflage. Akademische Druck- u. Verlagsanstalt. Graz 1952.

Nicolet, C. *The World of the Citizen in Republican Rome*. E.T. by P.S. Falla. London: Batsford 1980.

— 'Augustus, government, and the propertied classes' in Millar and Segal (1984) 89–128.

Nisbet, Robert G. *M. Tulli Ciceronis de Domo sua*. Oxford 1939.

Nisbet, R.G.M. *Cicero, in Pisonem*. Oxford 1961.

Nitzche, Jane Chance *The Genius Figure in Antiquity and the Middle Ages*. New York: Columbia U.P. 1975.

Ogilvie, R.M. *'Lustrum condere' JRS* 51 (1961) 31–9.

— *A Commentary on Livy, Books I–V*. Oxford 1965.

Ormerod, H.A. *Piracy in the Ancient World*. Liverpool U.P. London: Hodder and Stoughton 1924.

Page, T.E. *Virgil Aeneid I–VI*. London: Macmillan 1894.

Parke, H.W. *Festivals of the Athenians*. London: Thames and Hudson 1977.

Pearce, T.E.V. 'Notes on Cicero, *In Pisonem' CQ* 20 (1970) 309–21.

Pollini, J. *The Portraiture of Gaius and Lucius Caesar*. New York: Fordham U.P. 1987.

Purcell, N. 'Livia and the womanhood of Rome' *PCPhS* n.s. 32 (1986) 78–105.

— 'Tomb and suburb' in *Römische Gräberstrassen* (*Bayerische Akademie der Wissenschaften Phil.-Hist. Klasse* Abh. N.F. 96) edd. H. von Hesberg and P. Zanker. Munich 1987. 25–41.

— *'Atrium libertatis' PBSR* 61 (1993) 125–55.

Raaflaub, K.A. and Samons, L.J. II 'Opposition to Augustus' in Raaflaub and Toher *BRE* (1990) 417–54.

Ramin, J. and Veyne, P. 'Droit romain et société; les hommes libres qui passent pour esclaves et l'esclavage volontaire' *Historia* 30 (1981) 472–97.

Rawson, B. (ed.) *The Family in Ancient Rome. New Perspectives*. London: Croom Helm 1986.

Rawson, E. *Cicero: a Portrait*. London: Allen Lane 1975.

Reinhold, M. *Marcus Agrippa. A Biography*. Geneva, New York: The W.F. Humphrey Press 1933.

— *From Republic to Principate*. APA Monographs 34. Atlanta Ga: Scholars Press 1988.

Reynolds, Joyce *Aphrodisias and Rome*. London: Society for the Promotion of Roman Studies 1982.

Richardson, J.S. *'Imperium romanum*: empire and the language of power' *JRS* 81 (1991) 1–9.

Richardson, L. *A New Topographical Dictionary of Ancient Rome*. Baltimore: Johns Hopkins U.P. 1992.

Rickman, G.E. *Roman Granaries and Store Buildings*. Cambridge 1971.

Roddaz, J.-M. *Marcus Agrippa*. Bibliothèque des Écoles françaises d'Athènes et de Rome 253. Rome 1984.

Rose, H.J. 'Lustration' in *OCD* 626.

Rüpke, Jorg *Domi Militiae*. Stuttgart: Franz Steiner 1990.

Salmon, E.T. 'The evolution of Augustus' principate' *Historia* 5 (1956) 456–78.

Salway, P. *Roman Britain*. Oxford and New York: Oxford U.P. 1981. (corrected reprint 1982).

Sattler, P. *Augustus und der Senat: Untersuchungen zur römischen Innenpolitik zwischen 30 und 17 v. Chr.*. Göttingen 1960.

Schmitthenner, W. 'Augustus' spanischer Feldzug und der Kampf um den Prinzipat' *Historia* 11 (1962) 29–85.

Scott-Kilvert, Ian *Cassius Dio. The Roman History. The Reign of Augustus*. Harmondsworth: Penguin 1987.

Scullard, H.H. *Scipio Africanus: Soldier and Politician*. London: Thames and Hudson 1970.

— Revised edn of M. Cary *History of Rome*. London: Macmillan 1975.

— *From the Gracchi to Nero*. 4th edn London and New York: Methuen 1976. (3rd edn London 1970).

Seager, R. *Pompey. A Political Biography*. Oxford: Blackwell 1979.

Seston, W. 'Le *clipeus virtutis* d'Arles et la composition des *Res Gestae Divi Augusti*' *CRAI* (1954) 286–97.

Shackleton Bailey, D.R. *Cicero's Letters to Atticus* Vol. VI. *44 B.C. 355–426 (Books XIV–XVI)* Cambridge 1967.

— *Cicero, Epistulae ad Familiares*. Cambridge 1977.

Stanton, G.R. 'Tacitus' view of Augustus' place in history' in *Ancient History in a Modern University* (Festschrift for Edwin Judge). Sydney n.y.p.

Starr, C.G. *The Roman Imperial Navy 31 B.C. – A.D. 324*. 2nd edn Cambridge 1960 (New York: Cornell U.P. 1941).

Staveley, E.S. 'The *fasces* and *imperium maius*' *Historia* 12 (1963) 458–84.

— *Greek and Roman Voting and Elections*. London: Thames and Hudson 1972.

Stevenson, T.R. 'The ideal benefactor and the father analogy in Greek and Roman thought' *CQ* 42 (1992) 421–36.

Sutherland, C.H.V. *The Emperor and the Coinage. Julio-Claudian Studies*. London: Spink 1976.

— *Roman History and Coinage 44 B.C. – A.D. 69*. Oxford 1987.

Sutherland, C.H.V., Olçay, N. and Merrington, K.E. *The Cistophori of Augustus*. London: Royal Numismatic Society 1970.

Syme, (Sir) Ronald 'The Spanish war of Augustus (26–25 B.C.)' *AJPh* 55 (1934) 293–317.

— 'Imperator Caesar: a study in nomenclature' *Historia* 7 (1958) 172–88.

— 'Livy and Augustus' *HSCPh* 64 (1959) 27–76.

— 'The crisis of 2 B.C.' *Sitzungsberichte d. Bayerische Akademie der Wissenschaften (Phil.-hist. Klasse)* 7 (1974) 3–34.

Taylor, L.R. *The Divinity of the Roman Emperor*. Middletown, Conn: A.P.A. 1931.

Toynbee, J.M.C. *Roman Medallions*. New York: American Numismatic Society 1944.

Traub, H.W. 'Tacitus' use of *ferocia*' *TAPA* 84 (1953) 250–61.

Wallace-Hadrill, A. '*Civilis princeps*: between citizen and king' *JRS* 72 (1982) 32–48.

— 'Image and authority in the coinage of Augustus' *JRS* 76 (1986) 66–87.

— 'Roman arches and Greek honours: the language of power at Rome' *PCPhS* n.s. 36 (1990) 143–81.

— *Augustan Rome*. London: B.C.P. 1993.

Wardman, A. *Religion and Statecraft among the Romans*. London: Granada 1982.

Watson, Alan *Roman Private Law around 200 BC*. Edinburgh U.P. 1971.

Wells, C.M. *The German Policy of Augustus*. Oxford 1972.

Williams, R.D. *The Aeneid of Virgil Books 1–6*. Basingstoke and London: Macmillan 1972.

Wirszubski, Chaim *Libertas as a Political Idea at Rome during the Late Republic and Early Principate*. Cambridge 1950.

— 'Cicero's *cum dignitate otium*: a reconsideration' *JRS* 44 (1954) 1–13.

Wiseman, T.P. *Death of an Emperor*. (Exeter Studies in History 30). Exeter 1991.

Woodman, A.J. *Velleius Paterculus, The Tiberian Narrative (2.94–131)*. Cambridge 1977.

— *Velleius Paterculus: The Caesarian and Augustan Narrative (2.41–93)*. Cambridge 1983.

Yavetz, Z. *Plebs and Princeps*. Oxford 1969.

— *Julius Caesar and his Public Image*. E.T. London: Thames and Hudson 1983.

— 'The *Res Gestae* and Augustus' public image' in Millar and Segal (1984) 1–36.

— 'The personality of Augustus' in Raaflaub and Toher *BRE* (1990) 21–41.

Zanker, P. *Forum Augustum. Das Bildprogramm*. Tübingen: E. Wasmuth 1968.

INDEX OF PASSAGES NOTED

INDEX OF PERSONS (Selected)

Note: All persons are listed by whichever name is normally used in the text.

GENERAL INDEX